Empires and Indigenes

Empires and Indigenes

Intercultural Alliance, Imperial Expansion,
and Warfare in the Early Modern World

EDITED BY
Wayne E. Lee

NEW YORK UNIVERSITY PRESS
New York and London

NEW YORK UNIVERSITY PRESS
New York and London
www.nyupress.org

References to Internet websites (URLs) were accurate at the time of writing.
Neither the author nor New York University Press is responsible for URLs
thatmay have expired or changed since the manuscript was prepared.

Library of Congress Cataloging-in-Publication Data

Empires and indigenes : intercultural alliance, imperial expansion,
and warfare in the early modern world / edited by Wayne E. Lee.
p. cm. — (Warfare and culture series)
Includes bibliographical references and index.
ISBN 978–0–8147–5308–8 (cl : alk. paper) — ISBN 978–0–8147–5311–8 (pb : alk. paper) —
ISBN 978–0–8147–5309–5 (e-book : alk. paper)
1. Imperialism. 2. Indigenous peoples. I. Lee, Wayne E., 1965–
JC359.E4575   2011
325'.32—dc22   2010053654

New York University Press books are printed on acid-free paper,
and their binding materials are chosen for strength and durability.
We strive to use environmentally responsible suppliers and materials
to the greatest extent possible in publishing our books.

Manufactured in the United States of America

c   10 9 8 7 6 5 4 3 2 1
p   10 9 8 7 6 5 4 3 2 1

Contents

List of Maps

Projecting Power in the Early Modern World

The Spanish Model?

WAYNE E. LEE

Despite the near constant historical attention, the success of European expansion around the world continues to inspire debate over its meaning, consequences, and, of interest here, its causes and methods. The popular acclaim and subsequent academic criticism of Jared Diamond's *Guns, Germs, and Steel: The Fates of Human Societies* have highlighted the extent to which the subject continues simultaneously to fascinate and trouble. Western European states in the early modern era successfully hacked out trading and limited territorial empires in the Americas, Africa, and Asia, often at one another's expense, but primarily at the expense of the local peoples they encountered. The basic outlines of that story are well known, as are the arguments for the roles of disease, technology, military technique, and even a basic willingness to employ horrific violence. Imperial expansion, however, was not a Western prerogative in this period. The Russians, Ottomans, Mughals, Chinese, and others also were busily pushing the boundaries of their control, and they, too, confronted similar problems in managing the problems of conquest warfare in intercultural contexts. Local peoples proved to be essential determinants of imperial success or failure. Far from being mere victims, these peoples found ways to profit from imperial maneuverings: they could find employment and profit as allies, or they might direct the interests and energies of imperial powers against their traditional enemies. Indeed, imperial "expansion" was very often illusory, and Europeans' ability to project power actually depended entirely on local cooperation. In turn, that cooperative process shaped and reshaped the warfare and diplomatic practices designed to define and establish sovereignty and control, whether local or European. New cultures of power and cultures of war were born in the many crucibles of encounter around the globe, and this book, *Empires and Indigenes*, explores these themes and more.

The chapters in this book examine the problems of understanding imperial expansion in an early modern world still ruled primarily by organic energy.[1] Oceangoing sailing ships had harnessed the winds, and mills in Europe and elsewhere were using the power of wind or falling water to turn. Aside from these exceptions, though, wielding power meant harnessing organic energy derived from agriculture, timber, and pastoral products. Power required moving goods, feeding troops and animals, and extracting the wealth necessary to pay for and equip them. Accordingly, the problem of converting energy into military force and, in turn, converting force into a claim of sovereignty unifies these chapters.[2] The Ottomans and the Portuguese, the Muscovites and the English, all sought in some way to tap the labor of men and animals and to convert that labor into wealth. The process required asserting control over the space in which that labor was employed, and asserting control meant successfully projecting power. This indeed is a logical loop: projecting power required harnessing territorial space with its wealth and labor, and harnessing territorial space allowed for projecting power. One might imagine that "projecting power" meant dispatching a fleet or an army from the home country, but in fact, especially given the energy costs of early modern forces, it often was far easier to rely on local indigenous agents to act on the imperial behalf. It therefore was not always, or even mostly, a story of direct "conquest" but, rather, a story of convincing, cajoling, and coercing indigenous agents to harness their own resources and to project power, either at the imperial behest or at least in the imperial interest. The chapters in this book tell that story, as well as the story of some of the consequences of that process.

Empires and Indigenes is divided into three parts, proceeding from, roughly, the general to the more specific. Part I explores the interactive nature of imperial expansion from a wide perspective, presenting many of the broader themes that recur in the more detailed case studies. Essentially, how did intercultural contact, the meeting of empire and local, change diplomatic and military practices and cultures? In her chapter, Jenny Hale Pulsipher examines the blending of European and Amerindian diplomatic practices as both sides sought to find advantage in the other, and she finds that for most of this period, the Europeans adapted to Amerindian conventions rather than vice versa. Wayne E. Lee asks a similar set of questions about Amerindian military adaptation to European techniques and technologies, and Douglas M. Peers looks at the extent to which South Asian military practices determined and shaped British military capabilities there. In combination, these three chapters provide a broad synthetic analysis of how imperial "conquest" was complicated by the process of mutual diplomatic and military adaptation.

Part II also works from a broad perspective, but here Virginia H. Aksan and David R. Jones provide a comparative perspective on two non-Western European continental empires, those of the Ottomans and the Russians. As part of their imperial expansion, these two empires also came to recognize the necessity of diplomatic adjustment and compromise in order to foster intercultural alliances. Although historians specializing in the relatively new subfield of "Atlantic history" often compare the European oceanic empires with one another, they rarely compare them with continental empires, even those from the same era and resting on similar technological foundations.

Part III returns to the Portuguese, Dutch, and English Atlantic, but here John K. Thornton, Mark Meuwese, Geoffrey Plank, and Marjoleine Kars use a much more detailed approach, focusing on the problems and potentials of employing "indigenous" peoples in the cause of imperial expansion. Indigenous "allies" could play many different roles in solving the problem of projecting power in an organic economy, and these chapters explore that variability.

The Spanish Model?

In many ways the Spanish empire set the model to which other European powers aspired, and it also supplied the popular historical imagination with dramatic narratives of small numbers of Europeans seemingly "conquering" vast Amerindian empires.[3] Spain's (and Portugal's) apparent brilliant and enriching success motivated other European powers to try their hand at creating trading and territorial empires across the oceans. The Spanish story for a long time dominated the historical portrayal of the process of European expansion. Indeed, for many students and for most of the modern age, the Spanish conquest of Mexico and Peru defined the extent of European superiority. More modern scholarship, however, has battered that reputation and, furthermore, has begun to integrate fully into the story the (semi-)cooperative relations between the Spanish and the indigenous peoples of the New World.[4] In essence, we now see more and more clearly the extent to which Spanish imperial expansion both depended on extensive intercultural alliances and generated an adaptive exchange of warfare styles, which are the central themes of *Empires and Indigenes*. At the same time, however, Spain's experience turns out *not* to have been paradigmatic. Crucial aspects of their early successes could not later be duplicated, and so this book focuses on those empires that came afterward or that struggled for control elsewhere, outside the New World. Before we turn to those other empires, we will briefly examine the Spanish experience in the New World to review what was paradigmatic and what was not and, above all, to begin to discover the nature and limits of early modern European power.

In *Empire: How Spain Became a World Power, 1492–1763*, Henry Kamen argues that early modern Spanish, really Castilian, power derived from the efforts and contributions of many ethnicities, states, and peoples. More to the point, he notes that even using the word *power* too often conjures up images of troops, ships, and guns, when in fact power is more than "just the capacity to apply force." Power, he contends, derives from

> the underlying structures that made empire possible, factors such as the ability to supply finance and services. In other words, who gave the men, who supplied the credit, who arranged the transactions, who built the ships, who made the guns? . . . "Conquest" and power turned out frequently to be of less importance than . . . the ability to marshal resources.[5]

Kamen's thesis of the diffuse sources for Spanish power applies with even greater force to their activities in the New World. In 1519, when Hernando Cortés marched down out of the mountains into the valley of Mexico and approached Tenochtitlan, he brought with him several crucial advantages, all of which proved necessary in the ensuing contest. Those same advantages accrued to Francisco Pizarro in Peru in 1534 and to the other early conquistadors. First, the Spanish brought diseases, which, however unknowingly, proved potent allies in devastating populations and disrupting the normal processes of social mobilization and intergenerational cultural continuity.[6] Although the extent of the devastation by disease remains difficult to measure, it no doubt was worst in those centralized and urbanized states first encountered on the mainland in the valley of Mexico and in Peru. Second, the Spanish brought horses, steel swords, and a tactical system that proved to be remarkably resistant to indigenous methods, especially in the first part of the sixteenth century. After the initial shock response to their strangeness, firearms lost much of their importance, and unarmored horses in small numbers quickly proved vulnerable. But armored Spanish infantry, fighting in the close-order style associated with the European warfare of that era and armed with steel swords, functioned as a kind of impenetrable mobile core from which they could launch cavalry charges, or, more importantly, around which they could form their third advantage: large numbers of indigenous allies.[7]

Amerindians were equally or even more politically fragmented than the Europeans. The Spanish, though, had the advantage of arriving from the outside (literally) as a fresh variable into a tense system of competing indigenous powers. Even if we set aside the supposed material advantages of steel or horses, the Spaniards' strangeness allowed them to maneuver into the dual role of catalyst and tipping point. As numerically limited as Spanish military power was, it proved capable of mobilizing extant political struggles, and in doing so, the Spanish gained thousands of Amerindian allies. Certainly, the most famous example is the tens of thousands of Tlaxcalans who joined Cortés in overthrowing the Aztec state. But such aid persisted throughout the next two centuries and across the continent, even to the Spanish administrator in northern Mexico in 1693 who complained that "the soldiers absolutely cannot take the field without a number of Indian friends" and who asked that the salaries of eight Spanish soldiers instead be used to pay forty Amerindian fighters.[8] This lesson was particularly clear as a "model" for other European powers: seek out the divisions between indigenous peoples and use them to mobilize allies. The indigenous peoples' provision of numbers and intelligence could prove decisive. Later imperial powers in the New World, although also able to use local political divisions to their advantage, lacked the Spanish advantage of shock and surprise, so they were less successful at generating the kind of dramatic tipping point effect seen at Tenochtitlan.

There was another "side effect" of the Spaniards' outsider status. As Matthew Restall points out, Amerindians had the option of surrendering: a choice that would protect their families and their homes. To be sure, that same motive gave them extraordinary courage in fighting the Spanish, and thousands died resisting, but eventually they could choose submission and survival.[9] But the early conquistadors did not have that choice: if they failed, they died. These were men imbued with a crusading ideology, an energizing greed for hidden mineral wealth, and a profound, ends-of-the-earth, succeed-or-die desperation. Moreover, their consciences were fortified by an intricate and sustained religious-legalistic framework. As a result, the Spanish were pleased to accept native submission, but when resisted, they wielded violence swiftly, unhesitatingly, and with extraordinary cruelty. Like the "tipping point," the power generated by this sense of desperation also did not fully carry over to the later oceanic empires, whose explorers and soldiers could more reliably fall back to their ships (or coastal forts) and return home if necessary. And for the Old World continental empires discussed here, this power of desperation did not really apply at all.

Beyond the power of desperation and the potential power conferred by their outsider status, Restall suggests that the conquistadors' process followed a seven-part "method" that held true for most of the century and persisted in part because of deep precedent dating to the *reconquista* on the Iberian peninsula. This process also persisted because it succeeded. The Spanish began their campaigns (or *entradas*) in a quest for precious metals, which they framed with legalistic devices and appeals to distant, usually royal, authority that, as suggested earlier, fortified their consciences for the rest of their program of action.[10] Aware of their own vulnerability and local ignorance, the Spanish deliberately sought out interpreters and intermediaries, whom they then used to parlay Amerindian political divisions into active allies. Finally, at crucial moments of conflict, they sought to publicly seize and control the chief ruler and combined that act with the use of "display" violence designed to terrorize the population into submission (whom they wanted to tap for labor, after all, not eliminate).[11] To Restall's framework, I would add that appeals to the king's authority notwithstanding, throughout the seventeenth century virtually all these actions were conducted as private-enterprise ventures, although they were increasingly subject to rules set down in Spain—at least in theory.[12] What is crucial to note here is that this was a methodology applied *consciously*. Even if Spanish accounts later glorified their own role, the conquistadors' patterns of behavior clearly indicate their awareness of the necessity for interpreters and allies, as well as the efficacy of display violence and decapitation of the leadership.[13]

Although this "method" was repeated all around the hemisphere and was essential to Spanish success, the (in)famous conquests of Mexico and Peru were nevertheless *not* paradigmatic, even for Spain. Although often cited and also seen as the most in need of explanation, the victims of both "conquests" were complex, hierarchical, even imperial, states. These hierarchical states, especially in the shock of their first contact with an alien culture, proved to be more brittle and susceptible to overthrow by leadership decapitation than were the more diffuse tribal societies that Spain confronted in the rest of the Americas.[14] Much of the remaining Spanish expansion in the New World did not contend with state-based societies. It is true that there were other large contemporaneous Amerindian states, but many were eviscerated by disease or internecine warfare before full or continuing contact with the Spanish.[15] Furthermore, those tribal societies more distant from the first Spanish *entradas* had time to adjust to European technologies, if not fully adopting them, then at least understanding and coping with them. Indeed, even after those early spectacular successes in Mexico and Peru, for much of the sixteenth and into the seventeenth century the Spanish presence in the Americas remained confined to the fertile coastal zones of the Caribbean and Pacific or the urban centers that had formerly been the capitals of the Amerindian empires.[16] When and where the Spanish presence did expand deep into the countryside, it did so through a complex interactive process of administrative reform, missionary work, and small military garrisons, all engaged in elaborate and dependent interactions with the indigenous peoples.

During this long process of Spanish expansion, both Indians and Spanish adapted their forms of warfare to suit the new challenges. The seminomadic peoples of northwest Mexico and the Plains Indians of the North American Midwest and Southwest became famous horsemen and, in the case of the Comanches, arguably enabled them to build their own form of "empire."[17] Under Spanish pressure, the "Araucanian" Indians of Chile revamped their society politically, socially, and militarily to strengthen their ability to resist the Spanish, something they did successfully into the nineteenth century. Even considered from just the military perspective, their adaptations were remarkable: they learned to fight in pike-and-shot formations and deployed an excellent force of cavalry, superior in many ways to the Spanish cavalry in the region.[18]

"Spanish" forces adapted as well, vividly visible in the contrasting appearance, equipment, and background of two Spanish soldiers in the North American Southwest, one in 1598 and the other in 1663. In 1598, Captain Luis Gasco de Velasco presented himself for service equipped with two feathered hats, a suit of blue Italian velvet, eight pairs of cordovan leather boots, sword and gilded dagger, a silver lance signifying his rank, three sets of buckskin armor for his horse, and a silk standard (flag). In 1663 the Inquisition in Mexico City tried Nicolás de Aguilar, variously a field captain, sergeant, adjutant, and *alcalde* (mayor) of the district Las Salinas. As historian Andrew Knaut relates, he was a mestizo and accused heretic, "dressed in flannel trousers and woolen shirt and stockings—all crudely woven and in places badly frayed—and wearing a cotton neckcloth and buckskin shoes." In his possession, he also had some worn-out clothes, a bilingual catechism (Castilian and Timuquana), and several herbal cures.[19] In part, this process of mutual adaptation was carried out through the integration of armies. "Spanish" forces were usually more Amerindian than European, and tactics, weapons, and techniques were inevitably passed back and forth. Some Amerindian peoples became regular allies of the Spanish, accompanying them far afield on their campaigns. In fact, there is evidence that some Mesoamerican peoples fought with the Spanish in Peru and even in the Philippines.[20] In other cases, local peoples became the defenders of the Spanish "frontier." As Kamen argues, "The 'peace Indians' became the principal line of defence against the so-called 'war Indians.'"[21]

The existence of "peace Indians" leads to the next issue. Whether on the land of conquered Amerindian states or on the land of partially subdued or relocated tribal peoples, the Spanish had to create an ordered environment from which they could extract wealth and mobilize the population for its own defense. This hope, common to all the empires discussed here, required at least some territorial control in addition to internal stability. The modern U.S. Army refers to this post-"conquest" period as "Phase IV Operations." Then, as now, the most efficient method of consolidating an orderly territorial control was through local allies and existing local hierarchies. Even the infamous Spanish *encomienda*, a system of rewarding Spanish conquistadors with the control of native labor within a territorial grant, typically worked through agreements with local chiefs using existing networks of authority. As Susan Schroeder points out, in "Tenochtitlan, the king certainly died, but the four-part socio-political structure of governance was maintained with the traditional nobles as Spanish-styled elected officials in control much as they had before."[22] In the long, long, process of making the empire function, steel and disease lost the importance they had held during the initial conquest period. Instead, Spain's long-term power depended on exploiting indigenous networks for controlling or extracting wealth. That very process, however, also cemented the authority and privilege of the Spanish, who had violently positioned themselves at the top of the network. As a reward for their service, allied Amerindians might be granted certain levels of autonomy, or tax exemption, or regular access to Spanish cattle and other goods, but their actions nevertheless funneled profits into Spanish hands and thereby strengthened those hands.[23]

Some of those profits were funneled all the way back to the king in Spain, and the monarchs' hands were incomparably strengthened by this new access to the gold and silver mines of the New World (albeit with unforeseen costs).[24] In many ways, however, the shape of Spanish control in the New World presaged a future period of industrial imperial power, in which controlling strategic *locations* was sufficient to extract wealth, rather than an older form of empire, in which power derived from the expansive control of territory (and its rents, produce, herds, and so on). In one sense, the Spanish New World empire (and the trading-post networks of other early modern European oceanic empires) was merely a punctuated series of strategic locations from which influence inland was carried by indigenous hands. A certain minimal amount of territorial control was required to access the mines, grow food to feed the miners, and then move those resources to the ports. But Spain did not export Spanish settlers in the numbers required to make their empire demographically "Spanish." Nor until much later in the seventeenth century did the country exercise the kind of territorial control traditionally associated with "conquest" in an organic economy, in which the products and rents of the land were the reward for success.[25]

However un-paradigmatic they were in reality, contemporaries and historians often pointed to the spectacular early Spanish successes in Mexico and Peru and the *appearance* of gaining a vast territorial empire in a way that portrayed this experience as substantially different from those of the other "empires" discussed in this book. In the sense that those early successes produced unprecedented access to mineral wealth, the Spanish experience was indeed exceptional. Nevertheless, Spanish administrators and adventurers confronted the problems of controlling territory, of blending different cultures of war, and of depending on indigenous allies (with the parallel need to accommodate those allies politically). Each of those problems had parallels in the other empires of the era.

Intercultural Alliance, Imperial Expansion, and Warfare

Like Spain, all the empires discussed in this book depended on intercultural alliances to make their expansion work, and in so doing, they evolved new forms of warfare. Within these titular themes are a number of common concepts and terms. One of the most important has already been used in this introduction rather indiscriminately and perhaps needs some clarification. That term is *indigenous*. The Ottomans and Muscovites discussed here by Aksan and Jones, for example, almost never dealt with indigenous people, as that term is usually defined. But worries over whether any one people were truly autochthonous is less the issue here than the nature of the relationships generated by an expanding state-based society moving into the territory of a people with generations of experience with the local climate, terrain, and subsistence system. Even this definition is inadequate, however, as it might describe almost any conquest situation (for example, the Normans over the Saxons). So to that basic understanding of "local," we must add that the two societies operated according to different cultural systems, often set by the different scale of their social organization and especially by their use of different forms and even meanings of warfare.[26]

In most circumstances, it was this very difference in warfare styles that first attracted an imperial power to the task of recruiting indigenous allies.

They wanted "ethnic soldiers," meaning soldiers or warriors recruited for the skills they possessed as a part of their lifestyle and their regional or cultural form of warfare. In other words, they were recruited for who they were (or, at least, who they were perceived to be), rather than what they could become through training.[27] Jones shows that the Muscovites hoped to tap the remarkable military power provided by steppe horse archers through their diplomatic and alliance process with the steppe khanates. Aksan describes an Ottoman state less interested in specific military skills of the conquered (except for those of individual technicians) than in their local knowledge and therefore local mobility. Desert peoples and mountain peoples proved difficult to control, and so the Ottomans instead co-opted parts of their traditional leadership and used their skills within their own home territories. Kars's and Meuwese's studies provide valuable narratives of the details of how the Dutch gained and kept (and, in Brazil, later abandoned) ethnic soldiers, as well as the varying kinds of services that they could provide. Plank's chapter offers a slightly different viewpoint, one in which the British considered whether "ethnic soldiers" far outside their home territory could be valued for their inherent qualities, much as the Spanish deployed their Mesoamerican allies as far away as the Philippines. Indeed, it is fair to ask whether the Scots he discusses were a kind of hybrid of ethnic soldiers and indigenous people who merely served as a demographic pool for adding recruits to a uniformly trained army—something that Aksan sees as the Ottomans' eventual choice.

Kars's and Meuwese's chapters also highlight the many different ways in which indigenous allies could aid state power. Dutch military forces found it difficult to penetrate the interior of Berbice, or Brazil, and their campaigns were defined by the course of rivers or the shape of coastlines, places where they could project naval power, a term in this case meaning merely vessels carrying artillery and supplies. In the early modern era, European armies were increasingly designed around a combination of infantry, cavalry, and artillery, all supplied by animal-drawn four-wheeled wagons. Almost by definition, their armies and logistical systems depended on road-width paths. In Europe those roads existed because farmers moved their goods to market on the same form of wagon; that is, the vast network of local roads was a natural by-product of European subsistence and marketing practices. The Romans had built a strategic network of roads in part because the organic local versions did not yet exist. Only late in the early modern era (somewhat earlier for the Ottomans) were roads deliberately built by the state. In contrast, New World societies moved goods by canoe and porter. Although Europeans could use packhorses in a roadless environment, packhorses proved poorly

suited to early modern artillery. In this context, native allies not only provided the porters (sometimes enslaved), canoes, and knowledge necessary to
directly aid European movement, but more usually they operated independently as military forces within the interior, indirectly aiding Dutch power.
Understanding this logistical context suggests even more clearly that the fact
the Spanish were able to penetrate so much of the interior of two continents
speaks more to their success harnessing Amerindian power and labor than
to their own inherent abilities.[28]

Indeed, in many ways we might explain European successes and failures
entirely as an issue of logistics or, better, how well they succeeded in using
indigenous aid to overcome the logistical challenges. Thornton's chapter
shows the difficulty the Portuguese had in West Africa asserting almost any
kind of territorial control. In this case, the particular challenges of tropical
West Africa affected everyone, including the local Africans. Campaigns of
conquest in West Africa seemed to have had a limited range, and whatever
success the Portuguese did have reflected their ability to play the political
alliance game by African rules. Their style of warfare only marginally affected
regional African tactics, which already combined a heavy core of professional infantry with a larger crowd of missile-armed skirmishers. Horses in
that environment simply died. As a result, the Portuguese became merely
another regional power, although their possession of artillery and eventually
the modern European artillery fortress may have given them a kind of ultimate security, as they were difficult to force out of the region militarily.

In one sense, the Portuguese failed to convert their local allies into effective projectors of power. One route to imperial "control," as suggested by the
preceding discussion of Spanish and Dutch experience, was to avoid the costs
of direct state-funded or state-directed forces or administration and instead
to claim an indirect but comprehensive sovereignty through the more direct
sovereignty claims of indigenous peoples, who at least appeared to act as
imperial clients.[29] Pulsipher's chapter shows how the French and English in
North America sought that result by conforming to Amerindian diplomatic
practices. Both European powers learned to acknowledge the power of kinship (real and fictive), exchange, and ritual as part of the process of managing
trade but also as a means of asserting a broader "secondary" claim of sovereignty via Amerindian agency. Within the English colonies by the middle of
the eighteenth century, the military necessity to work through such indigenous agents declined as European settlers and European subsistence systems
penetrated the continent. As they did so, they naturally generated the food
supply and road networks necessary to move European-style armies, and

Amerindians found those armies increasingly difficult to resist. Jones's discussion of Muscovite diplomacy provides a neat parallel. The Musovites had a long history of accommodating steppe diplomatic systems, and although they needed European-style military systems to deal with their enemies to the west, expanding their coercive control over the steppe required steppe-style forces, at least until well into the eighteenth century.

Jones's essay thus joins Thornton's examination of West Africa and Peers's study of the British in South Asia as exemplars of the limits of the early modern "military revolution" in regard to enabling European expansive power.[30] Peers's is perhaps the most important in that respect because by the time of the period he examines (mid-eighteenth century), the British were using fully fledged, volley-firing, bayonet-equipped infantry in combination with cavalry and relatively mobile artillery. Even so, Peers does not find this particular tactical combination especially decisive, in part because of the logistical limits just discussed. Lord Wellington and his ilk instead adopted Indian logistical techniques and parlayed Britain's more developed financial capacities to successfully tap the local military labor market, a market, incidentally, with a long history of producing disciplined troops.

Nevertheless, European technological capabilities, not least the broadside-armed sailing ship and the bastioned artillery fortress, advanced their expansion. European firearms and artillery appealed to indigenous peoples, and this attraction, plus long experience as enemies and allies, led to a cultural blending of war practices. Wayne Lee's chapter focuses on how the input of new European technologies into North American Amerindian societies changed not only the way they fought but also aspects of their social organization. For all the arguments about the inadequacies of seventeenth-century firearms (for example), they proved irresistibly attractive and apparently useful to Amerindians, who adopted them at some cost to their security and cultural continuity. Technique transfer, however, was a two-way street. Peers demonstrates that a long history of "orientalizing" South Asians has downplayed and obscured the extent to which British forces in India incorporated local techniques and practices into their military system. Thornton and Jones similarly document the process of mutual adaptation in the Portuguese–West African and Muscovite-Nomad environments of confrontation and cooperation.

It is in this variety of approaches and perspectives that *Empires and Indigenes* has its greatest value. This volume provides not only comparative imperial studies but also comparison at the level of microdetail and synthetic overview. The complexity of the mechanics of intercultural interaction, mobilization, and adaptation are described here in both detailed narrative and theoretical structure. Imperial powers, for good or ill, successfully managed those complexities and mobilized indigenous power to their own benefit. Having placed themselves at the top of a co-opted network, they then used indigenous power to reinforce their own. Over the long term, they were able to assert a more direct and centralized form of control, which did not begin to break down until the twentieth century. Once again, Western military commanders now find themselves trying to mobilize local hierarchies and networks, perhaps without the same expansive imperial intent, but surely with strategic locations and security calculations in mind. It remains to be seen if they can master those complexities and adapt their own forms of logistics and warfare practices to fit indigenous needs, demands, and expectations.

NOTES

1. This conference was conducted under the auspices of the British Asia–British Atlantic Network, directed by Huw V. Bowen, Elizabeth Mancke, John G. Reid, and Emily Burton and sponsored by the Gorsebrook Research Centre, Saint Mary's University and the Milton F. Gregg Centre for the Study of War and Society, and the University of New Brunswick. See http://www.smu.ca/partners/baban/welcome.html. The authors of this book are grateful for their sponsorship and encouragement in publishing this volume. Cynthia Radding and John Thornton have been very helpful in guiding my discussion of Spanish colonization in this introduction but are surely blameless for its errors and inevitable omissions.

2. This discussion of preindustrial organic economies and their relationship to force and power was greatly influenced by John Landers, *The Field and the Forge: Population, Production, and Power in the Pre-Industrial West* (New York: Oxford University Press, 2003), which I modified here to apply it to the expanding imperial context of oceanic empires. I deal with this topic in more detail in my "Subjects, Clients, Allies or Mercenaries? The British Use of Irish and Indian Military Power, 1500–1815," in *Britain's Oceanic Empire: Projecting Imperium in the Atlantic and Indian Ocean Worlds, ca. 1550–1800*, ed. H. V. Bowen, Elizabeth Mancke, and John G. Reid (forthcoming).

3. In a volume that includes discussion of South Asia, "Amerindian" seems the most acceptable generic term for the indigenous inhabitants of North and South America.

4. A crucial starting point for this literature is Laura Matthew and Michel R. Oudijk, eds., *Indian Conquistadors: Indigenous Allies in the Conquest of Mesoamerica* (Norman: University of Oklahoma Press, 2008).

5. Henry Kamen, *Empire: How Spain Became a World Power, 1492–1763* (New York: HarperCollins, 2003), xxiii–xxiv.

6. The following analysis relies heavily on Matthew Restall, *Seven Myths of the Spanish Conquest* (New York: Oxford University Press, 2003), 140–45; Michel R. Oudijk and Matthew Restall, "Mesoamerican Conquistadors in the Sixteenth Century," in *Indian Conquistadors: Indigenous Allies in the Conquest of Mesoamerica*, ed. Laura Matthew and Michel R. Oudijk (Norman: University of Oklahoma Press, 2008), 28–64 (and the

other essays in that volume); John F. Guilmartin Jr., "The Cutting Edge: An Analysis of the Spanish Invasion and Overthrow of the Inca Empire, 1532–1539," in *Transatlantic Encounters: Europeans and Andeans in the Sixteenth Century*, ed. Kenneth J. Andrien and Relena Adorno (Berkeley: University of California Press, 1991), 40–69; Ross Hassig, "War, Politics and the Conquest of Mexico," in *War in the Early Modern World, 1450–1815*, ed. Jeremy Black (Boulder, CO.: Westview Press, 1999), 207–35; and Ross Hassig, *War and Society in Ancient Mesoamerica* (Berkeley: University of California Press, 1992).

7. John K. Thornton, *Cultural Encounters in the Atlantic World, 1400–1823* (Cambridge: Cambridge University Press, forthcoming), chap. 5; Guilmartin, "The Cutting Edge." John Thornton discussed his theory of this "armored core" with me, and I am grateful for him sharing his work in progress. Both he and Restall are somewhat dismissive of the power of cavalry, but for men on foot unaccustomed to them, horsemen could be a potent generator of fear. Thornton does not think cavalry could kill as many men as the sources credit them with doing, but battles are lost when armies run, not when they are killed while resisting. Generating panic wins battles, and then much of the killing occurs in the pursuit.

8. Kamen points out that the seizure of Atahualpa in Peru was unique in that Pizarro at that moment was not aided by Amerindian allies, but the longer-term conquest of the Incas did require such allies. See Kamen, *Empire*, 108, 110. See also Oudijk and Restall, "Mesoamerican Conquistadors," 32–37; and Susan Schroeder, introduction to *Indian Conquistadors Indian Conquistadors: Indigenous Allies in the Conquest of Mesoamerica*, ed. Laura Matthew and Michel R. Oudijk (Norman: University of Oklahoma Press, 2008), 16. Quotation is from Report of Joseph Francisco Marín, 15 June 1694, in Charles Wilson Hackett, *Historical Documents Relating to New Mexico, Nueva Vizcaya and Approaches Thereto, to 1773* (Washington, DC: Carnegie Institution of Washington, 1926), 2: 375–77 (my thanks to John Thornton for pointing me to this source).

9. Restall, *Seven Myths*, 144–45.

10. Restall does not assert the problem of "conscience" explicitly, but it is part of Patricia Seed's interpretation of the value of the "Requirement" (*requerimiento*), which stated the legal and religious authority for Spanish actions. See Patricia Seed, "Taking Possession and Reading Texts: Establishing the Authority of Overseas Empires," *William and Mary Quarterly*, 3d ser., 49 (1992): 204.

11. Restall, *Seven Myths*, 19–25, 91–92. The role of interpreters and "go-betweens" is a growing subject of interest in European-indigenous interaction. Pulsipher's chapter in this book deals with that literature for North America. For the Spanish regions, see Juliana Barr, *Peace Came in the Form of a Woman: Indians and Spaniards in the Texas Borderlands* (Chapel Hill: University of North Carolina Press, 2007); Alida C. Metcalf, *Go-Betweens and the Colonization of Brazil, 1500–1600* (Austin: University of Texas Press, 2005); and Yanna Yannakakis, *The Art of Being In-Between: Native Intermediaries, Indian Identity, and Local Rule in Colonial Oaxaca* (Durham, NC: Duke University Press, 2008).

12. Kamen, *Empire*, 84, 95; David J. Weber, *The Spanish Frontier in North America* (New Haven, CT: Yale University Press, 1992), 69, 81.

13. Cortés, for example, deliberately constructed a narrative designed to shine the light on him while downplaying his weakness and failings during the months before the Spaniards' (temporary) expulsion from Tenochtitlan. See Inga Clendinnen, "'Fierce and Unnatural Cruelty': Cortés and the Conquest of Mexico," *Representations* 33 (1991): 65–100.

14. Tzvetan Todorov is the most articulate on the role of culture shock in the early conquest, and although he has been rightly challenged on overplaying cultural difference as a source of impotence, there is still explanatory power in how strangeness and fear can be debilitating. See his *The Conquest of America: The Question of the Other* (New York: Harper Torch, 1992). Some historians and anthropologists prefer to avoid the descriptor "tribal," believing that it has acquired connotations of incivility or primitiveness. It nevertheless accurately conveys a relatively small society organized and mobilized through a broadly consensual political process nominally led by chiefs whose power was, at best, only partially hereditary.

15. For one example, see Grant D. Jones, "The Lowland Mayas from the Conquest to the Present," in *The Cambridge History of the Native Peoples of the Americas*, vol. 2, *Mesoamerica*, ed. Richard E. W. Adams and Murdo J. MacLeod (Cambridge: Cambridge University Press, 2000), 358–60.

16. Kamen, *Empire*, 96, 115, 122; Thornton categorizes European presence as one of conquest, colonization, or merely contact, reflecting different levels of European demographic presence and direct administrative control. He also points out that the category was at least in part determined by the nature of the indigenous people they faced, whether initially a state or a "free association" or a tribal society. See Thornton, *Cultural Encounters*, chap. 5. The Spanish in urban Mesoamerica or the high Andes did achieve a kind of "conquest," but much of the rest of their empire was more of a contested, interactive "contact" zone until at least the late seventeenth century. See also Daniel R. Headrick, *Power over Peoples: Technology, Environments, and Western Imperialism, 1400 to the Present* (Princeton, NJ: Princeton University Press, 2009), 131–32.

17. See especially Pekka Hämäläinen, *The Comanche Empire* (New Haven, CT: Yale University Press, 2008); Frank Raymond Secoy, *Changing Military Patterns of the Great Plains Indians* (Lincoln: University of Nebraska Press, 1953, 1992).

18. Kamen, *Empire*, 116–17; Robert Charles Padden, "Cultural Change and Military Resistance in Araucanian Chile, 1550–1730," *Southwestern Journal of Anthropology* 13 (1957): 103–21; Thornton, *Cultural Encounters*, chap. 8; G. V. Scammell, *The First Imperial Age: European Overseas Expansion, c. 1400–1715* (New York: Routledge, 1989), 73.

19. Andrew Knaut, *The Pueblo Revolt of 1680* (Norman: University of Oklahoma Press, 1997), 137–39. John L. Kessell provides another good discussion of the blending of military traditions, partly through intermarriage in the Mexican Northwest and the American Southwest, in his *Spain in the Southwest: A Narrative History of Colonial New Mexico, Arizona, Texas, and California* (Norman: University of Oklahoma Press, 2002), esp. chap. 3.

20. Oudijk and Restall, "Mesoamerican Conquistadors," 37.

21. Kamen, *Empire*, 257.

22. Kamen, *Empire*, 122; Schroeder, introduction, 12 (quotation).

23. For examples of what Amerindians gained from their aid to Spain, and Spanish attempts to provide some political reward, see Kamen, *Empire*, 124, 256; Schroeder, introduction, 17, 20, 22–23.

24. Paul Kennedy famously documented the temptations of "imperial overstretch" funded by bullion that eventually undermined Spanish power, in his *The Rise and Fall of the Great Powers: Economic Change and Military Conflict from 1500 to 2000* (New York: Vintage Books, 1987).

25. Landers, *The Field and the Forge*, 6–7.

26. Specifically excluded here are African slaves used as military auxiliaries in the New World. They were neither local nor indigenous, but from different cultural systems and warfare systems and acting as props to empire. For their use as military auxiliaries, see Peter Michael Voelz, *Slave and Soldier: The Military Impact of Blacks in the Colonial Americas* (New York: Garland, 1993); Christopher Leslie Brown and Philip D. Morgan, *Arming Slaves: From Classical Times to the Modern Age* (New Haven, CT: Yale University Press, 2006). Whether the Ottomans' use of slave soldiers in the Janissary corps is considered using "indigenous allies" is dealt with in Aksan's essay.

27. This differs from Cynthia H. Enloe's use of the term in her *Ethnic Soldiers: State Security in Divided Societies* (Athens: University of Georgia Press, 1980). Neil L. Whitehead uses the term to include almost any form of recruitment of a native people into imperial service; see his "Carib Ethnic Soldiering in Venezuela, the Guianas, and the Antilles, 1492–1820," *Ethnohistory* 37 (1990): 357. Part of the argument here is that "soldiering" is not "ethnic" unless the soldiers fight in their indigenous style. A generalized belief that certain peoples are fierce (that is, are a "martial race"), and likely to make good soldiers, and are then trained to fight in the European manner, represents a kind of hybrid of ethnic soldier with a uniform recruit. See Plank's chapter in this book, and Heather Streets, *Martial Races: The Military, Race and Masculinity in British Imperial Culture, 1857–1914* (Manchester: Manchester University Press, 2004).

28. Oudijk and Restall point out that providing porters to one's overlord was standard practice among Mesoamerican Amerindians. See their "Mesoamerican Conquistadors," 38–42.

29. Lee, "Subject, Clients, Allies, or Mercenaries?"

30. The literature on the military revolution is extensive but is amply discussed in Peers's, Jones's, Thornton's, and Lee's chapters and does not need additional citation here.

Military, Cultural, and
Diplomatic Exchange in the
Imperial-Indigenous Encounter

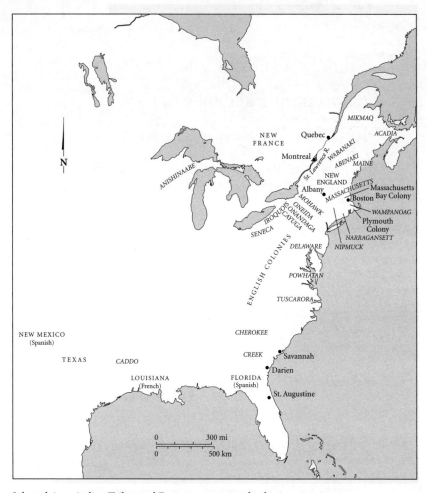

Selected Amerindian Tribes and European towns and colonies, 1650-1720.

Gaining the Diplomatic Edge

Kinship, Trade, Ritual, and Religion in
Amerindian Alliances in Early North America

JENNY HALE PULSIPHER

When a group of English separatists arrived on the shores of Cape Cod in 1620, weary from a long voyage and ill prepared for the coming winter, they were in desperate need of friends. The Wampanoags, an Amerindian people who occupied the region, were recovering from an epidemic that had sharply reduced their population. Their traditional enemies, the Narragansetts, had escaped the plague and were now more threatening than ever. For the Wampanoags, the English offered the possibility of help against their enemies, but at first the Natives kept their distance, warily observing the comings and goings of the English, felling trees and building a fort and houses.[1] In March 1621, after a winter of sickness and starvation had carried away half the newcomers, a few Wampanoags approached the settlement and indicated their interest in friendship and trade. Within days, Massasoit, the Wampanoags' paramount sachem (highest-ranking leader), and John Carter, the governor of the English colonists, sat down together, exchanged "salutations" and food and drink, and agreed to an alliance. The English promised that "if any did unjustly war against [Massasoit], we would aid him; if any did war against us, he should aid us," and by doing this, "King James would esteem of him as his friend and ally."[2] Most of the agreement's terms were reciprocal, and evidence suggests that the Amerindians viewed it as entirely reciprocal: an agreement of friendship and mutual defense between two parties whose shared needs made them approach each other as equals.[3] Gifts and trade both preceded and followed the treaty: the English gave Massasoit and his brother Quadequina knives, a copper chain with a jewel on it, a "pot of strong water," and some bread and butter, "which were all willingly accepted." Massasoit revealed his own view of the relationship through his announcement at the conclusion of the treaty that within eight or nine days, he would come with many of his people and plant corn on the other side of the stream from the English settlement. Their pact of friendship and alliance had seemingly made them one people.[4]

This early agreement reveals elements that were key to exchanges between Native Americans and Europeans in colonial-era northeastern America: kinship, exchange, and ritual.[5] Efforts to form alliances for trade, defense, or military assistance appear throughout records of interaction between Native Americans and Europeans during this period and in oral accounts and archaeological evidence of interactions between Native American groups before their contact with Europeans. War was physically and socially costly, and archaeological evidence suggests that the frequency of war increased in North America as Native American societies grew more complex.[6] In response, their efforts to maintain peace or gain allies for defense intensified and incorporated the same elements of kinship, ritual, and reciprocal exchange that supported peace and cooperation at the family and village levels. Whereas kinship was "the primary means of creating and extending ties between peoples," exchange and ritual helped create and maintain kinship.[7] These elements were mutually reinforcing and inseparable, their purpose being to create ties of obligation between groups that would nurture peace and promote mutual benefit.

Amerindian Diplomacy in the Precontact Era

Understanding how alliances between Native Americans functioned before their contact with Europeans helps us appreciate the enduring patterns of Native practice that structured their initial alliances with Europeans and— where the Amerindian population and power remained substantial—continued to maintain those relationships. David H. Dye's recent synthesis of archaeological and historical research on the Native Americans of eastern North America from 11,000 BCE to European contact reveals evidence of the long-standing presence of ritual, kinship, and trade practices that strengthened intergroup relationships and helped prevent conflict.[8]

Mortuary rituals are one example of the early mechanisms that enhanced relationships and helped maintain the groups' peaceful coexistence. Archaeological evidence of such rituals, including burial mounds and charnel houses, can be found throughout eastern North America, often on territorial borders. The importance of these centers is underscored by the evidence that they were targeted in enemy attacks.[9] But they also were sites of peace and exchange. In the Woodland period, rituals to honor and rebury the dead brought together people from different villages and kin groups. As they mourned the dead of their respective communities, they gave gifts to ease one another's grief and then symbolically raised their dead by adopting their visitors into their clans and communities, giving them names and kinship obligations that echoed those of their lost kin.[10]

Shared religious ceremonies honoring the dead united people fictively, but they also provided the opportunity to create real kinship ties. Because taboos prevented marriage within clans, or lineage groups, the large gathering of people was an ideal place to find marriage partners, and marriages across kin groups strengthened connections between villages and facilitated trade and alliance.[11]

Archaeologists believe that mortuary rituals dating back to the early Woodland period (as early as 1000 BCE) are the likely origins of rituals among Amerindian peoples at the time of contact, such as the Green Corn Ceremony, Sun Dance, and Calumet Ceremony.[12] Dye notes that mortuary ceremonialism and prestige goods exchange were markers of early and late Woodland societies. In fact, so widespread were these practices that they developed into what he calls an "international diplomatic protocol" in northeastern North America: a "standardized, international set of established rules, employed by strangers to avert violence and to weave alliances."[13]

Of course, specific ceremonies that supported alliances varied from place to place and over time. Amerindian groups differed from one another in language and cultural and religious practices. Some societies, like the Iroquois, were matrilineal, and others, like the Anishinaabes, were patrilineal, differences that affected their interpretation of kinship obligations and their expectations of those they adopted into fictive kin relationships.[14] While it would be foolish to assume that alliances operated identically for all Native peoples, for our broad overview, it is useful to acknowledge the common elements. The chief of these was the centrality of kinship. Most alliances involved ceremonies designed to create or renew bonds of fictive kinship. For example, the Calumet Ceremony, practiced by many midwestern Native groups, had ancient roots in burial mound ceremonies and retained a deep spiritual meaning, serving "to mediate a symbolic rebirth as part of an adoption ceremony to create fictional bonds of kinship between unrelated individuals and hence, indirectly, the social groups to which they belonged." Through this and other ceremonies, visiting leaders became fictive kin, "a metaphoric act which defined the relationship and obligations between two leaders and their respective communities or polities."[15]

Fictive kinship brought with it obligations that matched the specific roles of actual kin. For instance, Amerindians of the Iroquois League were divided into two groups, or *moieties*: The Mohawks, Onondagas, and Senecas were the "older brothers," and the Cayugas, Oneidas, and, later, Tuscaroras were the "younger brothers." Their reciprocal obligations to one another paralleled the obligations of the stated kin relationship: older brothers were superior in age and authority, so younger brothers were expected to defer to them (though not necessarily to obey them). But younger brothers could expect protection and generosity from older brothers. Similarly, when unrelated groups came together to negotiate alliances, the relationships they created through ritual adoption were expressed in kinship terms that signaled their position and obligations in relation to one another. In the matrilineal Iroquois society, maternal uncles exercised more authority over children than their fathers did. Hence, their role as "uncles" to the Delaware "nephews" was a symbolic demonstration of Iroquois dominance in the relationship.[16]

Most alliances also involved the exchange of sacred goods, ritual implements that symbolized peace and friendship and whose appearance signaled the "diplomatic intent and status" of visiting groups. In the Midwest, the calumet, or peace pipe; in the South, flutes; and in the Northeast, wampum strings and belts had this symbolic role.[17] Mediated by ritual, kinship and exchange nurtured peace and also offered material benefits: writing about the Delawares, Jane Merritt explained that they "recognized the importance of turning strangers into 'either actual or symbolic kinspeople' to strengthen political alliances or increase access to available resources."[18] In the precontact period, the gifts accompanying the creation or renewal of alliances were largely symbolic and small in quantity.[19] A wampum belt given to "cover the dead" in an Iroquois condolence ceremony, for instance, had deep spiritual value but no use outside the ritual context.[20] Rather, it displayed the friendship and generosity of the giver and, following an ancient pattern, helped requicken the dead through ritual adoption.[21] Accepting the gift was a symbolic representation that the receiver accepted the relationship and all the obligations and privileges that it entailed. As Daniel Richter explained, "Presents were assurances that promises made in the name of followers were likely to be carried out, for they proved that the speaker had the consent of the kin and followers who had banded together to produce them."[22] Failure to either accept or give gifts was regarded as a rejection of the relationship or the propositions made by the other party. Hence, ritual kinship and ritual exchange were inseparable.

Amerindian-European Diplomacy in the Postcontact Era

The strength of Native societies at first contact with Europeans allowed them to impose on the newcomers variations of the "international diplomatic protocol," with its symbolic meanings and kinship relationships. But maintaining these protocols over time was difficult. Amerindians in the coastal regions, such as Massasoit's Wampanoags, quickly lost their ability to make Europeans comply with their Native ways. European epidemics decimated coastal tribes, and within a generation, the rapid immigration and reproduction of settlers in New England had overwhelmed the Amerindian population.[23] Farther west, the situation was reversed. Natives of the Mississippi and Arkansas river valleys, where Spanish, French, and English settlement remained minimal through the eighteenth century, bent the Europeans to their expectations long after the Natives of the East had lost much of their negotiating power. Kathleen DuVal describes this Amerindian dominance as "the Native Ground."[24] Between the extremes of European and Native dominance was what Richard White called the "Middle Ground." There, Amerindians and Europeans of relatively equal power created new ways of coexisting, mutually modifying their cultural systems through their interaction. This middle ground was the province of such Native groups as the seventeenth- and eighteenth-century Iroquois, the Algonquians of the Great Lakes, the Cherokees, and the Creeks, whose distance from coastal traders and fishermen delayed their exposure to European diseases and whose value as allies allowed them to impose their diplomatic protocols on Europeans well into the eighteenth century.[25]

The well-documented relationship between the Iroquois and the Dutch, French, and English colonists in the seventeenth- and eighteenth-century Northeast demonstrates the continuing use of Native diplomatic protocols in their relations with Europeans and offers us a close look at how this protocol operated.[26] Despite population losses of more than 50 percent by the mid-seventeenth century, the Iroquois remained a people with significant power and influence among other tribes and neighboring Europeans, which enabled them to impose the same diplomatic protocols on Europeans that they used in their interactions with other Native peoples and among themselves.[27] Europeans learned that their negotiations with the Iroquois had to be carried out at a specific place and follow a specific sequence of actions. The Iroquois established their "council fire," the place where they carried out ritual diplomacy, at set places; in the mid-seventeenth century, Onondaga was home to the council fire. Here, representatives of the Five Nations met at regular intervals to renew their bonds with one another. Such meetings usually began with condolence ceremonies, with the host and visiting delegations on either side of the council fire. Those who had lost clan members received words of comfort and gifts of wampum and other goods from non-mourners, to "cover the graves" of the dead and to "requicken" them through ritual adoption.[28] For instance, the Iroquois bestowed the name "Corlaer" on the chief representative of the Dutch and, later, the English. As each bearer of this name died, he was ceremonially mourned, and the new representative sent to negotiate with the Iroquois was raised up in his place and given the name Corlaer.[29] Being adopted gave a stranger immediate access to the privileges and responsibilities of a reciprocal kin network, which might include rights to pass through tribal territory, access to trade, and assistance in war.[30] An example of how this might operate occurred in 1755, when the English were recruiting Native allies for the French and Indian War (known in Europe as the Seven Years' War). Hans, a Mohawk warrior and member of the Turtle clan, informed English officers that he and other members of the Turtle clan would assist in the English attack on the French. The reason they gave for joining was a kinship connection: one of those recruited by the English general William Shirley had previously been adopted into that clan. Thus his fellow clan members were obligated to come to his assistance.[31]

As they did in the precontact period, gifts accompanied the discussions between parties. They helped "cover the graves" of those who had died and "dry the tears" of mourners in preparation for the negotiations that would follow. In these discussions, too, gifts were exchanged to symbolically seal the promises one party made to another. As Denys Delage stated, "Speeches and presents were always symbolically linked. A gift was one's word, and one's word was a gift. To refuse a gift was to refuse the word that accompanied it."[32] Once an alliance was formed, the exchange of gifts continued through the periodic ritual renewal of the relationship at the council fire and through trade. Indeed, as Timothy Shannon noted, the Iroquois did "not distinguish between trade and alliance." If you were friends, you traded, a position explained by an Iroquois spokesman in Albany in 1735: "*Trade and Peace we take to be one thing.*"[33] Ritual and real kinship ties involved an exchange of sacred goods, but they also facilitated the exchange of ordinary goods, as kin were favored in trade, among both Amerindians and Europeans.[34] Over time, the quantity and commercial value of exchanged goods increased as each society accommodated the ways of the other. For a time, wampum became currency among Dutch and New Englanders, thereby greatly increasing its material value. And as Amerindians saw the quantities of goods circulating in European societies, they demanded more than token gifts in their diplomatic exchanges.[35]

From the time of first contact, both the Europeans and Natives showed great interest in ordinary trade.[36] The Pilgrims who settled southern New England needed access to the fur trade in order to repay those who had funded their settlement and food to sustain them until they could grow their own. Amerindians needed access to European weapons to defend themselves against more powerful Native groups, and they desired metal hunting and cooking implements for their labor-saving potential.[37] Although the first Native emissaries to the Pilgrim settlement insisted that they wanted both friendship and trade, they also made it clear that the two could not be separated. Therefore, when the English agreed to trade and ally with the Wampanoags, Massasoit declared his intention to come and live next to them.

Gifts and trade goods facilitated alliances by bolstering the authority of the Amerindian leaders who had formed agreements with European leaders. Many Native leaders' authority over their people was sustained as well by their redistribution of gifts, which demonstrated their generosity.[38] Daniel Richter calls this redistributive system among the Iroquois "upside-down Capitalism" because its goal was "not to accumulate goods, but to be in a position to provide them to others. Status and authority went not simply to those who possessed the most but to those able to give the most away."[39] The Europeans' failure to supply enough gifts to sustain a leader's authority, then, could lead to a change in leadership and, potentially, a disruption of the alliance.

As mentioned earlier, not all kinship roles were equal: the dominance of the Iroquois in their relationship with the Delawares was shown by their designation of the latter as nephews and of themselves as uncles.[40] Where did Europeans fall in the symbolic family structure? The answer, of course, is that their position varied over time and among different Native groups. The Iroquois addressed the French governor as "father," a title that, among Europeans, was applied to the ultimate authority figure, from the level of the family all the way up to God. For the matrilineal Iroquois, however, a maternal uncle held more authority than a father. Hence, applying the kinship term *father* to Onontio, the French governor, did not grant him the power to compel obedience from the Iroquois. It did impose on him, however, the obligations of generosity, protection, and mediation among his children.[41] Colonial officials explained this interpretation to the French court in 1730: "You know, Monseigneur, that all nations of Canada regard the governor as their father, which in consequence, following their ideas, he ought at all times to give them what they need to feed themselves, clothe themselves, and to hunt." The fact that the French governor was often willing to fulfill such expectations may explain why the Iroquois allowed him to retain a role whose intercultural ambiguity could not have been lost on them.[42] But not all Native groups were willing to use the term *father*. The Anishinaabes of the Great Lakes region, whose patrilineal kinship system gave more authority to fathers, refused to use this term for the French governor, preferring to refer to him by the more equal term *brother*.[43] In both cases, the Amerindians' interpretation of the kinship roles they used for their French allies precluded the status of subjection, which the French would have preferred but usually were unable to impose.[44] Well into the eighteenth century, a French colonial officer confessed that "if we do not agree or do not pretend to agree to [the Amerindians'] rights over the country which they occupy, never will we be able to engage them in any war for the defense of this same country which is the first line of defense of Canada."[45]

The English, too, preferred a dominant relationship with Amerindian peoples, but their initial weakness forced them to acknowledge the Natives' equality. For instance, the 1621 Plymouth-Wampanoag treaty speaks of Massasoit as the "friend and ally" of King James I of England. But within a generation, the English, whose population in North America had exploded, demanded that the Amerindians accept the status of subjects, not just of the distant king, but of themselves.[46] Similarly, the English of Jamestown, Virginia, initially bowed to the paramount sachem Powhatan, who insisted that they come to his home for negotiations and conform to Native diplomatic customs, actions that acknowledged his superior authority.[47] When the English and the Iroquois forged the Covenant Chain alliance in the late 1670s, the English hoped to be able to assume the same status of "father" to the Iroquois that the French governor had held. They were disappointed when the Iroquois repeatedly insisted that the relationship was one of "brothers."[48] Perhaps the size of the English population, which was so much larger than the French, made the Amerindians less willing to accept a symbolically weaker position. Or maybe they did not believe that the English were likely to fulfill the obligations of generosity and protection inherent in the role of a father. Either way, those Native peoples who remained strong relative to the Europeans consistently rejected symbolic statuses that undermined their autonomy.

The Natives also defended their autonomy by resisting exclusive alliances.[49] Exclusive trade or alliance meshed well with French and English hopes for a relationship in which the Amerindians were their subjects. Because subjection could not be shared with another power, subject peoples would have to restrict their trade or military assistance to one European power, a situation both French and English desired. But the region's Amerindians resisted exclusive relationships unless forced on them. In their view, they should be free to form an alliance—a tie between autonomous peoples—with anyone. Consequently, despite forming an alliance with the French, the Catholic Mohawks of Khanawake (near Quebec) continued to trade with the English, declaring that "they would rather be dead than deprived of English goods."[50] Similarly, the Wabanakis of Maine and Acadia "sometimes kept their options open, praying with the French yet traveling south to get better prices and goods at English trading posts."[51] Throughout the seventeenth century, the Narragansetts of southern New England made it a policy to have multiple alliances. Thus, even though they publicly acknowledged subjection to the English and promised to pay them tribute in the form of wampum, they defaulted on this obligation over and over again. The reason? They were sending their wampum to the Mohawks to recruit them as allies.[52]

Intermarriage and Alliance Formation

The Amerindians used ritual to create fictive kinships, or reciprocal relations that supported trade and military assistance between themselves and Europeans, but real kinship also was essential to forming alliances. Marriage between members of distinct groups was an important way of creating kinship and nurturing ties of alliance and mutual obligation.[53] Although intermarriage between Amerindians and Europeans was more common among the French, it could be found among other European groups as well. The French *coureurs de bois*, trappers and traders living among the Amerindians and adopting Native lifestyles, are well known.[54] By marrying an Amerindian woman in either the "manner of the country" or a Christian marriage, Frenchmen entered a reciprocal kin relationship. They received preferential treatment in trade from their wives' kin and were taken in and provided for by their new Amerindian families. In return, these men exchanged the first and best trade goods with their Amerindian relatives and provided lines of communication and contact with white society. The children of these marriages often continued in the same business as their parents: translating, engaging in trade, and acting as intermediaries between Amerindian and European governments.[55]

French officials had grave reservations about these traders' behavior, regarding their marriages to Amerindian women, which were usually unofficial and sometimes polygamous, as distasteful. But they did recognize that kin connections were an essential element in maintaining alliances.[56] In fact, on one occasion, the French denied military assistance to the Anishinaabes because of the absence of kin ties between them, complaining that "in the first place, you have not allied yourselves up to the present with our French people[;] your daughters have married with all the neighboring Nations, but not with ours."[57] Whether the lack of kin ties was really the "first" reason for the French denial of assistance is debatable, but their use of that reason is clear evidence that they recognized the vital role of kinship in Native society and, as a result, questioned the Anishinaabes' commitment to the French.

French willingness to create kinship ties, through either ritual adoption or intermarriage with Amerindian women, gave them an advantage in their dealings with Natives. Juliana Barr's *Peace Came in the Form of a Woman* contrasts the successful alliance of the French and the Caddo Amerindians with the failed relations between the Caddos and the Spanish in the late seventeenth- and early eighteenth-century Texas borderlands. The Caddos had well-developed practices for incorporating strangers into their community, including building houses for them and encouraging them to marry Caddo women and become part of their kinship network. Although the all-male Spanish colonists rejected intermarriage with Amerindians, they also did not send for their European wives to live with them. Among the Caddos, women were traditionally the emissaries of peace, providers of hospitality, and bulwarks of permanence. Without women, therefore, the Spanish appeared transitory and threatening, and their behavior soon proved the truth of this judgment. After several Spaniards raped or attempted to rape Amerindian women, the Caddos drove them out of the region. The Frenchmen approaching the same group of Natives took a very different tack, accepting offers of intermarriage and establishing permanent residences that demonstrated their commitment to the people and area. One French leader maintained his leadership position and residence near the Caddos for nearly forty years. The French participated in Caddo rituals that incorporated them into the Native community as brothers and confirmed the ties between them. As a result, they enjoyed long-standing peace and mutually beneficial trade and alliances.[58]

In contrast to the French, the largely Puritan New English colonists did not intermarry with the Amerindians, because of their cultural and religious aversion to the practice and also because their nearly equal sex ratios and rapidly growing population meant that they did not have to.[59] Outside Puritan New England, English intermarriage with Amerindians was more common. Traders in the Southeast, many of whom were of Scottish descent, frequently had Native wives, as did the English, Spanish, and French traders among Amerindians of the Mississippi and Illinois regions, and the French settlers of Acadia.[60] These ties facilitated peace, trade, and alliance among the immediate participants and also between their respective societies.

The Impact of Christianity on Amerindian-European Alliances

Like fictive and actual kinship, religion could also create ties between Europeans and Amerindians that were instrumental in forming alliances. A large number of Native groups and individuals converted to the Christianity of their European neighbors. For those converts, Christianity filled some of the same kinship-centered roles as the Native religion had. Evan Haefeli and Kevin Sweeney argue that at the Huron mission of Lorette, Catholicism "united the community of the living in peace and charity and kept its members connected with their ancestors" through such means as the Feast of All Saints, a holy day that commemorated the deceased, as had the Native Feast of the Dead.[61] The Catholic practice of godparenthood, too, had the same function as the Native practice of fictive kinship to bind Amerindian converts to European fellow believers.[62] Like the Native kinship bonds, the role of godparent was reciprocal, with the parent receiving respect and a degree of obedience from the godchild, and the child receiving protection, spiritual guidance, and generosity from the godparent. Both the French and the Spanish used this role to create ties that they expected would anchor the faith of young Amerindian converts and, in the process, cement their ties to them. John Kessell notes that the Spanish governor of New Mexico, Diego de Vargas, boasted that he "took advantage in all the pueblos of the ruse of being the compadre [godfather] not only of the headmen and leaders, but also of the other Indians" in an attempt to bind them to the Spanish.[63] Susan Sleeper-Smith asserts that "French authority over the North American interior rested on the hegemony" of the Catholic kinship networks of converts in Metis communities of the Illinois country. Links through godparenthood or marriage connected Catholics in both small and large trade outposts, creating a communication network. French traders married to Amerindian women were part of these networks, and French authorities used these chains of connection and communication to extend the reach of their authority and recruit warriors for military expeditions.[64]

Catholic priests living in Amerindian communities gained influence with their Native flock by assuming traditional familial and leadership roles, and as the "de facto representatives of the French government," they helped sustain Native ties with New France.[65] Father Gabriel Druillettes took on the role of a shaman among the mid-seventeenth-century Wabanakis, who declared of him:

> The Father is now one of our nation; that we have adopted him for our fellow-countryman; that we pay him consideration and love, as the wisest of our Captains, and respect him as the Ambassador of Jesus, to whom we wish to give ourselves entirely; and consequently, whoever attacks him, attacks all the Abnaquiois.[66]

The Oneidas ritually adopted the Jesuit priest Pierre Millet in the place of a sachem in 1689, and a pro-English Mohawk snarked, "The Jesuit hath as great authority in Oneyde as any Sachim of them all and rules the roast there."[67] The Mohawks of Kahnawake insisted on adopting all their Jesuit priests into clans and giving them Mohawk names, a practice the Catholic Church hierarchy reluctantly accepted.[68]

Most of the Catholic mission villages were located along the St. Lawrence River, but after the 1680s the French government directed some priests to set up residence farther south in Acadia, a region frequently in dispute between the French and English. In Acadia, where there were few European settlers, Mi'kmaq converts and colonists worshipped together, and the priests who served them "played a vital role in community life as a link to God, and as counselors, teachers, and intermediaries between themselves and French authorities. . . . Religious faith and practice bound the two peoples together in ways that complemented their familial ties." [69] Thus, priests in Wabanaki communities such as Sillery were able to use their roles as quasi family members to engage warriors for attacks on the English, keep trade flowing toward Quebec, and expand French influence in a crucial buffer zone.[70]

While religion provided a bond between some Europeans and Amerindians, it sometimes severed bonds between converted and unconverted Natives. Such was the case for the Massachusetts and Nipmucks of New England, whose conversion made them the targets of suspicion and animosity from fellow Natives.[71] Among the Iroquois, too, converts to Catholicism found their loyalties questioned, and with some cause.[72] The suspicions and occasional violence directed at converts by their unbelieving kin led some to flee their home villages for refuge in Catholic mission communities such as Kahnawake. Abandoning their former homes and associates demonstrated their greater loyalty to their fellow converts and their Jesuit teachers and made them a logical source of soldiers for French military expeditions.[73]

Religious affiliation, like other forms of alliance, had military consequences. By 1700, there were at least one thousand Iroquois converts in the St. Lawrence River valley and in the borderlands between Canada and New England; these became primary recruiting grounds for French military raids. Warriors from Kahnawake and other mission villages made up the bulk of French raiding parties against Deerfield, Massachusetts, during Queen Anne's War in 1704.[74] In New England as well, Protestant Amerindian "praying towns" supplied soldiers to English military forces from the time of King Philip's War (1676 to 1678) through the imperial wars of the succeeding century.[75]

The Wabanakis: A Case Study

Kin and kinlike connections made military assistance and trade natural, and positive interactions through alliance and trade could, in turn, strengthen ties. But the opposite held true as well. Disappointments in alliance and trade could undermine the carefully forged connections between peoples. Thus far, I have noted the general patterns in diplomatic interactions between Native peoples and Europeans throughout eastern North America. A more narrowly focused examination of one relationship, that between the Wabanakis of Maine and Acadia and the French and English in the late seventeenth century, provides a case study of the role of religion, trade, and kinship in European-Amerindian alliances, as well as the consequences of the failure of any of these elements.

Wabanaki is a collective term for several Algonquian Amerindian groups in the Maine/Acadia region and includes the Penobscots, Abenakis, Passamaquoddys, Maliseets, and Mi'kmaq.[76] Their location in an area contested by the English and French in the colonial period made them attractive as allies to both European powers. To the French, whose settlers in Acadia numbered only 885 as late as 1685,[77] the Wabanakis offered a buffer against the expanding English population north of Massachusetts, which exceeded 10,000 during the same time period.[78] Keeping the Wabanakis' loyalty might prevent them from becoming English allies who then could be used to attack Quebec. This was a reasonable fear. In 1690 the English had seized the French post of Port Royal, and months later, they directly attacked Quebec itself. Even though this attack was a dismal failure, the French knew that Providence—in the guise of an outbreak of smallpox among the English—had been their chief defense.[79] Having Wabanaki allies also was attractive as a counterbalance to the Iroquois, who were frequently at odds with the French and their Algonquian allies.[80]

For the English, too, maintaining good relations with the Wabanakis was important for both military reasons and trade. Although English fears of French-Catholic intrigues with Amerindians often outpaced reality, there was enough evidence of actual collusion to continue to fuel rumors.[81] Beginning in the 1670s, Catholic priests had taken up residence in a number of Amerindian towns, particularly those accepting refugees from King Philip's War in the south. There, they won many converts to Catholicism,[82] and the English feared, with good reason, that these religious and cultural ties would secure political loyalty to the French. Rumor had it that attacks on western Massachusetts communities in 1688 had involved both Maine Wabanakis and Native refugees of King Philip's War going south from their new villages in Canada.[83] Like the French, the English believed that securing the alliance of the Wabanakis would protect them from such attacks and secure the fur trade for themselves.

What about the interests of the Wabanakis? The choice between the English and the French was not clear-cut. On one hand, the English offered better trade—more goods at lower prices—and the Wabanakis, like most other Amerindians, had adapted to the convenience and superior performance of European metals and textiles. On the other hand, the rapidly growing English population was encroaching on Native lands, and with more and closer contact between English and Amerindians, the grievances between them grew. The tiny population of French, in contrast, offered no such threat, and some of them had married Amerindians. One such marriage was that of the daughter of the Penobscot sachem Madockawando to the French nobleman and trader Baron St. Castine. This and other marriages created kinship ties notably absent between the Wabanaki and English settlers.[84] In addition, the Catholic priests in such Wabanaki communities as Norridgewock and Medoctec forged kinlike relationships with Amerindians. Hence, it is not surprising that during most of the last decade of the seventeenth century, the years of King William's War, the Wabanakis favored an alliance with the French. But this was not always the case, nor was it the case for all Wabanaki peoples. Immediate circumstances—famine, French or English offenses, intertribal conflicts—could, and frequently did, sway the Wabanakis from one ally to the other.

The seesaw between the English and the French became particularly noticeable during King William's War, from 1688 to 1699. Compared with the small mountain of writing on King Philip's War, King William's War has attracted very little study, either in the past or today.[85] But it was an important transition between the local colonial wars and the imperial wars of the eighteenth century. In this war, in which imperial and local reasons for violence overlapped, Wabanaki Amerindians were, for the first time, pressed hard by the French and English governments to choose between them.[86] One leading element swaying the Natives' decision to ally with one or the other European power was access to trade goods.

European trade reached Wabanakia well before the English settled permanently in New England. As early as 1580, Natives had stockpiled large numbers of hides at Penobscot Bay for trade with passing Europeans, and they quickly recognized the utility of European metals for cooking and weaponry.[87] By the late seventeenth century, much of the Natives' traditional hunting practice had died with those who carried its specialized knowledge.[88] As a result, the Amerindians relied on European firearms for the hunting that supplied much of their diet in a region with a short growing season. While English governments periodically banned sales of guns and powder to Amerindians, Natives could simply turn to the French for supplies or, as frequently happened, to English traders willing to sell firearms despite prohibitions.[89] Thus the Wabanakis were dependent on European firearms by the time King Philip's War broke out in 1675. That dependency was increased by European expansion onto Amerindian lands. English settlements interfered with Wabanaki hunting and fishing grounds; their cattle trampled or ate Wabanaki corn, leaving the Natives susceptible to "perish of hunger."[90]

While the French had no official involvement in King Philip's War between 1675 and 1678, they did play a minor role, supplying Amerindians with powder and ammunition—or at least the promise of them.[91] During a peace parley in the fall of 1675, a group of Wabanaki sachems asked the English for supplies of guns and powder, as well as other assistance during the winter. This request was particularly urgent because the English had seized the Wabanakis' guns earlier in the war.[92] When the English refused these requests, the sachems warned that they might turn to the French for assistance and, in turn, shift their loyalty to them.[93] Again, as the war was drawing to an end, the Penobscot sachem Madockawando made the supply of guns and powder a condition of the peace treaty that his agent, Mogg Heigon, negotiated with the English in November 1676. He promised that if given this assistance, he would restrict his trade to the English government's authorized agents.[94] Such promises and threats were a preview of the critical part that competition for Amerindian trade would play in Native decisions about alliance in King William's and later wars.

The opening foray in King William's War in New England was a series of Amerindian attacks on English livestock, in direct response to significant English abuses, including their repeated failure to adhere to the terms of previous peace treaties (1678, 1685) and their expansion onto Amerindian lands. Among the rumors that preceded the violence was that a group of Wabanakis had gone to Canada to fetch ammunition.[95] Such rumors functioned as warnings to the English: Treat us well, give us the trade we need, and respect past treaties, or we will turn to the French. It is notable, however, that immediately after the first bloodshed of the war at North Yarmouth in September 1688, the Amerindians made overtures for peace, going so far as to travel to Boston to seek a renewal of relations, particularly trade with the English.[96] The English had refused to have any trade whatsoever with Amerindians in the aftermath of the North Yarmouth attacks, and the goods normally supplied by the English became desperately scarce, "by which means ye Indians were so distressed for want of fire-arms powder & lead yt they scarcely did subsist."[97] But the journey to Boston ended fruitlessly, as the town's response to news of the Glorious Revolution preempted negotiations.

Why, after suffering repeated abuses from the English, did the Amerindians not simply make good on their threats to turn to the French for ammunition, powder, and provisions? Why, if the French were willing to supply them, did the Amerindians so quickly seek reconciliation and renewed trade with the English? Because the French promised much but did not consistently deliver. One reason for this may have been that the French viewed the Wabanakis of Acadia as less important allies than the Algonquians and Christian Iroquois of the St. Lawrence River valley. These Natives, frequently employed in raids against the English, received the first and best of the limited French supply of gifts and trade goods.[98] Another reason that the French did not supply the Wabanakis consistently was the ongoing war between the French and English in Europe. Even though France's Louis XIV was the most powerful monarch in Europe, he was opposed by the "Grand Alliance" of England, the Netherlands, and Spain, whose navies interrupted regular trade to the French colonies in America. English colonial officials did their best to advertise this French disadvantage. For instance, in February 1692, Massachusetts officials directed their agents to contact Wabanaki leaders and inform them that two large ships had just arrived in the English port, laden with supplies, and that they were unlikely to be able to get any such goods from the French, "it being probabl[e] that ye ffrench will be incapacitated to afford them Succours most of ye Princes in Europe being joyned in a confederacy against ffrance."[99]

The Amerindians did not need English propaganda to tell them this. In August 1692, the Penobscot sachem Madockawando traveled to Quebec to visit the French governor, Frontenac, seeking the trade and supplies that he and other Wabanaki sachems had been unable to obtain from the English in

1689. Frontenac did provide some presents in return for Madockawando's gift of five English captives, but these were far less than the sachem and his people had expected.[100] John Nelson, an English captive then in Quebec, reported that Madockawando and other Amerindians "would often discourse their discontent, to some of us who understand their language." Frontenac's stinginess with gifts was a violation not only of the reciprocal relationship symbolized in Madockawando's gift of captives but also of the kinship role of father that French governors consistently claimed for themselves. A father should give generously to his children. If he did not, the Amerindian sachems allied to him would fail in their own roles as generous providers, and his people might shift their loyalties to others. With such a shift in mind, Nelson took the opportunity to promise Madockawando an English trading house on the Penobscot River, an answer to the "little satisfaction" the Amerindians had received from the French.[101]

Not only were French trade goods in shorter supply than English goods, but they were more difficult to find and consistently more expensive. While English traders regularly carried goods to various locations along the Maine and Acadian coasts, the French expected the Wabanakis to make the journey to Quebec—a fourteen-day trek overland—or wait for the yearly shipment of "presents" at the French fort on the St. John River.[102] Supplies sold to the Amerindians after presents were distributed were far more expensive than the same goods from the English: clothes and blankets were twice the English price, powder four times the price, and guns five times the price.[103] Compounding the problem were the furs that glutted the French market in the latter half of the 1690s.[104]

The French failure to give generous gifts and meet the Amerindians' demand for reasonably priced goods had swift and severe consequences. In 1693, Madockawando and other Amerindian sachems once again made peace overtures to the English, indicating their desire for trade and for the return of captives held in Boston.[105] Along with the sachems Moxes, Bomazeen, Edgeremet, and others, Madockawando signed a truce with the English at Pemaquid on July 21, 1693, then returned twenty days later to confirm the peace.[106] Reports from the English captives released in these negotiations confirmed the importance of trade goods and provisions to the Wabanakis' shift of loyalty. They said that for more than a year, the Amerindians had been discussing a design

to seek to the English to be in good terms with them, expressing their weariness of the War and lately resolved to cast off their Fryar who has laboured to push them forward in making further attempts against the English[,] giving them Expectation of receiving assistance from the French wherein they have found themselves to be deceived.[107]

The French leaders in Acadia knew what the Amerindians expected of proper allies. In September 1693, Acadian Commandant Villebon, who had learned of the English-Wabanaki treaty at Pemaquid, set about to restore the Wabanakis' loyalty to the French through a dramatic demonstration of his commitment to Amerindian expectations of allies, including establishing ties of fictive kinship, being generous with presents and regular with trade, and observing the ritual protocols that had long structured Amerindian-European relations. Promising him "presents," Villebon sent for the Penobscot sachem Taxous, who remained loyal to the French. When he arrived, Villebon "adopted him as my brother and gave him the best suit of clothes I had." In return, Taxous promised to provide warriors to fight for the French and to "induce Madokowando to join him, or render him contemptible to all the young Amerindians."[108] In June, in response to the efforts of Taxous and other sachems, Amerindians from many areas of Wabanakia, including Kennebec, Pentagoet, and Meductic, began to arrive at Nashwaak on the St. John River. Villebon held a great feast for them and gave them presents. At the feast, a Kennebec sachem, speaking for all the assembled Amerindians, excused their negotiations with the English, noting that "it was our need for many things and our distress at seeing our families destitute, which drove us to make overtures to the English." Then in an overt demand for favorable terms of trade from the French, the Kennebec sachem declared,

> It only depends on thee that we do not in future, have the same cause. Therefore, tell us what merchandise will be for sale on this river; when thou hast agreed with us on the price we promise to cease all negotiations with the English and to prevent our youths from trading with them.[109]

Faced with this demand, Villebon had little choice but to agree to fixed prices that "would not be changed while the war lasted, to make manifest the advantages they would derive from trading on this river."[110] The Natives' demand for fixed prices was a common one. Because the exchange of goods, ceremonial or otherwise, was linked to a kin relationship, Amerindians saw any change in the prices of goods as a betrayal: "What was a financial transaction for one party was a transaction of honour for the other."[111] French supply problems and preferences for other alliances had not changed, so this concession meant that either they would take significant losses or they would be unable to keep their promises to supply all that the Amerindians needed.

And that is what happened. For the remainder of the war, the French could provide "presents" worth only about 3,400 livres each year. Although this was barely enough to keep Wabanaki warriors in the field for two months, the French expected them to raid constantly. These constant raids cut into the hunting and planting that supplied Amerindian families still at home. Moreover, 3,400 livres a year was an average, and in some years the Amerindians received as little as 400 livres worth of supplies.[112] In a period in which the Wabanakis had adapted to European weapons, cooking implements, and other trade goods, these objects had become a necessity of life, so much so that even some Catholic missionaries—normally the chief advocates of French interests—urged the Wabanakis to trade with the English to sustain themselves.[113] Local Acadian officials were well aware of the shortfall and repeatedly requested more goods, but they were rarely supplied.[114]

Failing to provide sufficient gifts and reasonably priced trade goods violated reciprocal kinship expectations. The French compounded this failure by shifting their military strategy a few years into King William's War. In the initial skirmishes, French officers and soldiers had accompanied the Amerindians in attacks on English settlements. But by 1694, that practice had essentially ceased in Acadia. Instead, the French supplied the Wabanakis with powder and provisions and asked them to carry out raids entirely on their own, a request that the Norridgewock Amerindians claimed was a violation of the kin obligations that the provisions symbolized. Speaking to the French governor, Vaudreuil, the Natives declared, "A Father . . . when he sees his son engaged with an enemy stronger than he, comes forward, extricates his son and tells the enemy that it is with him he has to do."[115] Allies were expected to exchange presents, and they also were expected to come to each other's aid. Consequently, as the French began acting less and less like kin, the Amerindians began demanding trade goods *before* they would fight for them, thereby changing their relationship from a fictive kinship to a simple economic exchange: service rendered after receiving payment.[116] Thus, the French, who had always been more comfortable than the English with ritual and more adept at Amerindian protocols of kinship and exchange, squandered that diplomatic advantage. Under a commercial exchange system, the French could not compete with the English. The Wabanakis learned this lesson in King William's War, and it had a significant impact on their decisions about alliance in later wars.[117]

Conclusion

This brief overview of Wabanaki-European relations in the late seventeenth century demonstrates that the Europeans' failure to conform to the Natives' diplomatic expectations undermined the delicate balance of cross-cultural alliance. Similar experiences took place across North America. As the European allies failed to fulfill their kin obligations, the Natives shifted their loyalties to those who would fulfill them, thus maintaining a balance of power between themselves and the European powers vying for control of the continent. As long as the Amerindians retained power in relation to the Europeans, they could maintain their diplomatic protocols, incorporating Europeans into their kinship networks. The Iroquois did this well into the eighteenth century. Finally, however, two developments made maintaining the Amerindian ways of diplomacy increasingly difficult and, eventually, impossible. One was the booming European population, particularly in the English colonies. The other was the English defeat of France in the Seven Years' War, which resulted in the withdrawal of the French from the North American continent.

By the mid-eighteenth century, the non-Amerindian population in the English colonies had reached one million and was doubling every twenty-five years. As a result, the settlers had begun the inexorable process of spilling over the Appalachians into Amerindian territory.[118] When the Amerindians and the English met in council, the English requested land rather than furs or other Native goods as a demonstration of Amerindian friendship and loyalty. Under the impact of European expansion and diminishing resources, the Natives sometimes shifted to European modes of interaction, as the Wabanakis did by requiring pay before they would fight for the French. In another poignant example from eighteenth-century Pennsylvania, the Munsee spiritual leader Papunhank spoke against the traditional Native diplomatic system, which had become a tool for the English to extract land from Amerindians. He argued, probably with some irony, that Amerindians should adopt a trade system "ordered by the same ethical and moral principles that governed Christian behavior in white communities. Papunhank called upon God to shame the English into acting properly when dealing with Amerindians."[119] In other words, he challenged Christians to apply their religious principles, such as treating others as they would wish themselves to be treated, to their economic lives, as the Amerindians had long done. His plea is evidence that in an increasingly English-dominated world, Amerindian diplomatic protocols were failing to protect Native interests. By the middle of the eighteenth century, the growth of the English population, wars, and sporadic violence had driven many Amerindians from their homelands to refuges in Canada or to the west. Many of the Natives who stayed behind publicly acknowledged their subjection to local English governments, even if they privately continued to view themselves as sovereign peoples.[120]

The withdrawal of France from North America in 1763 had an even more profound impact on the Natives' ability to maintain their ways of diplomacy with Europeans.[121] Amerindians such as the Wabanakis, Iroquois, and others residing in borderlands between empires had grown adept at playing European powers off against one another by shifting (or threatening to shift) loyalties or, as the Iroquois did in 1701, achieving neutrality through skillful diplomatic negotiations.[122] Skill in negotiating with competing European empires and still sizable numbers in eastern North America allowed the Natives to maintain a balance of power with Europeans in many parts of the continent.[123] But that balance disappeared in 1763, and the English were quick to abandon the protocols that had shaped Native-European interactions for generations. The English had long complained that the extended councils, gift exchanges, and ceremonies of Native diplomacy were "tedious" and expensive, but they were compelled to conform to Amerindian expectations to keep them from shifting their loyalty and trade to the French.[124] Now, however, the English were free to ignore Amerindian protocols, an action that immediately sent the message that they neither respected Amerindians nor considered themselves in a relationship of mutual obligation.[125]

The withdrawal of the French also allowed the English to more openly assert their dominion over the Amerindians. Well before 1763, many of the Natives of eastern North America, like Massasoit's Wampanoags, had been forced to accept the status of subjects under the dominion of not only distant crowns but also local representatives of crown authority.[126] After 1763, even the status of subject was denied to many Amerindians, as the British increasingly considered the Amerindians unfit for the privileges and obligations of subjects of the crown. Instead of the relationship of mutual obligation that Native diplomatic protocols created, or even the ties of obedience and protection that the status of subjection to the crown implied, most Natives after 1763 were relegated to a lower category as racial others, and the world in which Amerindians and Europeans had intermingled and negotiated in relative equality disappeared.[127]

1. *Mourt's Relation: A Journal of the Pilgrims at Plymouth* (Bedford, MA.: Applewood Books, n.d.), 58; see also Jenny Hale Pulsipher, *Subjects unto the Same King: Indians, English, and the Contest of Authority in Colonial New England* (Philadelphia: University of Pennsylvania Press, 2005), chap. 1.

2. *Mourt's Relation*, 56–57.

3. Neal Salisbury, ed., *The Sovereignty and Goodness of God, by Mary Rowlandson, with Related Documents* (Boston: Bedford Books, 1997), 12. On the Amerindians' perception that the agreement was reciprocal, see Pulsipher, *Subjects unto the Same King*, 18–20.

4. *Mourt's Relation*, 55, 57–58. Following this agreement, Edward Winslow, representing Plymouth's governor, traveled to Massasoit's home with gifts to seal the alliance (60–65), and the Natives frequently visited the Plymouth colonists thereafter, most famously for the 1621 harvest feast now commemorated as the first Thanksgiving (82).

5. In this chapter, I place ritual and religion in the same category. Native rituals, shaped by Amerindian spirituality and beliefs, were used in diplomatic protocols to create ties of fictive kinship and loyalty.

6. David H. Dye, *War Paths, Peace Paths: An Archaeology of Cooperation and Conflict in Native Eastern North America* (New York: Alta Mira Press, 2009), 17.

7. Timothy Shannon, *Iroquois Diplomacy on the Early American Frontier* (New York: Penguin Books, 2008), 30.

8. Dye, *War Paths*.

9. Ibid., 73–78, 11.

10. Ibid., 166.

11. Daniel Richter, *The Ordeal of the Longhouse: The Peoples of the Iroquois League in the Era of European Colonization* (Chapel Hill: University of North Carolina Press, 1992), 14; Shannon, *Iroquois Diplomacy*, 21.

12. Dye, *War Paths*, 106, 149–50.

13. Ibid., 90, 162.

14. Richter, *The Ordeal of the Longhouse*, 19; Heidi Bohaker, "Nindoodemag: The Significance of Algonquian Kinship Networks in the Eastern Great Lakes Region, 1600–1701," *William and Mary Quarterly*, 3d ser., 63, no. 1 (January 2006), 23. Kathleen J. Bragdon argues that the patrilineal kinship system of many New England Natives preceded contact with patriarchal European societies. See her *Native People of Southern New England, 1500–1650* (Norman: University of Oklahoma Press, 1996), 153, 157–59.

15. Dye, *War Paths*, 150, 162.

16. Mary Druke Becker, "Linking Arms: The Structure of Iroquois Intertribal Diplomacy," in *Beyond the Covenant Chain: The Iroquois and Their Neighbors in Indian North America, 1600–1800*, ed. Daniel K. Richter and James H. Merrell (University Park: Pennsylvania State University Press, 2003), 33. See also Richter, *The Ordeal of the Longhouse*, chap. 1.

17. Dye, *War Paths*, 162.

18. Jane Merritt, *At the Crossroads: Indians and Empires on a Mid-Atlantic Frontier, 1700–1763* (Chapel Hill: University of North Carolina Press, 2003), 55.

19. Shannon, *Iroquois Diplomacy*, 23.

20. Ibid., 44.

21. Alan Greer, *Mohawk Saint: Catherine Tekakwitha and the Jesuits* (New York: Oxford University Press, 2005), 11; Shannon, *Iroquois Diplomacy*, 27–28.

22. Richter, *The Ordeal of the Longhouse*, 47.

23. On the New England Natives' inability to retain their diplomatic patterns with English settlers, see Pulsipher, *Subjects unto the Same King*, 22–29.

24. Kathleen DuVal, *The Native Ground: Indians and Colonists in the Heart of the Continent* (Philadelphia: University of Pennsylvania Press, 2006).

25. Richard White, *The Middle Ground: Indians, Empires, and Republics in the Great Lakes Region, 1650–1815* (New York: Cambridge University Press, 1991), x. A recent review of the impact of White's "middle ground" paradigm appears in "The Middle Ground Revisited," a forum in the *William and Mary Quarterly*, 3d ser., 63, no. 1 (January 2006).

26. On the Iroquois in this period, see Denys Delage, *Bitter Feast: Amerindians and Europeans in Northeastern North America, 1600–64*, trans. Jane Brierly (Vancouver: University of British Columbia Press, 1993); Richter, *The Ordeal of the Longhouse*; Jose Antonio Brandao, *Your Fyre Shall Burn No More: Iroquois Policy toward New France and Its Native Allies to 1701* (Lincoln: University of Nebraska Press, 1997); and Shannon, *Iroquois Diplomacy*.

27. Richter, *The Ordeal of the Longhouse*, 59.

28. Descriptions of this ceremony appear in Richter, *The Ordeal of the Longhouse*, chap. 2; Shannon, *Iroquois Diplomacy*, 26–44; as well as throughout *Documents Relative to the Colonial History of the State of New-York* (hereafter *NYCD*), ed. John Romeyn Brodhead (Albany: Weed, Parsons and Company, Printers, 1853).

29. Richter, *The Ordeal of the Longhouse*, 140.

30. Francis Jennings, *The Invasion of America: Indians, Colonialism, and the Cant of Conquest* (New York: Norton, 1976), 155–56.

31. Becker, "Linking Arms," 31.

32. Delage, *Bitter Feast*, 73, 102.

33. Shannon, *Iroquois Diplomacy*, 41, 22 (italics in original).

34. J. M. Sosin, *English America and the Restoration Monarchy of Charles II: Transatlantic Politics, Commerce, and Kinship* (Lincoln: University of Nebraska Press, 1980), 10.

35. Shannon, *Iroquois Diplomacy*, 44. On European use of wampum, see Lynn Ceci, "Native Wampum as a Peripheral Resource in the Seventeenth-Century World-System," in *The Pequots in Southern New England: The Fall and Rise of an American Indian Nation*, ed. Laurence M. Hauptman and James D. Wherry (Norman: University of Oklahoma Press, 1990); Neal Salisbury, *Manitou and Providence: Indians, Europeans, and the Making of New England, 1500–1643* (New York: Oxford University Press, 1982), chap. 5.

36. *Mourt's Relation*, 54–55; and Bruce J. Bourque and Ruth H. Whitehead, "Trade and Alliances in the Contact Period," in *American Beginnings: Exploration, Culture and Cartography in the Land of Norumbega*, ed. Emerson W. Baker et al. (Lincoln: University of Nebraska Press, 1994), 131–47.

37. From *Mourt's Relation*, we learn that Massasoit "hath a potent adversary the Narragansetts, that are at war with him, against whom he thinks we may be some strength to him, for our pieces [guns] are terrible unto them" (58). On the appeal of European metals and other trade goods, see Daniel K. Richter, *Facing East from Indian Country: A Native History of Early America* (Cambridge, MA: Harvard University Press, 2001), chap. 2.

38. Shannon, *Iroquois Diplomacy*, 44.

39. Richter, *The Ordeal of the Longhouse*, 22.

40. Becker, "Linking Arms," 33.

41. White, *The Middle Ground*, 184; Alan Taylor, *American Colonies: The Settling of North America* (New York: Penguin Books, 2001), 280; Merritt, *At the Crossroads*, 214.

42. White, *The Middle Ground*, 180–84, quotation on 180.

43. Bohaker, "Nindoodemag," 23, 26. Bohaker notes that Wendat, Mascouten, Nipissing, and Amikwa representatives also chose not to use the term *father* for the French. Peter Cook claims that "metaphors of brotherhood prevailed, rather than those of paternity" in French encounters with seventeenth-century Hurons, Algonquians, and Montagnais. Cited in Catherine Desbarats, "Following the Middle Ground," *William and Mary Quarterly*, 3d ser., 63, no. 1 (January 2006): 81–96.

44. Cornelius J. Jaenen asserts that while making no explicit claim of sovereignty over Amerindians, the French authorities nevertheless assumed it "through the usual symbolic acts of taking possession of terra nullius, or lands not claimed and settled by another Christian prince. French dominion was proclaimed through the recognition of the independence of the 'allied nations' who identified with the French in military, commercial, and missionary encounters." See Cornelius J. Jaenen, "Characteristics of French-Amerindian Contact in New France," in David B. Quinn et al., *Essays on the History of North American Discovery and Exploration*, ed. Stanley H. Palmer (College Station: Texas A&M University Press, 1988), 88–89.

45. Quoted in Jaenen, "Characteristics," 91.

46. Pulsipher, *Subjects unto the Same King*, 94–100.

47. Daniel K. Richter, "Tsenacommacah and the Atlantic World, " in *The Atlantic World and Virginia, 1550–1624*, ed. Peter C. Mancall (Chapel Hill: University of North Carolina Press, 2007), 29–65.

48. Richter, *Facing East*, 148; Shannon, *Iroquois Diplomacy*, 43. Juliana Barr notes that the Caddos, too, "cast trade alliances in terms of fictive kinship categories of 'brotherhood.'" See Juliana Barr, *Peace Came in the Form of a Woman: Indians and Spaniards in the Texas Borderlands* (Chapel Hill: University of North Carolina Press, 2007), 86.

49. Shannon, *Iroquois Diplomacy*, 44.

50. Evan Haefeli and Kevin Sweeney, *Captors and Captives: The 1704 French and Indian Raid on Deerfield* (Amherst: University of Massachusetts Press, 2003), 68.

51. Colin G. Calloway, *First Peoples: A Documentary Survey of American Indian History* (Boston: Bedford/St. Martin's, 1999), 155.

52. Neal Salisbury, "Toward the Covenant Chain: Iroquois and Southern New England Algonquians, 1637–1684," in *Beyond the Covenant Chain: The Iroquois and Their Neighbors in Indian North America, 1600–1800*, ed. Daniel K. Richter and James H. Merrell (University Park: Pennsylvania State University Press, 2003), 63.

53. Bohaker, "Nindoodemag," 27.

54. See, for example, Sylvia Van Kirk, *Many Tender Ties: Women in Fur Trade Society* (Norman: University of Oklahoma Press, 1983); Jennifer S. H. Brown, *Strangers in Blood: Fur Trade Company Families in Indian Country* (Vancouver: University of British Columbia Press, 1980); and, more recently, Susan Sleeper-Smith, *Indian Women and French Men: Rethinking Cultural Encounter in the Western Great Lakes* (Amherst: University of Massachusetts Press, 2001).

55. James Merrell gives the example of the mixed-race trader, translator, and negotiator Andrew Montour in *Into the American Woods: Negotiators on the Pennsylvania Frontier* (New York: Norton, 1999), 54–68.

56. On French concern over French settlers who married Amerindian women turning "savage," see Owen Stanwood, "Unlikely Imperialist," *French Colonial History* 5 (2004): 47–50.

57. Quoted in Bohaker, "Nindoodemag," 27.

58. Barr, *Peace Came in the Form of a Woman*, 35, chap. 2. On the key roles that women played in Native diplomacy as symbols and emissaries of peace, intermediaries, and clan leaders, see Nancy Shoemaker, "An Alliance between Men: Gender Metaphors in Eighteenth-Century American Indian Diplomacy East of the Mississippi," *Ethnohistory* 46 (spring 1999): 239–63; Sleeper-Smith, *Indian Women and French Men*; and Alice N. Nash, "The Abiding Frontier: Family, Gender and Religion in Wabanaki History, 1600–1763" (PhD diss., Columbia University, 1997).

59. David A. Smits, "'We Are Not to Grow Wild': Seventeenth-Century New England's Repudiation of Anglo-Indian Intermarriage," *American Indian Culture and Research Journal* 11, no. 4 (1987): 1–32; In his study of Martha's Vineyard, David Silverman found only one example of English-Amerindian intermarriage. See his *Faith and Boundaries: Colonists, Christianity, and Community among the Wampanoag Indians of Martha's Vineyard, 1600–1871* (New York: Cambridge University Press, 2005), 94.

60. Colin G. Calloway, *White People, Indians, and Highlanders: Tribal Peoples and Colonial Encounters in Scotland and America* (New York: Oxford University Press, 2008), chaps. 5 and 6; James H. Merrell, *The Indians' New World: Catawbas and Their Neighbors from European Contact through the Era of Removal* (New York: Norton, 1989), 24–25. Sleeper-Smith, *Indian Women and French Men*; Robert Conkling, "Legitimacy and Conversion in Social Change: The Case of French Missionaries and the Northeastern Algonquian," *Ethnohistory* 21 (winter 1974): 7.

61. Haefeli and Sweeney, *Captors and Captives*, 61–63.

62. Susan Sleeper-Smith, "Women, Kin, and Catholicism: New Perspectives on the Fur Trade," *Ethnohistory* 47 (spring 2000): 426.

63. John L. Kessell, "The Ways and Words of the Other: Diego de Vargas and Cultural Brokers in Late Seventeenth-Century New Mexico," in *Between Indian and White Worlds: The Cultural Broker*, ed. Margaret Connell Szasz (Norman: University of Oklahoma Press, 1994), 37.

64. Sleeper-Smith, "Women, Kin, and Catholicism," 436.

65. Christopher Bilodeau, "The Economy of War: Violence, Religion, and the Wabanaki Indians in the Maine Borderlands" (PhD diss., Cornell University, 2006), 206; Richter, *The Ordeal of the Longhouse*, chap. 5.

66. Bilodeau, "The Economy of War," 159, 106–8; Kenneth M. Morrison, *The Embattled Northeast: The Elusive Ideal of Alliance in Abenaki-Euramerican Relations* (Berkeley: University of California Press, 1984), 82–83; Conkling, "Legitimacy and Conversion," 15.

67. Cited in Richter, *The Ordeal of the Longhouse*, 176.

68. Haefeli and Sweeney, *Captors and Captives*, 69.

69. Jon Parmenter and Mark Power Robison, "The Perils and Possibilities of Wartime Neutrality on the Edges of Empire: Iroquois and Acadians between the French and British in North America, 1744–1760," *Diplomatic History* 31 (April 2007): 183.

70. Bilodeau, "The Economy of War," 260–63, 231–39; Morrison, *The Embattled Northeast*, 88.

71. See Jenny Hale Pulsipher, "Massacre at Hurtleberry Hill: Christian Indians and English Authority in Metacom's War," *William and Mary Quarterly*, 3d ser., 53, no. 3 (July 1996): 459–86.

72. Haefeli and Sweeney, *Captors and Captives*, 57; Shannon, *Iroquois Diplomacy*, 37; Richter, *The Ordeal of the Longhouse*, 118–19.

73. Richter, *The Ordeal of the Longhouse*, 106–10.

74. Haefeli and Sweeney, *Captors and Captives*, 100.

75. Jean M. O'Brien, *Dispossession by Degrees: Indian Land and Identity in Natick, Massachusetts, 1650–1790* (Cambridge: Cambridge University Press, 1997), 60–62, 69; Daniel A. Mandell, *Behind the Frontier: Indians in Eighteenth-Century Eastern Massachusetts* (Lincoln: University of Nebraska Press, 1996), 51, 85.

76. On the Wabanaki, see Morrison, *The Embattled Northeast*; Emerson W. Baker, "Trouble to the Eastward: The Failure of Anglo-Indian Relations in Early Maine" (PhD diss., College of William and Mary, 1986); Bilodeau, "The Economy of War"; Emerson W. Baker et al., *American Beginnings: Exploration, Culture and Cartography in the Land of Norumbega* (Lincoln: University of Nebraska Press, 1994); and Emerson Woods Baker, "Finding the Almouchiquois: Native American Territories, Families, and Land Sales in Southern Maine," *Ethnohistory* 51, 1 (2004): 73–100.

77. Censuses of Canada, 1665 to 1871, available at www.statcan.ca/english/freepub/98-187-XIE/earlyfre.htm. For French reports on the population in Acadia and efforts to secure additional settlers and soldiers, see John Clarence Webster, ed., *Acadia at the End of the Seventeenth Century: Letters, Journals and Memoirs of Joseph Robineau de Villebon, Commandant in Acadia, 1690–1700 and Other Contemporary Documents* (Saint John: New Brunswick Museum, 1934), 123, 125, 154.

78. Evarts B. Greene and Virginia D. Harrington, *American Population before the Federal Census of 1790* (Baltimore: Genealogical Publishing, 1932, 1981, 1993), 9–14; Emerson W. Baker, "'A Scratch with a Bear's Paw': Anglo-Indian Land Deeds in Early Maine," *Ethnohistory* 36, 3 (1989): 246; William D. Williamson, *The History of the State of Maine*, 2 vols. (Hallowell, ME: Glazier, Master, 1832), 1: 571; William Willis, quoting Pierre Biard, said that Maine's pre-epidemic Amerindian population was 9,000 to 10,000. See *History of Portland*, part 1, in *Maine Historical Society Collections*, vol. 1, 1st ser., 287.

79. Emerson W. Baker and John G. Reid, *The New England Knight: Sir William Phips, 1651–1695* (Toronto: University of Toronto Press, 1998), chap. 5; James Phinney Baxter, ed., *Collections of the Maine Historical Society (CMHS)*, 2nd ser., *Documentary History of the State of Maine*, vol. 5, *The Baxter Manuscripts*, 168.

80. Bilodeau, "The Economy of War," 226–27.

81. Owen Stanwood, "The Protestant Moment: Antipopery, the Revolution of 1688–1689, and the Making of an Anglo-American Empire," *Journal of British Studies* 46 (July 2007): 481–508.

82. Bilodeau, "The Economy of War," chaps. 2–4; Morrison, *The Embattled Northeast*, chap. 3.

83. "New England's Faction Discovered, or a brief and true account of their persecution of the Church of England," 1690, in *The Andros Tracts, Publications of the Prince Society*, vols. 5–7, 1868–1874 (New York: Burt Franklin), part II, 207; J. W. Fortescue, ed.,

Calendar of State Papers, Colonial Series (hereafter CSPCS) (Vaduz: Kraus Reprint, 1964), 12: 582–83, item 1868. See also Stanwood, "The Protestant Moment," 493.

84. Conkling, "Legitimacy and Conversion," 7; Owen Stanwood, "Unlikely Imperialist," 43–62.

85. On King William's War, see Cotton Mather, *Decennium luctuosum* [1699], in *Narratives of the Indian Wars*, ed. Charles H. Lincoln (1913; repr., New York: Barnes & Noble, 1952), 169–300); Samuel Adams Drake, *The Border Wars of New England: Commonly called King William's and Queen Anne's Wars* (New York: Scribner, 1910). The war appears as a subject in Thomas Hutchinson, *The History of the Colony and Province of Massachusetts-Bay*, ed. Lawrence Shaw Mayo, 2 vols. (Cambridge, MA: Harvard University Press, 1936); Morrison, *The Embattled Northeast*; and Bilodeau, "The Economy of War." See also Jenny Hale Pulsipher, "'Dark Cloud Rising in the East': Indian Sovereignty and the Coming of King William's War in New England," *New England Quarterly*, 80, no. 4 (December 2007): 588–613.

86. On the concept of parallel and overlapping wars, see Haefeli and Sweeney, *Captors and Captives*, 2.

87. Bourque and Whitehead, "Trade and Alliances," 131–47.

88. Baker, "Trouble to the Eastward," 193.

89. Ibid., chap. 4.

90. Williamson, *The History of the State of Maine*, 1:594.

91. Emerson W. Baker, "New Evidence on the French Involvement in King Philip's War," *Maine Historical Society Quarterly* 27 (fall 1988): 85–91. Both Kenneth Morrison and Christopher Bilodeau state that there is no evidence that the French government directed any Amerindian or French attacks in King Philip's War. But Bilodeau acknowledges that independent French traders and priests supported the Wabanaki in attacks on the English. See Kenneth M. Morrison, "The Bias of Colonial Law: English Paranoia and the Abenaki Arena of King Philip's War, 1675–1678," *New England Quarterly* 53 (September 1980): 363–87; Bilodeau, "The Economy of War," 65.

92. William Hubbard, "A Narrative of the Troubles with the Indians in New-England, from Pascataqua to Pemmaquid," in *The History of the Indian Wars in New England from the First Settlement to the Termination of the War with King Philip, in 1677*, ed. Samuel G. Drake (New York: Kraus Reprint, 1969), 2:148–49.

93. Hubbard, "A Narrative of the Troubles," 154.

94. Ibid., 190–92.

95. Fortescue, ed., *CSPCS*, 11: 633–35, item 1683, appended paper, May 14, 1684.

96. The conflict known as King William's War in the American colonies began in 1688, a year before its European counterpart, the War of the League of Augsburg, which began in 1689.

97. Coll. Ledgels Memoriall touching Trade wth the Indians &c., in Baxter, ed., *CMHS*, 2nd ser., 10: 1–6. Madockawando's negotiations with Edmund Andros in April 1689 were interrupted by the Glorious Revolution, which resulted in Andros's being deposed. Madockawando and the sachems accompanying him returned to Maine without making peace.

98. Daniel H. Usner Jr. notes that the same situation prevailed in another region on the periphery of French colonial America: the lower Mississippi Valley. Both the quantity and quality of trade goods coming into Louisiana in the eighteenth century were low because "government and merchants in France continued to give lower priority to this colony than to other American possessions." See Daniel H. Usner Jr., *Indians, Settlers, &*

Slaves in a Frontier Exchange Economy: The Lower Mississippi Valley before 1783 (Chapel Hill: University of North Carolina Press, 1992), 78.

99. Baxter, ed., *CMHS*, 2nd ser., 5: 321–23.

100. John Nelson letters, reprinted in Thomas Hutchinson, *The History of the Colony and Province of Massachusetts-Bay*, ed. Lawrence Shaw Mayo (Cambridge, MA: Harvard University Press, 1936), 1:321–22.

101. Ibid.

102. Tibierge's memoir of the present state of Acadia, 1697, notes yearly English imports of brandy, sugarcane, molasses, and utensils to Beaubassin, Minas, and Port Royal in Acadia, taking pelts and grain in exchange (Webster, ed., *Acadia*, 155). On the travel time to Quebec, see Bilodeau, "The Economy of War," 278.

103. Bilodeau, "The Economy of War," 277. Bilodeau's source for these trade comparisons is *NYCD*, 9: 408–9.

104. Bilodeau states that in the mid-1690s, the annual worth of fur production was 140,000 livres but consumption was only 74,000 livres. In response, the Ministry of the Marine closed all but one trading post in the *pays d'en haut* ("The Economy of War," 278).

105. Webster, ed., *Acadia*, 13, 53; Morrison, *The Embattled Northeast*, 128.

106. Baxter, ed., *CMHS*, 2nd ser., 10: 7.

107. Ibid., 23: 9.

108. Webster, ed., *Acadia*, 55.

109. Ibid., 78.

110. Ibid., 79.

111. Delage, *Bitter Feast*, 103.

112. Bilodeau, "The Economy of War," 270–71.

113. Webster, ed., *Acadia*, 5.

114. For instance, Tibierge, agent of the Acadia Trading Company, reported in 1695 that the goods sent that year "will not be sufficient" to supply the Amerindians, adding the warning, "It is very certain that the presents sent every year by the King to the Indians of Acadia do much to preserve their alliance with the French; without the aid they derive from it they would be in no position to resist the English and, in consequence, would be forced to make peace with them" (Webster, ed., *Acadia*, 141–43).

115. Quoted in Bilodeau, "The Economy of War," 369.

116. Bilodeau, "The Economy of War," 65. John Clarence Webster points out that French officials recommended reserving what goods they had for wartime, so the transformation from a kinship to a commercial relationship came from both sides (Webster, ed., *Acadia*, 4).

117. Christopher Bilodeau discusses the Wabanaki role in later imperial wars in chaps. 5 and 6 of "The Economy of War."

118. Colin G. Calloway, *The Scratch of a Pen: 1763 and the Transformation of North America* (New York: Oxford University Press, 2006), 24.

119. Merritt, *At the Crossroads*, 84–85.

120. Nancy Shoemaker notes multiple examples from the seventeenth- and eighteenth-century documentary record of Amerindians claiming sovereignty and a "scholarly consensus" on the fact that Natives saw their land as "sovereign territories." See Nancy Shoemaker, *A Strange Likeness: Becoming Red and White in Eighteenth-Century North America* (New York: Oxford University Press, 2004), 17–18. For an example of

Amerindians accepting subjection while simultaneously claiming sovereignty, see Pulsipher, "Dark Cloud Rising in the East," 595–97. Clashes of Amerindian and English views of subjection and sovereignty also appear in Gregory Evans Dowd, *War under Heaven: Pontiac, the Indian Nations, and the British Empire* (Baltimore: Johns Hopkins University Press, 2002), chap. 2.

121. For a detailed account of the consequences of the events of 1763, see Calloway, *The Scratch of a Pen*.

122. In "The Perils and Possibilities," Jon Parmenter and Mark Power Robison describe the diplomatic prowess of the Iroquois in establishing and maintaining sustained neutrality after 1701.

123. On this balance, see Richter, *Facing East*, chap. 5.

124. See Merritt, *At the Crossroads*, 214; Calloway, *First Peoples*, 151; Richter, *Facing East*, 187–88.

125. Dowd, *War under Heaven*, 74–78; Richter, *Facing East*, 187. Richter notes that by 1763, Spanish power north of Mexico was "feeble," so it could not counter English strength after the French withdrawal.

126. Pulsipher, *Subjects unto the Same King*, 97–100.

127. Dowd, *War under Heaven*, 170–75; Richter, *Facing East*, 187. See also Daniel R. Mandell, *Tribe, Race, History: Native Americans in Southern New England, 1780–1880* (Baltimore: Johns Hopkins University Press, 2008).

3

The Military Revolution
of Native North America

Firearms, Forts, and Polities

WAYNE E. LEE

Violent conflict almost inevitably accompanies interactions between imperial or colonizing powers and indigenous peoples.[1] Conflict in turn generates cultural exchange, as each side learns about the other's warfare practices and adapts to or adopts them. In the storybook version of their (especially the English) arrival in North America, the Europeans learned how to use canoes and snowshoes and (more slowly) to fight in the vast forested landscape by skirmishing, individually aiming, and hiding behind trees. Meanwhile, the Amerindians learned how to use firearms and to avoid direct battles with European conventional forces. Thus far, the story is an old and familiar one, and not entirely wrong. But it is possible to ask deeper questions about this process and to refine the story by adding detail. In this regard, it is helpful to apply a model of military change and its consequences that was developed for Europe in exactly this period. European historians have suggested that in the early modern era, the technology and techniques of war underwent a profound transformation and that this transformation in turn affected European social and political organization. Although it was primarily a *military* revolution, its consequences were far broader.

This chapter takes a similar analytical approach, asking what the consequences were of introducing new technologies and techniques to Native American warfare and whether their introduction changed their way of war and thereby changed their social and political organization. Did Native Americans experience a military revolution, with its accompanying social and political implications, based on technology introduced from Europe?

The European Military Revolution

For comparative purposes, it is best to begin with the European military revolution, or at least one version of it. The literature on the subject is extensive, primarily devoted to whether it had chronological limits, whether it was truly revolutionary, and whether it actually gave the Europeans significant advantages in the post-1500 global struggle.[2] Of the several different models, the one most relevant here is that developed by Geoffrey Parker in his landmark *The Military Revolution: Military Innovation and the Rise of the West, 1500–1800*. He suggests that the invention of castle-busting artillery in the late fifteenth century led rapidly to the creation in the sixteenth century of a new style of bastioned artillery fortress, known then and now as the *trace italienne* style. Almost simultaneously, handheld firearms became important on the battlefield, which, when combined with the new emphasis on siege warfare, put a premium on larger and larger armies. The horrific expense associated with the *trace italienne*, with artillery parks, and with larger and larger armies dominated the budgets and policies of the emergent European states, which were frequently locked in combat. Brian Downing pushed this argument even further, indicating that the states most often drawn into the kind of "arms race" inspired by the military revolution were those that tended toward absolutism, whereas those less threatened, primarily England/Britain, were left with political room to maneuver that allowed for a more cooperative relationship among the commons, aristocracy, and king.[3] Parker's argument goes on to emphasize that naval developments may have constituted the real military revolution in terms of European global power, but that approach is less useful here.

A key aspect of this "revolution" was the use of firearms on the battlefield and the consequences of their use. The first firearms were highly inaccurate and took an exceedingly long time to reload. As a result, to be useful on the battlefield, they had to be used in large masses, producing volleys of shot capable of hitting large blocks of enemy infantry or cavalry. Europeans turned to ancient Roman models of discipline, as they understood them, to produce new systems of synchronized collective movement designed to make these formations more efficient. This, too, had social consequences, since the advantage of firearms was that they opened up a much wider pool of the male population to recruitment. No special skills were required to be a musketeer, only institutionalized training.[4] In the period considered here, the radical possibilities of this widening of social mobilization were contained by placing the old aristocratic elite in charge as officers, who used their disciplinary tools for social and operational control over their men. In the long run, however, firearms made it possible for all men to serve usefully in the state's armed forces, which then led to a new kind of politics and even a new kind of state. All these arguments necessarily oversimplify the historical processes, but they at least prompt the questions to ask about the Native American experience.

One further technical detail arising from developments in Europe needs to be addressed as well. Most of the military firearms of the early colonial period, from roughly 1550 to 1690, were *matchlock muskets*, a composite term. Although *musket* could have a very specific contemporary meaning referring to a specific model of firearm, here and more generally it is a catchall term for any firearm with an unrifled barrel, loaded from the muzzle. The lack of rifling and the *windage*, or the difference in diameter between the bullets and the barrel, meant that these firearms were likely to hit a human-sized target only from a distance of no more than one hundred yards, and preferably fifty yards. *Matchlock* refers to the ignition mechanism, in which pulling the trigger dipped a prelit length of cord, or *match*, into the pan, which then ignited the charge at the base of the barrel. The obvious problem was preparing and lighting the match before needing to fire. *Flintlocks* (familiar to modern Americans from pioneer movies) and an early version of them called *snaphaunces* became available early in the seventeenth century. Although flintlocks were as inaccurate as matchlocks, they did not require a prelit match. They were not widely adopted for military purposes in Europe until the turn of the eighteenth century, but the colonists abandoned matchlocks much sooner. Planning for the Massachusetts Bay Colony in 1629 suggested that eighty snaphaunces and twenty matchlocks be provided for every one hundred men, while Maryland in 1641 required men who wanted title to land to come equipped with "one musket or bastard musket with a snaphance lock," ten pounds of gunpowder, and forty pounds of bullets, pistol, and goose shot (some required of each). Despite this kind of encouragement for the newer technology, however, matchlocks had a long life, even in the colonies.[5] As we shall see, flintlocks proved much more congenial to Amerindian warriors than matchlocks did.

By discussing the European military revolution as background to the changes in Native North America, I am not pretending that these were directly comparable experiences. We already know, for example, that Native American nations did not become transatlantic powers as a result of changes in military practice and naval technology. Nor am I arguing that Parker's model for Europe is correct. But the broader theoretical question remains: What were the social, political, and cultural implications of the new military technologies—firearms and fortresses—and techniques?

Protohistoric Native American Warfare
(The Cutting-off Way of War)

To discuss a revolution requires beginning with the prerevolutionary methods of war. Although this is a controversial topic, a new consensus is emerging among archaeologists, anthropologists, and some historians.[6] Older interpretations of Native American tactical techniques suggested that they were relatively innocuous and bloodless before the arrival of the Europeans. Some scholars have argued more specifically that before contact, Native Americans preferred to engage in linear pitched battles fought in a ritualistic manner, with a great deal of mutual firing and dodging of missile weapons, and not many casualties.[7] A corollary to this interpretation was that the arrival of European technology and more lethal metal arrowheads, rapidly followed by clumsy but lethal guns, led Amerindians to abandon the pitched battle and rely entirely on ambush. This line of thinking has occasionally been taken to extremes, with some arguing that the Europeans introduced the Amerindians to torture and scalping and even to the deliberate killing of enemies in battle.[8] For example, after describing the death of fifty Mohawks in battle in 1669, one of the most frequently cited historians of Amerindian warfare calmly asserts what is in fact unknowable: "Such heavy losses in a single action were unheard of before the arrival of the white man and his weapons."[9]

This older paradigm, often called the *skulking way of war*, has two fundamental flaws: It overemphasizes the tactical shift to ambush as the preferred form of war, and it inaccurately describes the level of lethality in precontact Amerindian warfare. Consider Jacques Cartier's testimony about one of the first contacts in the Northeast in the sixteenth century. In 1533, the Toudaman Amerindians surprised some *two hundred* sleeping Iroquoian persons (men, women, and children) inside a temporary palisade. They set fire to the palisade and then killed all those who rushed out, save five.[10] To account for this kind of warfare and for the growing archaeological evidence of extensive precontact warfare, recent anthropological work has developed a more complex, and more convincing, description of Native American warfare.[11] The basic argument is that highly lethal and highly ritualized warfare could coexist, with one superseding the other depending on the circumstance.

Explaining this coexistence of lethal and ritual war begins with acknowledging the small scale of Amerindian polities. Recognizing this demographic vulnerability, when Amerindian war parties went on offensives, whether to exact revenge, gain prestige, acquire prisoners, or perhaps administer a political lesson, they sought to achieve those goals at minimum cost. The preferred method was to "cut off" enemy villages or individuals through surprise and ambush. Repeated success at surprising a village could render it uninhabitable, cutting it off from its cluster of related villages. This "cutting-off way of war" followed the same basic techniques whether the war party was large or small.[12] The initial target for a large war party would probably be an entire enemy village. If the village remained unaware of its approach, as the Hurons of St. Ignace were unaware of the Iroquois approach in 1649, the attackers could sneak in before dawn and inflict considerable casualties. In the village of St. Ignace, 397 out of 400 people were killed or taken prisoner.[13] Although the Hurons' disaster took place well after contact, there is solid archaeological evidence for the long continuity of a style of war that *could* be highly destructive and lethal. Three examples are the large-scale massacre at Crow Creek in South Dakota in the fourteenth century; a cemetery site in Illinois from the same era indicating a persistent series of violent attacks; and a recent reexamination of 119 precontact southern New England burials showing that 15 percent died from violent trauma, 20 percent of whom were women or children.[14] Furthermore, the documentary and archaeological evidence for the Mississippian societies of the Midwest and Southeast strongly suggest a pattern of elaborate and deadly warfare.[15] In a later era, admittedly postcontact, the Narragansetts' advice to the English in 1637 was clear and stark: "'The assault would be in the night when they [the Pequots] are commonly more secure and at home, by which advantage the English, being armed, may enter the houses and do what execution they please." The Narragansetts did request, however, that women and children be spared.[16] Achieving this kind of surprise was relatively rare, and generally a threatened village learned of an enemy approach, sent for help, and tried to ambush the approaching warriors by "waylay[ing] the pathe." Or, as we will see, they could gather behind a palisade wall.[17]

On some occasions, if the defenders felt confident enough in their numbers and preparedness, they could offer open battle, lining up their warriors to oppose the approaching enemy. Such battles were documented on several occasions by early European explorers. Samuel Champlain participated in one against the Iroquois in 1609.[18] The Powhatans enacted a mock battle for the benefit of the early Virginia colonists.[19] And in the mid-sixteenth century, Jacques Le Moyne de Morgues provided both a drawing and a description of a Florida tribe lined up for battle in a deep, massed formation.[20] Even later witnesses in New England continued to describe Indians as occasionally lining up for battle. Roger Williams described their "pitch field" battles as seldom killing twenty men, since "they fight with leaping and dancing, that seldome an Arrow hits, and when a man is wounded, unlesse he that shot followes upon the wounded they soon retire and save the wounded."[21] These open battles, as Williams indicated, proceeded without much result. Very few casualties, and possibly even the first letting of blood, sufficed to end the battle, and each side would return home.[22] In this sense, *battle* could be ritualized and only marginally lethal, but this says nothing about the lethality of *war*.

Rather than view open battle as the main object of a military expedition, it is probably more accurate to consider these encounters as moments in which the expedition *already had failed*, having lost the benefit of surprise. Battle was thus a kind of face-saving measure, and perhaps also a test of strength, that in the right circumstances could have decisive results. An example was the battle of "Sachem's Field," fought between the Narragansetts and the Mohegans in Connecticut in the summer of 1643. Miantonomi led a force of some nine hundred to one thousand Narragansetts into Mohegan territory (apparently still primarily armed with bows and hatchets), almost certainly hoping to surprise Uncas, the Mohegan leader (or sachem). After learning of their approach from his scouts, Uncas sent for help from his tributary villages. Gathering together about six hundred warriors, he refused to be shut up in his fortified town (Shantok), which at sixty meters square probably could not have usefully accommodated six hundred men. He instead moved to meet Miantonomi on an open field, where the two sides approached to within bowshot. A parley was proposed, and Uncas offered to settle their dispute in a single duel. Miantonomi, with the greater numbers, declined, and Uncas gave the signal to begin the attack immediately. Miantonomi was wearing a European mail shirt and, slowed by its weight, was seized by Uncas. Some Narragansetts, perhaps thirty, were killed. The vast majority fled unhurt.[23]

Notice the key role of failed surprise and the defending Mohegans' appeal to their nearby allied or tributary villages. In this case, failed surprise and timely reinforcements allowed the defenders to offer open battle. In other circumstances, if warning came too late, the defender, perhaps consisting only of the targeted village's residents, might choose to remain behind walls and send for help. In that case, the attackers had three basic choices: assault the walls, blockade the fort, or go home, and they had to make that choice fully aware that other defenders could arrive from related villages at any time. The first option was relatively rare, particularly during the precontact era, because of the technological balance between offense and defense. There was no easy way to overcome the defenders without absorbing significant casualties. Fire could be used to speed the assault, and it was certainly used on occasion, even before the Europeans' arrival.[24] In general, however, attackers seemed to prefer the blockade, supplemented by sniping at the walls from the cover of the woods and trying to cut off any individuals who strayed outside as messengers or water carriers. The besiegers could keep this up as long as significant enemy reinforcements did not arrive. In this way, the blockade avoided casualties while offering the possibility of taking isolated prisoners or scalps and gaining the prestige and appearance of victory.

In short, the technological and tactical balance of offense and defense, in both siege warfare and open battle, meant that warfare before the arrival of Europeans *usually* was a relatively mild affair. Successful surprise, however, overcame that limitation and could immediately produce huge per capita casualty ratios while sustained harassment through smaller ambushes and raids could produce equally damaging casualty rates over the long term.[25] To conclude, a seventeenth-century dictionary of the Narragansett language, which, although it contains only a few phrases with tactical implications, nevertheless conveys a good impression of the most important issues in Native American warfare at the outset of European contact: "They fly from us / Let us pursue," "They lie in the way," "They fortifie," "An house fired," "An Halfe Moone in war," and, probably most important of all, "Keep Watch."[26]

A Native American Military Revolution?

The arrival of Europeans with their technologies, techniques, and attitudes toward war presented Native Americans with a series of challenges. But these challenges, too, changed significantly over time as the numbers of Europeans, their goals, and their military capabilities all shifted. To use the English as an example, the very first arrivals were mostly soldiers interested in rapid profits, who were quickly succeeded by settlers interested primarily in accumulating land and only secondarily interested in trade with the Amerindians. These settlers fought as a militia, with widely varying skills and persistence. Then in the mid-eighteenth century, professional military forces from Britain arrived, with more cannon and expeditionary capability, although they tended to strike and leave. Meanwhile, all Native American peoples continued to war with other Amerindians and thus had to take account of those groups' techniques and goals as well. Although European technologies did indeed produce some profound changes, especially at the outset of contact, cultural continuity and Native American sociopolitical structures limited their extent. Following the example of Parker's analysis of the European military revolution, I focus next on two major changes in military technique and then ask whether those innovations explain the postcontact changes in Native American polities. The first military shift is firearms, and the second is fortifications.

Firearms

The attractions of the gun versus the bow still elicit a surprising amount of disagreement. Elaborate and convincing arguments have been made that the musket, especially the matchlock and the snaphaunces of the early seventeenth century, held few advantages over the native bow. All experts admit that the advent of the flintlock made the gun more attractive, primarily because it was lighter and handier than the matchlock and did not require the bright, smelly, position-revealing match. Nevertheless, Brian Given contends that even the flintlock had more faults than virtues compared with the bow.[27]

The problem with Given's argument is the evident and persistent eagerness of native peoples to acquire guns and the services of gunsmiths and their equally strenuous efforts to secure and maintain their access to gunpowder.[28] Given proposes that guns were attractive for their psychological effect against those enemies not yet supplied with them, but this does not account for the persistent and long-term quest for guns.

As Given and others have pointed out, the native self bow and the seventeenth-century musket had comparable effective ranges (50 yards optimum, 100 to 150 yards at the outside). The bow, however, could be fired much more quickly, did not require extensive material infrastructure (such as that required for making gunpowder), was generally more accurate in the hands of a skilled user, was silent, could be reloaded while kneeling, and could even occasionally penetrate iron armor (especially when equipped with iron or brass arrowheads). Against an enemy accustomed to its noise, flash, and smoke, the argument goes, the musket held few advantages. Admittedly, early snaphaunces and the later flintlocks avoided the problem of the match, but they were prone to misfire more often than matchlocks were (that is, when the flint did not spark).

Europeans (especially Englishmen with their tradition of using longbows) had played out many of the same arguments with one another about the relative efficacy of the bow versus the early musket. It seems clear that in Europe the gun initially succeeded the bow for demographic and economic reasons, and Europeans then profited in the long term by the room for improvement inherent in firearms technology.[29] Whereas the bow required a lifetime's training to use effectively, the musket could be learned quickly. This relative simplicity of use allowed for a significant expansion in the pool of men suitable for military service, and this expansion is a key component of the argument for a European military revolution. Native societies, however, had little to gain by expanding the category of potential warriors, since virtually all men of a particular age were warriors anyway. Given all these disadvantages, why did Native Americans pursue guns so avidly?

Some of the answers are obvious, some less so. For Amerindians, because the bow or the musket had to serve in both war and the hunt, something in the technology had to satisfy the needs of both pursuits. Although the burning match of the matchlock was ill suited to hunting deer, a carefully prepared charge in a flintlock could be highly effective (a musket typically misfires because of dampness or repeated firing). A musket ball was less likely than an arrow to be deflected by vegetation, and it also had a greater kinetic impact on the target. A deer hit with an arrow receives a very deep wound (arrows from modern bows often pass through a deer), which, though eventually lethal, might require the hunter to pursue the bleeding deer for some distance. In contrast, a musket penetrates flesh, shatters bone, and creates a larger wound cavity.[30] It "smacks," whereas an arrow "slices." According to Given's calculations, a military musketball at 50 yards hits a target with 706 foot pounds of kinetic energy. An arrow from a typical modern bow hits at 50 yards with 50 to 80 foot pounds of energy. This is more than enough to penetrate flesh and tissue and produce a killing wound, but it is much less likely to drop an animal in its tracks.[31]

The musket has similar advantages against humans. Much of a human target is limbs, especially when walls or trees are used to cover the trunk of the body. An arrow wound to the leg or arm is rarely lethal, although it can be debilitating. But a musketball strike to the arm or leg may shatter the bone and is more likely to carry debris into the wound, lead to infection, sepsis, and death. In 1612 William Strachey described Powhatan fears of such a "compound wound . . . where . . . any rupture is, or bone broke, such as our smale shott make amongst them, they know not easely how to cure, and therefore languish in the misery of the payne thereof."[32] In the immediate term, a man with a shattered leg or arm, flung to the ground by the weight of a musket shot, also makes a better target for being taken prisoner or scalped. Unable to flee, he becomes vulnerable and may hold up his fellows trying to carry him away from the field. The musket's kinetic energy also made it a more reliable penetrator of wooden armor (a hardened steel arrow point may, in fact, penetrate steel armor better than a soft lead ball, despite the difference in kinetic energy). Although there is early anecdotal evidence for

Amerindian bows penetrating European armor, the systematic evidence of the disappearance of wicker-and-wood armor (and shields) from the Native American repertoire is more convincing proof of the difference in the penetrating power of musket and arrow against a semirigid surface.[33] More obviously, bullets cannot be dodged, whereas arrows in flight over any distance (especially on an arcing trajectory) can be seen and dodged. Modern film footage of the Dani people's arrow and javelin battles in New Guinea shows this process clearly, and numerous European witnesses commented on the Amerindians' ability to dodge arrows.[34]

Finally, the musket could be loaded with multiple small shot (or even, famously, "buck and ball"—a load of small shot combined with a normal musket ball).[35] This, too, could serve both hunting and warfare practices better than a bow. *Very* high levels of skill are required to take small game with a bow. An improvised "shotgun" load, however, greatly improves the odds, as it also does against humans at short range. The shotgun-style loading of a musket is described from the very beginning of the colonial experience and became famous during the American Revolution. Its ubiquity among the colonists surely informed the Amerindians' use of it as well. The Connecticut militia in the Pequot War of 1637, for example, was ordered to carry twenty bullets and four pounds of shot.[36] Excavations at the Monhantic Fort, a Pequot fortified village occupied from the mid- to late 1670s, has found small shot (4 mm to 5 mm) almost exclusively, with only one full-sized bullet so far recovered.[37]

All in all, there were considerable advantages to preferring a musket over the bow.[38] More important, we must ask what effect on tactics and strategy those advantages had. At one level, the musket's effects were few indeed. Strategically, the cutting-off way of war had always emphasized surprise as the best means of destroying unaware villages or isolated parties while also increasing the odds of successfully taking prisoners. Guns did not change that strategic preference. Late in the eighteenth century, John Norton, part Cherokee and an associate of the Mohawk Joseph Brant, described how the Iroquois raided the Cherokees and Catawbas in the early part of that century in a manner that perfectly captures the cutting-off method carried out from a great distance:

> The Warriors sought fame to the South of the Ohio, in desultory excursions against the Cherokee and Catawbas. . . . [They] left home in parties from two hundred to ten. . . . [and traveled until they] came upon the Head Waters of Holston, along the Banks of which the Cherokee Hunters

were frequently scattered; —these they often surprised, killing and taking them prisoners. At other times, they proceeded to the Villages, but only in small parties to prevent discovery, —the Main Body generally remaining [behind at various camps now in] the State of Kentucky. . . . When the party detached, had gained Scalps or Prisoners, they fled to where their comrades awaited their return, to support them in case they might be surprised by superior force. . . . Many of these Parties were overtaken [during their march home], —others triumphantly returned with Scalps & Prisoners.[39]

At this point, Iroquois raiders had been equipped with guns for some time, but surprise and efficient movement through the wilderness continued to dominate strategy. Tactically, guns also did not change the use of a shower of missile fire, followed by the close-in fight with ax and club, designed to disable individuals for capture or scalping. What guns did do, however, was to make an open battle—intended primarily to display power and numbers and to sustain prestige—excessively lethal. To fight in large massed numbers, in the open, and against guns, now meant that missiles could not be dodged, armor was no longer effective, and wounds were more likely to turn fatal from infection or shattered bones. Amerindian battles had never been fought to hold ground, and for a small-scale, relatively egalitarian society, the incentives to avoid fatal casualties were great.

"Battles" still were fought, but they tended to follow a pattern different from the massed open confrontation of the pregunpowder era, and they took place in three main contexts. In one pattern, a fortified native village could be persuaded that the raiding party lurking in the woods outside the fort was too small to be a real threat, and the inhabitants might sally forth to attack and drive them away. Like the steppe warriors of Eurasia, however, this often proved to be a feint; the raiders often had hidden larger forces out of sight, and the sallying villagers found themselves outnumbered and cut off from their fort. This exact scenario happened to a Squakheag town on the Connecticut River in southern New Hampshire in December 1663. An Iroquois war party, primarily Mohawks, appeared outside the fort, and fifty Squakheags emerged from the fort to challenge them, pursued them into the woods, and ran headlong into a much larger waiting Iroquois force. Eighteen Squakheags fought their way out of the trap and retreated into their fort, whereupon the raid became a siege (about which more later).[40] Nothing suggests that similar scenarios did not play out in a pregunpowder age, but without guns, an open confrontation in front of the walls of the fort (possibly in the cleared space around it) likely would have preceded the feint and chase (much like the 1643 battle on Sachem's Plain discussed earlier). For defenders who had walls to hide behind, such an open confrontation no longer made sense once guns were in play because the risks were now greater.

Another type of "battle" was the classic ambush: attacking a war party, or any other party, from behind cover when they were entirely unaware, and especially when the target was small enough to be hit simultaneously all along its length. Such attacks almost certainly had always been a part of Native American warfare and were probably the sort of attack that produced the most casualties over the long term. Surprising a whole village could generate a single high-casualty event, but such major surprises were probably rare. Smaller parties on the move were easier to catch. In this sense, the "skulking way of war" phrase continues to make sense, but especially when skulking is used in its alternate meaning of "waiting in hiding" rather than "sneaking." A war party traveled to the vicinity of an enemy and waited for an opportunity to strike.

Finally, there was the large-scale ambush or meeting engagement between two large armed and prepared groups. Exemplary in this category are incidents when large European military expeditions, too large and spread out to be ambushed all at once, suddenly found the head of their column under attack. As the battle progressed, Amerindian warriors moved from tree to tree, sliding along the flanks of the column and forming a horseshoe of fire, something that they called the *half-moon* formation.[41] Most infamously, this was the type of attack that General Edward Braddock's army encountered in 1755 at Monongahela. But the technique was widespread, and the half-moon apparently was an old method. Roger Williams recorded in 1643 that the formation could be referred to in Narragansett with a single world: *Onúttug*.[42] As the warriors moved around the flanks of the column, they also found that the half-moon allowed them to attack the key weakness in a European professional military expedition: their pack train.

European armies operating in the wilderness depended on bringing their provisions with them. Back in Europe, they could rely on strings of depots and magazines in preplanned locations, and when they moved beyond the resupply distance of a magazine, they could turn to the countryside for supplies. In northwestern Europe, or in the settled coastal areas of North America, the countryside was densely inhabited, farmed, and beribboned with local (if poor) roads, all of which facilitated the daily collection of food and forage.[43] But in the wilderness, both Braddock in 1755 and John Forbes in 1758 had to cut their own roads to accommodate their cannon and baggage.

Similar efforts slowed other such expeditions. Accordingly, when Amerindians attacked, they often deliberately focused not on killing large numbers of soldiers but instead on destroying their provisions, hoping thereby to turn the whole expedition around.[44]

If, on one hand, gunpowder had not changed tactics very drastically, on the other hand, the dependence on gunpowder undermined an already shaky Amerindian ability to sustain long, repeated campaigns. A society that sends out most of its men to war loses their productive labor (typically as hunters, whether for trade or subsistence). A war party on the move was therefore operationally much more mobile and logistically self-supporting than a European force, but strategically they did not have the reserves of provisions that could be shipped in from other locations to sustain campaigns over long periods. Worse, if their primary European source of gunpowder had become their enemy, they had to find alternative sources or risk running out—as seems to have happened to some groups in the Amerindian alliance in the Yamasee War in 1715 and to the Cherokees in 1761.[45]

The other major vulnerability for Amerindians created by the shift to gunpowder was in the field of artillery. There are very few examples of Native Americans successfully using artillery. The Susquehannocks' fort in 1663 and again in 1675 had cannon, but those were probably fired by European gunners the first time.[46] The Cherokees who successfully blockaded the British in 1761 in Fort Loudoun, South Carolina (now Tennessee), confiscated the fort's cannon and hoped to force the British gunners to help them attack Fort Prince George, but the gunners escaped.[47] In 1685 a village of French Catholic Iroquois at Sault built a pentagonal, bastioned palisade, with one 8-pounder cannon mounted.[48] Swivel guns seem to have been successfully adopted, but they are not often mentioned, and using them was not much of a technical leap from a musket.[49] But these instances were clearly exceptions. More common was the Europeans' ability to bring cannon to bear on Amerindian forts, which usually quickly ended the confrontation (although the Susquehannocks in 1675 held out for seven weeks). On the European side, a *trace italienne* style–fortress equipped with cannon was generally invulnerable to assault by Amerindians, although extended sieges and trickery did lead to the capture of several such European forts, and smaller stockades were vulnerable.[50] The combination of fort and cannon, especially backed by European transatlantic capabilities, provided a kind of ultimate guarantee of security and persistence in North America. But to discuss cannon here only points up the even more interesting and variable role that fortifications played.

Fortifications

It is generally agreed that the arrival of Europeans and their goods made conflict more frequent in North America. As discussed earlier, there is more debate over whether their arrival meant an increase in the lethality of warfare, but the arrival into an already competitive system of new players from an unexpected direction who bore desirable trade goods almost inevitably generated new conflicts while also incorporating the newcomers into old conflicts.[51] The proliferation of fortifications has long been understood as an archaeological marker for the intensification of conflict, and a major period of proliferation had begun across much of the eastern part of the continent beginning around 1100 CE.[52] The arrival of Europeans apparently created another burst of fortification and in new regions. Furthermore, Native Americans responded to European military capabilities by changing the design of their forts and then finally abandoning them. Next I consider the increasing use of forts and the shifts in their design, in preparation for then asking how those changes, in conjunction with gunpowder, may have changed the nature of Native American political structures.

Southern New England provides an informative case. The archaeological evidence strongly suggests that at least Connecticut, Long Island, and Rhode Island were devoid of native fortifications before extensive contact with the English and the Dutch in the seventeenth century.[53] Despite the absence of evidence for a tradition of palisading, archaeologists suggest that the "traditional" form of fort in the region, as was true for much of the Northeast and parts of the Southeast, was the circular palisade with a baffle gate, most famously represented in the woodcut of the Pequot fort at Mystic, destroyed by the English in 1637. Other Amerindian forts built in New England around this time and in the ensuing three or four decades took on a more European look: they were increasingly squared, combined a ditch and palisade, and were furnished with corner bastions projecting out from the wall that allowed the defenders to fire down the length of the wall.[54] They were not true European artillery fortresses, whose bastions could direct defensive artillery fire in crossing patterns at besiegers some distance out from the walls. These bastions were simpler, merely intended to give the defenders the ability to fire at enemies attacking through the ditch and trying to set fire to, or cut down, the base of the palisade. This need was almost certainly a result of European steel axes, which greatly improved the potential for success of this kind of attack. Furthermore, archaeologists have suggested that many of the forts in the Long Island Sound area were built to protect the production and accumulation of wampum, the carved shell bead that acquired tremendous importance in the mid-seventeenth century as a form of currency in the European-Native fur trade.

The need in New England for forts (not all of which were built *around* villages but instead were built *near* villages as refuges) may or may not have been driven by the wampum trade, but it seems clear that their design resulted from the arrival of European technology. Amerindians may not have been copying European fortification techniques when they adopted bastions or "flankers," which had long existed on prehistoric Mississippian forts in the Midwest and Southeast, but the suddenness and thoroughness of the change in fortifications indicate a response to a perceived threat. In these early contacts with Europeans, when a besieger was as likely to be an Amerindian as it was to be a poorly equipped European militia, it seems unlikely that the threat was cannon.

In this first phase of Amerindian fortress adaptation, as Craig Keener showed, the new threat was simply the iron ax. Keener analyzed shifts in Iroquois fortifications and assault techniques and found a process of evolution occurring in the seventeenth century similar to that discussed for New England, with the difference that Iroquoian and Huron precontact forts were already elaborate and common. Indeed, in the century before the arrival of Europeans, they had become progressively sturdier, using heavier poles in multiple lines (as many as four), with the earliest ethnographic sources describing watchtowers and wall platforms furnished with firefighting material.[55] Nevertheless, even a sturdy circular wall without projecting bastions was vulnerable to an enemy who gained the wall and was equipped with iron axes and mantlets to protect themselves from overhead fire. Keener outlines a series of successful Iroquois assaults in the 1640s, whose success he attributes primarily to their having iron axes.[56] In response, and under French tutelage, the Hurons in the 1640s began to "make their forts square and arrange their stakes in straight lines; and that, by means of four little towers at the four corners, four Frenchmen might easily with their arquebuses or muskets defend a whole village."[57] Squared, bastioned forts then proliferated in the last decades of the century, and as a result the Iroquois shifted their siege tactics and had fewer spectacular successes.[58]

The success of this kind of adaptation is revealed in the events at the same Squakheag fort discussed previously. This fort was new, built in the early 1660s when the Squakheags, actually several communities under pressure, were coalescing into one for mutual protection. The fort sat on a high, necked hill; it had a substantial palisade, flanking bastions, a "high standard" over the entrance, and covered access to a spring. After the initial disastrous battle outside the walls (described earlier), the Squakheags retreated inside while the Iroquois repeatedly assaulted the fort and even managed to set fire to one wall by throwing in a bag of gunpowder. Nevertheless, the attack failed, and the Iroquois later admitted to suffering at least one hundred dead.[59] A Jesuit source for the siege noted that shortly thereafter, the Senecas (the westernmost nation of the Iroquois) asked for French help in surrounding "their Villages with flanked palisades."[60]

Bastioned forts' successes against Native American enemies and ill-equipped militias, however, proved a false security. The Narragansetts famously relied on their new bastioned fort in the Great Swamp during King Philip's War, but it proved to be a death trap in the face of persistent attack by a large English militia army. In another example, from the early eighteenth century in North Carolina but still relatively early in the regional experience of military contact, the Tuscaroras went through a similar process. In just two years, they progressed from an initially successful adaptation of bastioned forts to catastrophic failure.[61] The Tuscaroras attacked English and Swiss settlers in eastern North Carolina in 1711 and then prepared to defend themselves against the inevitable counterattack. Their preparations included building a series of forts, one of which, Hancock's fort, was eventually besieged and assaulted by an expedition from South Carolina. John Barnwell, the English commander, was impressed with its complexity: it had

a large Earthen Trench thrown up against the puncheons [palisade poles] with 2 teer of port holes; the lower teer they could stop at pleasure with plugs, & large limbs of trees lay confusedly about it to make the approach intricate. . . . The Earthen work was so high that it signified nothing to burn the puncheons, & it had 4 round Bastions or Flankers.[62]

The Tuscaroras successfully defended themselves, and Barnwell marched away thinking that he had extracted a promise from the Tuscaroras to release their hostages and cease hostilities. For a variety of reasons, fighting broke out again, and Barnwell returned to Hancock's fort to find its defenses improved even further. This time he brought in artillery and mortars but again struggled to take the fort. He finally negotiated a temporary surrender and the right to march into the fort. The Tuscaroras likely saw this as a successful defense, and the next year, as hostilities continued, they built yet another, even more sophisticated fort at Neoheroka. They also gathered much of their population inside the fort, trusting in its protection. That decision, however, proved to be a disaster, as European siegecraft aided by hundreds of Amerindian allies eventually overwhelmed the defenders and killed or enslaved as many as five hundred to six hundred Tuscaroras.

Despite this record of failure, palisades were not abandoned all at once around the continent. Many native peoples continued to battle other Amerindians, and palisades remained functional against Amerindian enemies who lacked not only artillery but also the desire to engage in a protracted digging campaign designed to approach the walls. The Cherokees, for instance, expanded their own fortification system against the Creeks during their war from 1715 to 1752. When facing a competent European expedition, however, most Amerindians quickly learned to abandon their fortifications, as the Cherokees did in 1760 and 1761, and as the Iroquois did when the American revolutionaries invaded in 1779.[63]

And that is the point. Native Americans' technological and social infrastructure proved incapable of taking full advantage of the European components of the military revolution. They transformed their form of warfare in the field, and they initially transformed their fortifications with fair success. But without the ability to mount artillery on those forts or to provision them for the long term, forts could not provide the kind of frontier or homeland security that they did for the Europeans.[64] The forts instead became traps, soon regarded as useless. Without a reliable base of fortifications, Native Americans' strategic defensive options depended on their greater operational mobility in an undeveloped countryside. But that mobility came at the sacrifice of their cornfields and homes, left behind for European expeditionary forces to burn.

Polity Adaptation?

The story of how Native American social and political organization shifted and adapted to the many facets of the contact experience is varied, complicated, and often obscure. It was a long-term process perhaps best studied at the level of each individual people. The factors influencing the process were many, but the purpose of this chapter is to ask how changes in the techniques and technology of warfare shifted the structures of Native American polities generally.

First, the adoption of the gun meant a form of dependence, at least in the long run. Brian Given argues that no such dependence emerged in the mid-seventeenth century and perhaps for long after that. Less strident, but more widely cited, is Patrick Malone's evidence from seventeenth-century southern New England for Native Americans repairing guns and even having their own forges with which to do so. Indeed, New England Amerindians' long and close exposure to Europeans may have equipped them better than some other peoples to master certain smithing techniques. In addition to the forges that Malone discusses, excavations at Monhantic have revealed a forge site probably used by Amerindian smiths (although white militia operated cooperatively nearby with the Pequots, so the case cannot be certain). The blacksmithing tools recovered from the site and some small handmade gun-stock screws suggest that the smith there was capable of relatively sophisticated work.[65] It is nevertheless a striking and persistent truth in the records of Amerindian diplomacy across the eastern part of the continent that Native Americans sought out guns and gunsmiths. Broken gunstocks were easy enough for a woodworking society to repair, and matchlocks are extremely simple mechanical devices, as are the various tools used to clean muskets or make bullets. Flintlocks and barrels, however, were relatively complex metal objects and required a sophisticated knowledge base and tooling infrastructure to make repairs.[66] Ian Steele proposed that 20 percent of the inventory of actively used muskets had to be replaced or required significant repair every year. They simply broke.[67]

What was mostly true of guns and gun repair was unavoidably true of gunpowder. Even in Europe, its production was centralized in a relatively few locations, and the skills required were precise indeed, developed over a century and more of experimentation.[68] Even drying damp powder could be difficult and dangerous. Naturally enough, the records are replete with Amerindian requests for gunpowder (and at better prices).[69]

This dependency on Europeans for guns, gun repair, and especially for powder, had two related impacts on Native American polities. First, it emphasized maintaining diplomatic ties with Europeans in situations in which the response might otherwise have been hostility or even just simple disregard. It particularly emphasized inter-imperial diplomacy, so that if relations with the English, for example, deteriorated, the French could be turned to as an alternative source of powder. Long-range trade and diplomacy had always been important to Native American political and economic patterns and is amply attested in the archaeological record from the precontact era, but most long-distance goods had been used for prestige or ritual purposes. Although gunpowder had ritual functions, it was primarily a necessity.

As a corollary effect of this emphasis on diplomacy, many Native American polities experienced a shift in the relative power of war chiefs over peace chiefs and, in many societies, over the council of women. This is a complex subject, but the basic outlines are well known.[70] Most southeastern and northern Iroquoian polities divided political authority among men designated as war leaders, and the men and women who ran the domestic affairs of the clan, town, or tribe. Both civil and military powers were usually further separated from religious authority. Ultimate political authority depended on group consensus but was usually channeled through a semihereditary civil chief.[71] When European traders and soldiers entered the scene, as outsiders they were initially invited to deal with the war chiefs, the men tasked with external affairs and with raising warriors (often the point of a European visit). They then became the initial recipients of European diplomatic gifts, and as redistributors of those goods, they gained power and influence. In ignorance, Europeans tried to formalize this process by designating individuals as "kings" or "emperors," titles that meant little in the short run, but as those men became the redistributive authority for European goods, they did in fact acquire greater power and unbalanced the normal intragroup political relations. This process would no doubt have occurred in the absence of guns, axes, and gunpowder, since many European trade goods held appeal, but war and hunting were deeply significant.[72] Even given the remarkable successes that different Amerindian groups had in manipulating their European suppliers, or playing them off against one another, the Native American military revolution played a major role in reshaping the political structures within Native American polities.

The Native American military revolution also shifted settlement patterns. The failure of even improved fortress systems eventually led some native peoples either to ask that European forts and garrisons be placed in their midst or to relocate (especially in times of crisis) nearer to European forts. The Cherokees requested Fort Prince George in their Lower Towns, Fort Loudoun in the Overhill Towns, and even convinced the Virginia government to build another fort in the Overhill Towns, although Virginia did not garrison it.[73] For the Cherokees, having a British fort and garrison in their midst served a variety of purposes: they guaranteed a continuance of trade; they provided a refuge for the Cherokee people if attacked; and they certified the British alliance with the Cherokees to other Amerindians who might refrain from attacking them for fear of dragging the British into the fight. During the American Revolution, the British Fort Niagara became a magnet for refugee or threatened Amerindian populations. In part, this was because British subsidies were doled out from that location and also because of the kind of "ultimate security" that a British fort and garrison were thought to provide.[74] Even more dire circumstances persuaded the Saponis to move into the shadow of Virginia's Fort Christanna on the Meherrin River in 1714, hoping for regular access to the fort's smith as well as the protection of its cannon.[75] Native peoples similarly aggregated around the Spanish fort at St. Augustine and the French at Fort Toulouse in modern Alabama. Again, this partly reflected a desire for access to goods, but it also stemmed from the need for security in the face of failed Amerindian defensive systems.

Furthermore, with their own forts abandoned and under increasing pressure from Europeans' landownership patterns, Amerindian towns frequently became less nucleated, with individual farmsteads instead "straggling" across wide spaces in the same manner as backcountry European settlers. In one well-documented example, in the years between the building of Fort Loudoun (1756) and the American Revolution, and accelerating thereafter, Cherokee towns increasingly de-nucleated.[76] This was not a universal process, as not all native communities were nucleated in the first place. The process by which Amerindian corporate territory became individualized, Amerindian-owned parcels is not well understood and occurred in very different ways depending on local geography and local power relationships. Nevertheless it seems to have partially resulted from changes in the structure of military security. Villages inside palisades had become death traps, and nucleated towns and collective fields had become targets.[77]

But European military techniques represented more than dependence and disaster. For some Amerindian groups at some times, Europeans and access to their weapons represented opportunity. The specific histories of certain groups provide evidence that early access to the Europeans (and thus early participation in the Native American military revolution) provided a military advantage that these groups parlayed into greater power and influence over their neighbors. Most famously, a number of scholars contend that for the Iroquois, early access to guns (and axes) from Dutch suppliers gave them a decisive advantage over their traditional Huron enemies, whose French trading partners refused to supply them with guns. In contrast to decades of apparent relative balance, Iroquois campaigns from 1648 to 1652 forced a massive Huron displacement, essentially forcing them out of their homeland.[78] The New Brunswick Mi'kmaqs' readier access to French tools and weapons also seems to have enhanced the effectiveness and lethality of their raids on their agricultural neighbors to the south.[79] Similarly, the Amerindians of the coastal Southeast experienced what seems to have been a succession of positions of power enabled by the gun trade, as one people and then another raided for Amerindian slaves to sell to the South Carolinians in the late seventeenth century, using traded guns to enhance their power as raiders.[80] In New England the Mohegans blamed one defeat in 1645 on the Narragansetts' access to guns, although in general the Mohegans' friendly relations with Connecticut after the Pequot War in 1637 seems to have enhanced their overall power.[81] In this respect, it is difficult to separate the effects of the changes in military techniques and technology from the broader effects created by trade and/or actual military alliance with Europeans. Were the Mohegans able to parlay their alliance with Connecticut into a greater share of regional power because they had more guns? More trade? Better diplomatic choices? The wide-ranging successes of the Iroquois in the late seventeenth century are an even more marked example of the complexity of causes. Military superiority based on guns (and axes) and on a new ability to attack other Amerindian forts probably was a factor, but it seems unlikely to have been the primary cause of either their going to war or their success.

In this same vein of multiple and complex causes, the process by which Native peoples broke apart, coalesced, confederated, or otherwise reshaped their polities in the late seventeenth century and into the eighteenth century can hardly be attributed completely to shifts in military technique, although it was closely tied to the experience of European colonization. Disease and the broader demographic shocks caused by European intrusion, such as the Carolina Amerindian slave trade, created what Robbie Ethridge calls a "Shatter Zone."[82] In the Shatter Zone (which in many ways extended beyond the Southeast that Ethridge discusses), peoples broke apart, fled their traditional homes, and then recoalesced in new combined communities, reforming and renaming themselves. Sometimes these new peoples proved to be stronger than their individual parent groups, and so they persisted and survived. In particular, the eighteenth-century confederations created by the Creeks, Cherokees, Shawnees, and Iroquois were able to incorporate a host of other peoples and then use their position between competing imperial powers to assert their status as major military and diplomatic players.[83]

They did so by using the new technologies and new/old techniques of warfare, but the changes in those techniques were not themselves responsible for their coming together or for their status as regional powers in the eighteenth century. In Europe the introduction of chemical energy as a key facet of military power had produced a long-term change in the disciplinary structure of armies and a widening of social mobilization while initially retaining the social hierarchy. The resultant massive increase in the pool of labor that could be mobilized, however, eventually radically changed the political and social organization of the modern state. In smaller-scale Native American societies, in which virtually every male was already a warrior, the introduction of chemical energy did not change the mobilization of manpower. What socio-political changes did take place as a result of new military technologies and techniques paled beside the impact of the enormous Native American demographic decline and the equally enormous European demographic expansion.

NOTES

1. As always, Rhonda Lee played a significant role in smoothing my rough prose. Kevin McBride was a major help in exploring New England fortifications, and Jason Warren gave me new insights into Connecticut's alliance with Amerindians in the seventeenth century.

2. Key interventions are Geoffrey Parker, *The Military Revolution: Military Innovation and the Rise of the West, 1500–1800*, 2nd ed. (Cambridge: Cambridge University Press, 1996); Clifford Rogers, ed., *The Military Revolution Debate: Readings on the Transformation of Early Modern Europe* (Boulder, CO: Westview Press, 1995); Jeremy Black, *A Military Revolution? Military Change and European Society 1550–1800* (London: Macmillan, 1991). A recent reevaluation is Azar Gat, "What Constituted the Military Revolution of the Early Modern Period?" in *War in an Age of Revolution, 1775–1815*, ed. Roger Chickering and Stig Förster (Cambridge: Cambridge University Press, 2010), 21–48.

3. Brian M. Downing, *The Military Revolution and Political Change* (Princeton, NJ: Princeton University Press, 1992).

4. Wayne E. Lee, *Barbarians and Brothers: Anglo-American Warfare, 1500–1865* (New York: Oxford University Press, forthcoming), chap. 3; Geoffrey Parker, ed., *The Cambridge History of Warfare* (New York: Cambridge University Press, 2005), 1–11.

5. Harold Peterson, *Arms and Armor in Colonial America, 1526–1783* (New York: Bramhall House, 1956), 19, 43–46; Nathaniel B. Shurtleff, *Records of the Governor and Company of the Massachusetts Bay in New England* (Boston: W. White, 1853), 1: 26; William H. Browne, ed., *Archives of Maryland* (Baltimore: Maryland Historical Society, 1885), 3: 100–101. The Jamestown colonists had a mix of matchlocks, wheel-locks, and snaphaunces in 1609, but they rapidly moved away from matchlocks, as attested by a 1625 arms inventory. See J. Frederick Fausz, "Fighting 'Fire' with Firearms: The Anglo-Powhatan Arms Race in Early Virginia," *American Indian Culture and Research Journal* 3 (1979): 39, 44.

6. The following is adapted from a much longer treatment of these issues in my *Barbarians and Brothers*, chaps. 5 and 6. Note that the southeastern and midwestern precontact and protohistoric Mississippian peoples practiced a form of war different from that described here. In the wake of the Mississippian collapse in the late sixteenth century, however, southeastern peoples' practice of war grew to resemble their neighbors to the north more than it did their forebears a hundred years previous. See David H. Dye, "Warfare in the Protohistoric Southeast, 1500–1700," in *Between Contacts and Colonies: Archaeological Perspectives on the Protohistoric Southeast*, ed. C. B. Wesson and M. A. Rees (Tuscaloosa: University of Alabama Press, 2002), 141.

7. Daniel K. Richter, *The Ordeal of the Longhouse: The Peoples of the Iroquois League in the Era of European Colonization* (Chapel Hill: University of North Carolina Press, 1992), 35; Bruce G. Trigger, *The Huron: Farmers of the North*, 2nd ed. (Fort Worth: Holt, Rinehart and Winston, 1990), 54; Adam J. Hirsch, "The Collision of Military Cultures in Seventeenth-Century New England," *Journal of American History* 74 (1988): 1191; Fausz, "Fight-

ing 'Fire' with Firearms," 34; Patrick M. Malone, *The Skulking Way of War: Technology and Tactics among the New England Indians* (1991; repr., Baltimore: Johns Hopkins University Press, 1993), 29–31. Timothy Shannon repeats this older interpretation with more nuance in his "The Native American Way of War in the Age of Revolutions, 1754–1814," in *War in an Age of Revolution*, ed. Roger Chickering and Stig Förster (Cambridge: Cambridge University Press, 2010), 139–43.

8. Nathaniel Knowles, "The Torture of Captives by the Indians of Eastern North America," *American Philosophical Society Proceedings* 82 (1940): 151–225; Daniel P. Barr, "'This Land Is Ours and Not Yours': The Western Delawares and the Seven Years' War in the Upper Ohio Valley, 1755–1758," in *The Boundaries between Us: Natives and Newcomers along the Frontiers of the Old Northwest Territory, 1750–1850*, ed. Daniel P. Barr (Kent, OH: Kent State University Press, 2006), 32; Matthew C. Ward, *Breaking the Backcountry: The Seven Years' War in Virginia and Pennsylvania, 1754–1765* (Pittsburgh: University of Pittsburgh Press, 2003), 55.

9. Malone, *The Skulking Way of War*, 65.

10. Ramsay Cook, *The Voyages of Jacques Cartier* (Toronto: University of Toronto Press, 1993), 67–68.

11. Keith F. Otterbein, "A History of Research on Warfare in Anthropology," *American Anthropologist* 101 (2000): 800; William Tulio Divale, *Warfare in Primitive Societies: A Bibliography* (Santa Barbara, CA: ABC-Clio, 1973), xxi–xxii; Thomas B. Abler, "European Technology and the Art of War in Iroquoia," in *Cultures in Conflict: Current Archaeological Perspectives*, ed. Diana Tkaczuk and Brian C. Vivian (Calgary: University of Calgary Archaeology Association, 1989), 278–79; David H. Dye, *War Paths, Peace Paths: An Archaeology of Cooperation and Conflict in Native Eastern North America* (Lanham, MD: AltaMira Press, 2009), 111–13; Azar Gat, *War in Human Civilization* (Oxford: Oxford University Press, 2006), 116–32.

12. I develop the meaning of this phrase in greater detail in Wayne E. Lee, "Fortify, Fight, or Flee: Tuscarora and Cherokee Defensive Warfare and Military Culture Adaptation," *Journal of Military History* 68 (2004): 718–24.

13. Wayne E. Lee, "Peace Chiefs and Blood Revenge: Patterns of Restraint in Native American Warfare in the Contact and Colonial Eras," *Journal of Military History* 71 (2007): 707–9. Four hundred is clearly a rounded number, but the point is that only three men escaped.

14. George R. Milner, "Warfare in Prehistoric and Early Historic Eastern North America," *Journal of Archaeological Research* 7 (1999): 126–27; Patricia M. Lambert, "The Archaeology of War: A North American Perspective," *Journal of Archaeological Research* 10 (2002): 227–29; Maria Ostendorf Smith, "Osteological Indications of Warfare in the Archaic Period of the Western Tennessee Valley," in *Troubled Times: Violence and Warfare in the Past*, ed. Debra L. Martin and David W. Frayer (Amsterdam: Gordon and Breach, 1997), 241–66; Richard J. Chacon and Ruben G. Mendoza, eds., *North American Indigenous Warfare and Ritual Violence* (Tucson: University of Arizona Press, 2007). Kevin McBride, "The Evolution of Native Warfare in Southern New England: 1200–1637," paper presented to the Society of Military History conference, Lexington, VA, May 2010; Michael Strezewski, "Patterns of Interpersonal Violence at the Fisher Site," *Midcontinental Journal of Archaeology* 31 (2006): 249–80; Maria Ostendorf Smith, "Beyond Palisades: The Nature and Frequency of Late Prehistoric Deliberate Violent Trauma in the Chickamauga Reservoir of East Tennessee," *American Journal of Physical Anthropology* 121 (2003): 303–18.

15. Charles Hudson, *Knights of Spain, Warriors of the Sun: Hernando De Soto and the South's Ancient Chiefdoms* (Athens: University of Georgia Press, 1997); David H. Dye, "The Transformation of Mississippian Warfare: Four Case Studies from the Mid-South," in *The Archaeology of Warfare: Prehistories of Raiding and Conquest*, ed. Elizabeth N. Arkush and Mark W. Allen (Gainesville: University Press of Florida, 2006), 101–47; David H. Dye, "Warfare in the Protohistoric Southeast, 1500–1700," in *Between Contacts and Colonies: Archaeological Perspectives on the Protohistoric Southeast*, ed. C. B. Wesson and M. A. Rees (Tuscaloosa: University of Alabama Press, 2002), 126–41; David H. Dye, "The Art of War in the Sixteenth-Century Central Mississippi Valley," in *Perspectives on the Southeast: Linguistics, Archaeology and Ethnohistory*, ed. Patricia B. Kwachka (Athens: University of Georgia Press, 1994), 44–60; David H. Dye, "Warfare in the Sixteenth-Century Southeast: The de Soto Expedition in the Interior," in *Columbian Consequences*, vol. 2, *Archaeological and Historical Perspectives on the Spanish Borderlands East*, ed. David Hurst Thomas (Washington, DC: Smithsonian Institution Press, 1990), 211–22.

16. Roger Williams to Sir Henry Vane and John Winthrop, May 15, 1637, *Winthrop Papers* (Boston: Massachusetts Historical Society, 1943), 3:413–14.

17. George Chicken, "Journal of the March of the Carolinians into the Cherokee Mountains, in the Yemassee Indian War, 1715–16," *Yearbook of the City of Charleston* (1894): 345 (quotation).

18. Ian Kenneth Steele, *Warpaths: Invasions of North America* (New York: Oxford University Press, 1994), 64–65; Daniel P. Barr, *Unconquered: The Iroquois League at War in Colonial America* (Westport, CT: Praeger, 2006), 26–27.

19. Frederic W. Gleach, *Powhatan's World and Colonial Virginia: A Conflict of Cultures* (Lincoln: University of Nebraska Press, 1997), 43–44, reprints the colonists' descriptions of the battle, but Gleach does not believe it represented their normal way of fighting.

20. Paul Hulton, ed., *The Work of Jacques le Moyne de Morgues: A Huguenot Artist in France, Florida and England* (London: Trustees of the British Museum, 1977), 1: 144 and plate 105.

21. Roger Williams, *A Key into the Language of America* (1643; repr., Bedford, MA: Applewood Books, 1997), 188–89.

22. Richter, *The Ordeal of the Longhouse*, 35. This result is how ethnohistorians have described battles by other tribal peoples witnessed in the twentieth century. See Lawrence H. Keeley, *War before Civilization* (New York: Oxford University Press, 1996), 59–61.

23. The most detailed account of the battle is from an eighteenth-century letter by Richard Hyde. Hyde claimed to have heard it from men close to Uncas during his life. There are good reasons to believe that Hyde would have had those connections through his grandfather William Hyde, who was an original founder of Norwich in the 1660s, and was therefore connected to John Mason, who was close to Uncas. In addition, William Hyde's daughter Hester married Stephen Post, who had been at Fort Saybrook during the Pequot War and was also a friend of Uncas (thanks to Kevin McBride for confirming these connections). The letter is quoted in full in Daniel Coit Gilman, *A Historical Discourse Delivered in Norwich, Connecticut, September 7, 1859* (Boston: Geo. C. Rand and Avery, 1859), 82–84. The battle is also discussed in Edward Johnson, *A History of New England . . . (Wonder Working Providence of Sions Saviour)* (London: Nathaniel Brooke, 1654), 182–85; John Winthrop, *The Journal of John Winthrop, 1630–1649*, abridged ed. (Cambridge, MA: Belknap Press, 1996), 236–37; William Bradford, *Of Plymouth Plantation, 1620–1647*

(New York: Random House, 1981), 367; Michael Leroy Oberg, *Uncas: First of the Mohegans* (Ithaca, NY: Cornell University Press, 2003), 102–3; Herbert Milton Sylvester, *Indian Wars of New England* (1910; repr., New York: Arno Press, 1979), 1: 390–7.

24. Craig S. Keener, "An Ethnohistorical Analysis of Iroquois Assault Tactics Used against Fortified Settlements of the Northeast in the Seventeenth Century," *Ethnohistory* 46 (1999): 785; Hulton, *The Work of Jacques Le Moyne*, 1:149 and plate 123. Contra: Malone, *The Skulking Way of War*, 14; Alden T. Vaughan, *New England Frontier: Puritans and Indians, 1620–1675*, 3rd ed. (Norman: University of Oklahoma Press, 1995), xxv.

25. See note 14.

26. Williams, *A Key into the Language*, 184–86.

27. Steele, *Warpaths*, 13–14; Brian J. Given, *A Most Pernicious Thing: Gun Trading and Native Warfare in the Early Contact Period* (Ottawa: Carleton University Press, 1994); Armstrong Starkey, *European and Native American Warfare, 1675–1815* (Norman: University of Oklahoma Press, 1998), 20–21.

28. Abler, "European Technology," 275; James Hart Merrell, *The Indians' New World: Catawbas and Their Neighbors from European Contact through the Era of Removal* (Chapel Hill: University of North Carolina Press, 1989), 60, 153, 162–64; José António Brandão, '*Your Fyre Shall Burn No More*': Iroquois Policy toward New France and Its Native Allies to *1701* (Lincoln: University of Nebraska Press, 1997), 99–101. More evidence for this desire follows later.

29. Kenneth Warren Chase, *Firearms: A Global History to 1700* (Cambridge: Cambridge University Press, 2003), 199–202.

30. Clifford J. Rogers, "Tactics and the Face of Battle," in *European Warfare, 1350–1750*, ed. David Trim and Frank Tallett (Cambridge: Cambridge University Press, 2010), 203–35.

31. Given, *A Most Pernicious Thing*, 119 (for musket energy). The modern bow-hunting community has had an active and vigorous debate over the nature and type of kinetic energy expended by arrows. See http://www.huntingcircle.com/kinetic_energy.php (accessed June 9, 2009); Ed Ashby, "Momentum, Kinetic Energy, and Arrow Penetration (And What They Mean for the Bowhunter)," available at http://www.tradgang.com/ashby/ Momentum Kinetic Energy and Arrow Penetration.htm (accessed June 10, 2009). English longbows of the period delivered somewhat more kinetic energy, but there is no evidence that Amerindian bows were comparable to English ones. See Rogers, "Tactics and the Face of Battle"; Malone, *The Skulking Way of War*, 17–18.

32. Quoted in Fausz, "Fighting 'Fire' with Firearms," 37.

33. For the common use of armor and shields in nongun contexts, see Dye, *War Paths*, 14–15; and David E. Jones, *Native North American Armor, Shields, and Fortifications* (Austin: University of Texas Press, 2004), 57–62, 135–39. For the disappearance of armor as guns came into common use, see the summary in Barr, *Unconquered*, 27–29. Florida bowmen deeply impressed the Spanish in the early sixteenth century, penetrating their armor and as much as six inches of wood. See Steele, *Warpaths*, 12–13. At Jamestown, an Amerindian bowman pierced an English wooden shield but broke his arrow on a steel version. See George Percy, "Observations Gathered out of a Discourse . . . ," in *Jamestown Narratives*, ed., Edward Wright Haile (Champlain, VA: Roundhouse, 1998), 95–96.

34. Williams, *A Key into the Language*, 189; *Dead Birds* (1964 [2004], dir. Robert Gardner). Abler discusses this at greater length in "European Technology," 274–75.

35. Peterson, *Arms and Armor in Colonial America*, 227.

36. Alfred A. Cave, *The Pequot War* (Amherst: University of Massachusetts Press, 1996), 137.

37. Personal communication with Kevin McBride, June 2009.

38. More research is needed on who had access to rifled guns and when. Although rifling was a relatively old technology used in elite hunting weapons, it was uncommon even in Europe into the seventeenth century, and the famous American version, the "Pennsylvania Rifle," was not invented until the early eighteenth century. See Peterson, *Arms and Armor in Colonial America*, 192–93. Some sources from the Southeast (at least) indicate that they were only just becoming common among the Creeks in the 1750s. See Daniel Pepper to Governor Lyttelton, 30 November 1756; William L. McDowell Jr., ed., *Documents Relating to Indian Affairs* [*DRIA*], 2 vols. (Columbia: Colonial Records of South Carolina, ser. 2, 1958, 1970), 2: 296.

39. John Norton, *The Journal of Major John Norton, 1816*, ed. Carl F. Klinck and James J. Talman (Toronto: Champlain Society, 1970), 262.

40. Peter A. Thomas, "In the Maelstrom of Change: The Indian Trade and Cultural Process in the Middle Connecticut River Valley, 1635–1665" (reprint of 1979 diss.; New York: Garland, 1990), 248–50; Reuben Gold Thwaites and Edna Kenton, eds., *Jesuit Relations* (Toronto: McClelland & Stewart, 1925), 49: 139–41; E. B. O'Callaghan et al., eds., *Documents Relative to the Colonial History of the State of New York* [*NYCD*] (Albany, 1881), 13: 355–56; and David Wilton to John Winthrop Jr., December 25, 1663, *Winthrop Papers* (Boston: Massachusetts Historical Society). A similar feint outside a fort is recorded for the Narragansetts in 1645 in *Winthrop Papers*, 5: 19.

41. Leroy V. Eid, "'A Kind of Running Fight': Indian Battlefield Tactics in the late Eighteenth Century," *Western Pennsylvania Historical Magazine* 71 (1988): 147–71; *DRIA* 2: 467, 468; Gleach, *Powhatan's World*, 43.

42. Williams, *A Key into the Language*, 184.

43. John Landers, *The Field and the Forge: Population, Production, and Power in the Pre-Industrial West* (New York: Oxford University Press, 2003), esp. 98–100, 273–74.

44. Lee, "Fortify, Fight, or Flee," 769–70; for Braddock's defeat see Eid, "A Kind of Running Fight," 163; for Bushy Run, see Henry Bouquet to Jeffrey Amherst, 5 August 1763, in *The Papers of Col. Henry Bouquet*, eds. Sylvester K. Stevens and Donald H. Kent (Harrisburg: Pennsylvania Historical Commission, 1942), ser. 21649, part 1, 227; William Smith, *Historical Account of Bouquet's Expedition against the Ohio Indians in 1764* (1765; repr., Cincinnati: Robert Clarke, 1907), 20, 36, 82, 89–90. The Ohio Amerindian confederation opposed to General Anthony Wayne in 1794 waged a similar campaign, opening by attacking a pack train carrying flour to one of Wayne's logistical forts. Later, at Fallen Timbers, they attempted a one-sided half-moon envelopment (a river protected the other flank). Wayne's reliance on careful marches with daily fortified camps (explicitly following guidelines from his reading of Julius Caesar) helped lead to his eventual victory. See Allan R. Millett, "Caesar and the Conquest of the Northwest Territory," *Timeline* (Ohio Historical Society) 14 (1997): 17–21 (thanks to Allan Millett for pointing this piece out to me); John Sugden, *Blue Jacket: Warrior of the Shawnees* (Lincoln: University of Nebraska Press, 2000), 159, 164–66.

45. Merrell, *The Indians' New World*, 79; John Oliphant, *Peace and War on the Anglo-Cherokee Frontier, 1756–63* (Baton Rouge: Louisiana State University Press, 2001), 161.

46. See note 60.

47. Oliphant, *Peace and War*, 137–38. Henry Timberlake recorded the Cherokees firing "two pieces of cannon," as a salute when he departed Chote in 1762. These may have been swivel guns that the Cherokees had earlier received from the South Carolinians (see later). See Henry Timberlake, *The Memoirs of Lieut. Henry Timberlake* (1927; repr., New York: Arno Press, 1971), 118. The British were to sure to include a clause requiring the Cherokees to surrender those cannon in the 1761 treaty. See Treaty with Cherokees (18 December 1761) enclosed in letter from Gov. Boone to Amherst, January 18, 1762, Amherst Papers, WO 34/35, National Archives, UK.

48. *Jesuit Relations* 63: 245.

49. *DRIA* 2: 125, 127, 328. What appears to be a swivel gun ball emerged from excavations of a 1780s Catawba house site in summer 2009 (personal communication from Stephen R. P. Davis Jr.).

50. Matthew C. Ward, "'The European Method of Warring Is Not Practiced Here': The Failure of British Military Policy in the Ohio Valley, 1755–1759," *War in History* 4, no. 3 (1997): 258, notes that Amerindians in the summer of 1756 attacked nine small frontier stockades on the Virginia-Pennsylvania frontier and destroyed five, but these were not cannon-equipped *trace italienne* forts. From the late seventeenth century onward, combined French and Amerindian raids on the northeastern frontier regularly overwhelmed isolated forts and stockades. And most famously, several British forts were surprised and taken at the outset of Pontiac's War. See Steele, *Warpaths*, 141, 198–99, 237.

51. For the debate on the intensity and lethality of warfare, see Lee, "Peace Chiefs"; Chacon and Mendoza, *North American Indigenous Warfare*, 3–11; Keeley, *War before Civilization*.

52. Milner, "Warfare," 123–25.

53. Much of the following paragraph is based on the essays in Gaynell Stone, ed., *Native Forts of the Long Island Sound Area* (Stony Brook, NY: Suffolk County Archaeological Association, 2006), especially those by Kevin McBride, Ralph S. Solecki, and Charlotte C. Taylor. Lorraine Williams, however, argues that Fort Shantok had a precontact phase, although her argument is fragile, as it based on the use of trench-set posts, thereby implying a lack of European tools. Elizabeth Chilton states categorically that as of 2005, there is no evidence for "formal villages, palisaded settlements, intensive horticulture, or warfare . . . in New England prior to European contact." See her "Farming and Social Complexity in the Northeast," in *North American Archaeology*, ed. Timothy R. Pauketat and Diana DiPaolo Loren (Malden, MA: Blackwell, 2005), 50. I have discussed this issue extensively with Kevin McBride, research director for the Mashantucket Pequot, who also sees no evidence for fortification in southern New England in the precontact era. See as well Kathleen Bragdon, *Native Peoples of Southern New England, 1500–1650* (Norman: University of Oklahoma Press, 1996), 149.

54. See the reports in *Native Forts of the Long Island Area* for Forts Corchaug, Shantok, Massapeag, Fort Hill/Weinshauks, Monhantic, Ninigret, Block Island, and Montauk. For the Narragansetts' Great Swamp Fort and other similarly improved forts from the King Philip's War era, see Malone, *The Skulking Way of War*, 98–101.

55. In addition to Keener's broad survey in "An Ethnohistorical Analysis," see, for example, the three palisaded sites reported in Robert E. Funk and Robert D. Kuhn, *Three Sixteenth-Century Mohawk Iroquois Village Sites* (Albany: New York State Museum, 2003).

56. Keener, "An Ethnohistorical Analysis," 789–91.

57. *Jesuit Relations* 10: 53, quoted in Keener, "An Ethnohistorical Analysis," 786.

58. Keener, "An Ethnohistorical Analysis," 780–86, 800; Abler, "European Technology," 276–77.

59. See note 40.

60. *Jesuit Relations* 48: 141. An additional case study could be made of the Susquehannocks' successful use of European fortification technology, including cannon. The basic sources are Steele, *Warpaths*, 52–54; Michael Leroy Oberg, *Dominion and Civility: English Imperialism and Native America, 1585–1685* (Ithaca, NY: Cornell University Press, 1999), 195–99; Francis Jennings, *The Ambiguous Iroquois Empire* (New York: Norton, 1984), 127–28; William L. Shea, *The Virginia Militia in the Seventeenth Century* (Baton Rouge: Louisiana State University Press, 1983), 98–99; *Jesuit Relations* 68: 77; *Archives of Maryland* 2: 481–501; 3: 417, 420–21; 15: 48–49; Barry C. Kent, *Susuquehanna's Indians* (Harrisburg: Pennsylvania Historical and Museum Commission, 1984), 39–53; Charles M. Andrews, *Narratives of the Insurrections, 1675–1690* (New York: Scribner, 1915), 18–19, 47–48; CO 5/1371, f. 188, in Virginia Colonial Records Project microfilm collection. The Natchez built squared- or pentagonal-bastioned forts in the early eighteenth century. See *Plans des deux forts Natchez, Nouvelle Orléans* par Ignace broutin, Department des estampes, vd. 32, fol. T. 3. Bibliothèque nationale de France (copy provided to me by George Milne). Additional examples of modified forts in the Southeast are described in Jones, *Native North American Armor*, 130–35.

61. I analyze this case at length in Lee, "Fortify, Fight, or Flee," 724–45.

62. John Barnwell, "Journal of John Barnwell," *Virginia Magazine of History and Biography* 6 (1899): 44–45.

63. Lee, "Fortify, Fight, or Flee," 750–70; Max Mintz, *Seeds of Empire: The American Revolutionary Conquest of the Iroquois* (New York: New York University Press, 1999); Joseph R. Fischer, *A Well-Executed Failure: The Sullivan Campaign against the Iroquois, July–September 1779* (Columbia: University of South Carolina Press, 1997); Barbara Graymont, *The Iroquois in the American Revolution* (Syracuse, NY: Syracuse University Press, 1972); Lee, *Barbarians and Brothers*, chap. 8.

64. For another perspective on this problem, see George Raudzens, "Outfighting or Outpopulating? Main Reasons for Early Colonial Conquests, 1493–1788," in *Technology, Disease, and Colonial Conquests: Sixteenth to Eighteenth Centuries Essays Reappraising the Guns and Germs Theories*, ed. George Raudzens (Leiden: Brill, 2001), 31–58.

65. Malone, *The Skulking Way of War*, 93–95, cites the evidence for a Wampanoag blacksmith burial, as well as documentary evidence for a Narragansett blacksmith during King Philip's War. See Kevin McBride, "Monhantic Fort: The Pequot in King Philip's War," in *Native Forts of the Long Island Sound Area*, ed. Gaynell Stone (Stony Brook, NY: Suffolk County Archaeological Association, 2006), 331–32. The tools have not yet been published, but Kevin McBride kindly allowed me to examine the metal finds and tools from Monhantic (now stored at the Mashantucket Pequot Research Center and Library). In addition, a mid- to late seventeenth-century Narragansett cemetery in Rhode Island contains a man buried with a blacksmith hammer, a horseshoe, and other blacksmithing tools. See Paul Alden Robinson, "The Struggle Within: The Indian Debate in Seventeenth-Century Narragansett Country" (PhD diss., SUNY Binghamton, 1990), 285 (burial 38); Paul A. Robinson, Marc A. Kelley, and Patricia E. Rubertone, "Preliminary Biocultural Interpretations from a Seventeenth-Century Narragansett Indian Cemetery in Rhode Island," in *Cultures in Contact: The Impact of European Contacts on Native American Cul-*

tural Institutions, a.d. 1000–1800, ed. William W. Fitzhugh (Washington, DC: Smithsonian Institution Press, 1985), 120.

66. I make this judgment partly based on personal experience as an amateur blacksmith (forge-welding a barrel, for example, is a complicated task requiring specialized tools and precise temperature control), but the records of requests for gunsmiths are equally clear. See Wilbur R. Jacobs, ed., *The Appalachian Indian Frontier: The Edmond Atkin Report and Plan of 1755* (Lincoln: University of Nebraska Press, 1967), 8–10; Merrell, *The Indians' New World*, 60; *DRIA* 1: 104, 2: 372; *Jesuit Relations* 57: 29; *Propositions Made by the Five Nations of Indians* (New York: William Bradford, 1698), 5; Richter, *The Ordeal of the Longhouse*, 220–21; William Johnson, *Sir William Johnson Papers*, 12 vols. (Albany: University of the State of New York, 1921–1957), 1: 307.

67. Steele, *Warpaths*, 106.

68. Bert S. Hall, *Weapons and Warfare in Renaissance Europe: Gunpowder, Technology, and Tactics* (Baltimore: Johns Hopkins University Press, 1997), 41–104.

69. Examples can multiply endlessly. Consulting the indexes under "gunpowder" or even casual consultation focusing on recorded Amerindian speeches in such sources as *DRIA*, *NYCD*, and Peter Wraxall, *An Abridgment of the Indian Affairs . . . Transacted in the Colony of New York, From the Year 1678 to the Year 1751* (Cambridge, MA: Harvard University Press, 1915), conveys the extent of the problem.

70. Gleach, *Powhatan's World*, 142; Karen Ordahl Kupperman, *Indians and English: Facing Off in Early America* (Ithaca, NY: Cornell University Press, 2000), 102; Charles Hudson, *The Southeastern Indians* (Knoxville: University of Tennessee Press, 1976), 222–24; Rennard Strickland, *Fire and the Spirits: Cherokee Law from Clan to Court* (Norman: University of Oklahoma Press, 1975), 47–48; Bruce W. Trigger, ed., *Handbook of North American Indians*, vol. 15, *Northeast* (Washington, DC: Smithsonian Institution, 1978), 192, 315; Anthony F. C. Wallace, *The Death and Rebirth of the Seneca* (New York: Vintage Books, 1969), 40; James Axtell, "Making Do," in James Axtell, *Natives and Newcomers: The Cultural Origins of North America* (New York: Oxford University Press, 2001), 139; Fred Gearing, *Priests and Warriors: Social Structures for Cherokee Politics in the 18th Century*, memoir 93 (Arlington, VA: American Anthropological Association, 1962); Colin G. Calloway, *New Worlds for All: Indians, Europeans, and the Remaking of Early America* (Baltimore: Johns Hopkins University Press, 1997), 111; Kathleen DuVal, *The Native Ground: Indians and Colonists in the Heart of the Continent* (Philadelphia: University of Pennsylvania Press, 2006), 71–73, 90–91, 105; Bruce G. Trigger, *Natives and Newcomers: Canada's Heroic Age Reconsidered* (Toronto: University of Toronto Press, 1985), 93, 171.

71. Although northeastern Algonquians did not divide war and peace powers as strictly, they still ruled through a consensus-building process, something that European trade also disrupted. See Neal Salisbury, *Manitou and Providence: Indians, Europeans, and the Making of New England, 1500–1643* (New York: Oxford University Press, 1982), 42–43, 118–19; Bragdon, *Native Peoples of Southern New England*, 140–43, 146–48; Howard S. Russell, *Indian New England before the* Mayflower (Hanover, NH: University Press of New England, 1980), 19–20.

72. Nathaniel Sheidley presents a generational version of this argument in "Hunting and the Politics of Masculinity in Cherokee Treaty-Making, 1763–75," in *Empire and Others: British Encounters with Indigenous Peoples, 1600–1850*, ed. Martin Daunton and Rick Halpern (Philadelphia: University of Pennsylvania Press, 1999), 167–85.

73. Lee, "Fortify, Fight, or Flee," 757–60; Tom Hatley, *The Dividing Paths: Cherokees and South Carolinians through the Revolutionary Era* (New York: Oxford University Press, 1995), 94–98.

74. Bruce Wilson, "The Struggle for Wealth and Power at Fort Niagara, 1775–1783," *Ontario History* 68 (1976): 137–54.

75. Merrell, *The Indians' New World*, 57–58. The Catawbas also requested a fort from each of the Carolinas (162, 198). After 1648/1649, many Hurons coalesced around a new Jesuit stone fort on Christian Island, where the Jesuits built a new bastioned palisade for them. See Trigger, *Natives and Newcomers*, 269–70.

76. Roy S. Dickens Jr., *Cherokee Prehistory: The Pisgah Phase in the Appalachian Summit Region* (Knoxville: University of Tennessee Press, 1976), 15; H. Trawick Ward and R. P. Stephen Davis Jr., *Time before History: The Archaeology of North Carolina* (Chapel Hill: University of North Carolina Press, 1999), 187.

77. The process varied widely from locale to locale and people to people. Some lands never transitioned to private parcels (for example, the Pequot). Daniel R. Mandell studied this process for the Massachusetts Amerindians in the eighteenth century to include shifting settlement patterns. The details are complex and involved more than mere defensive needs, but those, too, played a role. See Daniel R. Mandell, *Behind the Frontier: Indians in Eighteenth-Century Eastern Massachusetts* (Lincoln: University of Nebraska Press, 1996).

78. Most of the debate on this war focuses on the motives for the Iroquois attacks, not on the reasons for their success. See Richter, *The Ordeal of the Longhouse*, 63–64; Keith F. Otterbein, "Why the Iroquois Won: An Analysis of Iroquois Military Tactics," *Ethnohistory* 11 (1964): 56–63; Keith F. Otterbein, "Huron vs. Iroquois: A Case Study in Inter-Tribal Warfare," *Ethnohistory* 26 (1979): 141–52; Elizabeth Tooker, "The Iroquois Defeat of the Huron: A Review of Causes," *Pennsylvania Archaeologist* 33 (1963): 115–23; Trigger, *Natives and Newcomers*, 266–69; George T. Hunt, *The Wars of the Iroquois: A Study in Intertribal Trade Relations* (Madison: University of Wisconsin Press, 1940). Brian Given, however, argues that European guns were irrelevant to the outcome (*A Most Pernicious Thing*, 8–10). Keener's conclusion, discussed earlier, that a combination of guns and iron axes made the difference, is probably correct. See Keener, "An Ethnohistorical Analysis," 789–91.

79. Salisbury, *Manitou and Providence*, 69–70.

80. Merrell, *The Indians' New World*, 40; Marvin T. Smith, *Archaeology of Aboriginal Culture Change in the Interior Southeast: Depopulation during the Early Historic Period* (Gainesville: University Press of Florida, 1987), 132–33. Alan Gallay is less certain that the gun provided the crucial advantage, but he follows Malone on the inefficacy of the gun versus the bow, and his own survey of the evidence suggests at least that Europeans believed the gun trade enabled the succession of slave-raiding peoples. See Alan Gallay, *The Indian Slave Trade: The Rise of the English Empire in the American South, 1670–1717* (New Haven, CT: Yale University Press, 2002), 41, 60–61, 147, 211.

81. Thomas Peters to John Winthrop, ca. May 1645, *The Winthrop Papers*, 5: 19; Jason W. Warren, "Connecticut Unscathed: An Examination of Connecticut Colony's Success during King Philip's War, 1675–1676" (master's thesis, Ohio State University, 2009), 23; Oberg, *Uncas*, 108–9.

82. Robbie Ethridge, "Creating the Shatter Zone: Indian Slave Traders and the Collapse of the Southeastern Chiefdoms," in *Light on the Path: The Anthropology and History*

of the Southeastern Indians, ed. Charles M. Hudson, Thomas J. Pluckhahn, and Robbie Franklyn Ethridge (Tuscaloosa: University of Alabama Press, 2006), 207–18.

83. The process of eighteenth-century confederation, reconfiguration, and even ethnogenesis has generated a large literature. For a summary, see Daniel K. Richter, "Native Peoples of North America and the Eighteenth-Century British Empire," in *The Oxford History of the British Empire*, vol. 2, *The Eighteenth Century*, ed., P. J. Marshall (New York: Oxford University Press, 1998), 356–61.

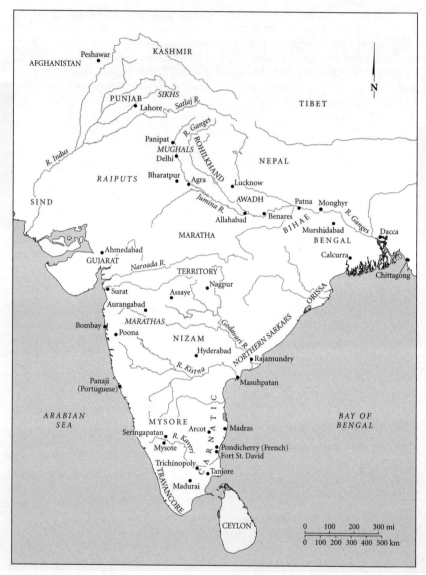

India in 1765.

4

Revolution, Evolution, or Devolution

The Military and the Making of Colonial India

DOUGLAS M. PEERS

Many of the chapters in this volume focus on indigenous aid to imperial expansion, partly to complicate the technological and military explanations for early modern European global expansion. Although this chapter contributes to that discussion, it also more broadly highlights the orientalist roots of assumptions about European military superiority in South Asia while simultaneously questioning the extent to which Europeans in fact enjoyed any decisive technological or organizational edge. British successes in India can perhaps better be explained by their long-term deeper financial capabilities and their consequent capacity to muster substantial forces from the Indian military labor market. In contrast, the dominant narrative has deep roots in eighteenth- and nineteenth-century orientalist writings on India and the East and now is inextricably entangled in discussions of the "rise of the West" or, more recently, the "Western way of warfare." This has systematically exaggerated the differences between "East" and "West" while overlooking or deliberately ignoring the extent to which the different parties learned and borrowed from each other.[1] When historians have acknowledged the transfer of technology, organizational methods, or tactics, the flow has almost always been presented as traveling from west to east.[2] Rarely has there been sustained attention to the actual flow from east to west or, for that matter, to the exchange and circulation of ideas and instruments within Asia as broadly defined. For example, shortly after their arrival in southern India at the end of the fifteenth century, the Portuguese found not only that artillery had preceded them but also that it had a remarkably cosmopolitan corps of gunners, including Turkish, Persian, Arab, and Abyssinian entrepreneurs. This blindness to Indian military sophistication and the resultant cultural blending of military practice has a long history.

Orientalism and the Trope of Western Military Superiority

The historiography of colonial India is replete with examples reaffirming the old adage that history is written by the victors. Triumphalist narratives celebrating various combinations of British arms, British organization, and, in some cases, British pluck, efface—arguably even deliberately—the hybrid characteristics of military cultures in India as allies and antagonists learned and borrowed from each other to the point that it was often difficult to identify any one power as enjoying a decisive military advantage over another. In seizing control over large parts of India, the British were dependent on local allies, local resources, and local manpower, and in a rapidly changing political, economic and strategic landscape, they were confronted by opponents who also were striving to adjust to conditions and introduce their own innovations. Consequently, any attempt to attribute the British conquest to inherent military superiority is not sustainable for a continent even when it might account for particular local successes. Especially when defined in technological or organizational terms, military superiority often had a relatively minor role. Instead, we need to look at a more complex matrix of economic and political factors to explain the British success, rather than at the more conventionally understood referents of military organization and technology.

As is still the case today, however, belief in such superiority all too often blinded the British to their opponents' military capacities, a blindness that subsequent historians all too often shared. The military has been particularly quick to use technology to contrast and compare different cultures. The historiography of imperial conquest and consolidation frequently resorted to military explanations to account for success, largely because military accounts could be fashioned in such a way as to bolster claims of European exceptionalism. These in turn buttressed subsequent orientalist renderings of Indian civilization. But this close relationship between militarism and orientalism was by no means limited to India. Patrick Porter highlighted the extent to which a society's military organization and culture became yardsticks by which civilizations could be measured and ranked, serving alongside such other colonial metrics as technology, political organization, status and treatment of women, and legal treatments of property.[3] Like these other tools for cross-cultural comparisons, the underlying impetus behind Western evaluations of indigenous modes of warfare may have been pragmatic, but the actual assessment and evaluation were shaped by deeply rooted prejudices and anxieties that have since become embedded in the historical record.

Explaining the Europeans' success in South Asia requires a word of caution: we must take care not to assume the accuracy of European estimates of the numbers of troops involved in colonial campaigns. The reason is that inflated estimates of the forces arrayed against them are more than simply a recurring feature of European accounts of colonial warfare; they are very often the basis for asserting Western superiority. Otherwise, how could we explain victory in the face of such alleged odds? We also must be wary of the systematic under-reporting of the numbers of indigenous allies that often were vital to European success. Plenty of evidence shows that the numbers of troops opposing the Europeans were deliberately exaggerated so as to accentuate and celebrate European superiority.[4] Equal caution is needed in regard to the common yet rarely substantiated references to European deserters and adventurers playing a decisive role in European defeats. One of the more extreme manifestations of this tendency came in the Burma War of 1824/1826: After encountering more resistance than they had expected, some British officers reported that the Burmese general, Maha Bandula, was a British deserter, as they apparently assumed that his tactical deployments could only have been the product of a European mind.[5] The *Oriental Herald* took this one step further, repeating a rumor that Maha Bandula was the illegitimate son of the previous governor-general of India, the marquess of Hastings.[6] Similar speculations were rife at the siege of Bharatpur (1825) when the skill with which the besieged used their artillery to hold the British at bay was attributed to British deserters.[7] Despite there being no evidence to support this claim, it lingered for some time. Some fifty years earlier, the author of one contemporary account of the Second Anglo-Mysore War claimed that "according to the best authorities [Haider Ali] was once a private soldier in the French army; in this situation he made such a rapid progress in the military art, that he soon thought himself qualified to fill a more respectable appointment under some of the country princes."[8]

But even after allowing for inflation and unsupported allegations, we still are faced with the fact that ultimately it was the Europeans who succeeded in dominating the world politically, economically, and militarily and that they often were outnumbered and operating at great distances from their home bases. It is therefore not surprising that historians have sought, and some have come to believe that there did exist, something that could be called a Western way of warfare, that its emergence amounted to a revolution of sorts, that its impact was truly global, and that it was not easily replicated by those over whom the European powers established their authority.

The idea of a military revolution excited considerable discussion during the 1980s and 1990s, and while the debate still trudges along, it appears to have lost some steam. As early as 1996, John Lynn was suggesting that "despite the recent flurry of new works, the discussion of the Military Revolution may have lost its intellectual validity."[9] Even though the outpouring of books and articles featuring "military revolution" in their title may have abated, it is not at all clear that the idea of the military revolution has lost currency, particularly among historians looking outward from Europe and seeking explanations for the chain of events that led to Western domination. At the same time, historians of Asia, Africa, and the Americas are working through the implications of this theory for their own fields of study and, in so doing, have posited a number of challenges to its proponents.

Unfortunately, the application of the idea of a military revolution(s) to world history by many historians has led to the normalizing of European political, organizational, and technological developments so that history has come to be understood, and progress has come to be defined, in very narrow and often unimaginative terms. And even though historians may quibble over the timing of such military revolutions, a broad consensus has emerged that it was superior technology and the infrastructure needed to support it that have distinguished Europeans from Asians. William H. McNeill based the rise of the West on its superior mobilization of resources in support of military activity.[10] Paul Kennedy, with a nod to Edward Gibbon, took this argument one step further, that the intensifying political rivalry in Europe triggered an arms race that, by drawing on the precociousness of market-driven economies, particularly in northern Europe, led to further innovation.[11] The end result, according to Geoffrey Parker, one of the chief proponents of the military revolution thesis, has been "the absolute or relative superiority of Western weaponry and Western military organization" that underpinned European conquest.[12] Elsewhere, he declared that "for most of the past 2,500 years, military and naval superiority rather than better resources, greater moral rectitude, irresistible commercial acumen or, until the nineteenth century, advanced economic organization underpinned western expansion."[13] In pitching his case, Parker asserts that what distinguished Europeans from the rest was the alacrity with which they looked to technology for solutions, their readiness to adjust their military organizations to take advantage of such opportunities, and the adaptability of their political and civic structures to the possibilities afforded by the more lethal weaponry at hand. In so doing, Parker's arguments assume positions that are strikingly similar to other neo-Weberians like David Landes.[14]

Yet such certainties about European military omnipotence that are commonplace today were rarely presented as unequivocally in the past, at least by those with battlefield experience. Was Wellington tempted to think that he was on the cutting edge of a military revolution? His experiences at the battle of Assaye in 1803, at which the British experienced a casualty rate topping 30 percent in what was, by any measure, a very hard-fought battle against an opponent that had plenty of skillfully deployed artillery and that took advantage of the terrain to secure two strong flanks. Like many of his contemporaries, Wellington may have been more impressed with his opponents than subsequent generations have been.[15] According to one of his confidants, "He [Wellington] used to say that it was the hardest fought affair that ever took place in India."[16] Yet many historians, with the benefit of hindsight and snug in the knowledge that Europe did indeed conquer much of the world, have too easily concluded that Europeans were somehow innately superior. In a letter written after the battle, the future duke of Wellington cautioned a fellow officer against underestimating the Marathas: "You must by all means avoid allowing him to attack you with his infantry," as "there is no position in which you could maintain your camp against such powerful artillery as all the Marattas have."[17] Wellington's respect for the Marathas' artillery was echoed by others, with one officer recounting that "never was artillery more destructively served or better defended."[18] And it was not only the Maratha artillery that compared favorably to European practice; Wellington also singled out the Maratha infantry for grudging respect.[19]

Shortly after the battle, Wellington provided a summary of the actions to Thomas Munro, an officer with the Madras army who later became the governor of the Madras presidency and who Wellington rated as one of the best informed on Indian affairs. The reason for this letter, in Wellington's words, was that Munro "was a judge of military operation, and [so] I am desirous of having your opinion on my side." In fact, Wellington anticipated criticisms of the heavy losses he had sustained, particularly given the prevailing tendency to disparage Indian armies as little more than armed rabbles.[20] Instead, Wellington cited the experience of one British officer who led an attack, insisting that "it was not possible for a man to lead a body into a hotter fire than he did the picquets on that day against Assaye."[21] Not only were Indian armies depicted as disorganized and undisciplined, they also were seen as deficient in such technical skills as those required by artillery and engineering. According to some, this deficiency accounted for the absence of Indian recruits in the company's artillery batteries, as they did not know that the company deliberately kept them out, fearing that Indian gunners would all too easily turn that knowledge, and even their weapons, against them.[22]

Nevertheless, several contemporary commentators offered opinions containing many of the assumptions about the differences between India and

Britain that continue to inform and inflame South Asian historiography. We should note, however, that not only were many of these writers writing for a domestic audience who had come to expect dramatic tales of the exotic but also that many of them had never even been to India, much less experienced battle firsthand.[23] The stark dichotomies they drew between European armies and their Indian counterparts became stock elements in a historiography that increasingly turned to such comparisons for reassurance of Western superiority, thereby helping stoke patriotic pride.

For example, in a rare comment on India, Sir Walter Scott wrote:

> I know it, said [Croftangry], kindling at the idea his speech inspired. I remember in the delightful pages of Orme the interest which mingles in his narrative, from the small number of English which are engaged. . . . They are distinguished among the natives like the Spaniards among the Mexicans. What do I say? They are like Homer's demigods among warring mortals.[24]

This exchange is grounded in a contrast between the small numbers of European adventurers who went to India and to New Spain and the masses that confronted them. Scott attributes this comparison to the writings of Robert Orme, whose histories of, or, rather, retrospectives on, the expansion and consolidation of colonial rule in mid-eighteenth-century India have had such a powerful influence on subsequent writings.[25]

Orme emphasized the discrepancies between the order and purposefulness of the Europeans, as well as their limited numbers, and the chaotic conditions that prevailed in an Indian camp. In so doing, he helped initiate one of the most pernicious rhetorical devices in colonial historiography, namely, the juxtaposition of a small and compact modern army against the large armed rabble, which was seen as the natural state of premodern military formations. As Javed Majeed eloquently argued, many writers in late eighteenth-century Britain used India as a metaphor for what could happen if reason and rational order were eclipsed by passion and other base emotions, a fear that was given added urgency by the upheavals occasioned by the French Revolution.[26] The armed rabbles that had come to typify Indian armies exemplify this metaphor, which is captured particularly well in the following passage by Orme:

> The rudeness of the military art in Indostan can scarcely be imagined, but by those who have seen it. The infantry consists in a multitude of people assembled together without regard to rank and file: some with swords and

targets, who can never stand the shock of a body of horse: some bearing matchlocks, which in the best of order can produce but a very uncertain fire: some armed with lances too long or too weak to be of any service, even if ranged with the utmost regularity of discipline.[27]

Such views were not confined to Orme but enjoyed widespread currency. In regard to Britain and India, Edmund Burke noted for the former: "The improved state of Europe, with the improved state of arts and the improved state of laws, and (what is more material) the improved state of military discipline," as contrasted to "the general fall of Asia, and the relaxations and dissolution of its governments, with the fall of its warlike spirit and the total disuse almost of all parts of military discipline."[28] James Mill, whose views of India and of Britain's responsibilities there were often at odds with Burke's, nevertheless broadly agreed with him on India's military organization and effectiveness:

Whether war is to be ranked among the fine or the coarse arts; and whatever the relative portion of the powers of mind which it requires; the art may be expected to exist in a state of higher perfection among a people who are more than a people who are less advanced in the scale of intelligence. When a number of people comparatively few, overcome and hold in subjection a number of people comparatively large, the inference is a legitimate one (unless something appears which gave the small number some wonderful advantage), that the art of war is in a state of higher perfection among the conquering people than the conquered. This inference, in the case of the Mahomedans and Hindus, is confirmed by every thing which we know with respect to both these people.[29]

Such a stark contrast between European and Indian modes of warfare became an integral element in colonial historiography and offered a ready-made yardstick by which Europeans could evaluate themselves. But not all agreed, and dissenting voices can be found, most often among those closest to the action. The editor of the *Mofussilite*, one of the most popular upcountry papers in India and a special favorite of army officers and soldiers, spoke disparagingly of James Mill's *History of British India*:

The history of those days has never been written, probably never will be, except after the fashion of Mill and Thornton, men who take the shilling from Leadenhall Street, and concoct what they call the philosophy of history by the yard and inch scale to suit all degrees of English ignorance of India.[30]

Explaining orientalist constructions of India in general, and its military history in particular, with reference to arrogance and/or ignorance is commonplace, and no doubt they were both in play. Not so well appreciated is the extent to which anxiety permeated the imperial culture in India. The sense of being beleaguered and constantly outnumbered and the consensus that the British must react to any and all challenges, out of fear that failing to do so would likely render their rule untenable, were equally important to shaping contemporary assessments of imperial rule in India. So it is not surprising that the historiography of early colonial India emphasized both providing evidence for and identifying the basis of British military superiority. Only then could the British reassure themselves of their security. Indeed, in many ways the militarism that informed British actions can be seen as the consequence of deep-seated anxieties about the permanence and stability of their rule.[31]

This tendency to evaluate and often inflate the differences between European and Indian military cultures was reinforced by commonly accepted notions of the inherently unstable and warlike nature of Indian polities. One of the reasons that John Malcolm, a military officer who eventually rose to become the governor of Mumbai (Bombay) and who wrote many works on India's strategic situation, was convinced that the British and Russians would eventually come to blows in Central Asia was because "there is an impelling power upon civilization when in contact with barbarism that cannot be resisted."[32] The reason for this, in the words of one of Wellington's confidants, is that "a too manifest determination to keep at peace is attributed by Orientals to weakness."[33] Not surprisingly, such conclusions helped entangle orientalist understandings of Indian society and strategic imperatives in imperial policymaking. This was a widely held view, remnants of which can still be glimpsed in assessments of the current situation in Afghanistan. As one commentator perceptively observed about popular treatments of the Afghans from the nineteenth century to the present, "They are the Red Indians of the East, the lurking menace waiting their chance to sweep down and eradicate civilization as we know it."[34]

This marriage of militarism and orientalism was further facilitated by the literary conventions and markets of the day, particularly the fascination with the exotic, the picturesque, and the romantic. Contemporaries were well aware of the ability of battlefield accounts to capture the public's imagination and so not surprisingly looked to accounts of battles in far-off places to trigger interest in India.[35] Such authorities as Robert Orme, J. W. Kaye, Henry Lawrence, and John Jacob deliberately wrote their accounts of India using the literary devices of the day. The frontier sagas of Sir Walter Scott, for example, furnished a template that could easily be adapted to the northwest frontier. Medieval tropes and motifs were common, especially in the nineteenth century (and here we also can find them in contemporary paintings and lithographs from India).[36] Biblical allusions and classical allegories were used with the aim of domesticating the exotic. One writer declared that the young men of the Pathans "represent to the modern world the rhapsodists of antiquity."[37] This romantic allure was picked up by less-gifted writers as well. One officer began his reminiscences by proclaiming: "How chivalrous, how charming, how poetical are all our early associations with distant Ind—that enchanting land of plantains, pine-apples and palm-trees."[38]

The modern version of the military revolution thesis would thus seem to have deep roots in eighteenth- and nineteenth-century writings. The historiographical step from Burke, Orme, or Mill to Parker, McNeill, or Charles Tilly is a short one, a shortness and a similarity that suggest a need to be wary. Nevertheless, next I shall consider the nature of the military revolution explanation so I can more accurately weigh it against the actual developments in South Asia.

Questioning the European Technological Edge

The arrival and introduction of gunpowder into European armies led to a number of developments, each having ripple effects throughout society. In Europe, for instance, gunpowder shifted the balance away from heavy cavalry toward an infantry carrying firearms. In turn, this required that the infantry be disciplined and drilled to maximize their firepower, which then prompted the raising of permanent and semipermanent infantry units. Firepower also threatened traditional styles of fortification, and the response was to build much stronger and more durable forts that over time shifted the balance in favor of the besieged. But successful sieges became increasingly costly, putting pressure on rulers to ensure that they had the resources at hand to undertake such operations. Moreover, gunpowder's revolutionary potential was not limited to land: heavy cannons at sea revolutionized naval warfare as suitably outfitted vessels preyed with relative impunity on unarmed merchant ships. Mobilizing the needed manpower and material resources consequently initiated political and administrative changes, and with modern warfare came the foundations of the modern state. In the words of Charles Tilly, "War made the state, and the state made war."[39] Works by Geoffrey Parker and others, drawing inspiration from Michael Roberts, explained the rise of absolutism in Europe by tying it to advances in military technology that forced states to devise new mechanisms for revenue mobilization and extraction.

That the idea of a military revolution is so appealing should come as no surprise, as it purports to answer some of the big historical questions about state formation and the transition from feudalism to absolutism and onward to more democratic forms of government. Military historians appreciate that this idea puts military history squarely at the center of major European and, by extension, world developments. Furthermore, it does so in ways that do not disturb some of our fundamental beliefs, particularly our faith in science and progress. For Parker, European military superiority can easily be summarized as follows: better weapons, better discipline, a more aggressive military tradition, a readiness to accept military innovation, and, finally, the erection of a financial infrastructure to sustain and advance modern weapons development. The military revolution approach allowed scholars of South Asia to account for British superiority using technological terms that seemingly promised objective and measurable criteria for comparative study.

The debate over military revolution cannot exist without the assumption that it is European military organization, European military technology, and European military mobilization that are the basis for any global comparison. The inner logic of the military revolution depends on a clear juxtaposition of tradition and modernity, and at first glance, India seems to offer many suitable examples. India has customarily, if inaccurately, been depicted as a culture (or many cultures) rooted in tradition. Again, this is not to say that proponents of this model routinely insist that the West is superior to the East (or the North to the South), and they are often quick to point to successful adaptations and innovations in the non-Western world.

Nevertheless, the parameters of the debate are European, and even those who chafe at the European bias and who are committed to overturning the more glaring manifestations of Eurocentrism often unwittingly find themselves entrapped by it. For example, Pradeep Barua begins his discussion of Indian military history by anchoring it in a universal framework, arguing that recent work now leads us to conclude that "Indian powers had progressed much further down the road to military equality with the West than previously believed."[40] That is, by focusing so closely on the structures and operations of the military, we have not allowed for the broader cultural, ideological, and social processes that inform, and are informed by, military organizations. Nor have we considered local conditions that often neutralize alleged advantages.

I do not deny that technology had an impact or that the introduction of new technology did not have wider ramifications. Yet some caveats are in order. First, there is a tendency to inflate the impact that technology had on its immediate surroundings. Geoffrey Scammell questions the extent to which conquest in Asia was predicated on military superiority.[41] Studies by Peter Marshall and Bruce Lenman show that until the mid- to late nineteenth century, many technological advantages attributed to Europeans were often short lived and, more important, largely confined to maritime warfare.[42] India's manufacturing sectors easily adapted to producing the kinds of weapons in use during much of this period and sometimes produced weapons of superior workmanship to those imported from Europe. In the late eighteenth century, for example, an English officer reported that locally made *bandooks* (a form of matchlock) used by the infantry serving under Shinde, a Maratha leader, were superior and that their rate of fire was somewhat lower but was more than compensated by their greater range and accuracy.[43] During the Sikh wars of the 1840s, the devastating artillery fire suffered by the British was partly due to the number and quality of guns manufactured by Sikh factories. One observer grudgingly conceded that "the Sikhs made very good fuzes, fuze composition, etc but all in a rather rough state; what can be well said of them is, that they were rough and ready soldiers and full of resources."[44]

Geoffrey Parker claims that European forts designed along Italian lines meant that "the small European enclaves perched around the coasts of Asia and Africa could defend themselves efficiently against their powerful neighbours until help arrived."[45] But were these forts really that significant in the broad strategic picture? British forts in India did not have a good track record for withstanding attack, nor were these forts the strategic linchpins that the forts in Europe often became. They might have had some success in fending off attacks from seaborne European rivals, but even during the most intense phases of the struggle between the French and the British in India, most of the critical campaigns took place inland, where the Europeans fought alongside their Indian allies. It is true that Europeans attempted to seize one another's principal factories and that this resulted in considerable investment in strengthening them. Fort William, for example, was constructed on a lavish scale to protect British interests from a possible French attack. Yet looked at from the landward side, its security, like that of other coastal forts, is less sure. Indigenous rulers could and did ignore these forts.

Haider Ali's army, for example, swept right up to the outskirts of Madras in 1780. Haider did not have to attack the actual fort, for his command over the surrounding territory deprived the British of much needed supplies and seriously undermined their claims of legitimate authority. Given the very fluid strategic conditions of south India, where political and military alliances were constantly in flux, the fact that the British were secure behind the walls of Fort St. George did little to reassure their allies that they would uphold their commitments. British fortifications in the south may have given them short-term relief, but in the long run, the British demanded a more vigorous and mobile strategy to create and sustain the alliances needed to achieve their military and political objectives.

At the same time, we should not simply assume that European standards of military architecture were significantly better than those in India. At the time of his death in 1799, Tipu Sultan had been rebuilding many of his fortifications on a "plan of such solidity, as, if completed, would have made it no easy capture."[46] And during the Sikh wars, the Sikhs' ingenuity in making embrasures led to their becoming the subject of considerable study by British engineers.[47] The withering fire that the Sikhs were able to deliver was so deadly at the battle of Ferozeshur that the governor-general ordered Prince Waldemar of Prussia, who had volunteered to serve with the British, to leave the battlefield.

We also must not extrapolate backward, that is, assign timelessness to the kinds of technological differentials so obvious in the late nineteenth and twentieth centuries. By then, the discrepancies between highly industrialized societies and recently conquered peoples in Asia and Africa had become unmistakably clear. Quick-firing artillery, breech-loading rifles with smokeless powder, machine guns, telegraphs, steam-powered vessels, and other innovations, which collectively comprise the kinds of weapons associated with modern industrial warfare, did not enter widespread service until late in the nineteenth century, after much of the conquest of India had already taken place.[48] The picture at the beginning of the century was much different, as Linda Colley reminds us, when only 5 percent of the British military budget in 1799 was allocated for guns, cannon, and ammunition.[49] The bulk went instead to more traditional accoutrements of warfare (horses, uniforms, swords) and to pay and feed the soldiers, a situation not unlike that prevailing in India's armies.

Europeans' assumptions about the preeminence of Western civilization were certainly already well entrenched by the mid- to late eighteenth century, but they did not have the same confident and, at times, complacent assertion of their military omnipotence. Not until much later in the nineteenth century did such unequivocal statements of Western military superiority as that presented in C. E. Callwell's *Small Wars* achieve canonical status.[50] A study of ordnance factories in India after 1857 shows that it was only in the aftermath of the rebellion that the British became convinced that they now had a monopoly over access to the superior firepower provided by more technically advanced small arms and artillery.[51] This is not to say that there were no technological differentials at work before that date, but they were not necessarily of the magnitude hitherto assumed, particularly when industrial modes of production were in their infancy.

A case in point is the arms race that broke out in Bengal in the 1760s. Mir Qasim, who the British brought in to replace Mir Jafar as the erstwhile ruler of Bengal when the latter failed to meet all the financial demands being placed on him, soon, and to the surprise of the British, began to assert his sovereign rights. Mir Qasim had come to appreciate the impact that musket-armed infantry could have on the battlefield, particularly when used in conjunction with the traditional Mughal heavy cavalry. He not only raised an infantry corps but also actively promoted the production of firearms. The muskets manufactured at Monghyr were said to be at least as good as, if not better than, the Tower-pattern muskets sent from England for use by the company's forces, apparently owing to the quality of the flints and steel used in their production.[52] Mir Qasim not only encouraged the growth of local weapons production, but he also tried to impose a monopoly over saltpeter production, as Bengal was then the principal source of saltpeter for the British.[53] The combination of superior weapons, a well-trained corps of troops whose salaries he was careful to keep from falling too far in arrears (a common failing in many Indian armies), and a more thoroughly supervised tax system to increase the flow of revenues into his treasuries made Mir Qasim a serious threat. As a consequence, when the British faced off against him at the battle of Buxar, they were confronted with a well-armed and well-motivated army that almost defeated them. Had they lost that battle, there was a very real chance that they could have been pushed out of Bengal.

Fifty years later, British officials still spoke admiringly of the craftsmanship of the Monghyr gunsmiths. In 1814, the marquess of Hastings reported that "the natives have imitated British fowling pieces and often with great skill. The articles which I saw did great credit to the ingenuity of the workmen."[54] But with the development of even more complex weapons, Indian manufacturing began to lag. By 1849, British officials were reporting that even though considerable numbers of firearms were still being produced at Monghyr, their quality had deteriorated.[55] This lends credence to Daniel Headrick's suggestion that the concept of a "breechloader revolution" may be more appropriate than a "military revolution" when discussing developments outside Europe.[56]

Furthermore, in the kinds of warfare in which Europeans often found themselves, local conditions often neutralized the putative edge that they enjoyed. In Burma and elsewhere in Southeast Asia, local rulers found that bamboo stockades could absorb many hits from roundshot without crumbling. Bamboo stockades and hit-and-run tactics worked very well in frustrating British designs, leaving an extremely irate British commander to complain that he could win the war if only the Burmese would fight according to the rules of military science.[57] This prompted a derisive reply from Thomas Munro, an experienced military officer then serving as governor of Madras, to the effect that even though the Burmese had not been properly educated, they appear to have worked things out for themselves. At issue here was the Burmese practice of avoiding pitched battles, preferring instead to harass their opponents, drawing them ever deeper into the interior, depriving them of food and transport, and subjecting them to ambushes. Such tactics, while incurring the commander in chief's disdain, did earn the grudging respect of some other officers. One ruefully noted that "the enemy, rarely to be seen in the open field, continually harassed the outposts, under cover of an impervious and incombustible jungle, and in the defensive system of stockades and breastworks, displayed no little skill and judgement."[58] Where technology did play a role, however, was in facilitating greater mobility. Steam-powered vessels were first used in this war, after strenuous advocacy by Captain Marryat and others. The steam-powered *Diana*, with barges in tow, proved invaluable in efficiently moving troops upriver.

The mobility afforded by the *Diana* highlights one of the challenges faced by the British in India, namely, their relative immobility as compared to many of their opponents. One advantage that the Europeans did enjoy that has often been overlooked is their capacity for what strategists today would label *power projection* or *ocean lift capacity*. In their suppression of the Indian rebellion of 1857/1858, for example, the British were hugely assisted by their ability to deploy troops to India rapidly. Waterborne transportation also was vital during the Burma war: command of the sea-lanes surrounding India was equally important to allowing the British to quickly, safely, and cheaply move troops between presidencies.

Once on land, however, the British all too often found themselves encumbered with large baggage and artillery trains, constrained by lengthy and very vulnerable lines of communication, and exposed to the harassing attacks of

Indian light cavalry, as was the case in their campaigns against the Marathas and against Mysore. Not surprisingly, some critics compared Britain's position with that of Gulliver in his encounter with the Lilliputians: "An armed man, unprovided with the means of moving, may not be inaptly compared to a giant chained to the ground, but still having his limbs at liberty, thereby retaining the power of lashing out at all within his reach."[59]

Much of Wellington's success in southern India can be attributed to his painstaking attention to logistics: he quickly came to appreciate India's practice of relying on long-distance trading communities like the *brinjaras* who, provided they were protected and adequately compensated, ensured a regular supply of food and fodder for an army in the field. As Wellington later commented, by adapting to local practices and introducing Indian conventions, he was able to achieve a mobility often denied Europeans. "If I had endeavoured in that war to carry about with me stores of grain sufficient for the consumption of the sepoys and the animals, I should have done nothing. It was difficult enough to transport my ammunition and supplies of meat and rum and bread for the Europeans."[60]

More contentious, however, from a historiographical perspective is that these attempts at tracing the diffusion and impact of technology have all too often started with the assumption that innovation began in Europe and that the flow of ideas was largely a one-way traffic between Europe and the rest of the world. This, not surprisingly, has often led to evaluating how successful the recipients were in incorporating the new technology. This fixation on narrow lineages with a single originating point obscures the complicated interaction of ideas and technologies. Jos Gommans persuasively demonstrated that military innovations in India were not exclusively inspired by Europeans. That is, until the end of the eighteenth century, gun-casting technology was more likely to be derived from Ottoman sources than from the Portuguese or other Europeans. While Portuguese sources quite openly admit this, most modern writers continue to assume a one-way flow of technology from western Europe to South Asia, ignoring the Ottomans as well as other routes that enabled the internal diffusion and exchange of technology within India.[61] Thus, for example, most of the firearms sold in Kerala in the seventeenth century were imported from northern India and the Arab peninsula; only a trifling amount came through the Portuguese.

Influence also came from the Ottomans, and the Safavids and the Durranis introduced some novel tactics such as outfitting cavalry with flintlocks. These were more than simply mounted infantry; their maneuvers were inspired by the tactics of Central Asian mounted archers.[62] Muskets, however, were easier to use than were bow and arrows, which enhanced their impact on the battle-field. For their part, Afghans introduced light cannon that could fire a two-pound ball and could be fixed to the saddle of a camel.[63] A number of Indian powers adopted this technology for their own use, including the Rajputs, Sikhs, and Rohillas. Tipu Sultan was reported in 1790 as having created a camel corps in which each camel carried two troopers, one of whom was armed with a "blunderbuss."[64] By introducing mounted musketeers and camel guns, the advantages offered by firepower were reconciled with Central and South Asian traditions of mobile warfare. These practices in turn spread deeper into India. Haider Ali, for example, recruited many of his cavalry officers from Persia.[65]

But the impact of new technology was not the same everywhere. Technology often had to yield to local circumstances and consequently what might prove decisive in Europe could have far less impact in South Asia. Richard Eaton, for example, questions the labeling of the Mughals as a gunpowder empire on the grounds that not only had firearms arrived before them in India but the nature of fighting in India, coupled with the technical limitations on firearms then in use, limited their usefulness.[66] Pregunpowder weapons were, nonetheless, still lethal. As the seventeenth-century French traveler François Bernier noted, Mughal mounted archers could discharge six well-aimed arrows in the time that a musketeer could get off two less-accurate shots.[67] Peter Lorge found a similar situation in China, where the arrival of guns did not immediately render horse archers redundant.[68] Questions also have been raised as to whether the latest generation of weapons always was superior. Randolph Cooper persuasively argued that long-barreled matchlocks, often seen as inferior to flintlocks, were in fact often more lethal in the hands of snipers.[69] Later in the nineteenth century, at the northwest frontier, the superior technology available to the British was largely neutralized by local conditions.[70] Nobody better captured this than did Rudyard Kipling. In his "Arithmetic on the Frontier," he cautions against technological triumphalism:

> A scrimmage in a Border Station—
> A canter down some dark defile
> Two thousand pounds of education
> Drops to a ten-rupee jezail.
> The Crammer's boast, the Squadron's pride,
> Shot like a rabbit in a ride!

Complicating our appreciation of the impact and diffusion of new technology is that while we may wish for readily definable boundaries between groups, armies, and states, these often prove to be very porous in practice. Part of the difficulty is the tendency of trying to distinguish between what is European and what is Asian, when in fact it was rarely a question of Europeans versus Asians in regard to soldiers, their weapons, their discipline, or their tactics. Close scrutiny of the early iconography of the Marathas, particularly some surviving friezes, reveal images of soldiers being drilled and disciplined.[71] These images predate the colonial era and thus question the long-standing assumption that only when European adventurers arrived in India did Indian states begin to introduce disciplined infantry.

Other Indian rulers demonstrated considerable ingenuity in applying technology to the battlefield. Like Mir Qasim, Haider Ali sought ways of harnessing local customs and traditions to forms of military organization introduced from Europe. As one noted historian observed, his military genius "lay in a brilliant combination of the mobile cavalry organized on the Mughal pattern with his increasingly disciplined musket-using infantry."[72] Again like Mir Qasim, Haider Ali introduced sweeping reforms to strengthen his administration and ensure a more reliable source of revenue. He also turned to indigenous technology. Studies of Haider Ali's arsenal show how he adapted and improved old pattern rockets, producing a weapon that not only plagued the British but also inspired them to develop the Congreve rocket. Haider's son Tipu Sultan recommended that each brigade include two hundred rocket men.[73] Rockets were useful as light artillery, were able to hit targets as far as away as one thousand yards, and could better keep pace with the infantry.

To understand the differences between European and Indian military cultures (recognizing the dangers inherent in generalizing about the diversity of local traditions in India), we should keep in mind that the two groups' strategic aims frequently differed, and consequently their organizational and operational imperatives cannot be easily compared. Simply put, Indian armies played to win whenever they fought, but their definition of winning was not always the same as that in Western military culture.[74] This was the case in India even when the ultimate objective of Mughal armies was annihilating the enemy's main force or their fortresses. The Marathas generally preferred battles of attrition, trusting to their mobility and loose organization to harass their opponents while simultaneously ensuring that they did not present their opponents with the possibility of a decisive battle. Europeans were aware of this, and Robert Orme explained how effective such a strategy could be.

It would be a very melancholy consideration for us who have made some considerable conquests in India if the enemy availed themselves properly of their superior numbers. They are somewhat inferior in discipline and in the nature of their arms, that under the command of an experienced officer, it is almost impossible to break our order of battle or withstanding our fire of cannon and musquetry. But it ought to be their principal object never to hazard a general action. Disperse their cavalry into small bodies of two or three thousand each, to destroy every village within your districts, to attack your convoys, to prevent the cultivation of the land and to impede and obstruct your manufacturers. In one year you would most sensibly feel the effects of such a change of conduct. It is with difficulty that you subsist your army, you would still be more distressed for the payment of it, and an entire stop would be put to all commercial transactions. In short you must enter into some kind of treaty with the enemy for it is impossible that the Company could long defray the expences of military expeditions, whilst they were deprived of their territorial revenues and their trade totally obstructed.[75]

Tapping the Indian Military Labor Market

Notwithstanding the discontent with simple technological explanations, there nevertheless is widespread agreement that European-style armies had to have some kind of advantage over their opponents; otherwise how could we explain the repeated battlefield successes and global European empires? Rather than dwell on technical differences, some historians have switched their emphasis to the Europeans' ability to raise and maintain military forces in such numbers and in such a state of efficiency that over time, they could overwhelm their opponents. In this context, in the case of India, we must remember that the bulk of the forces raised by the English East India Company were Indian and that they were drawn from India's traditional military labor markets. As Dirk Kolff found, a key characteristic of the late Mughal era was the superabundance of armed peasants, individuals who were willing to serve for a price and who could be quickly mustered by military entrepreneurs.[76] Although historians have customarily focused on the armed horsemen of North India, and although cavalry did constitute the dominant force in precolonial India (as well as enjoying greater status), it is a mistake to view Indian infantry at the outset of colonial rule as little more than an armed rabble. The rhythms of agrarian production in northern India allowed peasants to seek short terms of military service as a supplemental source of revenue. Add to such men the various adventurers, landless individuals, and other migrants, and the end result is a vast pool of potential soldiers who could be easily tapped by ambitious nobles eager to assert their authority in the very fluid conditions of eighteenth-century India.

The emergence of a series of successor states to the Mughal Empire in the first half of the eighteenth century fueled the demand for soldiers, horsemen as well as foot soldiers, and a number of these states made concerted efforts to better discipline and arm such levies.[77] Mir Qasim recognized the value of harnessing disciplined infantry firepower to traditional Mughal strengths in cavalry.[78] Although he retained the Mughal cavalry, he also raised a European-style infantry and cavalry, just as the British mixed together the European-style heavy cavalry shipped in from Europe with a light cavalry modeled on Indian *silladar* practices (in which the recruit provides his own mount and sometimes his own weapons). He also established a sound financial foundation, empowering auditors to sniff out corruption and check for leaks in his financial pipeline. Mir Qasim consequently earned the grudging respect of his opponents, one of whom noted that we "no longer had to contend against inefficient and undisciplined ranks, and traitorous leaders, but against well-equipped and well-organized forces, supported by powerful artillery, all trained after the fashion of his own troops."[79]

The military organization that sprang up in Mysore under Haider Ali and his son Tipu Sultan is another example of the hybrid military cultures that were emerging in eighteenth-century India. One of the more remarkable developments there was the production of a book compiled by one of Tipu's generals, Mir Zainul Abedeen Shushtari, which summarized and systematized the military reforms under way since the 1750s.[80] Standardization is one of its underlying themes, as is the realization that military effectiveness required the active engagement and coordination of various government departments. The end result was a book of impressive scope and considerable retrospection. It contains a long section on loyalty as well as detailed discussions about weights and measures, in addition to more practical sections on drill, tactical deployment, and the use of artillery.

Europeans were just another possible employer in this highly competitive market, though as time went on, the British earned a reputation as the least likely employer to default on salaries. This was something that many of their Indian opponents were increasingly unable to do, and it gave the British an edge. But initially at least, Europeans sought their recruits from a very buoyant military labor market, one in which they were initially dependent on middlemen, entrepreneurs who would raise a corps and then seek service with the highest bidder. Deeper pockets not only gave the British access to a ready supply of recruits, but the British also deliberately used their recruiting strategy, particularly the formation of various irregular units, as a means of absorbing what Wellington referred to as "freebooters."[81] Irregular units functioned as a form of sponge, drawing up thousands of armed and underemployed adventurers.

Through these processes, the British were able to raise a large number of recruits who were subjected over time to what historians have typically defined as European forms of discipline and organization. Historians, however, have tended to overplay the distinction between European and Indian forms of drill and discipline, either because they became preoccupied with the outward manifestations of discipline or because of the long-standing belief that discipline was something that did not come naturally to "orientals." I noted earlier that some surviving friezes confirm that drill already was used by precolonial military formations. Also, as some historians have observed, many of the states that emerged in the volatile eighteenth century were able to develop, with varying degrees of success, potent forces combining cavalry, infantry, and artillery.

Nevertheless, in such a fluid labor market, loyalty remained an elusive commodity, and until the British were able to dislodge their competitors, there always remained the possibility that the forces they raised would transfer their allegiance to a higher bidder. In the lead-up to the battle of Buxar, the British commander, Colonel Champion, recorded in his diary that "a subadar [Indian officer] of Capt McLean's Battalion was blown from a gun for endeavouring to seduce his company to desert to the enemy."[82] But lest disloyalty be thought of as something largely confined to the Indian rank and file, this same officer observed that European and Indian recruits alike were inclined to desert whenever they felt that their material expectations were not being met.[83] For many recruits, loyalty was negotiable.

A similar pattern of discretionary loyalties characterized alliance politics in India. Conflict was rarely a simple two-way struggle between a European and an Indian power. In many instances, it was not a single united enemy that the British were battling but a very loose coalition of interests that were continually reformulating their alliances and intentions. Jos Gommans aptly describes this as the "usual Indian politics of permanent sedition."[84] C. W. Malet, the British resident at Poona [Pune] in the late eighteenth century, was quick to realize that the "grand objective of our allies is to reap as much benefit as possible from the war and to stimulate Tipu's and our exertions to the exhaustion of our mutual force, so that they [Marathas and Nizam] may become the arbiter of future negotiations."[85]

Hence, any simple tally of troops on one side or the other has very little relevance. The struggles against the Marathas and even the battle of Plassey (1757) should be seen from this perspective. Wars of attrition were common-place, and many Asian armies employed tactics and organized themselves to fight what we would label as guerrilla wars. In such a situation, a decisive battle might have little meaning; instead, victory was often secured away from the battlefield. As General Paget reminded Lord Amherst after eighteen months of desultory fighting in Burma, "Success in negotiations is of much more importance than success in protracted warfare."[86]

In the end, what were the differences between British and Indian armies and styles of warfare? Some scholars, including myself, have argued that we should look less at the teeth of the army and concentrate more on the tail. The East India Company could outspend and outlast its opponents, financially and politically.[87] Can these differences be reduced ultimately to deeper pockets and wiser investments? To a large extent, what differentiated the East India Company's army, at least for the first century of colonial rule, was its ability to raise large numbers of Indian troops and ensure their loyalty through pay and other forms of support. Its ability to maintain an army in peace as well as in the field, properly equipped and regularly paid, was what distinguished it from its Indian rivals. As one mid-nineteenth-century observer commented, "The loose organization, uncertain and long-deferred payments, and feudal independence of parts, in the native armies previously existing, were among the chief causes of their inefficiency."[88] This is not to say that all Indian armies were feudal in nature. Transformations were already under way in mid-eighteenth-century India, just at the time when the British began to break out from their coastal enclaves. Military fiscalism was not an exclusively European import. Some of the conditions that were further refined by Haider Ali were laid down earlier in the eighteenth century in the Wodeyar state in Mysore.[89] Later generations had to contend with Ranjit Singh's Punjab, another quintessentially fiscal-military state. It is somewhat ironic that many of these new states created footholds for the British as they made available new opportunities for trade and service.

Conclusion

To suggest that the very idea of a military revolution has all along been anchored in the particularities of European history is by no means an original revelation. Other historians have spoken out strongly against this, though perhaps nobody as passionately as Peter Lorge in *The Asian Military Revolution*, in which he declares that "the cultural explanation of Asian technological inferiority is as pernicious as the racial explanations, since it denies Asia a military and political history before the arrival of the West."[90] The hyperbole notwithstanding, it is an important point, for neither technology nor institutions are as neutral a basis of comparison as we might otherwise think. Too often, European technology and institutions, either implicitly or explicitly, are accepted as the benchmark of progress, and then commonly it is the form rather than the function that attracts the historian's gaze. We need to acknowledge that the "military revolution" argument hinges on our continued acceptance of some of Orientalism's teleological, epistemological, and ontological legacies. In particular, the military revolution debate cannot exist without the a priori assumption that it is European military organization, European military technology, and European military mobilization that are the basis for any global comparison. The inner logic of the military revolution depends on a clear juxtaposition of tradition and modernity. With Europe pressed into service as the exemplar of modernity, this has left little scope for other societies to be anything but traditional.

But placing the emphasis here on the tail rather than the teeth, including the British successes in the Indian military labor market, is not completely at odds with a number of the conclusions inherent in the military revolution model. In fact, much of the military revolution model rests on the political, financial, and organizational modernization required to keep armies in the field, developments often subsumed under the heading of "military fiscalism." Nonetheless, many proponents of the military revolution model, besotted with technology, assume that technological revolution begat state formation, and their arguments regarding Europe can be quite compelling. Modernity before the rise of the modern welfare state can be understood, at least in political terms, as a combination of ideological and institutional developments that facilitated the efficient prosecution of war, as that was the principal preoccupation of the state. But this transformation does not necessarily require a technological jump start. The innovations and evolutions taking place in India were only partially tied to technology, and even then, they were not always predictable.

NOTES

1. Patrick Porter, *Military Orientalism: Eastern War through Western Eyes* (New York: Columbia University Press, 2009).

2. David B. Ralston, *Importing the European Army; the Introduction of European Military Techniques and Institutions into the Extra-European World, 1600–1914* (Chicago: University of Chicago Press, 1988).

3. Porter, *Military Orientalism*, 40.

4. The Victorian propensity to do this and the consequences for the writing of military history are the subjects of James Belich's "The Victorian Interpretation of Racial Conflict and the New Zealand Wars: An Approach to the Problem of One-Sided Evidence," *Journal of Imperial and Commonwealth History* 15 (1987): 123–47.

5. Douglas M. Peers, *Between Mars and Mammon: Colonial Armies and the Garrison State in Early-Nineteenth Century India* (London: I. B. Tauris, 1995), 159.

6. *Oriental Herald* 7 (1825): 567–68.

7. "The Siege of Bhurtpore," *East India United Service Journal* 10 (1835): 339. See also [G. R. Gleig], "The Siege of Bhurtpore," *Blackwood's Edinburgh Magazine* 23 (1828): 446.

8. John Le Couteur, *Letters, Chiefly from India; Containing an Account of the Military Transactions on the Coast of Malabar during the Late War* (London: John Murray, 1790), 111.

9. John A. Lynn, "The Evolution of Army Style in the Modern West, 800–2000," *International History Review* 18 (1996): 506, note.

10. William H. McNeill, *The Pursuit of Power: Technology, Armed Force and Society since a.d. 1000* (Chicago: University of Chicago Press, 1982).

11. Paul Kennedy, *The Rise and Fall of the Great Powers: Economic Change and Military Conflict from 1500 to 2000* (New York: Random House, 1987), 16–24.

12. Geoffrey Parker, *The Military Revolution: Military Innovation and the Rise of the West, 1500–1800* (Cambridge: Cambridge University Press, 1996), 115.

13. Geoffrey Parker, ed., introduction to *The Cambridge Illustrated History of Warfare* (Cambridge: Cambridge University Press, 1995).

14. David S. Landes, *The Wealth and Poverty of Nations: Why Are Some Rich and Others So Poor?* (New York: Norton, 1998).

15. Randolf G. S. Cooper, *The Anglo-Maratha Campaigns and the Contest for India: The Struggle for Control of the South Asian Military Economy* (Cambridge: Cambridge University Press, 2003), 292–93. Alfred Lord Tennyson later picked this up in his "Ode on the Death of the Duke of Wellington" (London, 1853), writing: "This is he that far away / Against the myriads of Assaye / Clash'd with his fiery few and won" (9).

16. G. R. Gleig, *Life of Arthur, Duke of Wellington* (London: Longman, Green, 1884), 37.

17. Wellesley to Colonel Murray, 14 September 1804, in Arthur Wellesley Wellington and John Gurwood, *The Dispatches of Field Marshall the Duke of Wellington: During His Various Campaigns in India, Denmark, Portugal, Spain, the Low Countries, and France, from 1799 to 1818* (London: John Murray, 1837), ii, 393.

18. Anonymous letter from an officer, 24 September 1803, in *The Maratha War Papers of Arthur Wellesley, January to December 1803*, ed. Anthony S. Bennell, Army Records Society (London: Sutton Publishing 1998), 290.

19. Gleig, *Life of Arthur, Duke of Wellington*, 38.

20. Wellington to Munro, 1 November 1803, in *The Life of Major General Sir Thomas Munro*, ed. G. R. Gleig (London: H. Colburn and R. Bentley, 1830), 1: 347.

21. Ibid., 1: 350.

22. "Indian Army," Asiatic *Journal and Monthly Register* 10 (1833): 221.

23. Douglas M. Peers, "'Those Noble Exemplars of the True Military Tradition'; Constructions of the Indian Army in the Mid-Victorian Press," *Modern Asian Studies* 31 (1997): 109–42.

24. Sir Walter Scott, "The Surgeon's Daughter," in *Chronicles of the Canongate* (Edinburgh: Cadell, 1871), 9–10.

25. These issues are the subject of Douglas M. Peers, "Conquest Narratives: Romanticism, Orientalism and Intertextuality in the Indian Writings of Sir Walter Scott and Robert Orme," in *Romantic Representations of British India*, ed. Michael Franklin (London: Routledge, 2006), 238–58.

26. Javed Majeed, *Ungoverned Imaginings: James Mill's* The History of British India and Orientalism (Oxford: Oxford University Press, 1992).

27. Robert Orme, *Historical Fragments of the Mogul Empire, of the Morattoes and of the English Concerns in Indostan* (1805; repr., New Delhi: Associated Publishing House, 1974), 268.

28. Edmund Burke and Paul Langford, *The Writings and Speeches of Edmund Burke* (Oxford: Oxford University Press, 1981), 6: 283.

29. James Mill, *The History of British India*, abr. ed. (Chicago: University of Chicago Press, 1975), 328.

30. "Is There to Be a War with the Seiks," *Mofussilite*, September 20, 1845, 142.

31. Peers, *Between Mars and Mammon*, chap. 3.

32. Malcolm to Count Woronzoff, 1820s, in *Life and Correspondence of Major General Sir John Malcolm*, ed. J. W. Kaye (London: Smith, Elder, 1856), 2: 360.

33. Gleig, *Life of Arthur, Duke of Wellington*, 18.

34. Ziauddin Sardar, *Balti Britain: A Journey through the British Asian Experience* (London: Granta, 2008), 203.

35. Peers, "'Those Noble Exemplars of the True Military Tradition.'"

36. Thomas R. Metcalf, *Ideologies of the Raj*, vol. 3, no. 4, of *The New Cambridge History of India* (Cambridge: Cambridge University Press, 1994).

37. "Military Tribes of Central Asia," *Colburn's United Service Journal* 3 (1850): 431.

38. Captain F. B. Doveton, "Palanquin Travelling in the East," *Colburn's United Service Journal* 2 (1846): 555.

39. Charles Tilly, ed., *The Formation of the Nation States in Western Europe* (Princeton, NJ: Princeton University Press, 1975). 31.

40. Pradeep Barua, "Military Developments in India, 1750–1850," *Journal of Military History* 58 (1994): 599.

41. G. V. Scammell, *The First Imperial Age: European Overseas Expansion, c. 1400–1715* (London: Unwin Hyam, 1989).

42. B. P. Lenman, "The Weapons of War in Eighteenth-Century India," *Journal of the Society for Army Historical Research* 46 (1968): 33–43; P. J. Marshall, "Western Arms in Maritime Asia in the Early Phases of Expansion," *Modern Asian Studies* 14 (1980): 13–28.

43. William Henry Tone, *A Letter to an Officer on the Madras Establishment, Being an Attempt to Illustrate Some Particular Institutions of the Maratta People* (London: J. Debrett, 1799).

44. G. G. Pearse, "The Seikh Artillery," 1849, MSS Eur E417/9, Asia, Pacific and Africa Collections (hereafter APAC), British Library.

45. Parker, *The Military Revolution*, 156.

46. An English Officer, *Narrative of the Operations of the British Army in India, from 21st April to the 16th July 1791* (London: printed for W. Faden, 1792), 16.

47. G. G. Pearse, "The Seikh Artillery," 1849, MSS Eur E417/9 (APAC).

48. The classic work on this is Daniel R. Headrick, *The Tools of Empire: Technology and European Imperialism in the 19th Century* (Oxford: Oxford University Press, 1981).

49. Linda Colley, "Size Does Matter: How a Few Islands Won an Empire," *Time Literary Supplement*, September 20, 2002, 12–13.

50. See also Michael Adas, *Machines as the Measure of Men: Science, Technology, and Ideologies of Western Dominance* (Ithaca, NY: Cornell University Press, 1989), which offers a very thoughtful discussion of how and when technology came to be such a pervasive measurement of the superiority of Western civilizations.

51. Kaushik Roy, "Equipping Leviathan: Ordnance Factories of British India, 1859–1913," *War in History* 10 (2003): 398–423.

52. Rajat Kanta Ray, *The Felt Community: Commonality and Mentality before the Emergence of Indian Nationalism* (New Delhi: Oxford University Press, 2002), 256.

53. Bengal Council to Mir Qasim, 23 February 1762, no. 1453, Imperial Record Department, *Calendar of Persian Correspondence . . . 1759–1767* (Calcutta: Government of India, 1911), 148.

54. Francis Rawdon, marquis of Hastings, and Sophia Frederica Christina Rawdon, *The Private Journal of the Marquess of Hastings* (London: Saunders and Otley, 1858), 54–55.

55. Captain Sherwill, *General Remarks on the District of Monghyr* (Calcutta: Military Orphan Press, 1849), 11.

56. Headrick, *The Tools of Empire*, 96–102.

57. Peers, *Between Mars and Mammon*, 161.

58. "Naval Operations of the Burmese War," *United Service Journal* 8 (1832): 13.

59. F. B. Doveton, *Reminiscences of the Burman War in 1824–5–6* (London: Allen & Unwin, 1852), 260.

60. Gleig, *Life of Arthur, Duke of Wellington*, 40.

61. S. Subrahmanyam, "The Kagemusha Effect: The Portuguese, Firearms, and the State in Early Modern South Asia," *Moyen orient et ocean indien* 23 (1986): 249–62.

62. Jos Gommans, "Indian Warfare and Afghan Innovation during the Eighteenth Century," *Studies in History* 11 (1995): 261–80; Jos Gommans, *Mughal Warfare: Indian Frontiers and High Roads to Empire, 1500–1700* (London: Routledge, 2002).

63. Jos Gommans and Dirk H. A. Kolff, eds., *Warfare and Weaponry in South Asia, 1000–1800* (Delhi: Oxford University Press, 2001), 381.

64. Captain Daniell's Diary, 1790, MSS Eur J788 (APAC).

65. Mark Wilks, *Historical Sketches of the South of India* (London: Longman, Hurst, Rees and Orme, 1810), 2: 718–19.

66. Richard M. Eaton, *The Rise of Islam and the Bengal Frontier, 1204–1760* (Berkeley: University of California Press, 1993), 152–53.

67. Ibid., 152, note.

68. Peter A. Lorge, *The Asian Military Revolution: From Gunpowder to the Bomb* (Cambridge: Cambridge University Press, 2008), 117.

69. Cooper, *The Anglo-Maratha Campaigns*.

70. T. R. Moreman, *The Army in India and the Development of Frontier Warfare, 1849–1947* (London: Macmillan, 1998); and Alan Warren, "'Bullocks Treading Down Wasps?' The British Indian Army in Waziristan in the 1930s," *South Asia* 20 (1997): 35–56.

71. Cooper, *The Anglo-Maratha Campaigns*.

72. Irfan Habib, ed., *Confronting Colonialism: Resistance and Modernization under Haidar Ali and Tipu Sultan* (Delhi: Tulika, 1999), xx.

73. Roddam Narasimha, "Rocketing from the Galaxy Bazaar," *Nature* 400 (1999): 123.

74. Cooper, *The Anglo-Maratha Campaigns*, 58.

75. Robert Orme, December 1764, MSS Eur 303/3 f.116 (APAC).

76. Dirk H. A. Kolff, *Naukar, Rajput, and Sepoy: The Ethnohistory of the Military Labour Market of Hindustan, 1450–1850* (Cambridge: Cambridge University Press, 1990).

77. Seema Alavi, *The Sepoys and the Company: Tradition and Transition in Northern India, 1770–1830* (Delhi: Oxford University Press, 1995), chap. 1.

78. Ray, *The Felt Community*, 256–57.

79. C. E. Oldham, "The Battle of Buxar," *Journal of the Bihar and Orissa Research Society* 12 (1926): 2.

80. Mahmud Husain, ed., *Fath-ul-Mujahideen: A Treatise on the Rules and Regulations of Tipu Sultan's Army and His Principles of Strategy* (Karachi: Urdu Academy, 1950).

81. Arthur Wellesley to Richard Wellesley, 2 November 1804, in *Selections from the Despatches, Memoranda and Other Papers Relating to India of Field Marshal the Duke of Wellington*, ed. Sidney J. Owen (Oxford: Oxford University Press 1880), 469–70.

82. Colonel Champion's Diary, 26 March 1764, H/MISC/198 (APAC).

83. Colonel Champion's Diary, 8 March 1764, H/MISC/198 (APAC).

84. Gommans and Kolff, *Warfare and Weaponry in South Asia,* 373.

85. Nirod Bhushan Ray, ed., *Poona Residency Correspondence*, vol. 3, *The Allies' War with Tipu Sultan, 1790–1793* (Bombay: Government Central Press 1937), vi.

86. Paget to Amherst, 27 October 1825, Campbell Papers, Scottish United Service Institute (Edinburgh).

87. Peers, *Between Mars and Mammon.*

88. John Chapman, "India and Its Finances," *Westminster Review* 4 (1853): 192.

89. Sanjay Subrahmanyam, "Profiles in Transition: Of Adventurers and Administrators in South India, 1750–1810," *Indian Economic and Social History Review* 39 (2002): 197–232; Habib, *Confronting Colonialism*, xxi–xxiii.

90. Lorge, *The Asian Military Revolution*, 2.

II

Warrior Peoples and Uniform Recruits in Old World Empires

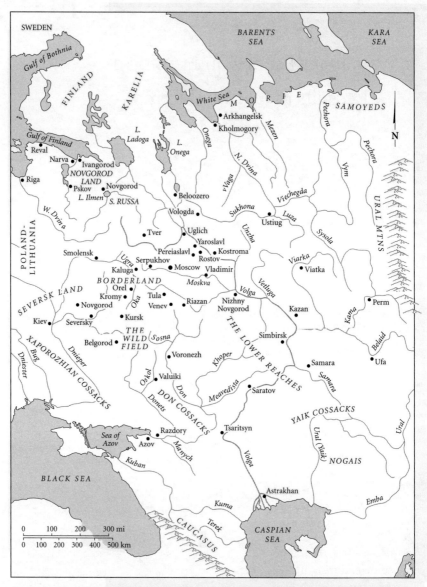

Russia in the early 1600s. From S. M. Soloviev, "Reign of Ivan the Terrible: Struggle against Bathory; Expansion into Siberia," in *History of Russia,* vol. 21 (Gulf Breeze, FL: Academic International Press, 2002). Courtesy Academic International Press.

5

Muscovite-Nomad Relations on the Steppe Frontier before 1800 and the Development of Russia's "Inclusive" Imperialism

—— DAVID R. JONES ——

Historians of Western Europe regard the "early modern" era culturally as that of the Renaissance and politically as that of the rise of centralized national monarchies. Many also credit this successful "state formation" and the creation of the first overseas commercial and colonial empires to the power unleashed by a "military (gunpowder) revolution." For the Muscovite state then emerging on Europe's periphery, however, the story was different. Largely isolated from Western developments, Moscow's rulers necessarily focused on their realm's survival in a brutal world of constant warfare, and not on colonial or imperial expansion. By 1800, Russia's empire stretched from the Baltic to the Pacific and from the Black Sea and to the Arctic, but the motives for its growth had differed significantly from those of the west European colonists. Meanwhile, differing geostrategic and military circumstances had produced an "imperial relationship" with the "natives" that differed considerably from those found in Europe's oceanic colonies.

Permanently Operating Factors

Any discussion of Muscovy's foreign and military policies involves recognizing some enduring historical elements. First, until the 1770s, Russian planners faced two distinct areas of threat. The first came from the west, initially from their Polish-Lithuanian and Swedish neighbors and later from their Austro-Hungarian and German rivals, and the second came from depths of the southern and eastern steppe. Since each posed its own mix of political problems, operational considerations, and often unique tactical imperatives, Russia developed "*two* foreign and military policies."[1] Furthermore, the burdens imposed by simultaneous and, until the late 1700s, nearly continuous conflict along both fronts left their imprint on Russian politics and culture and explain why the Russians carried out the two "military revolutions," each of which dealt with a particular enemy.

Second, the south-southeastern steppe front decisively shaped Muscovite military practice. Few scholars deny geography's impact on the Russians, and some even argue that since the broad Eurasian plain or steppe, which runs from central Germany to the Pacific, unites the European and Asian cultures, their state is more "Eurasian" than "European" or "Western."[2] Bordered in the south by mountain chains and the Black and Caspian seas, this great steppe is divided from north to south by distinctive vegetative bands. Besides the differing soils, its fertility varies with the rainfall, which diminishes when moving from the northwest to the southeast. Thus the Baltic region's poorer soils receive the most moisture, and the central steppe's excellent "black earth" has an irregular pattern of precipitation. Combined with the region's continental climate, this produces the cycles of famine interspersed by the bumper crops enjoyed by adventuresome sedentary pioneers and by the rich pastures valued by their nomadic herdsman rivals.[3]

The vast plain formed for the herdsmen an "international gallop" only partially interrupted by rivers such as the Elbe, Vistula, Dnieper, Don, and Volga and by the low ridges of the Ural Mountains. In fact, the Urals peter out into a wide east-west gateway open to movements from east to west and, more recently, vice versa as well. As William McNeill tells us, this extensive "grass sea" served as "broad and almost undifferentiated highway for those who had mastered the arts of horse nomadry."[4] In addition to the East Slavs or Rus (Ros), most migratory newcomers traversing this open road have been nomadic herdsmen, traders, and invaders. The earliest remain "unnamed in deep prehistory," and the first to be identified are the Indo-European Cimmerians, who appeared possibly as early as 1200 BCE. They were followed from 750 to 700 BCE by the Scythians and thereafter by a continuous parade of Sarmatians, Alans, Goths, Huns, Slavs, Avars, Magyars, and Bulgars, as well as the Turkic Khazars, Pechenegs-Patzinaks, Torks, Berendeis, Oghuz, Cuman-Polovetsy or Kipchaks, and, finally, the Mongol-Tatars.[5]

The promise of the steppe's rich black soil exerted an equally powerful pull on the farmer-peasants inhabiting its periphery. These included the Eastern Slavic ancestors of the later Ukrainians, Beilorussians, and Great Russians. The Great Russians' efforts to cultivate the region explain V. O. Kliuchevsky's celebrated description of Russia as a nation constantly colonizing itself.[6] Although for a long time, this "colonization" was largely unofficial, it was continually contested by the steppe's nomadic residents. The likelihood of conflict was increased by the fact that this vast arena's topographical lack of serious obstacles to east-west transit also meant a lack of geographical features to serve as a "natural frontiers." Consequently, the steppe is not easily subdivided territorially into stable states with demarcated borders. Rather, regional political entities were almost invariably separated from one another and, from the polities bordering the steppe, by "frontier zones" or "borderlands."

Within these polities, the steppe peoples competed for influence and clashed for dominance. Frustrated by their own fluid frontiers and their shifting, usually unpredictable relationships with their often hostile nomadic neighbors, the early Rus named the steppe the *dikoe pole* (wild prairie, field).[7] Hence, any Slav or other effort at steppe "governance" or "state formation," let alone "colonial" or "imperial" expansion, necessarily relied on some degree of frontier negotiation mixed with the conquest and integration of rivals, be they earlier established settlers or newly arriving migrants. The very name Ukraine itself translates literally as "on the edge" or "borderland," a fitting description for a territory that since the mid-1200s has been dominated by the Mongol Golden Horde, Cossacks, Crimean Tatars, Lithuanian-Poles, Muscovite Great Russians, and, during the last century alone, twice by German occupiers. Indeed, some scholars argue that this history leaves those living within its confines a "legacy of violence" and only a "tenuous, equivocal sense of national identity."[8]

Whatever the case, the very nature of the steppe clearly shaped the colonial or imperial ventures undertaken by those entering its vastness. As the changing cast of steppe peoples indicates, all the historical agents involved in Russia's imperial story have arrived from elsewhere.[9] In other words, during the 800s the allied Varangian (Norse) and East Slav Rus of Kiev were only one of many groups claiming the steppe as their home.[10] Also, as Boris Grekov observes, it is likely that the "ties linking the Eastern Slavs and the Turkic nomads were of long standing" and, furthermore, that whatever states rose or fell in the area were "poly-" or "multiethnic" in nature.[11] Indeed, only in Imperial Russia's last decades did "ethnicity" (in today's sense) gain any currency. So despite the strident claims of later nationalist publicists of all stripes, none of the identified inhabitants of the Eurasian steppe is "indigenous" in the same sense as are the Han Chinese of East Asia or the Amerindians of the Americas.

This brings us to a second major way in which the Russian "conquest" of the "wild prairie" differed fundamentally from the expansionist projects launched by early modern western Europe. Unlike the latter, Muscovite expansion from the more northern forest and steppe-forest zones after 1480 involved neither long-distance seaborne ventures against technologically inferior opponents, nor the creation of commercial and colonial empires composed of numerous overseas territories around the globe. Instead, it was a long, gradual process that Russian nationalist historians traditionally describe as being merely the recovery or "gathering in" of the earlier lands of medieval Kiev Rus. Some even note that in some ways, Muscovite expansion seemingly resembled that of the young American republic after 1783.[12] But whereas the Americans' push involved seizing new lands from a divided and reduced aboriginal populace, Russia emerged victorious only after three centuries of fierce competition with the other successor states to the Tatar Golden Horde. Furthermore, these hostile neighbors and rivals were initially Moscow's equals in material culture and military power and were often allies of Moscow's western (Polish-Lithuanian) neighbors as well. The goals, nature, and modes of Great Russian expansionism may well remain subjects for debate, but it seems clear that Moscow's rulers were not motivated by the same commercial, religious, and maritime-strategic ambitions that drove their west European contemporaries. In fact, as Michael Khodarkovsky concluded, Moscow's "colonialism" along the steppe frontier was "determined largely by its needs to secure and stabilize the empire's southern borderlands," or by the imperatives of state defense.[13]

Russian Conceptions of Defense

Given the particular problems posed by Russia's usually fluid and amorphous steppe frontier, the significance assumed by defense in Russian statecraft is hardly surprising. For Russian rulers, defense has been a near constant, dominating, and, frequently, the most pressing imperative. When Kiev Rus first emerged along the Dnieper River in the mid-800s, it began competing within an existing, complex regional state system. This included the stable Great Bulgar-on-the-Volga and Khazar polities to the east, the Muslim caliphate to the more distant southeast, and the powerful Byzantine Greek or Eastern "Roman" Empire to the south. Matters were equally fluid but less threatening in the west until the invasions by the Swedes and the crusading orders of German knights after 1200. But before the Mongol onslaught of 1238/1240, the only really mortal threat to Kiev came from the nomadic "hordes" roaming the Pontic Steppe between the Volga and Dnieper rivers.[14] Thereafter, despite the imposition of the so-called pax Mongolica on the devastated steppe in 1240 and Alexander Nevsky's celebrated victories over the Swedes and Germans,[15] by 1426 the small, struggling, and impoverished Muscovite principality had suffered another two hundred "attacks."[16] Nonetheless, after 1300 the new "Grand Duchy of Moscow" gradually grew in size and power at the expense of other Russian principalities, and the pace picked up after Ivan III's (1462–1503) annexation of Novgorod in 1478. With that event, Moscow's stake in the west rose significantly, and for a mix of motives—religious duty, prestige, and, possibly, an urge to break out to the Baltic—Moscow's rulers launched a prolonged series of border wars for the recovery of the lost Orthodox Slav lands of Kiev, Pskov, and Novgorod from Roman Catholic Poland and Lithuania (united as a commonwealth in 1569) and, later, Sweden. At the same time, the collapse of the great Kipchak or Golden Horde in the 1470s and 1480s led to a three-century struggle between Moscow and the Tatar successor states for control of the steppe.

The result was that by 1500, Muscovy was fighting offensively and defensively on both traditional fronts while remaining largely isolated, owing to the hostility of its western neighbors, from the intellectual and technological changes transforming the early modern West. This left the Poles and Swedes free to absorb and employ the new military techniques and tactics of western Europe's "military revolution" while simultaneously denying them to their Muscovite opponent.[17] As one Soviet scholar observed, by the 1500s Muscovy found itself "hemmed in by a ring of hostile neighbors": its "eastern and southern frontiers were assaulted by the Tatar khanates, founded after the collapse of the Golden Horde," and "on the western frontier, the struggle for the old Russian lands continued with the Grand Duchy of Lithuania, Poland and the Livonian Order, while Sweden posed a constant danger to the northeastern Russian territories."[18] Yet despite their state's seeming disadvantages, Moscow's rulers steadily expanded their realm.[19]

During this period, the terms *defense* (*oborona*) and *security* (*bezopanost*) acquired a peculiarly Russian sense, the latter acquiring connotations that make it better translated as "an absence of threat" or perhaps "absolute security."[20] For Russians, security became as much a state of mind as the product of some crude calculation of the balance of military and economic strengths and weaknesses. In reality, of course, such psychological serenity is unattainable, even for states with greater resources and more favored geostrategic circumstances than those allotted to the embattled Muscovy.[21] Even so, Russian leaders have often sought this goal, and their efforts frequently involved massive expenditures of state funds.[22] More practically, their spending after 1500 is explained by the necessity of maintaining three distinct defense and security establishments: two against their "external enemies" in the European west and the Mongol-Tatar south and southeast, and a third to check the simmering local and social resentments roused throughout society by efforts to centralize and mobilize the Muscovite state for waging wars on two fronts.[23] In retrospect, Russia's rulers' fears of this "internal enemy" sometimes seem absurdly exaggerated. Yet these, too, were "the fruit of harsh experience," and the danger of a combination of these three threats to the state's very survival were real.[24] This became clear to Muscovy's elite during the infamous "Time of Troubles" between 1604 and 1613, a perfect storm that united invasions from the west, Tatar raids from the Crimea, a dynastic crisis, and internal social-political rebellions. As a result, rebel peasant and Cossack armies controlled much of Muscovy; Poles twice held Moscow's Kremlin; and Swedes occupied the Russian northwest. Although order eventually was restored, for one long moment the Muscovite state seemed to be disappearing from the map of eastern Europe.[25]

Moscow's Bloody Steppe Frontier

Like Muscovite Russia's rulers before them, most military historians focus on the western or Polish-Lithuanian front. They do this despite the extreme vulnerability of the far-flung steppe front where Moscow waged nearly continuous war with its fellow rivals for succession to the one-time realm of the great khan. These were the Kazan, Astrakhan, Siberian, Nogai, and Crimean (Krim) Tatar khanates. Although now more sedentary, all retained the military skills of their nomadic Mongol forebears. They fought in a manner superbly adapted to the steppe environment, and even though they eventually succumbed to Russian power with the collapse of Kipchak power, they initially were more a threat than a victim. After 1468, they launched regular raids seeking slaves and booty, and apart from occasional periods of respite gained by skillful Muscovite diplomacy, "each year one waited for an attack, spoke of war," and a "year rarely passed without raids, fires, devastation."[26] This situation seemed about to improve after Ivan IV turned decisively eastward to destroy the Kazan and Astrakhan khanates from 1552 to 1556 and then began probing the defensives of the Crimean khanate. Yet in 1558 this ruler, too, turned westward.[27] Ivan IV's invasion of Livonia opened another drawn-out and exhausting conflict, whose burdens stoked the discontent that exploded in the Time of Troubles mentioned earlier. Even so, after this near-fatal catastrophe, John Keep rightly points out that Muscovy's true strategic necessity—"the life-and-death struggle" in the south—again took second place to the western conflicts,[28] and the frontier in the Pontic or Black Sea Steppe remained "a terrible gaping wound through which Russia's strength poured out" throughout the 1500s and 1600s while the state's leadership persisted in their westward enterprise.[29]

This focus is especially surprising when one realizes that throughout this era, Moscow's rulers were fully aware of the fates of the western Roman and Byzantine empires and were determined to avoid suffering a similar fate beneath the hooves of nomads storming out of the southern steppe.[30] Although a range of minor Tatar and Turkic nomadic opponents remained along the long steppe frontier after the collapse of the still nomadic Nogai horde, from the 1560s to mid-1700s the major threat came from the Crimean Tatars, or Krimtsy. They had formed a khanate in the early 1440s, and during the next three decades they extended its rule over the entire Crimean peninsula.[31] Their khan, who gained Turkish support in 1475 by recognizing the Ottoman sultan as his overlord, supposedly could field 30,000 men for occasional major campaigns like that which razed Moscow in 1571. More common, however, were the strikes launched by bands of some 150 to 200 mounted slavers. Described as "running about the list of the border as wild geese flie, invading and retiring where they see the advantage," such raiders posed a constant threat to the security of both Muscovy and Poland and were not decisively defeated until the early 1770s.[32] The damages they inflicted are evident from even the fragmentary data available. Between 1601 and 1655, Krimtsy slavers are credited with carrying off some 150,000 to 200,000 Ukrainians, Poles, and Russians,[33] and as late as 1710 to 1718, the Kharkov region was still subjected to almost annual attacks, one of which reportedly netted the Tatars some 14,000 prisoners.[34] Most were sold in Constantinople's slave marts, and others served as galley slaves in the Turkish Mediterranean fleets, but Moscow often ransomed particularly prominent or skilled prisoners. For this purpose, the tsars eventually maintained a special *prikaz*, or chancellory.[35]

Muscovy's Twin "Military Revolutions"

It is clear, then, that whatever view one takes of the Russians' subsequent expansion and "colonialism," after 1480 the Muscovite state faced real perils that demanded gigantic efforts. These dangers "kept the whole military establishment of Rus in a state of combat readiness," thanks to which a corresponding "tremendous material burden . . . lay heavily on the peasant and urban populace."[36] These conditions transformed Muscovy into a "military-national state" that, in practice, was "a permanent armed camp" supported by "a primitive economic base." Facing active enemies in both the west and south, from the latter 1400s onward Moscow's rulers made "obtain[ing] money and troops" their primary concern. Indeed, as Pavel Miliukov argues, the interrelated issues of finance and armed force "entirely absorbed the attention of the central authorities, and all the other central reforms, especially reforms of the state administration, . . . were in the end always called forth by these two demands."[37] If it is simplistic to explain the creation of Russia's autocratic tradition solely by the need to mobilize resources for constant warfare,[38] it nonetheless is reasonable to describe the newly centralized Muscovite polity as a "garrison" or "service state" directed by an "autocratic-bureaucratic" form of government.[39] Ivan III laid the foundations for this system, and his son Vasilii III (1502–1533) and his grandson Ivan IV "the Terrible" (1533–1584) completed his work. The same is true of the Muscovite program of military reforms, which ended in two interrelated but initially separate "military revolutions." Unlike their west European fellows, Russians planners faced two major opponents differing in social structures, military organization, and operational and tactical practices and therefore requiring two different responses.

Let us begin with what Richard Hellie and others call Muscovy's "gunpowder revolution." Since Muscovy's conflicts in the west resumed at precisely the time that the widespread introduction of firearms was transforming European armies, Muscovy also was required to radically reorganize its military in order to sustain its continuing conflicts with Poland-Lithuania. Despite their much-heralded isolation, Moscow's rulers were aware early of the implications of the new weaponry and its changes for battlefield tactics and military organization. Russians first reportedly used cannon in 1382, but Ivan III himself deserves credit for initiating a "massive introduction of more penetrating artillery" into his armies during the 1470s, along with such associated "significant technological advances" as granular gunpowder. Thereafter, Muscovite armies regularly used cannon for sieges, and in 1552 Ivan IV ranged 150 heavy and medium guns, along with numerous lighter weapons, against the Tatar stronghold of Kazan. Gun-toting infantry also appeared, first in the form of the *pishchalniki*, or arquebusers, and later in the *streltsy*, or musketeers. Ivan IV formed a corps of 3,000 *streltsy* in Moscow in 1550. Provincial units, largely for policing the "internal enemy," numbered some 50,000 by 1681, although they proved to be of little military value during the Time of Troubles. This led the new Romanov dynasty, beginning with the Smolensk war (1632–1634), to attempt intermittently to create new "foreign formation" regiments of Western-style infantry (*soldaty*) and cavalry (*reitary*), primarily for use in the west.[40]

Despite the Muscovite autocracy's concentrated powers, these measures had only mixed success. From at least 1550 to 1700, and sometimes thereafter, Moscow's western enemies usually were superior technologically. Aside from Muscovite conservatism and the resistance of vested interests,[41] this partly resulted from blockades imposed on technology transfers and imports into Muscovy by its western neighbors.[42] In any case, Russia's "gunpowder revolution" became a full European-style "military revolution" only after 1700 and Peter I's new round of Westernizing reforms. Having completely Westernized both his government and his armed forces, Peter I emerged victorious from the Great Northern War with Sweden (1700–1721), and his new "Russian Empire" won recognition as a major regional, if not yet a "great," power on the European stage.[43] Thereafter, the sense of constant and imminent mortal danger from the West dissipated somewhat, and as the cast of possible enemies changed, St. Petersburg, now an important player in the European system, maintained a large, usually forward-deployed, conventional European-style army in its western theater. There it supported Russian diplomacy and served to intimidate popular unrest in the recently annexed western provinces.[44]

This story of Russia's first military revolution is well known and needs little further comment. But I should note that in large part, the slow progress in creating a "modern" European type of army reflected the difficulty, if not the impossibility, of combining these forces with the "service class" or "gentry" militia created by Muscovy's other, second "military revolution." Also launched by Ivan III and completed by his immediate successors, this revolution aimed at providing the mass cavalry force needed for combat with the mobile Tatar raiders in the steppe. The result was the creation of a mounted militia force consisting of members of a military service class or social "estate," known as the "gentry" (*dvorianstvo* and *deti boiarskii*). Their service, in turn, was supported by hereditary, but still conditional (on service) *pomestie* land grants or fiefs, which were farmed by a peasantry that, by the mid-1600s, had been transformed into proper "serfs." In this manner, the gentry provided Muscovite rulers with the mounted "militia" army needed for the large mobile forces that were called up annually to act as strike forces backing the thin defensive fortress and outpost lines, known as the *zasechnaia cherta*, that Moscow maintained in the open steppe.[45] These first appeared in the early 1500s and then slowly began pushing farther south and east to protect the peasant-colonists who persisted in homesteading in the *dikoe pole* with the occasional support of semiautonomous (and at times fully autonomous) communities of non-Russian mercenaries, border-ers (*sevruki*), and the Slavic frontiersmen of the Zaporozh'e (Ukrainian) and Don Cossack "hosts."[46]

The "gunpowder revolution" may have given Muscovy a technological edge over the Tatars, but it had little initial impact beyond sieges like that of Kazan in 1552, and both cannon and handheld firearms long proved inef-fective against the swift Tatar horsemen. Worse still, by the mid-1650s the mounted gentry militia was as obsolescent and ineffective as the *streltsy*, but the gentry's social-political power prevented its reformation. Instead, Mos-cow experimented with "new formation" mounted units of European-style dragoons (*draguny*), lancers (*kopeishchiki*), hussars (*gusary*), and regular cavalry (*reitary*).[47]

Even these more "modern" troops did little to challenge the Tatar light cav-alry, which continued to dominate the Pontic Steppe well into the 1700s. Put simply, the Russian problem was that warfare on the steppe bore little resem-blance to the marches and countermarches, set-piece battles, and drawn-out sieges of the more constricted European military theaters. In the vast spaces of the steppe, the new linear infantry tactics made little sense. Despite the improved weaponry, the Russians' final success depended on their integra-tion of the tactical and logistical innovations borrowed from the West with the realities of the "wild field," and the development of a military tradi-tion and style very different from those prevalent elsewhere in Europe. An early experiment with more appropriate operational and tactical techniques was the "squares" employed by V. V. Golitsyn and Patrick Gordon in their Crimean campaigns of 1687 and 1689. These formations proved too cumber-some, but after 1760 the more flexible employment of smaller squares, as well as other "frontier" innovations introduced by generals such as P. A. Rumiant-sev and A. V. Suvorov, finally doomed the Krimtsy and permitted annexation of the Crimea in 1783.[48] Thereafter, Russian attention in the south turned to other Ottoman positions on the Black Sea coast, as well as the steppe fron-tier east of the Urals and the Caspian Sea.[49] While regular troops fought in both these new theaters, innovation again proved necessary. The struggle for Caucasia, for instance, rapidly evolved into a drawn-out series of bitter colo-nial wars involving repeated guerrilla-style skirmishes and actions with the Muslim mountaineers. As a consequence, during the 1800s the Caucasus and Central Asia became separate military regions in which war was waged by troops that, "like the colonial forces of England or France, maintained a vir-tually separate existence from the main body of the army," and had their own distinct, innovative and effective combat traditions.[50]

Imperialism on the Steppe Frontier before 1800

For many, Russia's "eastward movement" opened with Ivan III's formal break with the Golden Horde in 1480, and it scored its first major victories with Ivan IV's conquest of the rival Kazan and Astrakhan Tatar khanates between 1552 and 1556. But when Moscow's leaders became preoccupied with their wars in the west, they went on the defensive in the Pontic Steppe until the 1680s and left their interests east of the Urals largely to private "joint ventures," like that of the Stroganovs and the Cossack ataman Ermak who pushed into Siberia in the 1580s.[51] Continuing official neglect left later adventurers similarly free to pursue furs and glory across the Eurasian steppe into the Mongolian-Manchurian plain, on to Kamchatka and the Pacific, and finally into "Russian America," or Alaska. This Russian thrust into the Far East first created friction with Manchu (Qing) China in 1649, but a serious strategic threat to Moscow's position arose only when Manchuria and Korea also attracted Japanese imperial interest after 1894/1895.[52]

Discussions of this process must address the possible misconceptions and misinterpretations entailed by our accepted terminology. While Ivan III's annexation of Novgorod (1478) and his rejection of Tatar domination (1480) may, in retrospect, mark the beginning of Muscovite expansionism, it was hardly "imperialist" in the modern sense. Rather, Muscovy was immediately plunged into a life-and-death struggle with the other claimants—the various Tatar khanates—for the Mongol succession. These conflicts were as defensive as they were expansionist, and since they ended only with the annexation of Crimea in 1783, one might argue that Russia became explicitly "imperialist" (at least in the east) only after that date. It is in this context that Khodarkovsky uses the term *organic colonialism* to describe how Moscow absorbed other lands and peoples along the immediate borders of an eventual imperial metropolis simply as part of an effort to secure its steppe frontier in the context of these wars of succession.

Khodarkovsky's use of the specific term *colonialism*, rather than *imperialism*, seems appropriate in another way as well. As I noted, Moscow's eastward "movement" has superficial parallels to that of the United States' expansion westward to the same Pacific. But the United States, one scholar insists, sought to eradicate the conquered societies and assimilate their members in accord with some defined nationalist ideal or model, procedures better described as "nation building," not "empire building" or "imperialism." But until at least the late 1800s, the Russians consciously sought to avoid threats by expanding their state in such a way as to simultaneously incorporate the adjoining territories and their populations while leaving their cultures intact.

The result was a governance system of considerable ethnic and cultural diversity typical of many colonial empires.[53]

Furthermore, this diversity was a natural outcome of the manner by which Moscow sought to manage threats from the steppe. Given the perceived need to husband their resources for conflicts in the west, Muscovite strategists disliked devoting men and treasure to uncertain, usually futile, and invariably expensive military adventures against the Crimea.[54] So despite the limited effectiveness of their defensive frontier lines and the mobile militia detachments vis-à-vis the Tatars, after 1558 they usually initiated military actions only in response to enemy incursions. The officials charged with frontier defense preferred to avoid direct military action in favor of managing events beyond the frontier line through the time-honored practices of steppe diplomacy. When possible, the Muscovites used these techniques to influence dynastic and internal events within the Crimea as well. But with lesser hordes or bands, the Muscovites attempted to isolate, placate, or win over possible nomadic foes by manipulating, diffusing, and, if possible, neutralizing or eradicating all real or probable future threats. For this purpose, both before and after 1800, Russia's border agents employed a range of political initiatives that included negotiating alliances or treaties accompanied by solemn oaths that often implied vassalage (*shert*); the direct payment of tribute (*dan* or *yasak*), or a subsidy, often disguised as an act of reciprocal "gift giving"; and an exchange or taking of hostages (*amanat*). These direct diplomatic initiatives were then supplemented by an officially promoted intensification of trade and efforts to exert "cultural" influence through missionaries, translators, and the education of selected non-Russian students. If necessary, a pro-Russian party might receive support either indirectly through secret agents or directly by military intervention. In the end, an adjoining region might first be neutralized and then gradually absorbed into Muscovy's expanding realm as vassals or, if it proved necessary, safe, and politically advantageous, annexed outright. But whatever the mix of methods for each case of such "organic colonialism," possibly influential members of the opposite elite were usually wooed, subverted, and, one hoped, co-opted and eventually absorbed into Russia's own gentry or nobility.[55]

The Kievan Foundations of Muscovite Steppe Defense and Diplomacy

Until the fall of Imperial Russia, Muscovite and Imperial Russian officials used these diplomatic practices in one form or another along their Central Asian and Far Eastern frontiers. It is significant, however, that these practices were not devised by the officials but were inherited from an "international" steppe regime that had evolved centuries earlier. Their origins reflected the steppe peoples' common recognition of the need for an accepted social-political framework of customary behavior within which they could compete, cooperate, trade, and, if necessary, unite against an invading outsider. For example, almost all steppe regimes profited from maintaining trade routes, even in times of war, and acted accordingly. Consequently, the techniques of "organic colonialism" long predated the emergence of Moscow and, for Russians, represent a continuity in tradition dating from the foundation of Kiev Rus in the mid-800s, when their ancestors became part of the steppe's diplomatic regime.

This continuity in military policies is equally evident in the striking similarity between the fortified frontier lines deployed by Muscovy and the more modest "dragon walls" erected against the nomadic Pechenegs by Kiev's Grand Prince Sviatoslav the Great (ruled 957 to 972).[56] The frontier policies adopted by his son Vladimir I (980–1015) still more closely foreshadowed those adopted five centuries later. After a Pecheneg assault in 990 that "caused the Christians much harm,"[57] Vladimir rebuilt Kiev's circuit wall, began work on "towns and fortresses" along the neighboring rivers, and garrisoned his new strongholds by forcibly resettling there "the best warriors" from recently defeated tribes of East Slav rebels.[58] Like his Muscovite successors, Vladimir thus combined the needs of external defense with those of internal cohesion by transferring a recently disaffected elite from their traditional tribal homes as "military settlers" to a threatened frontier.[59] The continuing Pecheneg raids later compelled Vladimir to establish a second, ninety-mile line, which his son Yaroslav the Wise (1019–1054) extended still farther. Consequently, by the 1030s, Rus boasted a series of fortified river lines based on new fortress cities like Belgorod (991) and Pereiaslavl (992). From behind these, the grand prince and his war band conducted a mobile defense in depth or sallied forth to raid into the *dikoe pole* beyond.[60] Unlike their Muscovite successors, Kiev's *bogatyrs*—the knight-champions of the Rus frontier—regarded warfare as a way of life and gloried in launching expeditions against distant enemies. Although these lines later were less effective against the Polovtsians or Cumans,[61] these *bogatyrskie zastavy* (heroic frontier lines) nonetheless set a pattern for frontier defense that folk ballads and epics preserved for later Russians.[62]

The parallels between the Kievan and Muscovite techniques of steppe diplomacy are equally evident. As just noted, by origin these were not particularly Slavic or Russian, but simply the traditional modes of interaction developed by the ancient steppe peoples. Kiev's rulers adopted and adapted these practices to ensure the survival of their realm and the trade on which the new state's prosperity initially depended. The Varangian Rus were primarily traders, and at Kiev they held a strategic position within the web of river trade routes connecting northwestern Europe and the Baltic with the Black Sea and Constantinople in the south or, via the Volga Bulgars, Khazar kaganate, and Caspian Sea, with the Muslim caliphate.[63] Hence the primary task of Kiev's first rulers was to organize and defend their subjects' commerce and keep open their trade routes. Control of these commercial networks often involved armed conflict, but their long-term operation required the cooperation of all the major beneficiaries—the Rus, Bulgars, and Khazars—and so promoted diplomacy as well.

The nomads of the Pontic Steppe were in a similar situation. While the Rus wars with the nomadic Pechenegs, the East Slavs' first Turkic rivals, remained endemic for some 115 years, their relationship was much more complex than mere enmity. If nothing else, their "economic activities complemented one another," and a healthy commerce developed between the Slav farmers and nomad herdsmen. Thus the former provided the latter with grain in return for horned cattle and sheep, as well as the horses needed for steppe warfare and hunting.[64] Furthermore, the Pechenegs were enemies of the Khazars, the self-proclaimed overlords of Kiev when the Varangians arrived, and in 944/945 these nomads joined the Kievan Prince Igor in his successful campaign against Byzantium.[65] In addition, the steppe nomads were not insensible to the lure of the same trade that made their benevolent neutrality so necessary to the Rus. Later, when the Polovtsians became lords of the steppe, they too recognized the value of ensuring that caravan traffic across the southern steppe continued uninterrupted, sometimes even in periods of war.[66] Indeed, by the early 1200s they were "a major factor in the lively commerce between European Russia and Asia Minor" and facilitated, promoted, and possibly actively engaged in "the lively commerce" passing through the Crimean port of Sudak.[67]

Consequently, diplomatic relations between Rus and the two major Turkic nomad groupings in the steppe were inevitable. While merchants probably often acted as middlemen, other relationships between the Rus and the nomadic elites were equally natural. Whatever the cultural differences among the Norse Varangians, Slav farmers, and various steppe peoples, they had similar levels of socioeconomic development and lacked our modern concept of "ethnicity." After 988, when Prince Vladimir forcibly imposed Greek Orthodoxy on his subjects, only the Rus churchmen seemingly displayed any sense of "cultural" hostility toward their neighbors, and this was based firmly on religion rather than some ethnic, racial, or national consciousness. Furthermore, this hostility normally focused on the Turkic Pechenegs, Torks, and Polovtsians, referred to as either *chernyi klobuki* (black caps) or, more frequently, the "Sons of Hagar," "Sons of Ishmael," or "Sons of Moab." Yet they were condemned mainly as stubborn pagans, and because Ishmael was the bastard son of the prophet Abraham by the maid servant Hagar, even these designations implied a common biblical ancestry.[68]

Elite Integration before the Mongols

Although churchmen-chroniclers either deplored or downplayed the massive role of the Turkic nomadic "others" in Kievan politics, Vladimir's conversion in 988 had little impact on the traditional diplomatic and social relations of the steppe, and the chronicles are replete with accounts of treaties made (and broken) between princes with each other or with nomadic khans, and buttressed by the traditional practices of oaths (*shert*), "gift exchanges" (*yasak*), the exchange of hostages (*amanat*), and, on a number of occasions, dynastic marriages. Indeed, the integration of the Rus and the non-Slavic nomadic elites continued apace, and representatives of the latter continued to enter Kievan service, although they now usually converted to Orthodoxy.[69] This, Boris Grekov points out, suggests that Slavic-nomad ties "must inevitably have had a history" that already had "very naturally bred [a] similarity of interests" between "the two peoples."[70] Here are the origins of that afore-mentioned ethnic diversity, a tradition of Russian "imperialism," which, if not unique, is strikingly prominent. Throughout the history of the Russians' relationships with bordering peoples and regimes, including cases of outright annexation, they usually have decapitated the "colonized" by subsuming the alien elite within their own. Other imperialists occasionally acted similarly, but the ease and extent to which the Russians absorbed such "outsiders" and "newcomers" deserve serious attention.

The growing intimacy between the Rus and the nomads is most immediately evident in the *druzhinas*, or war bands, of the early princes. As the chronicles make clear, these began as an "ethnic" mix of Norse-Varangians and Slavs, and it is hardly surprising that they soon included Turkic nomads as well. After all, a man's skill and fame as a warrior mattered more than his ethnic origins. Over time, the recruitment of Norse as trusted *druzhniki* declined, and that of steppe nomads increased accordingly.[71] Whatever the impact of Orthodoxy on the self-identity of Kiev's secular elite, this trend continued even after Vladimir's conversion. In time, the chroniclers also honored valiant nomadic warriors with the title of *bogatyr*.[72]

Equally symptomatic of the close relations between the two elites was the frequency, both before and after 988, with which disgraced or defeated Russian princes sought refuge with their steppe neighbors and their aid when attempting to recover their thrones. For instance, when he was defeated in 1016, Vladimir's son Sviatopolk "fled to the Pecheneg people" and in 1019 returned "with a great many Pechenegs" to continue his struggle.[73] Thereafter, nomad interventions in Rus civil conflicts became commonplace, and from the latter 1090s on, all Polovtsian (Cuman) attacks were directly tied to internal rivalries within the Kievan state and often involved an exiled prince leading Turkic allies against his enemies within Rus. Remnants of the Pechenegs, Torks, and other earlier nomadic groupings were just as politically active when, defeated by the Polovtsians in the mid-1000s, they either served as mercenaries or settled as Kievan federates along Rus's borders. Like the independent Polovtsian khans from the deeper steppe, as well as many members of Rus's elite, their leaders usually supported the prince offering the best deal.[74]

In these cases, the interests of some of those in the parallel elites clearly coincided, but their growing solidarity is most evident in the respect often accorded to upper-class Rus hostages and prisoners of the nomads, and vice versa. Prince Igor Sviatoslavich, the hero of epic *Song of Igor's Campaign*, is iconic.[75] Defeated and captured with his son Vladimir by the Polovtsian "princes" Gzak and Konchak in 1186, Igor was honored, given freedom of the camp, taken hunting by his captors, and permitted to send for a priest to minister to his soul. Eventually he escaped, possibly helped by a Christian Polovetsian.[76] Gzak then suggested they execute Vladimir, "the falcon's son," but the more subtle Konchak instead proposed that they "entoil the falconet by means of a fair maiden."[77] This strategy succeeded and when young Vladimir arrived in Novgorod-Seversk that September, he had Konchak's daughter and an infant son in tow. Having presumably been married by Polovtsian custom, they then underwent the Christian rite, and the newly baptized bride, according to one later historian, received the name Svoboda, or "Liberty."[78]

This match was hardly exceptional. Other khans followed similar policies with other princes and with similar results. Although such unions clearly had diplomatic purposes, one estimate suggests that by the late 1100s, some "Russian" princes were seven-eighths Turkic by blood.[79] Furthermore, the tale of Igor suggests that just as in El Cid's Spain or along Digenis Akritas's Byzantine frontier, there was a "rapport between military aristocracies" on the Pontic Steppe that "could transcend religious and cultural barriers."[80] Like the commercial ties, these contacts between elites strengthened their interrelationships and fostered further diplomatic interactions. If the reticence of clerical chroniclers complicates a full analysis of the extent and significance of cooperative relations with non-Christian "others," there is evidence that both elites recognized the value of such ties, that "the Rus princes and the Polovtsian khans clearly had much in common, and [that] they demonstrated genuine respect for each other."[81]

Some princes seem to have "gone native." One who had a Polovtsian grandmother sought refuge with her people when uncles seized his patrimony in 1176, then presumably joined the Polovtsians serving in Georgia's army, and in 1185 married that kingdom's Queen Tamara.[82] Other princes seemingly became as Polovtsian as they were Slav and settled with the nomads after failing to recover their thrones in Rus.[83] Lesser figures, whether merchants, escaped slaves, or adventurous peasants, did likewise. Some created small settlements along the caravan routes and elsewhere,[84] and others adopted the nomadic lifestyle. Known as *brodniki* (wanderers), these frontiersmen were the direct forerunners of the later Don and Dnieper Cossacks. If they never achieved the Cossacks' status, by 1225 these *brodniki* were sufficiently organized and numerous enough to fight under their own commander, Ploskinia, alongside the victorious Mongols in the battle of Kalka.[85]

While the flexibility of the accepted practices of steppe diplomacy obviously promoted the growing complexity of these interactions between Russians and nomads, the role of Christianity is harder to assess. Its slow spread across the steppe hardly hindered closer relations,[86] and in a region where the Volga Bulgars' and caliphate's Islam sometimes offered serious competition, its expansion was more than a matter of faith.[87] Militarily, Rus's princes were merely equals of the steppe nomads. But Vladimir's conversion meant they had become culturally advantaged as cousins, albeit perhaps poor ones, of the Byzantine Greeks—a people fabled throughout the steppe for their riches and luxury. In matters of "nonmaterial" cultural influences, the flow therefore was largely from the Rus to the nomads, not vice versa.[88] In any case, by the 1100s the two elites were trading, treating, and often fighting together; their dynastic lineages and social traditions were increasingly intertwined; and there is evidence that growing numbers of Polovtsian princes were becoming Christian. Some undoubtedly entered a Kievan prince's service directly, but the khans retained their independence as Christian equals of the Rus within the wider world of a merging steppe elite. The progress made among steppe nomads by either Islam or Christianity remains uncertain, and the chronicles only occasionally mention baptisms.[89] Nonetheless, an increasing frequency of Russian names (such as Gleb, Yurii, and Danilo), as well as old Russian "princely" names (like Yaropolk Tomzakovich), among the nomad elite may be proof of successful conversions.[90] Examples are Khan Konchak's son Yuri, whose daughter also married a Russian prince in 1205 and who died fighting the Mongols alongside the Christian khan Danilo Kobiakovich.[91] Again, it seems likely that Khan Kotian, leader of the Polovtsian delegation seeking Russian support against the Mongols, from his brother-in-law of Prince Mstislav of Galich, was a Christian and that another leading Polovtsian prince was baptized on the eve of the Kalka battle.[92] All in all, it appears that these once contending elites were on the verge of a true merger, one that would have been sealed by blood on the field of Kalka, had the Mongols not returned between 1238 and 1242 to utterly transform life on the Pontic Steppe.[93]

Tsarist Russia's "Inclusive" Imperialism

With the Mongol onslaught, the Polovtsians and other Turkic steppe nomads disappeared from the historical stage. For the surviving Rus, the conquest was a cataclysm that left an enduring scar on Russia's national psyche, as earlier concerns about security paled in comparison with the new dangers. The center of the Rus's political recovery now became firmly rooted in the Vladimir-Suzdal region in the northeast where, under the suspicious eye of their new Mongol overlords, the surviving princes continued their internal struggles for supremacy. When the grand princes of Moscow at last emerged victorious, they turned first to the prolonged struggle to throw off the Mongol yoke and then to the conflicts for the Mongol succession and recovery of Kievan lands in the west. As noted earlier, the efforts required by both combined to create the conditions and attitudes necessary for the formation of the early Russian "service state" with its dual "military revolutions." Yet for all their faults, the Kiev Rus princes had left their Muscovite successors with useful techniques for surviving in the *dikoe pole*—techniques that helped transform their backwoods principality on the European fringe into a "great power."

It is these techniques that Khodarkovsky dubs "organic colonialism." But useful as this term may be in retrospect, we must stress again that rather than intended for expansion, "colonial" or otherwise, these practices and patterns of interaction emerged in response to the age-old patterns of steppe life. As practiced by Alexander Nevsky, among others, these techniques enabled him to buy off the Mongols while successfully repulsing the Swedes and Germans from 1240 to 1242, surely the nadir of Russian statehood. This same style of diplomacy proved equally invaluable as the surviving Russian principalities in the northeast jockeyed for local supremacy within the confines permitted by the Golden Horde. Operating politically from positions of military infe-riority, Moscow and its neighbors had no choice but to rely on diplomacy to neutralize possible threats and stay the Mongol-Tatar hand. Fortunately for the Russians, they were now a steppe people like the Mongols and so shared similar customs, styles, and modes of diplomatic intercourse. Needless to say, the conduct of these relations was the task of the elite, whose members were the only Russians to have regular direct social and political contact as subjects and vassals of the conquerors. Now princes from Moscow, Tver, and the other principalities journeyed to the great khan to his seek support by pledging their fealty, backed with hostages, payments of tribute or *dan*, the dispatch of contingents for the Mongol armies, and so on.[94] Since the Mongol khans selected and removed grand princes at will, in accord with the Horde's interests, over time the concerns of Russia's surviving elite again often merged with those of their opposites. "The people," though, could only watch, pray for peace and rain, fight when forced to do so, and flee when this was possible.[95]

Having honed their skills in waging war and conducting "power politics" on the steppe, and learned the techniques of imperial rule from their Tatar opposites, Moscow's grand dukes (tsars after 1550) faced a situation in the 1480s that resembled that of the Kiev Rus in the 900s. With the collapse of the Kipchak horde, Moscow emerged as only one of a number of the rival successor states, none of which could dominate the steppe. But post-Mongol Muscovy was already well on its way to becoming a highly centralized mon-archy. Its princes, though still plagued by internal opposition, proved adept at increasing their own authority while often holding external enemies at bay though their diplomatic dexterity. By a skillful combination of oaths, gift giv-ing, hostage exchanges, alliances, elite marriages, and, in time, the spread of Orthodoxy and Muscovite cultural values, they managed and reduced real and imagined threats while pushing their commerce and area of governance ever deeper into the *dikoe pole*. Combined with the judicious use of military force, these efforts eventually led to the destruction of the Kazan and Astra-khan Tatar khanates, promoted the disintegration of the Nogai horde, and opened an era of continuing expansion.[96] Thereafter, this advancing Musco-vite frontier, like "imperial" frontiers elsewhere, entailed the inclusion of a range of "colonial" peoples and territories within the borders of what became Imperial Russia. Apart from the Tatars, these included steppes neighbors like the Oriat Mongol-Kalmyks, the renegade Slav Ukrainian and Don Cos-sacks, various Caucasian tribesmen, and the Turkic Khirgiz-Kazakhs and Turkomens of Central Asia. In time, all found themselves at first contiguous to, and finally organic components of, Russia's growing Eurasian tsardom.

In line with the practices inherited from their forebears, the Muscovite princes often promoted close relationships with members of the elites in bordering territories. As it had done earlier, this intercourse gradually created a convergence of interests that paved the way for Moscow's absorption of the "other's" leadership within its own. One technique was accepting a foreign "prince" and, with him his principality, as a protected vassal. For example, after the Tatar tsarevich Kasim of Kazan had supported Grand Prince Vasilii II in a civil conflict during the 1440s, he received as a fief in return the small enclave, or client "tsardom" of Kasimov on the Oka River.[97] Over the next three centuries, Russian rulers made similar arrangements of mutual interest with a number of other non-Slav and non-Christian princes and khans. Thus the treaties negotiated between 1731 and 1741 by Empress Anna's government with leaders of all three Kazakh hordes were initiated by Khan Abulkhair (1693–1748), who was seeking a powerful ally in his wars with the invading Oriat-Jungars. Although the Kazakhs had no desire for direct rule by Moscow, this diplomatic vassalage eventually integrated their elites and led to Kazakhstan's incorporation, the treaties allegedly having signaled their "voluntary" union with Imperial Russia.[98]

Whatever the occasion for each such agreement, it usually involved a treaty of alliance, along with an oath implying vassalage or fealty (*shert*) and often exchanges of "gifts" and hostages as well. On this basis, the ongoing interaction among elites was then reinforced by growing social intercourse and even personal contacts between rulers. The extent to which these lands and peoples became "colonies" in the usual sense remains debatable. Unlike "settler societies" in the Americas and elsewhere, Muscovy's acquisitions more resembled medieval European provinces and feudal principalities than the west Europeans' overseas colonial domains. Beyond the fact that he and his fellows served in a different army, a new Muscovite subject's life thus probably changed little after his own sovereign became a subordinate "vassal" of the tsar.

When listing the "oriental natives" serving Muscovy and contributing "a colourful touch to the military scene during the latter 1500s–early 1600s," John Keep mentions the Tatars from the annexed Kazan, Astrakhan, and Sibir khanates; mercenaries from the still independent Nogai and Crimean hordes; units from the Chuvash, Mari (Cheremis), and Mordvians of the middle Volga region; and, less important, Bashkirs from the Ural foothills, Caucasian Karbardians, and non-Tatar Siberian tribesmen. Although such mercenaries, allies, and vassals sometimes supported pretenders, rivals, or other rebels opposing the tsar, on the whole they proved both useful and remarkably reliable auxiliaries in Muscovy's foreign wars. As a result, the Muslim Kasimov principality finally disappeared only with the death of the last "tsarevich." The roles of the other "oriental" units gradually diminished and then largely disappeared with reforms instituted after 1680 and with the subsequent rise of Peter I's regular, European-style military.[99] Later, however, the Imperial regime raised new "native" formations, and these, too, fought loyally alongside their Great Russian and other Slavic counterparts. Units made up of Crimean Tatars (the once-feared Krimtsy), for example, fought well in the wars between 1783 and 1878 and thereafter continued serving in the elite Crimean (Tatar) Escort or Convoy of His Imperial Majesty. Again, as late as 1914 to 1917, other once-hostile nomadic or mountain peoples filled the Dagestan Cavalry Regiment and the Ossetian and Turkestan Cavalry Divisions.[100]

Muscovy's successful absorption of neighboring elites also was fostered by the second "military revolution" and the creation of a "garrison" or "service" state. As explained earlier, this had established a mounted militia based on the gentry or *dvorianstvo*. Membership in this social "estate" (or class) reflected an individual's personal vassalage to the ruler and his obligation to serve militarily, in return for which he was granted a conditional landholding or estate (*pomestie*, or fief). As reorganized by Ivan IV in the 1550s, this new land regime abolished the private property of the former local princes and *boiar*-nobles and instead made conditional holdings available to anyone, regardless of "ethnic" and social origin, whom the tsar or his officials deemed to be sufficiently loyal and capable of military service. Like Prince Vladimir of Kiev in the 980s to 990s, Moscow's rulers forcibly moved former princely and *boiar* private landowners from elsewhere to new conditional *pomestie* grants along the frontiers. In this way, they both strengthened their realm's defenses from its "external enemies," and deprived possible "internal enemies" in annexed regions like Novgorod of their traditional leadership.[101]

More significant still, Moscow's rulers also offered land grants to non-Russian outsiders who volunteered to serve their throne. This also obviously helped promote and ease the integration of local native elites from newly incorporated or annexed, non-Slav lands into the Muscovite *dvorianstvo*. By converting a "native" prince or khan lands into de facto *pomestie* fiefs, Muscovite rulers transformed the secular native leaders and their subordinates into personal vassals of the Muscovite ruler and so also deprived potential rebels of their traditional leaders. Once accepted into the tsar's service, these newcomers usually proved worthy of their new master's trust, and some advanced to the highest offices of state. Here the case of the Tatar tsareviches of Kasimov is hardly exceptional. In 1575, for instance, when Ivan IV briefly "retired," he set another trusted Tatar servitor, Khan Simeon Belbulatovich, on the throne in his stead.[102] Ivan also welcomed foreigners from the west into his service, and two—Albert Schlichting and Heinrich von Staden— served in that tsar's dreaded security force, the *oprichnina*.[103] But again, these Germans were not exceptional, and especially after 1630, numerous foreigners entered Muscovite service to organize European-style military units.[104]

Conclusions

This chapter began by noting that geography and history combined to place Russia in an exposed position in the northwest corner of the Pontic Steppe, itself an extension of the larger Eurasian Steppe. Because the Eurasian Steppe served for centuries as a high road for invaders, "defense" and "security" have naturally been primary concerns for any Russian government. Consequently, what we call Muscovite "imperialism" on the steppe differed from the colonial empire building of the early modern west European states in two vital respects. First, Russian expansion and colonialism before 1800 in the south and east (though not necessarily in the west) was largely inspired by the desire to neutralize or remove any perceived or real threat by managing it, absorbing it, or pushing it further away. Thus the locales of early Russian "imperialism" were always in an adjacent (not some distant maritime) theater, and any "colonies" acquired were in the immediate proximity of the "imperial metropolis."[105]

Second, unlike the situation in the Americas and most cases elsewhere, all the rival claimants to power on the Pontic Steppe after 1480 had originally arrived from elsewhere. All therefore were "settler" (rather than "indigenous") societies, and by that date all shared a history of more than two centuries of interaction.[106] Lacking the military power to secure their extensive steppe frontiers, Moscow's rulers were forced to resort to the traditional modes of steppe diplomacy and elite interaction with its treaties and alliances, buttressed by sacred oaths, acts of gift giving, exchanges of hostages, and, on occasion, dynastic marriages. Thanks to these traditions and to the introduction of the *pomestie* form of landholding, Moscow gradually absorbed as vassals the elites of new lands acquired before 1680 and then integrated them into the Russian upper class or gentry.[107]

This transition of elites was further eased and regularized by Peter I's creation of the Table of Ranks in 1722. By opening careers in state service to almost everyone with sufficient qualifications, Slav and non-Slav "others" alike, this provided a reorganized Russian Empire with a "multinational" and "polyethnic" ruling class. To this end, Peter's "table" established parallel "ladders" of ranks (*chiny*) that offered everyone entry into Imperial Russia's hereditary noble "estate" (the *dvoriane*) through service in the armed forces, the civil bureaucracy, the diplomatic corps, the education system, the court, and so on. Henceforth, the only formal obstacles to state careers were based on education, ability, and religious belief, not ethnic or social origin.[108]

As a result, many of the best and the brightest of the "subject" elites were incorporated and assimilated into the empire's nobility. This policy was perhaps most spectacularly successful among the Baltic provinces' German nobility, whose contributions to Imperial Russia's military, bureaucratic, and cultural elites are incalculable.[109] Yet they were not exceptional in accepting a new "liege lord" in the person of the Russian ruler. Despite the rise of nationalist, non-Russian intelligentsias during the latter 1800s, or the irritation provoked by official policies of "Russification" after 1883,[110] numerous members of almost all nationalities served the Imperial regime until its collapse in February 1917.[111] Indeed, we might see Nicholas II's abdication as marking the end of the Russian elite's age-old obligation of personal service to the monarch in war, governance, and diplomacy. First developed by the princes of Kiev Rus and then refined by their Muscovite and Imperial successors, this tradition had provided Imperial Russia with a vast, military and civil bureaucracy, whose members were drawn from all the "colonies" acquired through Russia's "imperialist" expansion since 1480. Perhaps ironically, within a decade of its destruction, Peter I's empire was replaced by the new Soviet Union of supposedly proletarian and socialist "nations" and by the variegated, polyethnic, Imperial gentry-bureaucracy by that new multinational elite known as the Communist Party.

NOTES

1. John L. H. Keep, *Soldiers of the Tsar: Army and Society in Russia, 1462–1874* (Oxford: Clarendon Press, 1985), 15 (italics added).

2. A useful introduction to this "Eurasian" debate is by Mark Bassin, "Russia between Europe and Asia: The Ideological Construction of Geographical Space," *Slavic Review* 50 (spring 1991): 1–17.

3. From north to south, the main vegetative bands are the Arctic tundra, taiga or forest, mixed forest-steppe, "Black-Earth" open steppe, and arid desert or "hungry" steppe.

4. William H. McNeill, *Europe's Steppe Frontier, 1500–1800* (Chicago: University of Chicago Press, 1964), 3.

5. Barry Cunliffe, introduction to *The Oxford Illustrated History of Europe*, ed. Barry Cunliffe (Oxford: Oxford University Press, 1994), 3; Rene Grousset, *The Empire of the*

Steppes: A History of Central Asia, trans. Naomi Walford (New Brunswick, NJ: Rutgers University Press, 1970), 3–17, 171–89; Erik Hildinger, *Warriors of the Steppe: A Military History of Central Asia to 1799 a.d.* (New York: Sarpedon, 1997), 33–90; and Paul M. Barford, *The Early Slavs: Culture and Society in Early Medieval Eastern Europe* (London: British Museum Press, 2001), chaps. 1–4, 13.

6. This "colonization" school of Russian historians is briefly and critically reviewed in Nicholas V. Riasanovsky, *A History of Russia*, 2nd ed. (New York: Oxford University Press, 969), 102–3.

7. V. V. Kargalov, *Narod-bogatyr* (Moscow: Voenizdat., 1971), 10–70. This limited Pontic zone is itself only one section of a still larger territorial entity known to Arabs and Persians from the 900s to 1400s as the Desht-i Kypchak, or to the early Russians as the Kipchakskaia step (Kipchak Steppe). It ran from the lower Syr Darya, Lake Balkhash, and the Irtysh River in Central Asia and Kazakhstan in the east, to the mouth of the Danube in the west, and north from the Crimea to the "Great Bulgarian" state on the Volga River. As its name indicates, from around 1050 to 1238 it was dominated by the Kipchak-Polovtsy nomads (and not the Rus). Its eastern extension later became known as the Kirghiz or Kazakh Steppe. See Sh. F. Mukhamed'iarov, "Desht-i-Kipchak," in *Sovetskaia istoricheskaia entsiklopediia*, ed. E. M. Zhukov, 18 vols. (Moscow: Izd. Sovetskaia entsiklopediia, 1964), 5: 143.

8. Anna Reid, *Borderland: A Journey through the History of the Ukraine* (London: Orion Books–Phoenix, 1998), 1–2.

9. Exceptions are the Finns, Balts, and other scattered dwellers of the northern forest or tundra.

10. Nicholas V. Riasanovsky, "The Norman Theory of the Origin of the Russian State," *Russian Review* 7 (1947): 96–110; and, more recently, Barford, *The Early Slavs*, 232–42. In this context, "Varangian" means "Norman," Norse, or Scandinavian.

11. Boris D. Grekov, *Kiev Rus* (Moscow: Foreign Languages Publishing House, 1959), 468.

12. Joseph L. Wieczynski, *The Russian Frontier: The Impact of Borderlands on Early Russian History* (Charlottesville: University of Virginia Press, 1976).

13. Michael Khodarkovsky, *Russia's Steppe Frontier: The Making of a Colonial Empire, 1500–1800* (Bloomington: Indiana University Press, 2002), 224.

14. On early Rus' "ethnic" composition and "international" position in the steppe, see Grekov, *Kiev Rus*, 569–650; Barford, *The Early Slavs*, 227–49; and, more concisely, Janet Martin, *Medieval Russia, 980–1584* (Cambridge: Cambridge University Press, 1995), 1–5; and Charles J. Halperin, *Russia and the Golden Horde: The Mongol Impact on Medieval Russian History* (Bloomington: Indiana University Press, 1985), 11–12.

15. For Russians, the Swedish and German attacks at the time of the Mongol invasion was an unforgivable "stab in the back." See, for instance, Igor P. Shaskol'skii, *Bor'ba Rusi protiv krestonosnoi agressii na beregakh Baltiki*, vols. xii–xiii, ed. A. G. Man'kov (Leningrad: Izd. "Nauka," 1978); and Kargalov, *Narod-bogatyr*, 70–72, 154–58.

16. Serge M. Soloviev, *Istoriia Rossii s drevneishikh vremen*, 15 vols. (Moscow: Izd. Sots.-ekonomicheskoi lit., 1959–1966), 2: 514–15.

17. A useful introduction is by Jeremy M. Black, *A Military Revolution? Military Change and European Society, 1550–1800* (London: Macmillan, 1991).

18. K. V. Bazilevich, *Vneshniaia politika russkogo tsentralizovannogo gosudarstva vtoraia polovina XV veka* (Moscow: Izd. MGU, 1952), 2. Many non-Russians agree, and one American

insists that the "basic continuous elements of Russian history are the people, the Great Russians, surrounded by real or imagined enemies in a country without suitable natural frontiers and without adequate resources—material and human—for their own defense." See Richard Hellie, "The Structure of Modern Russian History," *Russian History* 4, no. 1 (1977): 3.

19. On the rate and extent of the Muscovite-Great Russian "imperial" expansion, see Rein Taagepera, "An Overview of the Growth of the Russian Empire," in *Russian Colonial Expansion to 1917*, ed. Michael Rywkin (London: Mansell Publishing, 1988), 1–7.

20. David R. Jones, "Soviet Concepts of Security: Reflections on Flight KAL 007," *Air University Review*, November/December 1986, 33–36; and David R. Jones, "Soviet Strategic Culture," in *Strategic Power: USA/USSR*, ed. Carl G. Jacobsen et al. (Basingstoke: Macmillan, 1990), 35–49.

21. There are parallels with the United States. See James Chace and Caleb Carr, *America Invulnerable: The Quest for Absolute Security from 1812 to Star Wars* (New York: Summit Books, 1988); J. E. Kaufmann and H. W. Kaufmann, *Fortress America: The Forts That Defended America, 1600 to the Present* (Cambridge, MA: Perseus–Da Capo Press, 2004).

22. In budgetary terms, our first hard but incomplete data on defense spending relate to 1680 and suggest a figure of 62 percent. Four decades after Peter I's reforms, defense still comprised 63.3 percent of the 1762 budget. This is a wartime figure, but the norm for this period still was around 40 percent. Even during the three decades before 1914, after the economy had modernized and expanded with industrialization, defense spending accounted for roughly 27 percent of total outlays, a figure intriguingly close to the estimates of 25 to 32 percent made by the Central Intelligence Agency and other Western specialists for Soviet defense spending during the 1950s to 1970s. On this issue, see David R. Jones, "The Soviet Defence Burden through the Prism of History," in *The Soviet Defence Enigma: Estimating Costs and Burdens*, ed. Carl G. Jacobsen (Oxford and Stockholm: Oxford University-SIPRI, 1987), 151–74.

23. This third establishment began with Ivan IV's *oprichniki* (internal security force) in the 1560s, the streltsy (musketeers) in the 1600s, and, finally in the militarized gendarmes, secret police, and so on of modern Imperial Russia. All officially stood guard against the "internal" enemy. Later radical "intellectuals" aside, this "internal threat" was posed by both rebellious non-Russians and a frequently restless peasantry, whose revolts are chronicled in Paul Avrich, *Russian Rebels, 1600–1800* (New York: Schocken Books, 1972). See also Erik Amburger, *Geschichte der Behördenorganisation Russlands von Peter dem Grossen bis 1917* (Leiden: Brill, 1966); Ronald Hingley, *The Russian Secret Police: Muscovite, Imperial Russian and Soviet Political Security Operations, 1565–1970* (London: Hutchinson, 1970).

24. Keep, *Soldiers of the Tsar*, 15.

25. Sergei F. Platonov, *The Time of Troubles: A Historical Study of the Internal Crisis and Social Struggle in Sixteenth- and Seventeenth-Century Muscovy*, trans. John T. Alexander (Lawrence: University Press of Kansas, 1970); and Ruslan G. Skrynnikov, *Time of Troubles: Russia in Crisis* (Gulf Breeze, FL: Academic International Press, 1988).

26. N. Khlebnikov, *O vliianii obshchestva na organzatsiiu gosudarstva v tsarskii period russkoi istorii* (St. Petersburg: Tip. A. Kotomina, 1869), 5–6.

27. Henry R. Huttenbach, "Muscovy's Conquest of Muslim Kazan and Astrakhan, 1552–56: The Conquest of the Volga: Prelude to Empire," in *Russian Colonial Expansion to 1917*, ed. Michael Rywkin (London: Mansell Publishing, 1988), 45–69. On these campaigns and Ivan's strategic decisions, also see George Vernadsky, *The Tsardom of*

Moscow, 1547–1682, 2 vols. (New Haven, CT: Yale University Press, 1969), 1: 51–58, 63–64, 87–100; Sergei F. Platonov, *Ivan the Terrible*, trans. Joseph L. Wieczynski (Gulf Breeze, FL: Academic International Press, 1978), 79–96; and Ruslan G. Skrynnikov, *Ivan the Terrible*, trans, Hugh F. Graham (Gulf Breeze, FL: Academic International Press, 1981), 49–57.

28. Keep, *Soldiers of the Tsar*, 15.

29. T. Szameuly, *The Russian Tradition*, ed. R. Conquest (London: Secker and Warburg, 1974), 25.

30. Khodarkovsky, *Russia's Steppe Frontier*, 1, 224.

31. Alan W. Fisher, *The Crimean Tatars* (Stanford, CA: Hoover Institution Press, 1978), 1–10.

32. Benedict Humphrey Sumner, *Survey of Russian History* (London: Duckworth, 1947), 42. The style of warfare of the Krimtsy is discussed in Hildinger, *Warriors of the Steppe*, 203–13.

33. A. A. Novosel'skii, *Bor'ba moskovskogo gosudarstva s tatarami v pervoi polovine XVII veka* (Moscow: Izd. "Nauka," 1948), 434–36. He admits that fewer Russians were taken as compared with the inhabitants of Poland and present-day Ukraine. Also see Alan W. Fisher, *The Russian Annexation of the Crimea, 1772–1783* (Cambridge: Cambridge University Press, 1970), 20, who cites another Russian claim that in 1575 a single Tatar raid cost Muscovy 15,000 prisoners and 40,000 horses.

34. Sumner, *Survey of Russian History*, 42, adds that this last figure is "suspiciously high." Also see the review of raids carried out after 1468 in Keep, *Soldiers of the Tsar*, 15–16, who agrees that Russia's vulnerability "in this era scarred men's minds and left lasting traces." McNeill, *Europe's Steppe Frontier*, chaps. 3–4, provides a clear account of events on the disputed Pontic Steppe from 1570 to 1740. Bohdan Baranowski's study, *Polska a Tatarszczyzna w latach 1624–1629* (Lodz: Lodzkie Towarzystwo Naukowe Societas Scientiarum Losziensis, 1948), 114–17, concludes that despite its seeming power, Poland lacked the strength to maintain its position on the Baltic and simultaneously pursue its ambitions vis-à-vis the Crimea.

35. Keep, *Soldiers of the Tsar*, 15–20.

36. Bazilevich, *Vneshniaia politika russkogo*, 2.

37. Pavel N. Miliukov, *Ocherki po istorii russkoi kul'tury*, 5th ed., 3 vols. (St. Petersburg: Tip. I. N. Skorokhodova, 1904), 1: 145.

38. For alternative views of the origins of Russia's "autocracy," see Michael Cherniavsky, "Khan or Basileus: An Aspect of Russian Medieval Theory," in *The Structure of Russian History: Interpretive Essays*, ed. Michael Cherniavsky (New York: Random House, 1970), 65–79.

39. Richard Hellie, *Enserfment and Military Change in Muscovy* (Chicago: University of Chicago Press, 1971), 3; Keep, *Soldiers of the Tsar*, 13–15.

40. Hellie, *Enserfment and Military Change*, 151–64, 202–10; and Keep, *Soldiers of the Tsar*, 60–73, 75–9. On issues of Muscovite military technology in general, see Thomas Esper, "Military Self-Sufficiency and Weapons Technology in Muscovite Russia," *Slavic Review* 28, no. 2 (1969): 185–208.

41. Werner Philipp, "Russia's Position in Medieval Europe," in *Russia: Essays in History and Literature*, ed. Lyman H. Letgers (Leiden: Brill, 1972), 36, insists that for variety of reasons, geography included, Muscovite "Russia became the conservative country par excellence in Europe."

42. Sergei F. Platonov, *Moscow and the West*, trans. J. L. Wieczynski (Hattiesburg, MS: Academic International Press, 1972), 5; and Thomas Esper, "A Sixteenth-Century Anti-Russian Arms Embargo," *Jahrbucher fur Geschichte Osteuropas* 15 (1967): 180–96. On Sweden's role, see Ragnhild Marie Hatton, "Russia and the Baltic," in *Russian Imperialism: From Ivan the Great to the Revolution*, ed. Taras Hunczak (New Brunswick, NJ: Rutgers University Press, 1974), 108–19. Hatton points out that the Polish "ban on military and technological contacts between Russia and the West" was lifted only in 1686, thus ending "Russia's isolation from Western technological advances" (119).

43. G. A. Nekrasov, "Mezhdunarodnoe priznanie rossiiskogo velikoderzhaviia v xviii v.," in *Feodal'naia Rossiia vo vsemirno-istoricheskom protsesse.Sbornik statei, posviashchennyi L'vu Vladimirovich Cherepinu*, ed. V. T. Pashuto et al. (Moscow: Izd. "Nauka," 1972), 381–88; and the analysis in John P. LeDonne, *The Russian Empire and the World: The Geopolitics of Expansion and Containment, 1700–1917* (Oxford: Oxford University Press, 1997), sec. I.

44. David R. Jones, "Russian Military Traditions and the Soviet Military Establishment," in *The Soviet Union: What Lies Ahead? Military-Political Affairs in the 1980s*, ed. Kenneth M. Currie and Gregory Varhall (Washington, DC: USAF-US GPO, 1984), 38. William C. Fuller Jr., *Strategy and Power in Russia, 1600–1914* (New York: Free Press, 1992), provides the fullest Western account of Imperial Russian military planning. Russia's "Western Provinces" are discussed in detail in Edward C. Thaden with Marianna Forster Thaden, *Russia's Western Borderlands, 1710–1870* (Princeton, NJ: Princeton University Press, 1984).

45. The creation of this service gentry is detailed by Hellie, *Enserfment and Military Change*, 25–47.

46. Keep, *Soldiers of the Tsar*, 16–17, map 1; Hellie, *Enserfment and Military Change*, 174–80; Platonov, *Ivan the Terrible*, 119–24. For a more detailed account, see A. I. Yakovlev, *Zasechnaia cherta Moskovskago gosudarstva v XVII v.: Ocherk iz istorii oborony yuzhnoi okrainy Moskovago gosudarstva* (Moscow: Tip. G. Lissnera i D. Soiko, 1916). From the 1700s to the 1800s, similar chains of border posts protected the Ural and Siberian steppe frontiers as well.

47. Hellie, *Enserfment and Military Change*, 198–200; Keep, *Soldiers of the Tsar*, 81–91. This issue also is examined extensively in Carol Belkin Stevens, *Soldiers on the Steppe: Army Reform and Social Change in Early Modern Russia* (De Kalb: Northern Illinois University Press, 1995).

48. Bruce W. Menning, "Russia and the West: The Problem of Eighteenth-Century Military Models," in *Russia and the West in the Eighteenth Century*, ed. A. G. Cross (Newtonville, MA: Oriental Research Partners, 1983), 289; Bruce W. Menning, "Military Institutions and the Steppe Frontier in Imperial Russia, 1700–1861," *Acta* no. 5: Bucarest 10–17 VIII 1980 (Bucharest: International Commission of Military History, 1981), 174–94; and David R. Jones, *The Advanced Guard and Mobility in Russian and Soviet Military Thought and Practice*, SAFRA Paper no. 1 (Gulf Breeze, FL: Academic International Press, 1985), 22–25, 32–35.

49. Fuller, *Strategy and Power in Russia*, 147–50.

50. Robert F. Baumann, "The Russian Army, 1853–1881," in *The Military History of Tsarist Russia*, ed. Frederick W. Kagan and Robin Higham (New York: Palgrave Macmillan, 2002), 146. Also see Robert F. Baumann, *Russian-Soviet Unconventional Wars in the Caucasus, Central Asia, and Afghanistan*, U.S. Army Command and General Staff College, Leavenworth Papers, no. 20 (Fort Leavenworth, KS: Combat Studies Institute, 1993); and

W. E. D. Allen and Paul Muratoff, *Caucasian Borderlands: A History of Wars on the Turco-Caucasian Border, 1828–1921* (Cambridge: Cambridge University Press, 1953).

51. On the Siberian Tatars, other natives, and conditions along this section of Russia's expanding frontier, see Terence Armstrong, ed., *Yermak's Campaign in Siberia: A Selection of Documents*, trans. Tatiana Minorsky and David Wileman (London: Hakluyt Society, 1975).

52. George V. Lantseff and Richard A. Pierce, *Eastward to Empire: Exploration and Expansion on the Russian Open Frontier to 1750* (Montreal: McGill–Queen's University, 1973). This process is usefully summarized in James R. Gibson, *Feeding the Russian Fur Trade: Provisionment of the Okhotsk Seaboard and the Kamchatka Peninsula, 1639–1856* (Madison: University of Wisconsin Press, 1969), 3–33; Daniel R. Brower and Edward J. Lazzerini, eds., *Russia's Orient: Imperial Borderlands and Peoples, 1700–1917* (Bloomington: Indiana University Press, 2001); George Alexander Lensen, ed., *Russia's Eastward Expansion* (Englewood Cliffs, NJ: Prentice-Hall, 1964).

53. This distinction is drawn by Ivan Eland in *The Empire Has No Clothes: U.S. Foreign Policy Exposed* (Oakland, CA: Independent Institute, 2004), 3–4, who warns that "nation-building can be more brutal than the quest for empire [where] conquered populations are left intact and dominated, at least partially, using local elites. They often keep their own language and laws." Despite occasional bouts of "Russification" in the 1800s, tsarist Russia remained essentially an "empire," and not a "nation-state," until its collapse in 1917.

54. The real logistical and other problems of a full-scale campaign against the Crimea also discouraged this course, see Platonov, *Ivan the Terrible*, 83–85.

55. Khodarkovsky, *Russia's Steppe Frontier*, 46–82, 184–222 (esp. 224); Michael Khodarkovsky, *Where Two Worlds Met: The Russian State and the Kalmyk Nomads, 1600–1771* (Ithaca, NY: Cornell University Press, 1992). These same techniques were employed east of the Urals throughout the 1800s and also still later in Central Asia and the Far East.

56. Barford, *The Early Slavs*, 146, 247.

57. Serge A. Zenkovsky with Betty Jean Zenkovsky, ed., intro., and trans., *The Nikonian Chronicle*, 3 vols. (Princeton, NJ: Kingston Press, 1984–86), 1: 990.

58. Samuel H. Cross, *The Russian Primary Chronicle*, Harvard Studies and Notes in Philology and Literature, no. 12 (Cambridge, MA: Harvard University Press, 1930), 206; Grekov, *Kiev Rus*, 626–27; Barford, *The Early Slavs*, 246–47; and Anatolii N. Kirpichnikov, *Voennoe delo na Rusi v XIII–XV*, vol. 5 (Leningrad: "Nauks," 1976), 51–61.

59. Zenkovsky and Zenkovsky, *The Nikonian Chronicle*, 1: 109; Martin, *Medieval Russia*, 18.

60. Kargalov, *Narod-bogatyr*, 17–22, and esp. the map of frontier defenses on p. 21; Barford, *The Early Slavs*, 247–48.

61. On the Polovtsians or Cumans, Thomas S. Noonan, "Polovtsy (Polovtsians)," in *The Modern Encyclopedia of Russian and Soviet History*, ed. Joseph L. Wieczynski (Gulf Breeze, FL: Academic International Press, 1982), 29: 12–24; Martin, *Medieval Russia*, 48–55; A. I. Popov, "Kypchaki i Rus," in *Uchenye zapiski Seriia istoricheskikh nauk*, vyp. 14, ed. S. I. Kovalev (Leningrad: Izd. Leningrad. Gos. Ordena Lenina Univ. im A.A. Zhdanova, 1949), 94–119; and Peter Golden, *The Polovci Dikii*, Harvard Ukrainian Studies, nos. 3–4 (1979–80): 296–309.

62. Martin, *Medieval Russia*, 19. For typical epics and ballads, see Dimitri Obolensky, ed., *The Penguin Book of Russian Verse* (Baltimore: Penguin, 1962), 1–42; and Serge A. Zenkovsky, ed., *Medieval Russia's Epics, Chronicles, and Tales*, rev. ed. (New York: Dutton, 1974), 15–21, 49–65. Both contain the famous epic *The Lay of Igor's Campaign*, which also

is translated, with a commentary, by Vladimir Nabokov as *The Song of Igor's Campaign* (New York: Random House-Vintage Books, 1960). Also on *bogatyrs* and ballads, see L. A. Magnus, *The Heroic Ballads of Russia* (London: Kegan Paul, Trench, Trubner/Dutton, 1921), 13–118; and Kargalov, *Narod-bogatyr*, 23–26.

63. Rus's initial seaborne activities on the Black and Caspian seas are detailed in Vladimir V. Mavrodin, *Russkoe morekhodstvo na yuzhnykh moriakh* (Chernom Azovskom i Kaspiiskom s drevneishikh vremen i do XVI veka vkliuchitel'no) (Simferopol: Krymizdat, 1955), chaps. 1–4.

64. Martin, *Medieval* Russia, 17–18; Grekov, *Kiev Rus*, 626–28; Grousset, *The Empire of the Steppes*, 182–85; Thomas S. Noonan, "Pechenegs," in *Modern Encyclopedia of Russian and Soviet History*, ed. Joseph L. Wieczynski (Gulf Breeze, FL: Academic International Press, 1982), 27: 126–33. On the early Slavs' use of horses in warfare see Barford, *The Early Slavs*, 143–44.

65. Cross, *The Russian Primary Chronicle*, 160–64; Grekov, *Kiev Rus*, 463, 69.

66. A. I. Popov, "Kypchaki i Rus," in *Uchenye zapiski Seriia istoricheskikh nauk*, vyp. 14, ed. S. I. Kovalev (Leningrad: Izd. Leningrad. Gos. Ordena Lenina Univ. im A.A. Zhdanova, 1949), 103–4.

67. Noonan, "Polovtsy (Polovtsians)," 20, 22–23.

68. Zenkovsky and Zenkovsky, *The Nikonian Chronicle*, 1: 109. The newly Christianized Slavs borrowed these terms from the Byzantines, who used them for Muslim Arabs and other non-Christian nomads. Moab was Lot's son by his own daughter.

69. This practice continued until 1917. Even under the supposedly anti-Semitic Nicholas II, baptized Jews reached high positions in the military. See, for example, General M. Grulev, *Zapiski generala-evreia* (Paris: Author, 1929–30).

70. Grekov, *Kiev Rus*, 468–69.

71. For example, when Oleg marched south to make Kiev the capital of a unified Rus in 881, he reportedly "had with him the Varangian men and the Slavic men, and that is the reason why they are all called Russians." See Zenkovsky and Zenkovsky, *The Nikonian Chronicle*, 1: 29–30. On Kiev's rulers and their *druzhinas*, and their membership, see Grekov, *Kiev Rus*, 382–411, 450–61; and David R. Jones "Central Military Administrative System and Policy-Making Process" in David R. Jones, *The Military-Naval Encyclopedia of Russia and the Soviet Union* (Gulf Breeze, FL: Academic International Press, 1978), 2: 41–45. Grekov traces the decline of Varangian and an increase of nomad steppe warriors, both as mercenaries and *druzhniki* (461–63). For examples of nomad recruitment, see Zenkovsky and Zenkovsky, *The Nikonian Chronicle*, 1: 73, 107, 109–11; and Cross, *The Russian Primary Chronicle*, 204–13.

72. Zenkovsky and Zenkovsky, *The Nikonian Chronicle*, 1: 118, 2: 7.

73. Robert Mitchell and Nevill Forbes, trans., *The Chronicle of Novgorod, 1016–1471* (Hattiesburg, MS: Academic International Press, 1970), 2; Zenkovsky and Zenkovsky, *The Nikonian Chronicle*, 1: 75, 131–33.

74. The chronicles are replete with accounts of exiled princes and their role in Polovtsian attacks interventions; also see Noonan, "Polovtsy (Polovtsians)," 16–21; and Martin, *Medieval Russia*, 52–54, 129–32.

75. On the background to this event, see Martin, *Medieval Russia*, 129–30.

76. According to *The Song of Igor's Campaign*, 66, and Nabokov's note to line 751 (p. 130), Igor's escape was facilitated by one "Ovlur," or Lavor (Vlor), "a friendly Cuman."

Popov, "Kipchaky i Rus," 105, suggests that he helped the prince because he was a Christian, who fled with Igor back to Rus.

77. Nabokov, *The Song of Igor's Campaign*, 70. Zenkovsky and Zenkovsky, *The Nikonian Chronicle*, 2: 186–88, see this disaster as punishment for the prince's pride, regard his escape as evidence that God "will not destroy a humble and meek heart," and ignore his son's later nuptials to Konchak's daughter.

78. Entry for 1187 in the *Ipatiev Chronicle*, cited in Nabokov, *The Song of Igor's Campaign*, 134, n. 856. One authority suggests that such brides were also hostages; see "The Testament of Vladimir Monomakh," as printed in Basil Dmytryshyn, ed., *Medieval Russia: A Source Book, 900–1700* (New York: Holt, Rinehart and Winston, 1967), 69.

79. D. S. Likhachev, *Velikoe nasledie: Klassicheskoe proizvedeniia literatury drevnei Rusi* (Moscow: Izd. "Mysl," 1975), 158. Even Grand Prince Yuri Dolgorukii was grandson of a Polovtsian khan. Also see the comments by Popov, "Kypchaki i Rus," 103.

80. Halperin, *Russia and the Golden Horde*, 19.

81. Noonan, "Polovtsy (Polovtsians)," 17.

82. This was Andrei Bogoliubskii's son Yuri; see Noonan, "Polovtsy (Polovtsians)," 17.

83. For example, the princes Oleg Sviatoslavich and David Igorevich. See Cross, *The Russian Primary Chronicle*, 292–95; Zenkovsky and Zenkovsky, *The Nikonian Chronicle*, 1: 221–24.

84. Popov, "Kypchaki i Rus," 102.

85. For the brodniki, see Popov, "Kypchaki i Rus," 113–14. For Kalka, see Kargalov, *Narod-bogatyr*, 83–7; Martin, *Medieval Russia*, 132; Zenkovsky and Zenkovsky, *The Nikonian Chronicle*, 2: 289 and n. 25.

86. Although Barford remarks that with Vladimir's conversion, "Russia was flooded with missionaries, clergymen, craftsmen and artists" (*The Early Slavs*, 248,), Martin points out that these missionaries initially met considerable resistance from the Rus, which undoubtedly long militated against sustained efforts among the steppe nomads (*Medieval Russia*, 73–76).

87. On the spread of Islam on the steppe, see Noonan, "Pechenegs," 131; and Noonan, "Polovtsy (Polovtsians)," 22.

88. On the evidence of cultural interactions, see Halperin, *Russia and the Golden Horde*, 16–20; and Popov, "Kypchaki i Rus," 104–5, 114–17. Although Muscovite and Imperial regimes launched more sustained missionary efforts, these were more culturally than religiously successful.

89. For example, "the Polovets prince" in Zenkovsky and Zenkovsky, *The Nikonian Chronicle*, 2: 2.

90. Popov, "Kipchaki i Rus," 105.

91. Zenkovsky and Zenkovsky, *The Nikonian Chronicle*, 2: 228, n. 6. Zenkovsky and Zenkovsky insist that "like several other Polovetsian khans of that time, [he] already had become Christian."

92. Zenkovsky and Zenkovsky, *The Nikonian Chronicle*, 2: 285–86. On this issue, see Noonan, "Polovtsy (Polovtsians)," 23.

93. Noonan, "Polovtsy (Polovstians)," 22–23.

94. Halperin, *Russia and the Golden Horde*, chaps. 4–10; Martin, *Medieval Russia*, chaps. 5–7. On Moscow's emergence, see John L. I. Fennell, *The Crisis of Medieval Russia, 1200–1304* (London: Longman, 1983), esp. 98–124; and John L. I. Fennell, *The Emergence*

of Moscow, 1304–1359 (Berkeley: University of California Press, 1968). The actual Mongol invasion is described in James Chambers, *The Devil's Horsemen: The Mongol Invasion of Europe* (New York: Atheneum, 1979); and the long-term impact of the Mongol yoke is discussed in Sumner, *Survey of Russian History*, 87–92; and George Vernadsky, *The Mongols and Russia* (New Haven, CT: Yale University Press, 1953).

95. Martin, *Medieval Russia*, 199–201; Halperin, *Russia and the Golden Horde*, 106–7.

96. Martin, *Medieval Russia*, 302–26, 351–59.

97. Keep, *Soldiers of the Tsar*, 79; Halperin, *Russia and the Golden Horde*, 29, 59, 109–10. The term *fief*, of course, is west European.

98. For the range of views of this process, see the discussions in G. A. Akhmedzhanov's *Sovetskaia istoriografiia prisoedineniia Srednei Azii k Rossii* (Tashkent: FAN, 1989); N. G. Apollova, *Prisoedinenie Kazakhstana k Rossii v 30-kh godakh XVIII veka* (Alma-Ata: AN KSSR 1948); N. G. Apollova, *Ekonomicheskie i politicheskie sviazi Kazakhstana s Rossii v XVIII-nachale XIX veka* (Moscow: "Nauka," 1960); and Martha Brill Olcott, *The Kazakhs* (Stanford, CA: Hoover Institution Press, 1987).

99. Keep, *Soldiers of the Tsar*, 77–79; and, more visually, Angus McBride's "Plate D" in Viacheslav Shpakovsky and David Nicolle, *Armies of Ivan the Terrible: Russian Troops, 1505–1700* (Oxford: Osprey Publishing, 2006), 28, and commentary, 44–45.

100. Fisher, *The Crimean Tatars*, 87–88; E. Messner et al., *Rossiiskie ofitsery* (Buenos Aires: South American Section of the N. N. Golovin Institute for the Problems of War and Peace, 1959), 17.

101. After annexing Novgorod, Ivan III created this system partly for this purpose, and Ivan IV did likewise by exiling alleged opponents to Kazan in the 1560s. See Skrynnikov, *Ivan the Terrible*, 88–93.

102. Skrynnikov, *Ivan the Terrible*, 162–71.

103. Both left accounts of their service. See Hugh F. Graham, ed., "A Brief Account of the Character and Brutal Rule of Vasil'evich, Tyrant of Muscovy (Albert Schlichting on Ivan Groznyi)," *Canadian American Slavic Studies* 9, no. 2 (1975): 204–72; and Heinrich von Staden, *The Land and Government of Muscovy*, trans. Thomas Esper (Stanford, CA: Stanford University Press, 1967).

104. The Muscovite regime's efforts in this regard are outlined in Keep, *Soldiers of the Tsar*, 80–92; and Hellie, *Enserfment and Military Change*, 176–257.

105. In this respect, Russian "imperialism" more resembles England's expansion in Scotland and Ireland than its colonial ventures overseas, and we therefore might compare Russian Poland with England's Ireland!

106. Since the Mongol-Tatars did not arrive and settle in the Pontic Steppe until after 1240, in this case the Muscovite-Russians, perhaps ironically, might claim "aboriginal" status!

107. Opposition to this process did develop after the Time of Troubles. As a result, conversion to Orthodoxy increasingly became a requirement for membership in the service class of late Muscovite Russia and for a grant from the land fund; see Hellie, *Enserfment and Military Change*, 55–56. There were, of course, occasions when policies of elite integration failed. Such was the case with the religiously motivated Muslim Caucasian mountaineers, who in the 1860s preferred mass exile in Ottoman Turkey to becoming subjects of the Christian tsar.

108. Keep, *Soldiers of the Tsar*, 123–28.

109. The indispensable introduction to the role of the Baltic Germans in Russian life is that by Wilhelm Lenz, et al., eds., *Deutschbaltisches biographisches Lexikon, 1710–1960*

(Cologne/Vienna: Bohlau Verlag, 1970). Many of these German Balts believed that they served the emperor personally, not Russia, and therefore that they became free agents after the overthrow of Nicholas II in February 1917!

110. See Peter A. Zaionchkovsky, *The Russian Autocracy under Alexander III*, trans. David R. Jones (Gulf Breeze, FL: Academic International Press, 1976), 59–77.

111. Concepts of "national" origins meant nothing to tsarist bureaucrats, and the category is often ignored in official records. Later estimates based on official sources therefore use statistics on religious denomination, which were recorded; see Sergei V. Volkov, *Russkii ofitserskii korpus* (Moscow: Voenizdat., 1993), 273–79. Emigré historians after 1917 did discuss the national issue and Messner, et al., *Rossiiskie ofitsery*, 15–18, report that between 1911 and 1914 the officers of the Fifteenth Artillery Brigade (based in Odessa) were nineteen Great Russians, twelve Little Russians (Ukrainians), nine Poles, six Germans, two French, two Greeks, one Tatar, and one Bulgarian. Bon-Russians—seven Germans, five Little Russians, four Swedes, two Finns, three Caucasians, and one Karite, Swiss, Frenchman, and Tatar, respectively—made up some 40 percent of total in the elite Life Guards Grenadier Regiment. As noted earlier, religious prohibitions on serving as an officer referred to Jews and, in some periods, Polish Catholics, but these disabilities disappeared with baptism.

6

Ottoman Ethnographies
of Warfare, 1500–1800

VIRGINIA H. AKSAN

In the long sweep of Ottoman imperial history, the Ottomans seriously addressed the question of warrior (or indigenous) societies in their military organization only when minority groups in the empire, such as the Greeks and Serbians, began to define themselves as "nations." That does not mean that the Ottoman dynasty lacked definitions of ethnicity but rather that such labels, while continuously applied to warrior groups, were not central to the ways in which the Ottomans understood or officially organized their armies until at least the late eighteenth century. Nevertheless, the Ottomans wrestled extensively with how to control and/or incorporate conquered peoples, coreligionists or otherwise, and their attempted solutions speak to the broader problem of understanding imperial expansion in the early modern world. A coercive Ottoman strategy of local elite cooptation is evident in specific locales of the empire such as the Balkans, though less so in areas where Muslim populations predominated, such as Anatolia or the Arab world until after 1700. As with all other early modern empires, the need for manpower and supplies remained an imperative catalyst of negotiations with local indigenous forces.

This chapter begins by examining the state of Ottoman historiography on warfare and warrior societies (assumed here are their origins as Turks in Turco-Mongol societies of Asia in general), and then by schematizing the Ottoman "difference" in a comparative imperial context around two further nodes: a consideration of how the Ottomans extended power in the Balkans and Arab world through their understanding of "ethnicity" or "indigenous" peoples as part of their coercive strategy of conquest, settlement, and resource extraction; and then a discussion with examples of the use of auxiliary/militias/indigenous forces by the Ottomans over time. The chapter concludes with some thoughts on the question of indigenous warriors and theories of military reform.

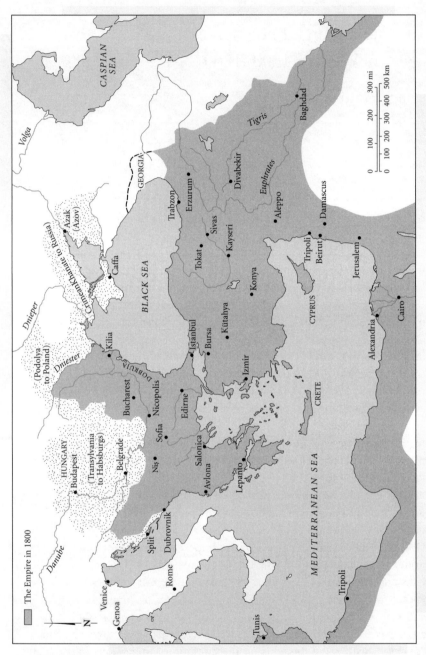

Ottoman Empire, 1683–1800.

Studies of the relationship between warfare and indigenous or "native" peoples in the Ottoman Empire (or the Middle East, for that matter) are few and far between. There are a number of reasons for that, not the least of which is the way in which Ottoman and Middle Eastern historiography has evolved. First, it is a small field with a handful of practitioners across the world. We Ottoman historians in particular suffer from empire envy and are invariably catching up with our *confrères* in imperial studies. Second, the internal debate about the very nature of the "empire" remains alive and well. Was the Ottoman Empire really an empire? And if so, when? Did it have universal aspirations to European or world domination? Compared with the other empires of the premodern era, the Ottomans remained small (maybe 40 million subjects) at its largest, certainly more like the latter-day Austro-Hungarian Empire than the Romanovs of Russia. That it encompassed a diverse population is evidenced by the twenty-seven successor states that have emerged from the Ottoman territories since 1789.[1] More specifically, the history of premodern violence in the Middle East in general is still in its infancy, largely because of avoidance of such topics by a majority of Ottoman specialists and the utter obsession in both professional and public arenas with political debates about the Armenian massacres, Palestine, and modern so-called Islamic terrorism.

The post-imperial animus to the Ottomans varies from country to country, but in general, the ambivalence regarding the Ottoman past has given rise to a series of what we might call jangled and often hysterical national historiographies, often focused on a semimythical narration of the abuse and destruction of local population(s) through warfare and conquest. The "Ottoman yoke," as it is often called in Balkan historiography, remains a black hole of shame and oppression in most post-1918 regional historiographies. Hence, there has been a cultural resistance to acknowledging the impact (other than in negative terms) of Ottoman rule on large parts of the premodern Middle East. The most egregious example of this is the Serbian nationalist evocation of the 1389 Ottoman-Serbian battle of Kosovo, which Slobodan Milosevic used as a call to arms in 1989. Similarly, until very recently, Turkish Republican historians have eschewed the study of violence and the Ottoman past, not least because of the international pressure to accept the Armenian genocide. This pressure is and has been fiercely resisted by the present-day Turkish government, and it remains intellectual suicide for scholars to address the issue in Turkey itself. In other words, national stories (and current events) have inhibited the robust critique and reconstruction of the premodern Ottoman military past.

The question of whether or not the Ottomans were a "colonial" power is a related subject that has gained some traction only in the last two decades or so, but the discussion usually addresses a very late moment in the empire when efforts to retain (or regain) Albania and Yemen were made during the so-called First Constitutional period in the late nineteenth century, and hence is beyond the scope of this chapter.[2] In fact, many scholars who work on the Ottoman Arab pre-1918 provinces, especially those interested in the Bedouin tribes of eastern Turkey, Iraq, Syria, Jordan, and northern Saudi Arabia, are beginning to argue that the southern tier of the empire became a site of an Ottoman colonial project starting in the 1850s.[3] I have argued elsewhere that when manpower demands forced the recognition of ethnic differences, the colonial project and military conscription went hand in hand from 1830s forward. The attempt to incorporate (and civilize) the border-lands (or nomadic peoples) is most evident, however, in the reign of Sultan Abdülhamit II (1876–1909), when the matter of survival and definitions of *citizenship* in the remaining Ottoman territories had become the dynasty's overriding concern.[4]

The focus on the Ottoman administration of the late frontier/border ter-ritories has also produced new work on earlier centuries concerning tribes (native, or national identities). The most recent example of this broadly inter-disciplinary work is a new volume published in the proceedings of the British Royal Academy, the result of an international conference on frontiers.[5] This volume will set the parameters for further study, as it includes contributions concerning all aspects of "middle ground" Ottoman life: geography and map-ping, administration, peoples and opportunities, and investments in and maintenance of material culture, especially of garrisons and fortresses. Sur-prisingly, the volume (and the literature at large) lacks the kind of remark-able studies concerning the astonishing range of ethnicities and religions of the Russian Eurasian frontier, or the settlement of frontier warriors as border defensive systems in Habsburg territories. The closest are Rossitsa Gradeva's essay on Vidin, the Ottoman-European border fortress after 1699, in the *Fron-tiers* volume, and other work elsewhere on the Hungarian marches. But a new edited collection on Ottoman ransom slavery promises to help fill the gap.[6]

It is remarkable, too, that we have so few closely detailed monographs on the nature and strategic objectives of the Ottoman military system in gen-eral, given that the empire is invariably described as a society constructed exclusively around warfare.[7] Most modern military historians acknowledge that the organization and administration of warfare (manpower and logis-tics) were the primary occupation of all early modern imperial entities, an essential aspect of coercive strategies of imperial ambitions, and that violence was a matter of everyday life. The long contest between the Ottomans and Europe, however, has given the Turks the special status of most warlike, and their society is seen as occupying the top rung (or bottom rung, depending on one's point of view) of (warrior) civilizations along with the Mongols. Even early Turkish republican histories of the "Turk" embraced the European labels and constructed the ten great Turkic civilizations, starting with the Hittites and culminating with the Republic, to bolster the new definition of Turkishness in the young nation-state. Younger generations of scholars, however, are nibbling around the edges of a somewhat ossified view of the national histories of the region.

For decades, Hungarian scholars have led the way in analyzing the rich archives of the Habsburgs concerning their own period of contact with the Ottomans from the 1540s to 1699, but Hungary is a special case, as it probably was the only territory the Ottomans systematically constructed as a garrison state and as a territory removed early from Ottoman dominion through the imperial contest and treaties with Austria. Recently, thanks largely to the efforts of Edward Erickson, the Ottoman experience in World War I has become a publishing industry in English. Apart from the remarkable number of World War I memoirs and studies of warfare, a whole new generation of young Turkish scholars also are concentrating on the transformative period of the empire under Selim III (1789–1807) and Mahmud II (1808–1839).[8] We soon should see a deeper analysis and new interpretations of the Ottoman military system from the 1700s to the 1860s.

The Ottoman Extension of Power into the Balkans and the Arab World

Historians have long studied Ottoman attitudes toward new subjects brought under their aegis by conquest and negotiation, but largely from the point of view of religious identities and then as the national groups they became in the contest over the late Ottoman territories, as suggested earlier. A hypothesis posed by Metin Kunt decades ago has not been adapted to the military context. He argued that ethnicity was crucial to cohesion in the Ottoman context and was particularly relevant as a regional identity. In military lore, Bosnians and Albanians, he contended, became the "Westerners," whereas Circassians and Kurds were the "Easterners" of warrior rivalries. All were prized for their martial abilities and loyalty to the sultan. Other scholars have described the rivalries as one of the Rumeli (European territories of the Ottomans) versus the Rum, or Anatolian (Asian), troops.[9] For students of the

Ottoman military organization, however, the problem is that in official documents, ethnic characteristics are generalized and undifferentiated, although the importance of such a label to the individual member of such a group is obvious.

The debates for earlier centuries generally revolve around two questions that do arise from the evidence: What was the status of Christians and Jews as non-Muslims in the imperial hierarchy, and how did that change over time? The fault line of the debate, as we might imagine, is tolerance versus intolerance of the central ruling elite, as determined by taxation differentials, categories of dress, prohibition of rituals, and the like. Non-Muslims always paid an extra head (or poll) tax and, in theory, were not obliged to serve in (were excluded from) the army. The historiographical fault line after 1800 concerns which groups benefited from the Ottoman constitutional (and Westernization) movement and how that led to a bifurcated Muslim/non-Muslim society. Studies of Ottoman attitudes toward Muslim "minorities," or "natives," such as the Kurds, Circassians, or Albanians, are much more recent and much more closely related to the manpower needs of the transformed modern military.[10]

To press more deeply into the Ottoman use of conquered peoples, particularly their use of them centered on their "ethnicity" or indigeneity, we must first examine three key characteristics of the Ottoman imperial system in the era of expansion and construction: the origins and nature of the dynasty itself, the legal systems as imposed in newly conquered territories, and the use of slaves in the military.

The official Ottoman story dates to 1300, but its beginnings were not recorded until a century later, when official chroniclers traced the dynasty's origins to a Turkish tribe of Central Asia, the Oghuz. This tribe reputedly converted to Islam as it crossed the Oxus River into Anatolia, part of a great human flow from Eurasia into the Middle East between 1000 and 1300 CE. Hence, the original "aristocracy" was Turkic, and the house of Ertuğrul (Osman's father) adopted Islam as its official ideology.[11] These Turkish warriors were superb horsemen and expert bowmen, and they gained prominence as mercenaries for hire by the rival Seljuks and Byzantines, the latter confined largely to the territories around Constantinople and Thrace by 1300. The Turks encountered "native" peoples—Greeks, Armenians, Kurds, and other Turcoman tribes (it should be stressed that all these names are generic)—as they expanded their early power base in Anatolia. In the Balkans, they eventually subdued other "natives": Albanians, Bulgars, Bosnians, Serbians, Croats, and Thracian Greeks, to name just a few.

"Ottoman," the dynasty and the language, are constructions. Osman and his successors acknowledged their lineage as Turkic but projected a Muslim cosmopolitanism based on the trilingual foundation of the Islamic educational system: Arabic, Persian, and Turkish, and training in all the disciplines of the Muslim civilized world. Until the mid-nineteenth century, to be a "Turk" was to be a country bumpkin. In 1500, Turkic dynasties stretched from eastern Europe to southwest Asia and included the Safavids and Mughals, to name the most prominent, but shortly after 1500, the Ottomans acquired sovereignty over the Egyptian world, the gateway to Mecca and Medina, which gave them a legitimate claim to the title of protector of the sacred cities and caliph of the Muslim world.

The Ottomans chose to constitute and rule newly conquered territories by invoking three legal sources: the *sharia*, or Islamic law, which was supplemented with sultanic prerogative (*kanun*), and, on occasion, with the existing laws of newly conquered lands. The first official appointed to new territories was the Islamic judge (*kadi*), assigned the responsibility of organizing the new district (*sancak*) for his masters in Constantinople. When the *sharia* failed to provide guidance, *kanun* was often employed, as in the rules and regulations concerning the organization of imperial armies. New territorial acquisitions were often constituted as well by determining local practices (*örf*, or customary law), most often relating to taxation. By this means, the early sultans proved simultaneously adaptive and innovative, learning from their predecessors and often relieving overtaxed populations of excessive burdens, such as the *corvée*, or forced labor, of previous rulers. This tripartite legal system, a synthesis of Muslim and Christian influences, is most evident in the Balkans and Anatolia proper and is counted as a significant contributor to the longevity of the Ottoman Empire.

If we are to believe the later theorizing around the so-called circle of justice evoked by philosophers and historians alike, the Ottomans understood society to be divided into various classes in harmonious balance, with individuals relegated to their class of birth. Ottoman Muslim ruling elites were classified as the military class (*askeri*), as opposed to the ruled, or peasant, class (*reaya*, the flock).[12] The *askeri* were not taxed, but the *reaya,* producers of the empire's (agricultural) wealth, were. The division was further legitimated by the Muslim principle of tolerance of subject non-Muslims, recognizing fellow believers of other sacred texts. (It is worth remembering that Christians outnumbered Muslims in large parts of the Ottoman Balkans well into the seventeenth century.) Formal recognition was thus extended to the monotheistic "people of the book." Non-Muslims were under the jurisdiction of the sultan and Islamic law when dealing with Muslims, and were governed by the chief religious figures of their own religion for religious practices and familial law. For most of the history of the empire, the *millets*, as the religious confessional groups were called, numbered three in Ottoman documents: Jews, Orthodox Greeks, and Armenians. The Greek Orthodox patriarch of Istanbul made the first such pact with Mehmed II shortly after 1453. Such arrangements, largely ad hoc, were later extended to the Catholic (in the mid-eighteenth-century) and Protestant (mid-nineteenth-century) communities of the empire.

Although some historians argue for a long history of racialized Ottoman attitudes toward the Christian *reayas*, it was not until Ottoman bureaucrats turned to constitutionalism in the nineteenth century that they learned the new ethnoreligious categories of emerging nationalism(s).[13] Mahmud II (1808–1839), for example, always referred to his subjects as his *reaya*, even when they rebelled, not as "Serbians" or "Greeks," as the great powers preferred. His successors, however, *did* move to an ethnic understanding of their "citizens." From there, it was but a short step to ethnographic categorization of *aşiret*, for example, the ubiquitous and generic word for *tribe* until the mid-nineteenth century when Ottoman reforms and the arm of centralization reached into Arab Bedouin communities in Syria and Iraq, or Kurdish communities in eastern Anatolia and Iraq, some of whom developed a sense of ethnohistorical identity for the first time.[14] The grand paradox of the Ottoman nineteenth century is that all central attempts to implement egalitarianism actually created more fissures in the relations between the Muslim and non-Muslim communities.

In some ways the turbulent cosmopolitanism of Constantinople itself provided a means for overcoming nominal ethnic and religious divides. After the Ottoman conquest in 1453, Constantinople came to resemble a "renegade city" where any enterprising young individual, as long as he professed Islam, could enter the entourage of the sultan. Stories abound of the early sultans spotting raw young talent while out hunting or on campaign, the "boon-companion" tradition of much of Muslim civilization. A recent article explores the origin myths, conversion to Islam, and service in the Mughal court of the Kyamkhani, a Muslim warrior community of northern India. This discussion of the evolution of religious identities resonates with our understanding of the early Ottoman warrior context in Anatolia. Converts were a ubiquitous part of the court, some coerced and others voluntary.[15]

What is most important here is that non-Muslims were not obliged to serve in the army (or, more accurately, were prohibited from such elite status). So who was fighting for the Ottomans? Answering that requires a further digression into Ottoman difference: the use of slaves. The earliest armies of the sultan were (free) Turkic tribal groups, horsemen, and volunteer warrior aristocrats of many of the indigenous groups who joined the young empire or were subdued by it. They were rewarded with noninheritable fiefs, or *timar*, as a means of support for military service and were generically called *sipahis* (also *timariots*). This body of warriors was the backbone of Ottoman provincial defense and the heart of their campaign armies in the early centuries. At its greatest extent, the sultan could count on some 80,000 such *sipahis*. The system worked as long as the agricultural revenues could support the *sipahi*, who was required to show up at imperial campaigns with his retinue, which was self-sufficient in weapons, food, and fodder. Indeed, one explanation for an instance of provincial chaos in the seventeenth century, the so-called Celali rebellions, was the too-rapid demobilization following decades of campaigning, marked by an inability to feed the returning soldiers. Campaign records after 1700 indicate alarming rates of desertion, with thousands of names being removed from the *timariot* registers when they failed to report for duty. One reason for this has to do with the precipitous decline in agricultural revenue, which could no longer support the *timariot* system.

As early as the late fourteenth century, the sultans recognized the need for firepower and infantry. From this recognition emerged the most formidable armed force of the Ottomans, the Janissaries, or "new troops." Some historians argue that the Janissary corps was created as a counterweight to the "native" Turkish aristocracy, but more recent studies have argued that massed and disciplined firepower was the primary aim. Slave infantries such as the Janissaries suited a culture that prized horses and whose elite resisted dismounting and disdained firearms.[16]

Recruits for the new service were Christian boys, either war captives or conscripts, often part of the capitulatory agreements made with newly conquered (largely European) territories. Circumcised and raised as Muslims, they remained slaves of the sultan (*kul*),[17] even though graduation into the ranks of Janissaries after an extended apprenticeship was accompanied by emancipation. The periodic roundup (*devşirme*) of young boys and its presumed catastrophic effects on Balkan villages is a fundamental trope of all nationalist narratives of the Balkans. In its first two to three hundred years, some of these military slaves ended up running the empire as grand viziers and Janissary *aghas* and even occasionally endowed their (Christian) homelands with charitable institutions. Most such recruits secured an assignment in one of the ninety-six Janissary regiments. Note that we are not talking about depopulating depredations here, as the *devşirme* was not an annual event and did not involve huge numbers. For example, the Janissary army of Sultan Süleyman (1520–1566) numbered some 20,000 elite troops.

The roundups of young Christian boys had largely ceased by the mid-seventeenth century, once major conquests by the Ottomans ceased. Instead, sons of Janissaries and other Muslim notables, clamored for and received membership in the elite organization, which guaranteed extraordinary privileges. Everyone and anyone could be a Janissary as long as he claimed to be Muslim. Hence, it also became a shelter for renegades of all stripes. Indeed, contemporary observers linked the decline of the corps (and the empire) to the indiscriminate registration of all and sundry in the Janissary rolls. The corps functioned most efficiently in its heyday, between 1400 and 1700, when its size was restricted to some 30,000 at most, although the study of Janissaries stationed in provincial garrisons, as distinct from the sultan's corps in Istanbul, is in its infancy. As the force grew in size and was deployed across the empire in garrison cities and frontier forces, its military prowess declined and its members melted into the countryside economies, until it had become a huge financial burden to the sultan without much military effectiveness. Other forces emerged in the mid-seventeenth century to supplement or replace both *sipahis* and Janissaries, which I discuss later.

Eastern Europe (Poland and Ukraine mostly, but the principalities of Wallachia, Transylvania, and Moldavia on occasion, as well as other Habsburg territories) was subject to extensive predations in periodic slave raids by the Muslim Tatar khan of the Crimea and his famed horsemen. Having submitted to Ottoman clientage at the end of Mehmed II's reign, the khan served as an advance guard for Ottoman campaigns, simultaneously profiting from their human trafficking. The khan could command as many as 80,000 horsemen for campaigns and was essential to the Ottoman military until 1783, when Catherine II unilaterally annexed the Crimea and dispersed or co-opted Tatar military prowess.[18]

An interesting aspect of the Ottoman-Habsburg frontier was the thriving business of ransom slavery, especially in the quieter moments of the Ottoman-Austrian border, from 1606 to 1683, when raiding across borders was fairly continuous. This affected all classes of society, but the main (and profitable) target for both sides was the middle-level soldier, who could be sold as a galley slave or returned to his native land for a considerable sum. Such captives, like Osman of Témesvar, might spend years in an enemy's household, as one of the few Ottoman records of the system available to us revealed, before the details (and legalities) of captive exchanges were worked out.[19] Thus there was a continual stream of slaves to populate imperial and notable households across Ottoman territories. Such a system obviously led to the considerable intermingling of ethnicities.

This variety of institutional contexts for Ottoman slavery erased the boundary between slave and free. Enslaving fellow Muslims (and even fellow monotheists) was technically against the *shari'a*. But in this, as in other things, the Ottoman went their own way. As the introduction to the recent volume on ransom slavery notes,

> Slaves' lives were made more bearable by the peculiarities of Muslim social development. As different layers of society—especially the militarised governing apparatuses—absorbed slaves in huge numbers, the borderline between free men and slaves was gradually blurred, or, more precisely, lost its significance (to such an extent that, for example, in the Ottoman state even dignitaries who were legally slaves could hold slaves themselves).[20]

For the Janissaries, the experience of "slavery" was conditioned by their relationship with the sultan. Taken from their mothers generally from the ages of ten to eighteen, Ottoman iconography always described their relationship with the sultan as one of father and son, and early members of the corps could be relied on for unswerving loyalty to their master. It was a self-governing community, in both financial and legal terms. Like comparable premodern military organizations, each regiment saw to the welfare of its members, including maintaining a regimental treasury and seeing to the dispersal of an individual's inheritance in case of death. Janissary discipline was administered within the corps and hence was beyond the legal hand of the Ottoman court system. This "slave" army became the empire's moral compass, capable of seating and unseating sultans, and many of the rebellions attributed to them were based on real abuses: limiting their privileges, debasing their coinages, and, particularly, sending them on long and futile marches into eastern territories.[21]

In the case of other slaves, Islamic law teaches that emancipation is an exceptionally good deed, and many households were liberated upon their master's death. Children of concubines, as another example, were considered free. What we understand as the political household system of the ruling class was an extensive network of clients beholden to their leader through slave bonds as much as through blood. As Ehud Toledano explains,

The purchase of enslaved persons for various roles was one of the four most important channels of recruitment to imperial-center and Ottoman-local households. The other three modes of recruitment-cum-bonding to a household were biological-kin relationships, marriage, and the voluntary offer of loyalty and service in return for patronage. . . . Attachment to a household gave an individual protection, employment and social status. Not less significantly, it gave household members (*kapı halkı*) a sense of belonging and an identity, both social and political.[22]

Purchased slaves who achieved prominence as servants or retainers were often married to the daughters of the head of their households. In the royal house itself, the practice was called *damatlık* (status of bridegroom of the sultan), which was obligatory for the highest officials of the court by the eighteenth century.

The growth of elite provincial households, partly from this commerce in manpower, had important consequences for the Ottoman military. The devolution of revenue collection and responsibility for regional and border defense to the frontier provinces, which accelerated after 1650, led to local centers of power emerging around powerful families with extended networks in urban and rural areas alike. These local powers organized personal entourages/armies with the mixture of slave and free-born military systems just described. By the end of the eighteenth century, both the Janissary army (in garrisons outside Constantinople) and the *timariots* had been largely eclipsed by a parallel federative, contractual, highly mobile, and notably undisciplined military system, which became the main source of their military manpower.[23]

What the array of provincial forces looked like depended on the region. Egypt, for example, had three sources of military power by the mid-seventeenth century: the local Egyptian elite, with largely Caucasian Circassian slave households and legacies deriving from their Mamluk past; six Janissary regiments, assigned to Egypt under the centrally appointed Ottoman governor and originally consisting of *devşirme* recruits; and the Rum *uşağı*, the free-born, mobile "Turkic, or Anatolian" soldier for hire, who might just as often be Kurdish or Albanian. This gave rise in the eighteenth century to the well-known Qazdağlıs family, which amassed enough power to regularly challenge the court-appointed governor and his Janissaries.[24]

As another example, the system in Vidin, Bulgaria, situated on the Danube, the gateway to Europe, looked somewhat different. What had been a frontier march, with some five hundred *sipahis* in the sixteenth century, had become a large fortress town by 1750, with more than five thousand Janissaries garrisoned there once the territory stood on the Habsburg-Ottoman frontier. Evegenii Raduschev and Rossitsa Gradeva marshal substantial evidence to argue that Christian locals converted to Islam out of a desire to join the prestigious Janissaries. All the *reaya* along the Danube River were engaged in one way or another in paramilitary activities, and after 1700, many were in some way attached to a Janissary regiment.[25] This transition to a militarized society allowed for the rise of such warlords as Osman Pazvantoğlu of Vidin, who could command thousands of voluntary soldiers as needed and who fought off three successive armies sent against him by Selim III between 1790 and 1810. His ambitions and predations set off the Serbian revolt of 1804 in Belgrade, which was just one example in which a powerful local force, in his case known for his tolerance of both Christian and Muslim mercenary bands in his ranks, stimulated the emergence of an ethnic nationalism.

This trend in the eighteenth century has also been identified in Aleppo, Damascus, and Acre, among other places,[26] though Greece represents something of an exception. There the use of Christian paramilitary groups by the Ottomans continued longer than elsewhere, especially in the Peloponnese and on the Adriatic Sea, where Ottoman control was often quite tenuous and contested by the Venetians until the mid-eighteenth century. An entrenched Greek/Albanian culture of banditry, piracy, and resistance to local and imperial officials blurred the boundaries of legitimate and illegitimate legal forces, even though the general trend toward the formation of large households and of bonds of obligation and trust look very similar to that in other regions of the empire. The lack of systemic control over that region produced a particularly strong paramilitary culture in which "the development of strong patron-client relations seemed the only socio-political mechanism left for survival. Hence, despite their shortcomings as far as the maltreatment of the Greek peasants is concerned, men who bore arms in such difficult times were highly respected by the agrarian population."[27] Such groups became the "freedom fighters" of the Greek independence movement in 1821. Here as elsewhere, the Ottomans created, financed, and deployed new semiautonomous military groups to counteract resistant or nuisance warrior populations.[28]

The Ottomans' Use of Indigenous Forces over Time

Conquered subjects, or "indigenous" forces, always were essential to the Ottoman military machine, but there were multiple paths into that system, and those paths changed over time. Aside from their "own" *sipahis*, or the slave-subject Janissaries, whom the Ottomans remade into something also their "own," the Ottomans extensively used other mercenaries and auxiliaries from the very beginning of their expansion out of Anatolia. An interesting shift in the understanding of the characteristics and motivation of paramilitaries occurred around 1700, as the sultans came to rely on such forces for major campaigns.

The early conquests of the Balkans were enabled by the encounter with, submission of, and subsequent employment of these martial populations. The Ottomans themselves began as mercenaries for the beleaguered Byzantine emperor. Military historians point to the Ottomans' early use of some raiding groups such as the *martelos* or *akincis* (cavalry and raiders) in the Balkans. Many are considered to have been largely Christian groups, although the *akincis* in particular were Turkomen horsemen from Anatolian territories who moved with their families to the Balkans in the early centuries of the Ottoman expansion. The *derbend* service (guardians of the mountain passes) is another example of a privileged military status, largely derived from local notable warlords but often conferred on peoples in high mountains whose full conquest of and incorporation into *timar* estates proved not worth the effort. Even some of the first postconquest *timariots* were local notable Christians, rewarded for their service on behalf of the sultan, whose descendants usually converted to Islam.[29] The *serhad kulu* (frontier troops) were another category of local military manpower who could serve as frontier guards or permanent garrison troops, as well as campaign contingent auxiliaries. Again, depending on the territories, they could be Christian or Muslim. Determining which ethnicities filled these roles (or even whether they were necessarily Christian) has been difficult because of the records' lack of specificity.

The Tatars' military importance to the imperial army cannot be underestimated. Tatar is a generic name for several tribal lines of Turkic-Mongolian descent. They may have constituted the most visible of Ottoman ethnicities, though they too operated semi-independently in a capacity as a client, frontier territory. Because their Turco-Mongol and Muslim lineage gave them special status as possible successors to the Ottomans should the line die out, the Ottoman sultan formally recognized each new khan with elaborate ceremonials. The crescent-shaped Ottoman imperial army encampment recognized the importance of the horsemen by deploying the Tatars on one side and the *sipahis* on the other of the imperial (first the sultan's and later the grand vizier's) tent.

Auxiliaries other than these natural warriors also were coerced into Ottoman service. In addition to directly hiring locals into military service, the Ottomans also forced the local populations to serve in the garrisons, and not always as slave labor. Quite often it was to their benefit. Sometimes such services were contracted on a more or less permanent basis; sometimes the contract was contingent on a particular campaign, when sappers, road and bridge repair crews, and wagons and cattle drovers were much in need. The return for locals was in tax relief or, more infrequently, in wages or rents.

The Bosnians are a unique case, as it was one of the territories that completely converted to Islam, thereby achieving an unusual contractual status with the imperial center and preserving their much vaunted local military system by guaranteeing to supply the Ottoman army with one thousand to two thousand troops as needed on the large campaigns. The Bosnians remained loyal and were very important to eighteenth-century confrontations with the Habsburgs. Consequently, when pressed to conform to the new military regulations and uniforms of the modernized army after 1826, the Bosnians' rebellion was significant.[30]

Later conquests required other sorts of negotiations. Wallachia and Moldavia (present-day Romania), both Christian lands, negotiated a tributary status with the Ottomans, which until the early 1700s meant a semiautonomous status for territories vital to the Ottomans' military supply needs, especially grain. The *voyvoda*, or administrator, of each principality maintained a small army and occasionally supplied troops to the Ottomans. In return, the Ottomans installed a small garrison of Janissaries in each territory (some two hundred men) and otherwise prohibited Muslim settlement north of the Danube.

In the southern and eastern tier of the empire, where the Ottomans confronted Muslim rivals, we find a different set of agreements upon their conquest. The Ottomans' enemies were fellow Muslims, but Shiite under the Safavids. Kurdish and Bedouin (mostly Arab, both Christian and Muslim) tribesmen were given a great degree of autonomy to run their own tribes, headed by sheikhs, as long as they contributed to the Ottoman purse or performed essential services. They also were called on to defend against the *kızılbaş* (red heads, or red hats), the Ottomans' generic name for Shiite rebels. Such contractual arrangements were ad hoc, involving a submission ceremony and a commitment of mercenaries (usually tribal confederations) to protect, for example, the pilgrimage route through Damascus. A major campaign was undertaken when the territories became too unruly, such as that of Murad IV in 1640, when the center reacquired Baghdad and established what has continued more or less as the frontier with Iran.

The Kurds and Arabs contributed to imperial campaigns in the Balkans in a number of ways. Their commitment to the call to arms meant that provincial governors (or tribal equivalents) arrived at headquarters on the

Danube with a contingent of their warriors. Some of these regiments began to be called *yerli kulu,* or local troops, used to protect governors and other officials of the provinces. These local troops became more common in the seventeenth and eighteenth centuries as central control over garrison Janissaries and *sipahis* slipped away and they were replaced by locally raised and financed troops under the aegis of ambitious warlords.[31]

The evolution from *timariot* to "private" or "contracted" regional armies was partly enabled by the Ottomans' fairly constant use of local irregular bands, militias labeled *levend* (one of many terms in the documentation), as early as the sixteenth century.[32] *Levend,* a term that originally denoted armed, vagrant, and landless peasants, evolved into its military usage as "independent soldiery companies."[33] Deriving at least partially from demobilized *sipahis,* the *levend* turned to marauding and were the cause of rebellions across the empire for a hundred years. This cycle of rebellion (*fitne*) and calm is found throughout the chronicles, which describe *fitne* as the most heinous crime of the countryside. The Ottomans mastered the art of eliminating those militias that had turned to banditry by arming the countryside for its own protection and then enlisting these bands for the next campaign, a process that has been characterized as the Ottomans' effectiveness in "embodying within itself the potential forces of contention."[34]

Such groups of roving mercenaries began to join local powerful households that could pay and feed them more regularly, especially during peacetime. They acquired the name of household *levend* or state *levend,* the distinction being whether they were part of the provincial governors' forces (*kapılı* or *kapı halkı*) or were paid from provincial revenues or directly by the state (*miri levend*).[35]

By the late seventeenth century, a provincial governor was expected to arrive for a campaign with two hundred of his private entourage and one thousand to two thousand *levend* recruits, both infantry and cavalry. By the 1720s, the latter were paid either through tax privileges (and cash) for the provincial official or directly out of the sultan's purse. In other words, the local official had become a military contractor. According to the statistics, this system grew a hundredfold from the siege of Vienna in 1683 to the first Russo-Ottoman campaign of the 1768–1774 war.[36] The reliability and loyalty of such troops was an acute problem, especially as determined by the state's financial stability and whether it was able (or willing) to redistribute provincial revenues for the benefit of local officials.

It is easy to see how such bands might acquire semi-independent status and organize regionally as ethnic bands. Most historians agree that the phenomenon reached its peak in the eighteenth century. Around the turn of the nineteenth century, the term *levend* disappeared from usage and was replaced with other words such as *başıbozuks* (broken heads, without a master) and *delis* (crazy). Often, those who acquired special names like *delis* were identified as Albanians, Kurds, or Circassians.

The Albanians, for example, are ubiquitous in the annals of the dynasty. Reşat Kasaba raises the chicken-and-egg question about the Ottomans' settlement policies by suggesting that in some cases,

> the Ottomans did not even have to channel or harness the movements of local tribes but simply followed them. This was the case with the 10,000 nomads [Turkomans] who spontaneously moved from northwestern Anatolia and settled in the Balkans, where they linked up with the semi-nomadic communities of the Vlachs and Albanians in the fourteenth century.[37]

Skanderbeg, Albania's national hero, began his career as an Ottoman general. He rebelled, however, and his long resistance only ended after his death in 1468, when the Ottomans incorporated large parts of Albania into their central imperial territories, and much of the population progressively converted to Islam. Albanians can be found in the Janissaries, as *sipahis* and as chief officers of the empire, and the greatest of the grand vizierial families, the Köprülüs, were of Albanian stock.

Albanian (*Arnavut*) became a label of opprobrium only because of these people's wild, unruly ways in eighteenth-century Ottoman armies, especially after 1770, when bands of *levends* headed for the Danubian campaigns against the Russians were diverted to put down a (Greek) rebellion in the Peloponnese.[38] In mercenary bands, Albanians tended to demand payment up front and, like many of their ilk, were the first to vanish when the fighting began. They naturally cohered around their regional brethren and traveled from one end of the empire to the other. Their troop or company commanders were local, and their loyalties easily shifted to the highest bidder, but they often were known in Constantinople for their ability to raise troops and get them where they were needed. One of the empire's greatest difficulties during the era of reform after 1800 was addressing the culture of such proud and voluntary warriors, who in many instances became the symbol of resistance to Ottoman tyranny, the *hayduts* (bandits or freedom fighters, depending on one's point of view) found in all Balkan languages and literatures.[39]

Up into the nineteenth century, the Ottomans essentially exercised only loose control over the southern and eastern tiers of their empire. Although they managed and played off provincial household rivalries, this system began to spin out of control after 1700, and from 1831 to 1840, the Arab army of Egypt's Mehmed Ali threatened the empire's very heartland. As a result, facing an acute shortage of manpower and dealing with a potent "internal" threat, the Ottoman commanders saw the necessity of subduing various formerly semiautonomous warrior populations.[40] Indeed, it is possible to talk about a "conquest" or incorporation of mountainous Albania and hitherto remote and largely autonomous Kurdish territories during this period. Huge rebellions required a significant effort by the newly formed Ottoman regimental army, which "conscripted" Kurds by dragging them to the battlefront in chains. In this new regimental army, especially after about 1826, ethnicities were incorporated into a more or less uniform army that deliberately effaced ethnicity, even though more than half the armies fighting for Mahmud II were made up of irregular bands.[41]

In conclusion, the Ottoman Empire might be better described until the 1830s as a contractual, negotiated state. Far from holding the Weberian "monopoly of armed force," the sultan relied on the military qualities and services of peoples only partially or barely subservient to the state. Although coercive in its initial conquest, demanding submission, the empire proved to be highly adaptable to local situations and attempted no real integration except as related to *sharia* law and taxes. The Janissary system was arguably a coercive strategy aimed at creating a force totally dedicated to the security and perpetuation of the Ottoman house. Nevertheless, other tributary, clientage, or patronage relationships were essential to the initial conquests of Ottoman territories. Unlike the later European Atlantic empires, however, such relationships were not necessarily thought of or organized around "ethnicities." Incorporating regional (some ethnically based) systems of defense and awarding tax breaks initially was attractive to frontier populations, but religious affiliation turned out to have a more prominent role than did ethnicity in the extension and projection of Ottoman power. Mobility and nomadism also were important to the initial stages of such gathering in, and the Ottomans' recognition of the status of "nomad" may well have contributed to its perpetuation within the Ottomans' territories.

The redistribution and devolution of agrarian revenues to the provinces in the seventeenth and eighteenth centuries unintentionally diminished the Ottomans' capacity to organize warfare and contributed to the eclipse of the *sipahi* system. Simultaneously, the loss of control over the size and discipline of the Janissary forces required new methods of raising manpower, which in turn led gradually to the increased use of ethnically based autonomous bands. That they came to be such a large part of actual campaign forces testifies both to the Ottomans' inability to settle large parts of the population of seminomadic, tribal forces in the seventeenth century and to its loss of central control over mobile warriors as its imperial borders shrank after 1700.[42] Ironically, the consequences of the shift to a contractual military system facilitated the final elimination of the Janissary corps in the second decade of the nineteenth century.

Accordingly, we could argue that after 1750, the Ottomans' military weakness was largely administrative and not technological, as is commonly thought. In other words, just as Europe moved to social discipline and uniformity in its military forces, incorporating "native" troops, the Ottomans came to rely on a federative, paramilitary force to maintain its territories on the Danube and in greater Syria. Those forces and their powerful leaders posed one of the single greatest threats to the Ottomans' central power confronting Mahmud II after 1807, especially when they came to be seen as the liberators of their ethnic brothers and sisters.

NOTES

1. Şükrü Hanioğlu, *A Brief History of the Late Ottoman Empire* (Princeton, NJ: Princeton University Press, 2009), 210.

2. Thomas Kühn, ed., "Borderlands of the Ottoman Empire in the 19th and Early 20th Century," *MIT Electronic Journal of Middle Eastern Studies* 3 (2003) [special issue], available at http://web.mit.edu/cis/www/mitejmes, with articles by Thomas Kühn, Isa Blumi, Ryan Gingeras, and Charles Herzog. (This journal has been discontinued.)

3. Eugene Rogan, *Frontiers of the State in the Late Ottoman Empire* (Cambridge: Cambridge University Press, 1999); Ussama Makdisi, "Ottoman Orientalism," *American Historical Review* 102, no. 3 (1997): 786–96; Reşat Kasaba, *A Moveable Empire: Ottoman Nomads, Migrants & Refugees* (Seattle: University of Washington Press, 2009).

4. Virginia Aksan, *Ottoman Wars, 1700–1870: An Empire Besieged* (Harlow: Pearson Longman, 2007); Engin Akarli, "The Tangled Ends of Empire: Ottoman Encounters with the West and Problems of Westernization: An Overview," *Comparative Studies of South Asia, Africa and the Middle East* 26, no. 3 (2006): 353–66.

5. A. C. S. Peacock, ed., *Frontiers of the Ottoman World* (London: British Royal Academy, 2009).

6. Rossitsa Gradeva, "Between Hinterland and Frontier: Ottoman Vidin, Fifteenth to Eighteenth Centuries," in *Frontiers of the Ottoman World*, ed. A. C. S. Peacock (London: British Royal Academy, 2009), 331–51; Géza David and Pal Fodor, eds., *Ransom Slavery along the Ottoman Borders: Early Fifteenth through Early Eighteenth Century* (Leiden: Brill, 2007). Géza Dávid and Pál Fodor have also edited two volumes on Hungarian-Ottoman military affairs: *Hungarian-Ottoman Military and Diplomatic Relations in the Age of Süleyman the Magnificent* (Budapest: Loránd Eötvös, 1994); and *Ottomans, Hungarians and Habsburgs in Central Europe: The Military Confines in the Era of Ottoman Conquest* (Leiden: Brill, 2000). See also Rossitsa Gradeva, *War and Peace in Rumeli: 15th to Beginning of 19th Century*

(Istanbul: Isis Press, 2008); Kemal Karpat and Robert Zens, eds., *Ottoman Borderlands: Issues, Personalities and Political Changes* (Madison: University of Wisconsin Press, 2003); Caroline Finkel and Victor Ostapchuk, "Outpost of Empire: An Appraisal of Ottoman Building Registers and Sources for the Archeology and Construction History of the Black Sea Fortress of Özü," *Muqarnas* 22 (2005): 150–88; Frederick F. Anscombe put together a collection of essays, *The Ottoman Balkans, 1750–1830* (Princeton, NJ: Markus Weiner, 2006), which includes his own "Albanians and Mountain Bandits," 87–133, and Virginia H. Aksan, "Whose Territory and Whose Peasants? Ottoman Boundaries on the Danube in the 1760s," 61–86; Michael Khodarkovsky, *Russia's Steppe Frontier: The Making of a Colonial Empire, 1500–1800* (Bloomington: Indiana University Press, 2004); Willard Sunderland, *Taming the Wild Field: Colonization and Empire on the Russian Steppe* (Ithaca, NY: Cornell University Press, 2004); Carol B. Stevens, *Russia's Wars of Emergence 1460–1730* (Harlow: Pearson Longman, 2007); Michael Hochedlinger, *Austria's Wars of Emergence: War, State and Society in the Habsburg Monarchy 1683–1797* (Harlow: Pearson Longman, 2003).

7. Gábor Ágoston, "Ottoman Warfare in Europe, 1453–1812," in *European Warfare*, ed. Jeremy Black (New York: St. Martin's Press, 1999), 118–44; Rhoads Murphey, *Ottoman Warfare 1500–1700* (London: UCL, 1999); Virginia H. Aksan, "Ottoman War and Warfare, 1453–1812," in *War in the Early Modern World, 1450–1812*, ed. Jeremy Black (London: UCL, 1999), 147–75; Caroline Finkel, *The Administration of Warfare: Ottoman Military Campaigns in Hungary 1593–1606* (Vienna: VWGÖ, 1988); Gábor Ágoston, *Guns for the Sultan: Military Power and the Weapons Industry in the Ottoman Empire* (Cambridge: Cambridge University Press, 2005).

8. Edward Erickson, *Ordered to Die: A History of the Ottoman Empire: Prelude to Collapse, 1839–1878* (Stuttgart: Steiner, 2001); also Edward Erickson, *Defeat in Detail: The Ottoman Army in the Balkans, 1912–1913* (Westport, CT: Praeger, 2003); and Edward Erickson with Mesut Uyar, *A Military History of the Ottomans, from Osman to Ataturk* (Westport, CT: Praeger, 2009); Mustafa Aksakal, *The Ottoman Road to War in 1914: The Ottoman Empire and the First World War* (Cambridge: Cambridge University Press, 2008).

9. Metin Kunt, "Ethnic-Regional (*Cins*) Solidarity in the Seventeenth-Century Ottoman Establishment," *International Journal of Middle East Studies* 5 (1974): 233–39; Gabriel Piterberg, *An Ottoman Tragedy: History and Historiography at Play* (Berkeley: University of California Press, 2003); Jane Hathaway, *A Tale of Two Factions: Myth, Memory and Identity in Ottoman Egypt and Yemen* (Albany: State University of New York Press, 2003).

10. Robert W. Olson, *The Emergence of Kurdish Nationalism and the Sheikh Said Rebellion, 1880–1925* (Austin: University of Texas Press, 1989); Isa Blumi, 'The Commodification of Otherness and the Ethnic Unit in the Balkans: How to Think about Albanians," *East European Politics & Societies* 12: (1998): 527–69; Michael A. Reynolds, "The Ottoman-Russian Struggle for Eastern Anatolia and the Caucasus, 1908–1918: Identity, Ideology and the Geopolitics of World Order" (PhD diss., Princeton University, 2003).

11. Cemal Kafadar's *Between Two Worlds: The Construction of the Ottoman State* (Berkeley: University of California Press, 1995), remains the best review of the literature and the *ghazi* thesis.

12. Reşat Kasaba argues for the role of movement and mobility as central to the explanation for many Ottoman state policies over time. He reminds us that beyond religious identities, subjects were categorized as peasants, townsmen, or nomads (*A Moveable Empire*, 28). He goes on to say that Kurds and gypsies, both mobile communities, were

generally identified by ethnicity and not religion, even when those labels included both Muslim and Christian groups (29).

13. Bruce Masters, for example, holds that Ottoman discrimination against *millet* populations was no different in the sixteenth or the nineteenth century, whereas Ussama Makdisi sees the development of (Christian) sectarianism as a direct result of the Ottoman rescript (Hatt-i Humayun) of 1856, which recognized the freedom of religion. Others who examined *shari'a kadi* court records, which touched the lives of all subjects, Muslim or non-Muslim, see a preference among Christian women for divorce and inheritance adjudication in Muslim courts, and still others read racial and ethnic degradation (Dhimmitude) in the epistemology of court language referring to non-Muslim plaintiffs and defendants. See Bruce Masters, *Christians and Jews in the Ottoman Arab World: The Roots of Sectarianism* (Cambridge: Cambridge University Press, 2001); Ussama Makdisi, *The Culture of Sectarianism: Community, History and Violence in Nineteenth Century Ottoman Lebanon* (Berkeley: University of California Press, 2000); Iris Agmon, *Family and Court: Legal Culture and Modernity in Late Ottoman Palestine* (Syracuse, NY: Syracuse University Press, 2005); Bat Ye'or, *Islam and Dhimmitude: Where Civilizations Collide* (Madison, NJ: Fairleigh Dickinson University Press, 2002); Avigdor Levy, ed., *The Jews of the Ottoman Empire* (Princeton, NJ: Darwin Press, 1984).

14. Reuven Aharoni argues that Mehmed Ali used Bedouin regiments with Başıbozuks as their commanders, in his *The Pasha's Bedouin: Tribes and State in the Egypt of Mehemet Ali, 1805–1848* (London: Routledge, 2007), 5, 27, 163.

15. Cynthia Talbot, "Turning Turk the Rajput Way: Conversion and Identity in an Indian Warrior Narrative," *Modern Asian Studies* 49, no. 1 (2009): 211–43.

16. For the latest on Janissaries and firearms, see Günhan Börekçi, "A Contribution to the Military Revolution Debate: The Janissaries and the Use of Volley Fire during the Long Ottoman-Habsburg War of 1593–1606 and the Problem of Origins," *Acta Orientalia Academiae Scientiarum Hungaricae* 59, no. 4 (2006): 407–38.

17. In fact, all members of the sultan's entourage were technically called *kul*, as was the case of the Russian court of Catherine the Great.

18. The Ottoman court prized slavic beauties for the harem, making the sultan himself no more pure-bred Turkish than his ethnic subjects.

19. Osman Ağa and Richard Franz Kreutel, *Die Autobiographie des Dolmetschers 'Osmān Ağa aus Temeschwar* (London: E. J. W. Gibb Memorial Trust, 1980); Osman Ağa and Frédéric Hitzel, *Prisonnier des infidèles: Un soldat ottoman dans l'empire des Habsbourg* (Paris: Sindbad, 1998).

20. David and Fodor, *Ransom Slavery*, x–xi.

21. Virginia Aksan, "War and Peace," in *The Cambridge History of Turkey*, vol. 3, *The Later Ottoman Empire 1603–1839*, ed. Suraiya Faroqhi (Cambridge: Cambridge University Press, 2006), 81–117.

22. Ehud Toledano, *As If Silent and Absent: Bonds of Enslavement in the Islamic Middle East* (New Haven, CT: Yale University Press, 2007), 29.

23. Virginia H. Aksan, "Whatever Happened to the Janissaries? Mobilization for the 1768–1774 Russo-Ottoman War," *War in History* 5, no. 1 (1998): 23–36.

24. See Hathaway, *A Tale of Two Factions*; and Gabriel Piterberg, "The Formation of an Ottoman Elite in Egypt in the 18th Century," *International Journal of Middle East Studies* 22, no. 3 (1990): 275–89.

25. Evegenii Raduschev, "'Peasant' Janissaries?" *Journal of Social History* 42, no. 2 (2008): 447–70; Gradeva, "Between Hinterland and Frontier," 341–42.

26. Charles Wilkins, *Forging Urban Solidarities: Ottoman Aleppo 1640–1700* (Leiden: Brill, 2010); James Grehan, *Everyday Life and Consumer Culture in Eighteenth Century Damascus* (Seattle: University of Washington Press, 2007); Thomas Phillip, *Acre: The Rise and Fall of a Palestinian City 1730–1831* (New York: Columbia University Press, 2001).

27. Gerassimos Karabelias, "From National Heroes to National Villains: Bandits, Pirates and the Formation of Modern Greece," in *Subalterns and Social Protest: History from Below in the Middle East and North Africa,* ed. Stephanie Cronin (London: SOAS/ Routledge, 2008), 266.

28. A scholar of post-Ottoman Greece described a similar problem for the Greek state after 1821. The newly independent government struggled to

> impose a monopoly of the means of coercion led to what can be characterized as a case of "inverse racketeering": a situation in which the state becomes the client and not the supplier of protection against internal and external adversaries. On the one hand, the "racketeers" (i.e., bandits-irregulars) provided the state, via a patron client relationship, with protection against themselves and other bandits/irregulars. In other words, bandits-irregulars directly and indirectly stimulated an internal threat.

See Achilles Batalas, "Send a Thief to Catch a Thief: State-Building and the Employment of Irregular Military Formations in Mid-Nineteenth-Century Greece," in *Irregular Armed Forces and Their Role in Politics and State Formation*, ed. Diane E. Davis and Anthony Pereira (New York: Cambridge University Press, 2003), 150.

29. Halil Inalcik, "Ottoman Methods of Conquest," *Studia Islamica* 2 (1954): 103–29.

30. Michael Hickok, *Ottoman Military Administration in Eighteenth Century Bosnia* (Leiden: Brill, 1997); Odile Moreau, "Bosnian Resistance against Conscription in the Nineteenth Century," in *Arming the State: Military Conscription in the Middle East and Central Asia, 1775–1925,* ed. Erik Jan Zürcher (London: I. B. Tauris, 1999), 129–37.

31. The Ottoman term for these provincial figures is *ayan,* which is most often translated as "notable," "grandee," or "warlord." The literature describing the phenomenon has grown immensely in the last decade. See Antonis Anastasopoulos, ed., *Provincial Elites in the Ottoman Empire* (Rethymno: University of Crete Press, 2005); Anastasopoulos and Elias Kolovos, eds., *Ottoman Rule and the Balkans, 1760–1850: Conflict, Transformation, Adaptation* (Rethymno: University of Crete Press, 2007). *The Cambridge History of Turkey,* vol. 3, devotes several chapters to households: see Fikret Adanir, "Semi-autonomous Provincial Forces in the Balkans and Anatolia," 157–85; and Bruce Masters, "Semi-autonomous Provincial Forces in the Arab Provinces," 186–206. Masters concludes that paradoxically, the rise of local elites and the devolution of economic resources (in the eighteenth century) made for widening the identity of the Arab *ayans* "to include the possibility of being Ottoman for the first time" (206). In this volume, also see Carter Findley, "Political Culture and the Great Households," 65–80.

32. Halil İnalcık, "Military and Fiscal Transformation in the Ottoman Empire 1600–1700," *Archivum iOttomanicum* 6 (1980): 292; Mustafa Cezar, *Osmanlı Tarihinde Levendler* (Istanbul: Güzel Sanatlar Akademisi, 1965), 351–56.

33. İnalcik, "Military and Fiscal Transformation," 295.

34. Karen Barkey, *Bandits and Bureaucrats: The Ottoman Route to State Centralization* (Ithaca, NY: Cornell University Press, 1994), 241.

35. Cezar, *Osmanlı Tarihinde Levendler*, 214–16.

36. Aksan, "Whatever Happened to the Janissaries?" and Virginia H. Aksan, "Ottoman Military Recruitment Strategies in the Late Eighteenth Century," in *Arming the State: Military Conscription in the Middle East and Central Asia, 1775–1925,* ed. Erik Jan Zürcher (London: I. B. Tauris, 1999), 21–39.

37. Kasaba, *A Moveable Empire,* 34.

38. Kasaba notes that more than a hundred years after trying to settle mobile populations, the Ottomans were still negotiating with the "mountain rebellions (*dağlı isyanları*) organized by fugitive soldiers in the Balkans" (*A Moveable Empire,* 80).

39. For a discussion of the problem in a comparative imperial context, see Aksan, *Ottoman Wars,* 58.

40. Mehmed Ali himself represents the very conundrum of ethnicity, as Khaled Fahmy's recent biography demonstrates. He is known to Turks as Kavaklı Mehmed Ali from his birthplace in present-day Greece. Fahmy does not answer the question of ethnicity but says that some believe that Mehmed Ali was Kurdish, others, Albanian. The important thing is that he made his way to Egypt as part of a contingent of three hundred irregular troops, themselves Albanians, at the order of the sultan, following the invasion of Alexandria by Napoleon in 1799. See Khaled Fahmy, *Mehmed Ali: From Ottoman Governor to Ruler of Egypt* (Oxford: Oneworld, 2009), 9.

41. See particularly Virginia H. Aksan, "Ottoman Military and Social Transformations, 1826–28: Engagement and Resistance in a Moment of Global Imperialism," in *Empires and Autonomy: Moments in the History of Globalization*, ed. Stephen M. Streeter, John C. Weaver, and William D. Coleman (Vancouver: University of British Columbia Press, 2009), 61–78.

42. Kasaba, *A Moveable Empire*, 86.

Variations

Types of Indigenous-Imperial

Alliances in the Atlantic Empires

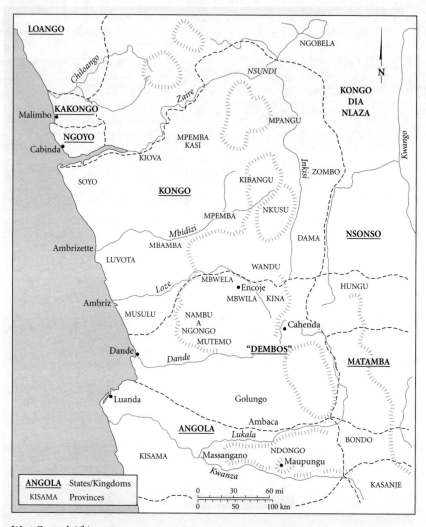

West Central Africa, 1650.

Firearms, Diplomacy, and Conquest in Angola

Cooperation and Alliance in West Central Africa, 1491–1671

JOHN K. THORNTON

The Spanish conquests in the New World in the sixteenth century often set the model for our assumptions about the interaction of Europeans with those they met during the period of expansion. Europeans, generally considered to have great military superiority, attacked and destroyed vast empires with teeming populations and powerful armies in a matter of weeks with only a few hundred brave and beleaguered soldiers. As Jared Diamond saw it in his prize-winning and much admired book, their success was based largely on the workings of geographical alignments and chance developments over the long past, which gave Europeans the guns, germs, and steel that allowed them to overwhelm Americans in short order.[1]

Historians have never been particularly happy with this triumphalist model, and recent historiography has turned strongly against it, most notably with regard to the role of indigenous allies that helped the Spanish achieve their conquests and, at times, might even have guided it.[2] Under newer visions of conquest in the New World, the arrival of the Spanish was more like a tipping point in an old deadlocked military struggle in which they, with their allies, were able to achieve victory. That tipping point was the product, however, of crucial military advantages that Spanish brought to America, first, their cavalry and, second, their armor and powerful missile weapons like crossbows and muskets.

The European encounter with Africa also is rarely considered in the discussion of the conquest period, mostly because they did very little conquering in that continent. Even though the slave trade required a military balance, historians recognize that the majority of the slaves were acquired by African armies, bandits, or judges and that even though imported European military technology may have played a role in the development of the trade, it was more or less a secondary one. The historical literature has said relatively little about conquest in Africa, mainly, of course, because before 1850, European conquests had reached only Angola and South Africa. This lack of conquest has often been attributed to a hostile disease environment. Indeed, Kwame Nkrumah's famous statue to the anopheles mosquito in Accra (Ghana), as a hero sparing the Gold Coast/Ghana from European settlement is a telling reminder of this theory.

Europeans did attempt conquests in Africa, of course, or at least tried to use military force to advance their interests. As early as 1488, for example, the Portuguese sought to provide military support to Bemoim (baptized as João Bemoim), a pretender to the throne of the Great Jolof, although it was thwarted when the captain of the expedition killed Bemoim in an argument while he was on the way to Senegal.[3] Portuguese mercenaries also interfered in the affairs of various African powers, often as individuals, such as the Portuguese who assisted the king of Benin in the early sixteenth century or those who could be found in the Sierra Leone region a bit later.[4]

Not unlike the many minor Spanish encroachments, recorded and perhaps unrecorded, these small European interventions in Africa produced no real results. The one significant European conquest was that of Angola, which Portugal commenced in 1575 (though its roots go back to 1483) and, in many respects, completed in 1671.[5] The conquest of Angola was hardly spectacular by Spanish standards, as it took over only about half the kingdom of Ndongo, its principal target, and at the end of the wars, Portugal controlled just a small sliver of land, mostly along the coast and the banks of two rivers, whose course was largely through inhospitable semidesert land. Even here, however, Portugal achieved its results only with major assistance from indigenous armies, and it fit into the regional politics as just one of the players in a system of interstate relations. To the degree that Portugal could expand its coercive authority through space, it was required to make major concessions to its allies and to accept alliances that had a high cost in regard to Portuguese control.

What Portugal Brought: European Warfare in the Sixteenth and Seventeenth Centuries

Many discussions of warfare in the early Atlantic world focus on technology, with the possession of guns and horses (not exactly technology but treated as if they were) a crucial component. Europeans developed this technology in the context of a particular art of war that had grown up in the continent since the Middle Ages, starting with armored cavalry and elaborate fortifications.

As Robert Bartlett noted in his study of medieval Europe, those who think of the Middle Ages as being about knights and castles have pretty well got it right.[6] Starting in about 1100, European iron workers and horse breeders began simultaneously both creating stronger armor that incorporated steel and sheet metal and breeding stronger and faster horses to accommodate the greater weight of the armored riders. At the same time, European elites focused a great deal of attention, in part in reaction to the dominance of battlefields by armored cavalry, to fortifying the bases of their power. Simple fortified towers gradually gave way to more elaborate fortifications that took years and thousands of man hours to construct.

While European innovation and effort were directed to creating defensive arms, both personal and collective, another set of innovations pushed in the other direction. More and more powerful armor-piercing weapons were developed, first the crossbow and eventually firearms, whose principal task was to penetrate the stronger and thicker armor that protected the horsemen. A parallel development started with catapults and ended with cannon that were designed to knock down castle walls. By the time Columbus set sail and the Portuguese went to support João Bemoim, Europeans were carrying powerful armor-piercing weapons to assist them. The earliest wave had crossbows, and those who followed in the sixteenth century had firearms. Armor-piercing weapons had had a considerable impact by then, and in fact, many European cavalries had begun to shed much of their armor, since firearms made it less protective, and its weight (and related heat factors) made it less attractive in other ways. The Spanish *jinete*, the lightly armored lancer who terrified and routed indigenous armies from Hispaniola to Peru, was the natural evolution of this process.

Another process that immediately preceded the first European voyages was the complex of tactical and organizational changes that European rulers developed in the late Middle Ages, perhaps especially during the Hundred Years' War, which qualifies as the start of what is widely called the "Military Revolution."[7] In this development, infantry forces were augmented, trained to carry pikes and to stand in close order so as to deter cavalry charges and to protect other soldiers, either archers or crossbowmen, whose missile weapons might be able to penetrate the cavalry's armor. The infantry square, with musketeers in the interior, had just started to become ascendant on the battlefield when the Portuguese ships reached Angola.

A great deal of what Europe brought with it into the Atlantic, then, was the product of a specific military environment. For example, in order to counteract the armored cavalry, Europeans had developed ever more powerful missile weapons, but at a cost. While the penetrating power of a crossbow was great, it was so because of a complex loading and cocking procedure in which a winch was attached to the front in order to pull its impossibly stiff bow out to its extension. This time-consuming operation did result in the capacity to kill armored horsemen, or at least to unhorse them through sheer impact (which was good enough). However, it required that crossbowmen be protected during the long reloading period, and to this end, a fairly large mass of infantry primarily equipped to repel cavalry with long pikes in a close order formation was required. The early harquebus and musket were even more effective at penetrating armor, so much so that their appearance on the battlefield caused most cavalry to shed their armor altogether, but like the crossbow, they required a lengthy time to reload. In addition, firearms misfired frequently, thus greatly reducing their effective rate of fire and requiring more protection still. Thus the pike-and-shot combination, complemented by lightly armored cavalry, came to dominate battlefields in the Thirty Years' War.

Warfare changed from primarily cavalry-on-cavalry actions to infantry-on-infantry actions. In the Thirty Years' War, masses of pikemen pressed on each other until by the "push of a pike," one or the other formation broke ranks and fled. Once out of formation, the cavalry moved in to hack up the fleeing infantry, who could not outrun the horses and, moreover, could not defend themselves while fleeing facing away from their pursuers. As muskets with bayonets replaced pikes, and volley fire with flintlocks replaced the slower-firing matchlock in the late seventeenth century, European war took a final shape, infantry forces advancing against each other, firing volleys and then charging with bayonets, in which the first side to break ranks was mowed down by the cavalry. This course of action was typical of battles from the War of the Spanish Succession until the Napoleonic Wars.

Again, weapons, organization, and tactics revolved around a complex interplay of forces involving armor, missile weapons, and cavalry. Changes in the balance might be a result of technological change, but often it was also organization and even social change that brought about the changes. All this explains European military evolution, but how did it work when the Europeans left their home environment?

In Angola, the evolution of warfare was quite different from that of Europe, and not surprisingly, their reaction to the arrival of Europeans with their weapons and tactics was not the same as Europeans meeting each other at Agincourt, Breitenfeld, or Blenheim.

African Warfare in Angola: The Foundations

According to our somewhat limited documentation, there were two styles of war in the region now occupied by Angola and its immediate neighbors where the Portuguese made their conquest. In the north part of the region, the Kongo style prevailed, and in the south of the region, the Mbundu style held sway.[8]

The Kongo style involved two sorts of troops. The first were archers, recruited in the thousands from villages, mostly by conscription in the weeks before a campaign. They carried only a bow and arrows and perhaps another sidearm, but not necessarily. They used fairly weak self bows whose range and penetrating power were quite limited. In some areas, such as the eastern parts of Kongo, the effectiveness of archery was enhanced by adding poison, though poison was apparently not used everywhere.[9]

The core of a Kongo army was the "heavy infantry," or the shield bearers (*adargueiros*), as the Portuguese called them. These were trained and professional infantry, nominally considered as nobles and living at state expense. They were protected by long shields that extended from approximately their knees to their necks, but without other body armor. The shields were adequate to prevent injury from direct hits of their opponents' arrows and to ward off sword blows as well. Their principal weapon was a scimitar-shaped long sword, which they were trained to wield expertly.[10] This training included a martial dance, called *nsanga*, which involved some aesthetic display but was primarily a demonstration of virtuosity with the sword and shield.

Kongo armies usually deployed with the archers on the flanks or covering the front and the heavy infantry in the middle. Action commenced with arrow strikes from the archers with the intent of causing some casualties and shaking their opponents' nerve. This was followed by a determined advance of the heavy infantry against the opponent's heavy infantry. The outcome of the action was decided in this relatively brief encounter, in which one formation of heavy infantry would force the opposing one to flee, inflicting more casualties from behind as the attacker pursued those who were fleeing.

The Mbundu region had a slightly different art of war. Like Kongo, it had both elite and non-elite troops, with the non-elite being hordes of archers hastily recruited from villages. As in Kongo, they commenced the battle with arrow strikes, and as in the northern area, they might flee when this task was done. The Mbundu did not, however, deploy a heavy infantry. Their elite fighters carried no defensive armor but used a curved-bladed battle-ax as their principal weapon. They relied heavily on personal maneuver to avoid their enemies' blows and thus trained extensively to develop their fencing (if that is the word for fighting with battle-axes) skills. For them, as in Kongo, the decisive phase in battle came when the elite troops engaged, and the winner of that tangle would emerge as the victor on the battlefield.

All the Central African armies, including the Portuguese once they entered the war, relied solely on human porterage to move supplies, a situation generally exacerbated by the low population density and the mobile rural population, which made living off the land very difficult. An army had a hard time maintaining itself in the field for more than a few weeks, and indeed, the capture of the opposing armies' supplies was an important objective in forces that were often fighting hungry as well as tired. Accordingly, this limitation made long campaigns and deep penetrations into enemy lands very difficult.[11]

Portugal Arrives

The Portuguese realized that some part of their art of war had great effect in Africa, especially firearms. In Benin art of the sixteenth century, Portuguese musketeers carrying several guns were prominent, suggesting that these weapons and their defensive armor made them interesting and perhaps effective. Of course, we know very little about what they did in these early encounters and how they did it.

Portuguese sailors under Diogo Cão first visited Kongo in 1483, where they hoped to be able to offer a combination of armor-piercing weapons and defensive armor. During this first encounter, they took some high-ranking Kongos back to Portugal and left some Portuguese behind them, as a sort of system of mutual hostage taking and leaving.[12] During the next few years, the Portuguese in Kongo described Europe to the king of Kongo, enabling the Kongolese nobles to learn about Europe at first hand. When Cão returned to Kongo in 1488 to reexchange hostages, the king of Kongo, Nzinga a Nkuwu, asked to be baptized and to form an alliance with Portugal. When a new expedition returned to Kongo in 1491, the king was baptized, and an alliance was formed. As a part of the new alliance, Portuguese troops accompanied Nzinga a Nkuwu, now baptized as João, in a war to defeat some rebels.[13] There was never any thought given to the idea that the Portuguese would fight on their own or that they would command the expedition in question. We know these troops marched with crossbows, not firearms, but the rebels, whose lands lay along the Congo River, could be reached by water, and a Portuguese ship equipped with a bombard may have helped in the successful action. Portugal sent a second military-political mission to Kongo in 1509, and the instructions to its commander, Gonçalo Rodrigues, make clear that the mission was to assist the king of Kongo in whatever wars he fought and to accept any payment that he might offer.[14] Again, there was no thought of his operating independently or outside the king's authority, nor was he instructed or advised to attempt a conquest. Clearly, the idea was to make Portuguese troops useful to Kongo in the hopes that greater opportunities might follow, but no one appears to have considered that this alliance would extend the coercive authority of the Portuguese or even project their power in Kongo.

Portuguese troops might not have been overwhelmingly effective in this early phase—when João I died and his son Afonso Mvemba a Nzinga took over in 1509, no Portuguese forces contributed at all to the civil war that briefly kept Afonso from the throne. Moreover, in 1514 Afonso pointedly accused the Portuguese of cowardice in a war that they had helped him wage in the south a year or two earlier. They had lagged behind his army, had made demands for payment, and had arrived too late to be of much value in the action. Other Portuguese, entrusted with carrying slaves back to the capital from the battlefield, had carelessly let them escape, and the queen had to deploy Kongo security forces to round them up.[15]

How much more Portuguese military forces may have contributed to Kongo's expansion and warfare in the following half century is unknown, but despite this false start, they must have proved to be of some value. When King Álvaro I was driven from his throne by mysterious invaders or rebels, called Jagas, in 1568 or 1570, he wrote to Portugal to seek military assistance in restoring him to his throne, and King Sebastião I responded by sending Francisco de Gouveia Sottomaior, governor of the island colony of São Tomé, with six hundred soldiers to relieve the king. Duarte Lopes, a Portuguese New Christian (converted Jew) who served as Álvaro's ambassador to Rome in 1584 and contributed to a history of Kongo published in 1591, noted that Gouveia Sottomaior's men successfully repelled the Jagas and restored Álvaro to his throne.[16] As the others had, he worked with the Kongo army, and his forces finally left Kongo in 1576.[17] But the Gouveia Sottomaior expedition had not been without costs to Kongo and gains for Portugal, and it was through his efforts that the Portuguese began their conquest of Angola.

Indeed, the Portuguese response to the Jaga invasion or rebellion did allow Portugal to claim some authority in Africa, in part though its alliance with Kongo. Gouveia Sottomaior was ordered to demand some sort of vassalage arrangement from Kongo and to place Portuguese residents in the kingdom under the authority of the Portuguese king and outside the jurisdiction of Kongo's rulers. Although Gouveia Sottomaior was ordered to "protect the king and gather the Portuguese so that they would not be insulted as in the past," the Portuguese residents, led by a priest named Francisco Barbudo, persuaded Álvaro not to allow either action to be taken.[18]

Our knowledge of the exact arrangements is hazy; upon ordering Gouveia Sottomaior to withdraw his forces in 1574, the Portuguese king Sebastião noted with apparent satisfaction that the captain had "reduced that Kingdom to my obedience," though such a "reduction" seems hardly to be justified by the immediate withdrawal of what might have been a garrison.[19] When the Jesuit priest Garcia Simões arrived in Luanda in 1575, he heard that Gouveia Sottomaior had papers in his possession "confessing he [Álvaro] was his [the King of Portugal's?] vassal."[20] Álvaro did at least refer to the king of Portugal as "my lord and brother," suggesting that he had accepted some sort of vassalage,[21] but no record of a vassalage agreement survives today. Álvaro probably agreed to pay Portugal for the services of Gouveia Sottomaior's forces by allowing Portugal some rights over its "mine" of *nzimbu* (shell money current in Kongo) on the island of Luanda, as Kongo's King Ambrósio I (1626–1631) explained in 1630 to Portuguese ambassadors who sought concessions on the basis of this treaty. When told that the ambassadors had "seen and read" a letter of Sebastião making a donation of the "fifth" of the *nzimbu*, Ambrósio countered by asserting that Sebastião had refused the offer, saying that he had intended only to "augment and extend Christianity in those parts."[22] In fact, secondhand reports of Gouvia Sottomaior's instructions stated that he was to locate mines of precious metals and secure them for Portugal, though Álvaro apparently persuaded him that Kongo possessed no precious metals.[23] It therefore is possible that some sort of undocumented compromise was worked out, in which a portion of the proceeds of the shell mines were paid to Portugal, although in fact the mines remained firmly and fully in Kongo's hands.

It may also be true, although it is not elucidated by a clear documentary record, that Kongo agreed to assist Portugal in building a real colony in Angola, as the lands on the coast around Luanda and the mouth of the Kwanza River were known. Perhaps the mysterious references to vassalage refer to a military alliance that would promote the expansion of coercive Portuguese powers in Africa and perhaps allow Kongo to share in the benefits. In fact, what seems clearest as the events played out is that the language of whatever agreement was reached included a state of vassalage and dependent ally for Kongo, if it could be obtained. But it was quite evident that Portugal could not sustain a dependent alliance with Kongo, that the best they could hope for was some assistance in the conquest of Angola.

The core of what became the colony of Angola was the land known as Mbundu, an ethnically defined region that lay to the east and south of the modern city of Luanda and whose language, Kimbundu, is one of Angola's major languages. The region of Mbundu was dominated by a major kingdom called Ndongo.[24] In the early sixteenth century, Ndongo had risen to power and conquered a wide swath of land westward from its core in the highland region around the modern city of N'dalatanda to the region just east of modern-day Luanda. In the early sixteenth century, Kongo claimed authority over the area and, indeed, over Ndongo itself, and Afonso I viewed the expansion with some trepidation. The war of 1512, in which he had accused Portuguese participants of cowardice, was waged against an Mbundu lord named Munza, who perhaps was somehow connected with the rise of Ndongo. Moreover, in 1518, Ngola Kiluanje (ca.1515–1556), the ruler of Ndongo, had sent a mission to Portugal seeking baptism and, in effect, recognition by Portugal of equality with Kongo. When Portugal responded by sending a missionary and ambassador, Afonso managed to upend the mission and installed his own missionary in Ndongo's capital in 1526. At the same time, he complained vociferously to Portugal about the initiative.[25]

Nonetheless, in the next few years, Ndongo managed to form more informal alliances with Portugal. In 1548 Afonso's successor, Diogo I (1545–1561), conducted a full-scale inquiry into trade from his ports and concluded that Portuguese merchants in Ndongo were redirecting the slave trade to their area and away from his own port of Mpinda.[26] Ndongo tried diplomacy again in 1560 by sending a second mission to Portugal, this time headed by Paulo Dias de Novais, the future conqueror of Angola, to consolidate an alliance. Again it failed, but Dias de Novais returned to Portugal seeking another chance.[27]

The Jaga invasion and Álvaro's embarrassment gave Dias de Novais and Portugal another chance to firm up a relationship with Ndongo and expand their influence in central Africa. Dias de Novais was granted a charter to make a real conquest in Angola, and although none of this is stated in the charter, the events in Kongo must certainly have raised hopes in Portugal that an alliance like that of Cortes and Tlaxcala to conquer the Aztecs might be in the works.

Dias de Novais's mission was not like those that had been sent to Kongo earlier. He had obtained from Sebastião I a charter of conquest representing a definite intent, for the first time in Portugal's relations with central Africa, to take over land and power. Dias de Novais's charter did not envision a direct attack on Ndongo. Instead, it called on him to settle in Luanda, to build forts, and also to take control of a wide stretch of land that lay south of the Kwanza River, in a region known as Kisama.[28] Kisama, though claimed by Kongo since the 1530s, was actually firmly in Ndongo's control, and any serious attempt to found a colony there would surely meet determined resistance from Ndongo.

Dias de Novais knew the landscape of power and control in central Africa well enough to realize that he could not attack Ndongo, and so he presented himself to both Kongo and Ndongo as being a mercenary expedition intent on assisting each country in its wars. His first attempt to do this, on behalf of Kongo, was an effort to subdue a rebellious district called Kansanze that lay just east of Luanda, but it was a failure and his troops had to be bailed out by Kongolese forces.[29] If the understanding that Kongo and Portugal had developed as a result of the Jaga invasion and Gouveia Sottomaior's assistance to Kongo had any hope of creating a dependent ally, it was lost on that day. Dias de Novais had more success fighting on behalf of Ndongo in the following years and resisted an attempt by Álvaro II to co-opt his forces by refusing the Kongo ruler's offer of ten thousand heavy infantry to help him in his wars.[30]

In 1579, however, Dias de Novais's efforts to appear to be an ally of Ndongo fell apart. Francisco Barbuda d'Aguiar, who had been a chaplain in Kongo for many years, had been a steadfast opponent of Gouveia Sottomaior's mission when he resided there, and had recently transferred his activities to Ndongo, denounced Dias de Novais's plan to the king Njinga Ngola Kilombo kia Kasenda (1575–1592). After the ruler heard about Barbuda's contentions, he launched a full-scale surprise attack on all the Portuguese forces stationed in his land. The attack was successful, and the troops were routed—Dias de Novais was at Luanda at the time and thus spared, but the losses were heavy. The Portuguese regrouped around Luanda and hoped they could stave off an attack from Ndongo.[31]

Dias de Novais was fortunate in that Álvaro II had seen his operation as a further opening for Kongo to expand its authority and recover from the Jaga debacle, perhaps even turning the tables and putting Portugal in his service. As he had in Kazanze, he offered Dias de Novais help: a large army to attack Ndongo in conjunction with whatever Dias de Novais could offer.

In the dry season of 1580, Álvaro's army, a great expedition of conquest, sallied forth from its mobilization points and headed toward Ndongo. This was a large force, however, so logistics was a problem, as the army was moving north to south and thus could not use rivers to move supplies or support the porters. The army was met by an Ndongo army as it sought to cross the Dande River, probably in the mountainous region called the Dembos, and was defeated. Álvaro withdrew in shame, and Dias de Novais was left once again to fend for himself.[32]

It is from this point that the real conquest of Angola can be said to begin. The alliance with Kongo, especially if conceived as having been along the lines of the Spanish expansion of coercive authority in America, had failed to produce the results intended. Kongo was not a real vassal; there were no Portuguese forces in the country; and in any case, its king had been unable to rescue Dias de Novais. The grand politics of Ndongo and Kongo and their struggle for regional hegemony was behind them, and Dias de Novais was left clinging to a few small forts ringing Luanda, protected from Ndongo's full onslaught only by the considerable distance and logistical problems that an army of Ndongo would face advancing so far toward the coast.

The Portuguese, in contrast, were able to use the Kwanza River as a transport corridor, and this undoubtedly explains how they were able to succeed in Angola. In an environment where the navigable rivers, primarily the Congo and the Kwanza, ran east to west, the only prospect of using riverine transport was on the lower courses of the Kwanza, which indeed they did. The Kwanza corridor allowed them to move forces and supplies rapidly at least as far as the river could be navigated by large vessels. But just as the river allowed this easy penetration, the Portuguese faced real logistical problems attacking very far from it—either to the north into Kongo, as Kongo discovered with Álvaro's defeat in 1580, or east beyond the heads of navigation in the Kwanza, or even south into the central highlands of Angola.

Dias de Novais did what any Spanish conquistador would do, as we now understand the conquest of the New World: he looked for dissatisfied local rulers who could give him men and supplies. He was at the hinterland of Ndongo's authority: the coast held little value for Ndongo, and in any case, the real sovereignty around those parts had been in Kongo's hands. The local rulers, *sobas*, as they were styled, had been under Ndongo's authority as tribute-paying subjects and might be persuaded to accept a new master under perhaps better terms. Dias de Novais began to recruit them. One or two joined him, accepted baptism, and offered arms. More important perhaps, individual Kongolese nobles offered their services to Dias de Novais and brought with them seasoned soldiers to fight on his behalf. Dias de Novais used his larger ships on the Kwanza to transport them farther inland, and in 1582, using forces of his own Kongolese allies, plus those of several Angolan *sobas* who were rebelling against Ndongo, he fought a battle against a detachment of the Ndongo army at Massangano and won.[33]

The presidio of Nossa Senhora da Victoria at Massangano became Dias de Novais's inland base. His large vessels could sail on the Kwanza with impunity, and the local *sobas* accepted his authority. For the next eight years, Dias de Novais carefully garnered his forces, using his allies to good effect and attacking those who opposed him with his own and their forces. In the process, he had these allies sign vassalage treaties, making them subjects of the king of Portugal and promising to render Portugal military assistance, labor service when required, and nominal tributes. These treaties were affirmed in a variety of ways throughout the coming years and envisioned a change of sovereignty. But even though few such changes took place, the Portuguese considered any further warfare against these allies as "rebellions."

Ndongo did dispatch troops to defend the vulnerable areas, but logistical problems surely prevented a large deployment, just as logistical problems had kept Kongo from defeating Ndongo in 1580. By 1589 Dias de Novais had managed to win nominal control over most of the dry lowlands between Massangano and Luanda north of the Kwanza. He now decided on the most difficult task: a direct attack on Ndongo's core region, but his death in 1590 precluded his carrying it out personally. Such an attack would have allowed Ndongo to defend his core province on its own ground without the logistical difficulties of mounting an attack on the lowland provinces.

Ndongo's heartland was on an inland plateau, bounded on the south side by the Kwanza River and on the north by the Lukala River, both of which ran through deep canyons to the sea. Luis Serrão, who had taken over Dias de Novais's enterprise on his own behalf, led his army up the plateau and advanced rapidly on Ndongo's capital at Kabasa, located south of N'datatanda, the modern capital of Cuanza Norte Province. The two armies met near the Lukala River, and Serrão was totally and completely defeated. Only through sheer determination to survive were the defeated soldiers were able to limp back to Massangano. When news of the defeat spread to the lowlands, many of the *sobas* who had given their allegiance to Portugal reconsidered and withdrew from the alliance (an action the Portuguese called *rebellion*).[34] The first phase of the Portuguese conquest was over.[35]

During the fifteen years of war that Dias de Novais and his men fought in Angola, they developed an art of war that was specific to them and their political system. It is possible that the roots of the art of war were laid during the time when Portuguese served in Kongo's armies, although Dias de Novais and the men he brought with him seem to have had little experience in the northern kingdom (and in fact, the Portuguese residents there were lukewarm, to say the least, about Dias de Novais's enterprise). He may also have learned this art from the Kongo forces that served in his army, but in any case, it was an innovation in Mbundu.

In effect, the Portuguese soldiers were to the Mbundu armies what the heavy infantry was to Kongo's army. The Portuguese soldiers, protected by some body armor, including shields, and backed up by musketeers, formed a square more or less in the center of the battlefield. Using the sort of training that would have been appropriate in a European battlefield to keep the cavalry away, they still became something of a fortress in a battlefield where there was no cavalry. Standing in close order, shields next to one another and attacking, as in the Kongo heavy infantry, with long swords, they were a defensive formation that was hard to break. They then arranged the archers that they recruited from allied *sobas* on their flanks, and the battle proceeded as usual.[36]

When they fought relatively small Ndongo armies, they could easily hold their own, even against the skilled professionals. In one engagement in 1585, Jesuits who accompanied the Portuguese to Angola noted they had defeated the "flower" of the Ndongo nobility, in a force that now contained its own musketeeers.[37] From these accounts, it is unclear whether the Portuguese deployed any skilled Mbundu infantry on their side or whether their Kongolese allies joined them as heavy infantry. Tactical descriptions written by priests do not dwell on the specifics of troop deployments, and Portuguese pride gave little credit to African soldiers fighting alongside them.

The defeat at the Lukala River, however, suggests that Portugal, even with its varied allies, was not able to take on a fully deployed royal army on its home ground. It probably was recognition of this problem that led the governors following Dias de Novais and Luis Serrão to accept a peace, negotiated and ratified in 1599, accepting Portuguese control along the Kwanza and some areas near Luanda but denying them much of the land that Dias de Novais claimed in 1590.[38]

Then, in the early seventeenth century, Portuguese policies toward Angola shifted. The idea of making a real conquest, establishing real administrative control with effective coercive mechanisms in place instead of the often unenforceable vassalage agreements, including governing large areas, and perhaps profiting by the discovery of mines was abandoned in favor of a different sort of colony, one that was oriented toward trade, in particular the slave trade, but did not involve participating in warfare or seeking allies to make wars. Governors' instructions of that period stressed the need to avoid aggressive war against the Africans and tried to limit their activities to trade. From the beginning of Dias de Novais's operations in 1575, the wars in Angola had been funded largely by the export of the captured as slaves. By most accounts, Dias de Novais had done quite well on this front, even if his taking of territory had been more nominal than real. As long as he could win battles and capture the losers, he could continue financing his expedition. But defeat in 1590 made this strategy less appealing, though some limited wars still were fought along the upper Kwanza, and the presidio of Cambambe was founded in 1602 in what was hoped (vainly, it turned out) to be the base of a silver mine.[39]

If the crown were prepared to abandon conquest in favor of trade, the governors were less interested in peaceful trade. They still hoped that they could locate allies that were not as powerful and independent as Kongo or as weak and fickle as the *sobas* who had fought with them up to the battle of Lukala and then abandoned them, only to be slowly won back in the years following their defeat. To this end, Portuguese governors sought to intrigue with members of Ndongo's elite in hopes of benefiting from the splits created by rivalries, as Pizarro had in Peru. It was fairly clear that only by working within the elite of Ndongo, provoking or benefiting from civil war, and backing one or the other of these, could they win allies who would be beholden to them in a way that would allow an extension of authority over some areas through the concession of some authority in others.

Whether or not Portugal conquered territory, Angola did provide value to the Portuguese crown as a commercial colony. Portugal could project power through wars, which, though not extending its authority, nevertheless did provide the "by-product" slaves for export and sale, as indeed had been the case in earlier periods too. Angola's export of slaves to the Spanish territories and Brazil grew steadily from 1575 and continued to grow or at least to remain steady through the early seventeenth century. Wars in the trading area around Luanda were frequent enough that even if the Portuguese themselves did not fight, they could obtain as many as ten thousand slaves a year for the region, the single largest slaving region at the time and the supplier of the vast majority of enslaved workers to both Brazil and the Spanish Indies.[40]

The military impasse that had prevented the Portuguese conquest in Ndongo was broken, at least for a time, in the early seventeenth century by the simultaneous emergence of the Imbangala and the development of serious dissidence among Ndongo's elite. The first step was the formation of an alliance with the Imbangala. Portuguese first heard of these military nomads in the early seventeenth century, when trading along the coast south of the Kwanza River. An English sailor, Andrew Battell, who had been captured and forced into Portuguese service, went with his master on a trading voyage to them and was subsequently left in their hands for sixteen months until escaping and returning to Portuguese-held territory. His account of his adventures, published in full in 1625, describes the Imbangala.[41]

The Imbangala offered apparently no particular military innovations, in either weapons or tactics. They formed their bands by kidnapping youths from the populations through which they traveled. According to Battell, they lived by rapine and were particularly fond of palm wine, which they consumed in a wasteful manner before moving from one district to another. They fought with both arrows and the same sort of battle-ax that the Mbundu used, although perhaps more of their bands were elite troops than the typical army would be. Aside from their fighting skill and training, the Imbangala also cultivated a reputation as cannibals, which perhaps gave them a psychological advantage augmenting the fear that their arms alone generated.[42]

Battell's Portuguese colleagues persuaded the Imbangala to sell their captives to them in exchange for the usual trade goods and large quantities of alcohol. In his day, their activities were confined mostly to the area south of the Kwanza; Battell once came close to the river when he was traveling with one of the bands, but he never crossed it. Both the governor Bento Banha Cardoso, who took over in 1611, and, following him, Manuel Cerveira Pereira thought that there might be military value in an alliance with the Imbangala. Both had used them to win wars. But this alliance did not come to fruition until 1617 when Governor Luis Mendes de Vasconcelos arrived in Luanda. A skilled soldier with long service in India and the author of a treatise on the art of war, Mendes de Vasconcelos initially rejected the idea of an alliance with heathen cannibals. But he soon changed his mind and brought several bands across the Kwanza River to serve him in a new assault on Ndongo's heartland.

The new attack, aided by dissident nobles from within Ndongo's core district and bolstered by the terrifying new allies, was remarkably successful. Mendes de Vasconcelos's troops sacked Kabasa and burned it, captured royal wives, and sent Mbande a Ngola, the king, fleeing. Powerless against the new forces arrayed against him, he set up a makeshift capital in the Kindonga islands, a group of islands in the Kwanza River, but despondent at the loss of his capital and so many of his subjects (Mendes de Vasconcelos exported fifty thousand slaves during his three years as governor), he committed suicide in 1624.[43] Mendes de Vasconcelos hoped that he could then govern through a puppet king from among the dissidents and tried to place a certain Antonio Correa Samba Antumba on the throne, but "it had no effect, because he was not obeyed," since his birth and legitimacy were not sufficient to win supporters, as the people did "not obey anyone who is not a child or descendant of a king."[44]

Although the Portuguese governors had failed to find noble allies among the Mbundu elite, they did find an effective military force in the Imbangala and perhaps could succeed with their aid. Following the defeat of Ndongo, they explored the possibility of turning the tables on Kongo. Luis Mendes de Vasconcelos had ended his administration in an attempt to take over Kasanze, an always rebellious area where thousands of runaway slaves had been taken in. The territory was nominally Kongo's, and it was this connection that led João Correia de Sousa, Mendes de Vasconcelos's successor, to use it as a wedge to enter Kongo. In 1622 Correia de Sousa launched a successful and treacherous attack on Kasanze and then accused Kongo of supporting the rebels. Kongo's King Álvaro III died during the initial phases of the Kasanze war, and his successor, Pedro II, was elevated to the throne from the duchy of Mbamba, in whose lands Kasanze lay. Correia de Sousa made untenable demands on the new king, including claiming that he had the right to enthrone and dethrone Kongo kings (although de Sousa did not invoke the vassalage claim that might have dated back to the Jaga period), and then invaded. His army of twenty thousand included a detachment of Imbangala, and they met a Kongo frontier force at Mbumbi, south of Mbamba's capital. In a hot battle, the outnumbered Kongo force was routed, and several prominent Kongolese nobles were eaten by the Imbangala soldiers.[45] In this battle, the first that matched Portuguese against Kongo forces, one witness recalled the value of Portuguese musketry, which was that it could easily penetrate the shields of the Kongolese heavy infantry.[46]

Outraged, Pedro moved his army down to meet the Portuguese, and in an undescribed battle waged near the town of Mbanda Kasi in early January 1623, he completely defeated and routed the Portuguese force.[47] Pedro next moved his army into the Dembos region and reclaimed the allegiance of several districts that had been brought under Portuguese vassalage in the earlier campaigns.[48] The military combination that had been so successful against Ndongo could not crack Kongo's combination of heavy infantry backed with musketeers and archers. Although the last phase of this campaign is poorly recorded, it is quite possible that the Portuguese force was unable to sustain itself for logistical reasons, and just as at Lukala, such a force could not withstand an attack by a fully prepared African army on its own land with short supply lines.

Meanwhile, affairs in Angola moved forward as Ndongo's leaders responded to the shock of the Imbangala intervention. In 1622, before he ended his life, Mbande a Ngola had sent his sister Njinga Mbande to Luanda to negotiate a peace. She had been forced to agree to vassalage to Portugal, payment of a tribute in exchange for assistance in removing the Imbangala scourge from her lands. But the Portuguese government never kept its side of the bargain, and thus when he died, Njinga Mbande, who took over her brother's throne as regent to his seven-year-old son, likewise refused to honor the Ndongo portion of the treaty. Soon afterward, Njinga killed her protégé and declared herself queen.[49]

Upon Njinga's accession to the throne, warfare in Angola entered a new phase. Njinga had been her father's favorite and had accompanied him to the wars. She was well known to and liked by the army, who accepted her as their queen and leader. But her accession also was controversial. Although no one had stepped forward to support Samba Antumba when Mendes de Vasconcellos proposed him as king of Ndongo, Njinga's opponents were willing to work with Portugal. Hari a Ndongo, from a rival lineage and opposed to a female occupying the throne, was one of the dissidents who had aided Mendes de Vasconcellos's penetration of the plateau. Hari a Ndongo accepted vassalage from Portugal in exchange for its assistance in driving Njinga from Ndongo, much as Pizarro had worked stepped into the rivalries between Atahualpa and Huascar and subsequently between Manco Inca and Paullu Inca to win Peru. Between Hari a Ndongo, who accepted baptism as Felipe I when he swore vassalage, and the Imbangala, the Portuguese now had what appeared to be a winning combination of allies, one with royal pretensions and the other with military might.

But the alliance proved to be less effective than the Portuguese hoped. Njinga was sufficiently popular that many *sobas* did not abandon her. She worked out her own alliance with some of the Imbangala bands and was thus in a position to defy the Portuguese and Felipe. Felipe, Njinga, and the Portuguese fought back and forth across the eastern end of Ndongo's territory, and while the Portuguese were able to drive Njinga from her island capital of Kindonga, she withdrew successfully to Matamba, another interior kingdom, which she conquered and converted into her base.[50] The Portuguese also were at the end of their logistical capacity. Because they were no longer able to use river transport, their forces could not pursue even broken Mbundu armies beyond the islands of Kindonga, and in that area at least, the initiative was in Njinga's hands.

By the end of the 1630s, this war also was stalemated. The Imbangala bands were now divided into three groups: one was with Njinga, incorporated into her state through Njinga Mona (Njinga's son); another remained with the Portuguese; and a third band, led by Kasanje, founded its own independent state south of Njinga's capital in Matamba. Another round of diplomacy in 1639, although not formally successful, recognized a status quo among these three powers.[51]

Meanwhile, in the aftermath of the failed invasion of Kongo, Pedro II had written to the Dutch Estates General proposing a military alliance with them to expel the Portuguese from Angola. He promised the Dutch that if they sent a fleet to attack Luanda, he would not only pay for their efforts and support it with ground forces, but he would allow them to establish a post in Luanda under his authority. Although the first attempt to make good on this alliance in 1624 had failed, in part due to Kongo's own politics and the conciliatory tone that Portugal took to Kongo in the aftermath of the war, a second military alliance led to the Dutch seizure of Luanda in 1641.

In many respects, the Dutch were attempting to repeat what the Portuguese had done sixty-five years earlier. They hoped to cooperate with Kongo to conquer Angola, and as the Portuguese before them had, at least some of the Dutch saw it as a commercial colony that would thrive off the slave trade. The new king of Kongo, Garcia II, dispatched an army to help them, and the Portuguese were soon driven from the coast to their interior post at Massangano. Heartened by this setback, Njinga sent an embassy to the new Dutch government in Luanda promising them aid, and soon she moved her army from Matamba back to the lands she had controlled earlier in her reign.[52] The wars between the Portuguese, Njinga, and the Dutch during the Dutch occupation period (1641–1648) were not unusual for the period and were well described by a Portuguese soldier, António de Oliveira Cadornega, who came to Angola in 1639, just in time to witness them.[53]

Cadornega's military descriptions are sufficiently detailed that we can see how the various military components brought by Europe to Africa, as well as the alliances they forged, worked. The Portuguese fought more or less as they had earlier, with a tightly formed square in the center of their army, now often backed by light artillery that fired grapeshot into the advancing attackers. Although the Portuguese were often aggressive strategically, they preferred to fight battles defensively, forcing their opponents to attack their central square if they expected to succeed. The decisive moment in battle was when Njinga's army, having swept away the allied archers, launched itself fully into the Portuguese square, with her elite forces and the Imbangala as the shock troops. The Portuguese soldiers in the square sought to hold off her forces primarily by maintaining their formation and using their swords, as firearms were useful only in the earlier stages of battle when missile weapons were deployed by African archers. Generally, Portuguese generals deployed their allied archers, supplied by *sobas*, on the wings of the battlefield and had them engage fully in the opening stages. The Imbangala were kept usually as a reserve force, to intervene if things went poorly for the Portuguese square or, more often, to counterattack when the attackers wavered and seemed about to break.[54]

These armies were fairly evenly matched. Even though Njinga's army included musketeers from the Netherlands, she did not win all her battles. In the battle of Kombi in 1647, however, she crushed the Portuguese army and forced the remaining Portuguese forces and their allies to fall back into their three fortified presidios of Ambaca, Massangano, and Muximo.[55] She laid close siege to all three but, lacking artillery, was unable to storm them and, lacking naval superiority on the river, was also unable to cut off their supplies. In 1648, a new Portuguese force from Brazil, under the command of Salvador de Sá y Benevides, landed in Luanda.[56] Frustrated by the expenses of the long war and disappointed in the commercial results, the Dutch capitulated and left Africa.[57] Unable to maintain her siege of the forts, Njinga withdrew to Matamba. Although further but indecisive actions continued for some years, she and the Portuguese negotiated a treaty of peace in 1657, establishing the borders more or less where they had been in 1639, before the Dutch invasion.

The new Portuguese governor sought a punitive peace, even though he had not won any real battles, and in fact, Portugal's military efforts were directed primarily against the dry lowlands south of the Kwanza rather than in the highlands or against Ndongo or Matamba. When Kongo appeared to be on the verge of civil war in 1658, a Portuguese force was dispatched to assist one of the pretenders to the throne, but the troops, remembering the defeat at Mbanda Kasi more than thirty years earlier and recognizing the logistical difficulties they would face if they advanced farther, refused to pass into Kongo's territory.[58]

If logistical difficulties had upset Portugal's plans to invade Kongo, the same issues surely hampered Kongo's own plans for attacking Portugal. In 1665 Kongo sought to reestablish its authority in a succession dispute in the small state of Mbwila, sandwiched between lands claimed by Kongo, Matamba-Ndongo, and Portugal. When Garcia II's son and successor, António I, sent an army to intervene, the Portuguese dispatched their own to counter it. The two armies met in a cataclysmic battle on the shore of the small Ulanga River in Mbwila's territory. Both armies were operating far from their main bases, though many of Kongo's troops came from far away to the battlefield, and the battle proceeded as was now typical of Angolan wars. The first stages of the engagement saw the archers on the Portuguese side swept from the field, and António, accompanied by his heavy infantry and musketeers, assaulted the Portuguese square. The Portuguese, aided by two field pieces, managed to repel two attacks, and on the third one, a shot from one of the musketeers hit and killed the king. The Kongolese attack broke, the Imbangala counterattacked, and Kongo suffered a military disaster of the first order, leaving thousands of dead on the field.[59]

Despite this seemingly decisive victory, the usual logistical problems prevented the Portuguese from maintaining their army in Mbwila and completely ruled out a follow-up into Kongo. Kongo dissolved into civil war following António's death, and five years later, a disappointed pretender to Kongo's throne named Rafael appealed to Portugal to restore him. Francisco da Távora agreed to help and mounted an attack on Kongo in 1670. The army followed a daring campaign strategy, aimed at subduing Kongo's coastal province of Soyo. After an engagement with Kongo forces in the southern end of the country favored the Portuguese plan, Rafael marched with his own forces to the Kongolese capital in São Salvador. The Portuguese field commander, thinking he had broken Kongolese resistance, continued farther into the country, intent on capturing slaves and perhaps extending Portuguese authority, but well beyond its capacity to support the army logistically. The prince of Soyo's army met him in battle at Kitombo, on the banks of the Congo River, and totally destroyed the Portuguese force. Even the Imbangala fought to the last man while hundreds of Portuguese drowned trying to retreat across a swollen river, and the Kongolese offered Dutch merchants Portuguese captives as slaves.[60] Just as Kongo had suffered its worst defeat in Mbwila, Portugal endured its worst setback at Kitombo just five years later. Although a formal treaty of peace was not signed until 1690, Portugal abandoned any further offensive action aimed at its northern neighbor until 1857.

One final action ended the period of Portuguese colonial invasion. During the first war with Njinga, Portugal had systematically aided a dissident branch of Ndongo's royal family, the Hari family, in their claims to the throne of Ndongo. Hari a Ngola's troops provided the bulk of Portugal's fighting forces in both the first wars against Njinga and the Dutch wars. But with the treaty of 1657, Portugal had to recognize Njinga as ruler of Ndongo and Matamba, and she insisted that they no longer recognize Hari a Ngola. Hari's bitter disappointment with their abandoning his claims was compounded by the fact that Portuguese settlers near his domains had illegally diverted his subjects to their estates.[61] No one in Portugal listened to his complaints, and just as the disastrous campaign against Kongo ended, he formally revolted against Portugal.

The Portuguese managed to scrape enough soldiers together to attack Hari in his heavily fortified capital at Mpungo Ndongo in 1671. The campaign took a year and cost heavily, but at last Hari sued for peace and accepted Portuguese control over his domains. A presidio was built at Mpungo a Ndongo to symbolize the occupation of his lands.[62] But it was a Pyrrhic victory at best, for Portugal was no longer capable of waging successful wars against any of its African neighbors. The country's inability to sustain deeper penetration was revealed again when a Portuguese army sought to intervene in the succession of Matamba in 1683 but was defeated and forced to withdraw by Queen Verónica I, one of Njinga's successors.[63] A peace treaty following the war only reestablished the status quo ante, and a similar long-range and unsuccessful campaign was waged against Matamba in 1744.[64] Portugal redirected its military efforts to the smaller states of the Dembos region to the north or to Kisama to the south and reverted more and more to obtaining slaves by trade rather than warfare.[65]

Conclusion

Like other European conquests in the early modern period, the Portuguese conquest of Angola relied heavily on local military forces, political and military cooperation by indigenous elites, and a concomitant reward to the collaborators in the postconquest government. But in many respects, it also was radically different. Portugal's alliance with Kongo has no real parallels, in large measure because it realized so little gain from it. Likewise, although we can find ready parallels to Portugal's policies in the conquest of major American kingdoms, like the Tlaxcala alliance in Mexico or the exploitation of the civil war in the Inca Empire in Peru, these politics foundered on the ultimate failure of all the alliances to advance Portuguese territorial claims very far.

Portugal achieved no real conquest in its wars and contributed only marginally to the way in which war was fought, but it did benefit from war. Although Angola's disease environment was different from that of Europe and its soldiers died from tropical diseases, Portugal's defeats were usually strictly military. The greatest Portuguese military asset was probably the use of tightly formed infantry supporting firearms as a central feature of the battlefield, a formation designed originally in Europe to oppose cavalry but employed very differently in Africa as a means of supporting allied infantry. The "imperial" benefit to Portugal was *not* in the territorial expansion of coercive control. The Portuguese were more or less unable to control territory anywhere beyond the banks of the rivers, thanks to the significant logistical difficulties facing all parties engaged in armed conflict in west Central Africa. Even there, Portuguese power was compromised by alliances with its allies. The only real benefit to Portugal was its access to the fruits of campaigns waged by Africans, Africans with whom this country often had solely diplomatic relationships, not "control" relationships. Those "fruits" were the prisoners fed into the slave trade. Thus although the wars were not always successful, the very existence of wars, and even those wars in which Portugal had only a partial hand in creating, nourished the slave trade, which ultimately paid its way through the empire.

NOTES

1. Jared Diamond's *Guns, Germs and Steel: The Fates of Human Societies* (New York: Norton, 1997) won many prizes, including the Pulitzer Prize for best nonfiction book in 1998, and was the subject of a PBS documentary in 2005.

2. Ross Hassig, *Mexico and the Spanish Conquest,* 2nd rev. ed. (Norman: University of Oklahoma Press, 2006); Mathew Restall, *Seven Myths of the Spanish Conquest* (Oxford: Oxford University Press, 2004), esp. 44–64 and 131–46; Laura Matthews, *Indian Conquistadors: Indigenous Allies in the Conquest of Mesoamerica* (Norman: University of Oklahoma Press, 2007).

3. Avelino Teixeira da Mota, "D João Bemoim e a expedição Portuguesa ao Senegal em 1489," *Boletim cultural da Guiné Portuguesa* 36 (1971): 63–111. This is a detailed study publishing all relevant documents.

4. On early Benin and Portugal, see A. F. C. Ryder, *Benin and the Europeans, 1485–1897* (New York: Humanities Press, 1969).

5. The initial study in English is David Birmingham, *Trade and Conflict in Angola: The Mbundu and Their Neighbours under the Influence of the Portuguese* (Oxford: Clarendon Press, 1966). More recent studies include Graziano Saccardo [da Legguzzano], *Congo e Angola con la storia dell'antica missione dei Cappuccini,* 3 vols. (Venice: Curia provinciale dei Cappuccini, 1982–83); Ilídio do Amaral, *O reino do Congo, os mbundu (ou Ambundos), o reino dos "ngola" (ou de Angola) e a presença portuguesa, de finais do século XV a meados do século XVI* (Lisbon: Ministério da Ciência e da Tecnologia, Instituto de Investigação Científica Tropical, 1996); and Ilídio do Amaral, *O Consulado de Paulo Dias de Novais. Angola no último quartel do século XVI e primeiro do século XVII* (Lisbon: Ministério da Ciência e da Tecnologia, Instituto de Investigaçao Cientifica Tropical, 2000); and Linda Heywood and John Thornton, *Central Africans, Atlantic Creoles and the Foundation of the Americas, 1585–1660* (New York: Cambridge University Press, 2007).

6. Robert Bartlett, *The Making of Europe: Conquest, Colonization and Cultural Change, 950–1350* (Princeton, NJ: Princeton University Press, 1993).

7. Clifford Rogers, "The Military Revolution of the Hundred Years' War," *Journal of Military History* 57 (1993): 341–78, with a brief review of the long debate on the "military revolution."

8. John K. Thornton, "The Art of War in Angola, 1575–1680," *Comparative Studies in Society and History* 30 (1988): 360–78; John K. Thornton, *Warfare in Atlantic Africa, 1400–1800* (London: UCL Press, 1999), 99–126.

9. On poison arrows in the east, see [Mateus Cardoso] "Relação do Alevamentamento de D. Affonso, Irmão del rei do Congo D. Alvaro," 24 January 1622, in António Brásio, *Monumenta Missionaria Africana* [*MMA*], 15 vols. (Lisbon: Agência Geral do Ultramar, Divisão de Publicações e Biblioteca, 1952–88), 15: 531.

10. An illustration can be found in António Oliveira de Cadornega, *História geral das guerras angolanas (1680)*, ed. José Matias Delgado, 3 vols. (Lisbon: Agência-Geral do Ultramar, 1940–42, facsimile edition, 1972), 3: facing page.

11. For fuller details on logistics, see Thornton, "The Art of War," 369–71; Thornton, *Warfare*, 119–20. There is no useful description of logistics for the sixteenth century, and my argument is based on seventeenth-century evidence.

12. Heywood and Thornton, *Central Africans*, 60–61.

13. Italian translation of an untitled Portuguese chronicle of Rui de Pina, ca. 1492, written from the ship's book and six witnesses shortly after the return of the mission. It is published with a Portuguese translation in Carmen Radulet, ed. and trans., *O cronista Rui de Pina e a "Relação do reino do Congo." Manuscrito inédito do "Códice Riccardiano 1910"* (Lisbon: Comissão Nacional para as Comemorações dos Descobrimentos Portugueses, 1992), fols. fol. 98rb, 99rb (foliation of original ms); also the different material in de Pina's Portuguese chronicle of 1515, *Crónica del Rei D Joham Segundo . . .* , also in Radulet, *O cronista*, 152.

14. Despacho de Gonçalo Roiz . . . 1509, in Brásio, *Monumenta*, 4: 61.

15. Afonso to Manuel, 5 October 1514, in Brásio, *Monumenta*, 1: 312–13.

16. Filippo Pigafetta, *Relatione del reame di Congo et delle circonvicine contrade; tratta dalli scritti e ragionamenti di Odoardo Lopez portoghese* (Rome: Appresso Bartolomeo Grassi, 1591), 59–60. The origins of the "Jagas" and their relationship to Kongolese politics has been a long and contentious issue. See the summary in the long footnote by Michel Chandeigne in his new translation of *Pigafetta, Le royaume de Congo et les contrées environnantes (1591)* (Paris: Chandeigne UNESCO, 2002), 291–95.

17. Gouveia's epitaph gives his service in Kongo as five years (1571 to 1576) and places his death shortly after the end of the expedition, on September 24, 1577. See Esperança, *Historia Serafica* in *MMA* 3: 122. He certainly was still in Kongo in October 1575 and had left by November 1576, according to letters of Garcia Simões of 20 October 1575 and 7 November 1576, *MMA* 3: 142 and 146.

18. Pigafetta, *Relatione*, 61.

19. Sebastião I to Francisco de Gouveia, 19 March 1574, reproduced by the royal chronicler, Manuel dos Santos, in *Historia Sebastica* (Lisbon, 1735), 197–98, reprinted in *MMA* 3: 120. Similar language also can be found in Gouveia's epitaph in Lisbon in 1577, recorded in 1656 in da Esperança, *Historia Serafica* (Lisbon, 1656), part 1, pp. 245–46, reprinted in *MMA* 3: 121–22.

20. Garcia Simões letter of 7 November 1576, *MMA* 3: 146.

21. Álvaro to Garcia Simões, 27 August 1575, *MMA* 3: 127.

22. Reminiscences of Fernão de Sousa, 23 February 1632, *MMA* 8: 147. Given Sebastião's own commitment to expansion of the Portuguese empire, it is extremely unlikely that he did in fact refuse such an offer.

23. Pigafetta, *Relatione*, 62. The initial concession is confirmed by Garcia Simões to Luis Perpinhão, 7 November 1576, *MMA* 3: 145.

24. Background can be found in Heywood and Thornton, *Central Africans*, 49–102.

25. Baltasar de Castro to João III, 15 October 1526, *MMA* 1: 485–87; João III to Afonso, ca. 1529, *MMA* 1: 532; Saccardo, *Congo e Angola*, 1: 76–77, see also do Amaral, *O reino do Congo*, 75–82.

26. Inquest into trade of Angola, 7 May 1548, *MMA* 2: 197–205.

27. Saccardo, *Congo e Angola* 1: 79–82; do Amaral, *O reino do Congo*, 208–10.

28. Its text is in *MMA* 3: 36–51; for further context in the Portuguese world, see the study of do Amaral, *Consulado*, 49–72.

29. Pero Rodrigues, "Historia da residência dos Padres da Companhia de Jesus em Angola, e cousas tocantes ao reino, e conquista," May 1, 1594, *MMA* 4: 571.

30. Rodrigues, "Historia," *MMA* 4: 556, 577; Garcia Simões to Luis Perpinhão, 7 November 1576, *MMA* 3: 146 (an action in 1576); Baltasar Afonso letter, 9 October 1577, *MMA* 3: 157; Paulo Dias de Novais to Sebastião, 3 January 1578, *MMA* 4: 295–96 (refusing Álvaro's offer of 10,000 troops. He did accept the assistance of Portuguese residents in Kongo, who brought their own soldiers and a good number of private Kongo nobles. Garcia Simões to Provincial, 20 October 1575, *MMA* 3: 140–41.

31. Heywood and Thornton, *Central Africans*, 86–87.

32. Baltasar Afonso to Miguel de Sousa, 4 July 1581, *MMA* 3: 205; Baltasar Afonso to Sebastião de Morais, 31 January 1582, *MMA* 3: 208; Pigafetta, *Relatione*, 19–20, 22.

33. Heywood and Thornton, *Central Africans*, 87–88.

34. Rodrigues, "História," *MMA* 4: 574–76; letter to Gaspar Dias de Beja, March 1591, *MMA* 3: 423–24; Domingos de Abreu de Brito, "Svmario e descripção do reyno de Angola," 1591, fols. 33–35v, in *Um Inquérito à vida administrativa e económica de Angola e do Brasil*, ed. Alfredo de Albuquerque Felner (Coimbra: Imprensa da Universidade, 1931), 41–42 (this section also is reproduced in *MMA* 4: 533–35).

35. The documentation on this area does not, in my opinion, support any contention such as David Birmingham made in *Trade and Conflict in Angola*, 50–53, and elsewhere, that the Portuguese army was defeated by disease. Of course, it, like all armies, undoubtedly suffered serious losses from disease, but the battlefield record strongly points to military defeat as the source of many of its losses.

36. Thornton, "The Art of War."

37. Rodrigues, "Historia," *MMA* 4: 568–70.

38. Pierre du Jarric, *Histoire des choses les plus mémorables advenues tant es Indes Orientales . . .* , 3 vols. (Bordeaux: Simon Millanges, 1608–14), 2: 103.

39. Heywood and Thornton, *Central Africans*, 88–94.

40. Ibid., 93–98.

41. Samuel Purchas interviewed Battell and read his manuscript before 1614 and incorporated his work into a longer work, *Purchas His Pilgrimage* (London: Printed by William Stansby for Henrie Fetherstone, 1614). Then in 1625 Purchas published Battell's whole manuscript. E. G. Ravenstein published a critical edition of the two in *The Strange Adventures of Andrew Battell in Angola and Adjacent Regions* (London: Hakluyt Society, 1901).

42. Heywood and Thornton, *Central Africans*, 93–94.

43. Ibid., 117–24, 160.

44. Fernão de Sousa, "Lembrança," in *Fontes para a história de Angola*, ed. Beatrix Heintze, 2 vols. (Stuttgart: F. Steiner Verlag Wiesbaden, 1985–88), 1: 195.

45. Jesuits of Luanda to the Lord Collector of Portugal, 23 October 1623, *MMA* 15: 512–19. Other Jesuit letters provided less detailed accounts with a few variations. See Mateus Cardoso to Manuel Rodrigues, 1624, *MMA* 7: 291–97; and Mateus Cardoso, "Relação do que se passou em Angola no anno de 623 . . . ," *MMA* 7: 177–79.

46. António de Oliveira de Cadornega, *História geral das guerras angolanas (1680–1681)*, ed. Alves da Cunha and José Nattias Delgado, 3 vols. (Lisbon: Agência-Geral do Ultramar,

1940–42, reedited, Lisbon, 1972), 1: 105. Cadornega came to Angola in 1639 and was not himself a witness, but in this passage he cites the recollection of a participant, Francisco de Soveral, who gave him a detailed account as he recalled it.

47. Nationaal Archief Nederland (formerly Algemeen Rijksarchief), Staten Generaal, 5751, meeting of 27 October 1623.

48. Pedro II to Licenciado André de Morais Sarmento, 23 March 1623, *MMA* 7: 105–6.

49. This period is covered in great detail in Beatrix Heintze, "O fim de Ndongo como Estado independente," in *Angola nos séculos XVI e XVII*, ed. Beatrix Heintz (Luanda: Kilombelombe, 2007). An original German version of this article appeared in 1981, and a revised version without footnotes was published in 1994. This version is a translation with notes that includes the revisions.

50. Heintze, "O fim," 352–61.

51. Heywood and Thornton, *Central Africans*, 124–35.

52. Ibid., 145–52.

53. Cadornega, *História geral.*

54. Thornton, "The Art of War," 367; Thornton, *Warfare*, 120–24.

55. "Extract van seeckeren brief, gheschreven uyt Loando . . . (The Hague, 1648). This is in the collection Pamflet Knuttel 5780, published as an appendix in S. P. L'Honoré Naber, "Nota van Pieter Moortamer over het gewest Angola . . . ," *Bijdragen en mededeelingen van het Historisch Genootschap* 54 (1933): 41–42. See also Cadornega, *História geral*, 1: 498–500; and testimony taken on 30 August 1648 from Portuguese survivors, published in *Arquivos de Angola*, 2nd ser., 2 (1945): 149–64; see also Testimony of Pilot Manuel Soares, 11 November 1647, *MMA* 10: 69–70.

56. For a full background, see Charles R. Boxer, *Salvador de Sá and the Struggle for Brazil and Angola, 1602–1686* (London: University of London Press, 1952).

57. The Dutch perspective can be found in Klaas Ratelband, *Nederlanders in West-Afrika 1600–1650: Angola, Kongo en São Tomé,* ed. René Baesjou (Zutphen: Walburg Pers, 2000).

58. Cadornega, *História geral*, 2: 131–35.

59. Thornton, *Warfare*, 121–22, and map, xi.

60. Cadornega, *História geral*, 2: 266–85; Girolamo Merolla da Sorrento, *Breve e succinta relatione del viaggio nel Congo* (Naples: Per F. Mollo, 1692), 124–27.

61. José Curto, "A restituição de 10000 súbditos *ndongo* 'roubados' na Angola de meados do século XVII: uma análise preliminar," in *Escravatura e transformações culturais: África, Brasil, Caribe*, ed. Isabel Castro Henriques (Lisbon: Ed. Vulgata, 2002), 185–208.

62. Cadornega, *História geral*, 2: 298–325.

63. Arquivo Histórico Ultramarino (Lisbon) Caaixa 12, documento 71, João da Silva e Sousa to King, 18 March 1682; Luis Lobo da Silva to King, 25 November 1684, *MMA* 13: 582–86. The treaty is Capitulações de Paz, 6 September 1683, *MMA* 13: 542–43.

64. Silva Corrêa, *História*, 1: 363–66; AHU, Cx. 34, doc. 73, Devasa of Doutor Ouvidor geral e provedor da Fazenda Real Antonio Per.a Corte Real,18 March 1745; and its response, Biblioteca Publica de Évora, Códice CXVI/2-15, peça 14, fols. 40v–44, "Informação q. se da ao Sapientissimo Patrono do Cappam Mor de Campos.

65. For details of the events, see Saccardo, *Congo e Angola*, 2: 299–306.

Dutch Territory in Brazil, 1643.

8

The Opportunities and Limits of Ethnic Soldiering

The Tupis and the Dutch-Portuguese Struggle for the Southern Atlantic, 1630–1657

MARK MEUWESE

The Dutch colony in northeastern Brazil was governed by the West India Company (WIC) during the entire history of its brief existence from 1630 to 1654. The WIC depended on a strong navy and army to maintain its colony in South America. Without enormous investments in soldiers, ships, and weapons, the company would never have been able to wrest away the rich sugar provinces of northeastern Brazil from the Iberian powers, to which Brazil belonged as part of the Spanish-Portuguese Doublemonarchy from 1585 to 1640.

In addition to European company soldiers, however, the WIC greatly depended on indigenous allies in Brazil. Like the Portuguese, the Dutch identified two types of native peoples in Brazil.[1] One type included the autonomous indigenous communities that the Portuguese called "Tapuyas," a term used by the coastal Tupi-speaking peoples and referring to any natives speaking a non-Tupi language. The term Tapuyas covered a wide range of peoples, most of whom lived in the Sertão, the dry, rugged, and uncolonized backcountry of northeastern Brazil. The WIC viewed the Tapuyas as uncontrollable allies because of their nomadism and cannibalistic practices, so only in desperate circumstances did the company call on them as military allies.[2]

The other indigenous allies were the Tupi-speaking peoples who lived along the coast. The Dutch consistently called the various Tupi peoples "Brazilians," to distinguish them from the Tapuyas. The most prominent Tupi people who fought for the WIC were the Potiguares (shrimp people), who inhabited the coastal zone from Pernambuco to Rio Grande do Norte at the time of first contact with the Portuguese in the early sixteenth century. In contrast to the Tapuyas, the Potiguares were integrated into colonial society.

After the Potiguares and other Tupis had been defeated by the Portuguese at the end of the sixteenth century, they were concentrated in *aldeias*, mission villages established and run by Jesuits. In the *aldeias*, the Tupis received instruction in the principles of the Catholic faith as well as reading and writing.[3] Although the *indios aldeados*, the mission Amerindians, were legally free, many were used as a cheap labor force by the *moradores*, the Portuguese colonists. The Portuguese also recruited *indios aldeados* as military auxiliaries to fight hostile indigenous groups. Unlike the Tapuyas, the WIC regularly and on a large scale called on the military services of the Brazilians.

Although some historians, such as Evaldo Cabral de Mello, have examined the role of native allies of the Portuguese during the "Dutch wars," the significance of indigenous allies for the WIC in Brazil has so far received comparatively little attention.[4] Here I use the recently developed concept of "ethnic soldiering" to examine the widespread military participation of the Potiguares and other Tupi peoples on the side of the WIC in Brazil. *Ethnic soldiering* has been broadly defined as the military use of indigenous peoples by colonial powers. As defined in this book, however, the term refers more narrowly to those men recruited or persuaded to provide skills considered specific to their ethnicity or way of life.

Recruitment can take various forms (coercion, co-option, alliance, economic reward) but always applies to native peoples, using native skills, to enforce the colonial order. For example, in most of the European colonies in the American tropics, indigenous allies were recruited to track down runaway slaves, in order to prevent the emergence of a dangerous aboriginal alliance with African slaves. As described by ethnohistorian Neil Whitehead, at first the European powers only weakly controlled the process of ethnic soldiering but over time increased their influence over indigenous peoples. Ethnic soldiering served to intensify the native peoples' dependence on colonial administrations.[5] In what ways, then, did ethnic soldiering and its consequences apply to the Tupis/Potiguares? Did the Tupis/Potiguares become more dependent on the WIC by serving as military auxiliaries, or were they able to expand their political autonomy in return for military service?

Traditional Tupi Warfare

The basic unit of the Tupis' sociopolitical organization was the village. Each village, made up of several families, varied in size from several hundred to a few thousand residents. War played a central role in the Tupis' life. Although the independent Tupi villages frequently waged war on one another, sometimes they formed alliances. The primary motive for war was revenge; economic motives such as control over fisheries, hunting territories, agricultural fields, or paths were secondary. When warriors of one village inflicted casualties on an enemy village, the residents of the latter community were bound by honor to take revenge. Since no institution existed to regulate intervillage raids, this retaliatory warfare continued unabated. Moreover, for the village chiefs, warfare was an opportunity to strengthen their position and to forge unity in the community. Whenever enemies attacked a village, its chief called the community together and delivered a long speech, in which he reminded his audience of their ancestors' martial prowess. The talk then ended with a call to avenge the relatives who had been killed.[6]

Military raids were carried out according to long-standing practices. The number of warriors varied from a few dozen to several thousand. Attacks on enemy villages usually took place at night to take advantage of the element of surprise and to minimize the attacker's own casualties. Pitched battles took place on the fields or on the water in canoes. During expeditions traveling over long distances, women usually accompanied the men to carry supplies and prepare food. Some campaigns lasted for weeks, and others could stretch out for several months. The most common weapons were longbows and two-handed, oval wooden clubs that were sharpened at the top, a deadly weapon in close combat.[7]

One aspect of traditional Tupi warfare that shocked and intrigued European observers during the sixteenth century was their treatment of captives. Upon their return to the village, warriors exposed their captives to a series of public rituals, which included humiliation and torture. Women often participated in what were long and festive ceremonies. Afterward, the captives were integrated into the community as social inferiors, and after one year, they were executed in a ceremony attended by the entire village. After the execution, the bodies were cut up, and their parts were grilled and consumed by the community. By cannibalizing the victims in this way, the Tupis inflicted the ultimate form of revenge on their enemies.[8]

The Tupis' Militarization during the Portuguese Colonization

The Tupis underwent great changes as the Portuguese colonized northeastern Brazil during the sixteenth century, of which undoubtedly the most dramatic were caused by the infectious diseases introduced by Europeans and Africans. Through interactions with European colonists, African slaves, and imported cattle, diseases such as cholera, measles, and especially smallpox were transmitted to the indigenous Brazilians. Lacking either immunity or medical remedies, the Tupis' mortality rate was horrific.

Because outbreaks of deadly epidemics occurred frequently throughout the late sixteenth century, the Tupi communities were never able to recover demographically, Moreover, the number of epidemics increased when the European colonization of the region intensified. Although no exact numbers are available, from anecdotal European observations and comparative experiences with deadly epidemics among native peoples elsewhere in the Americas during the sixteenth century, disease probably reduced the coastal Tupi population by half by the end of the century.[9]

Despite the massive depopulation, the Tupi peoples remained essential trading partners and allies as well as military opponents of the Portuguese. After Pedro Álvares Cabral's discovery of Brazil in 1500, Portugal's interest in Brazil remained limited to the coastal trade in brazilwood, a reddish dyewood valued in Europe to color textiles. Portuguese merchants set up factories along the Brazilian coast where they exchanged iron tools for brazilwood harvested by Tupis. The profitable dyewood trade soon attracted competitors from the French maritime province of Normandy. The French obtained dyewood primarily through *truchements* (interpreters) who were dropped off by ships to live in native communities. In the 1530s, to reap more profits from Brazil and to keep out the Normandy-based traders, the Portuguese crown encouraged the private colonization of coastal Brazil, and sugarcane plants and skilled workers were imported from Madeira to develop a profitable cash crop. Although private colonization was largely unsuccessful due to widespread Tupi resistance, because the colonists required a workforce for their sugarcane plantations, the decision for permanent colonization set in motion a rapidly developing trade in Amerindian slaves. The Portuguese-French rivalries and the Amerindian slave trade destabilized the coastal Tupis. The Portuguese encouraged their Tupi trading partners to raid their traditional enemies, especially those allied with the French, in order to obtain captives for the slave trade. The Portuguese and the French then made the revenge wars even deadlier by introducing firearms, cannon, and metal-bladed weapons.[10]

During the second half of the sixteenth century, the Tupis faced even more aggressive Portuguese colonization efforts. In 1549, seeking to strengthen stability and pacify the coastal Amerindians, the Portuguese crown imposed royal control over the private colonies. Native groups who resisted colonization or remained allied with the French became the targets of ruthless Portuguese reprisals, which included the torching of villages, large-scale enslavement, and the killing of noncombatants. Beginning at the colonial capital of Salvador de Bahia in the Bay of All Saints, Portuguese military expeditions steadily pacified the captaincies, or provinces, of northeastern Brazil. But because Portuguese manpower remained limited, colonial officials recruited subjugated Tupi groups as military allies against hostile Amerindians and the French. Portuguese officials effectively used *mamelucos*, children born from liaisons between Tupi women and Portuguese men, to mobilize Tupi warriors against the French and hostile Amerindians. In this way, by 1600, the entire coast from Bahia to Cabo de São Roque in Rio Grande do Norte was brought under Portuguese control. The pacification of northeastern Brazil in turn opened the fertile coastal region for expansion of the sugar economy. As the indigenous population declined precipitously owing to epidemic diseases, resettlement, land loss, and the violent Portuguese campaigns, the indigenous labor force on the sugar plantations was gradually replaced by imported slaves from West Central Africa.[11]

The resistance and subjugation of the Potiguares illustrates the process of Portuguese pacification. As part of the dyewood trade, the Potiguares aligned themselves with the French, and during the last quarter of the sixteenth century, the Potiguares fiercely defended themselves against the Portuguese. But despite successful ambushes and French military aid, the Potiguares were ultimately defeated by ruthless and relentless Portuguese attacks. The Portuguese also persuaded defeated communities to attack those Potiguares who still were resisting. In 1585, the Portuguese defeated the Potiguares in the captaincy of Paraíba. After ten more years of intense fighting, in 1597 the Portuguese subjugated the Potiguares in the adjacent captaincy of Rio Grande do Norte. Whereas many Potiguares were sold as slaves, others were resettled in Jesuit mission villages across the northeast. The Portuguese used these *índios mansos* (tame Indians) as auxiliaries against hostile Amerindians, runaway African slaves, and European privateers. For example, during a Dutch maritime raid on Salvador in 1604, mission Amerindians ambushed Dutch sailors and soldiers who had landed in the Bay of All Saints.[12]

Besides the many defeated Tupi groups who became auxiliaries for the Portuguese, an unknown number of Potiguares sought refuge in the rugged interior of Brazil's northern coast. In this arid region, unsuitable for sugarcane, all the previous Portuguese colonization attempts had failed. Many Potiguares and other Tupi groups settled in the Serra de Ibiapaba, a mountainous area in the captaincy of Ceará, from where they continued to resist the Portuguese. Here the Potiguares also maintained their ties with French traders interested in dyewood as well as precious minerals believed to be located in Ceará. The lure of minerals, ongoing Tupi resistance, and the presence of French traders compelled the Portuguese to bring the northern coast of Brazil under control. Portuguese planters in the northeastern captaincies also were interested in pacifying Ceará to obtain Amerindian slaves for their sugar mills. Finally, Jesuit missionaries were attracted to northern Brazil to bring back mission Amerindians to the faith. Once again, successive Portuguese campaigns, supported by subjugated Potiguares warriors, defeated the Amerindian-French alliance. In 1615, the last French stronghold, on the island of Maranhão, was destroyed. After that, Portuguese colonization in the region was limited, although the Portuguese retained many Tupi and Tapuya groups until the Dutch colonization.[13]

From Reluctant to Loyal Allies, 1625–1635

During the late sixteenth century, Dutch merchants first became active in the Atlantic, when a growing number of Dutch vessels participated in the lucrative Brazilian sugar trade to Europe. Then, around 1600, through the sugar trade as well as Dutch shipping and trade in the Caribbean, a few Dutch merchants came in contact with the Tupi refugee groups on the northern coast of Brazil. In Ceará, Dutch traders exchanged ironware for dyewood with the Potiguares and other Amerindians, and some of the Dutch visitors also showed an interest in locating silver mines in the interior.[14]

In addition to trade, Dutch merchants and navigators also were interested in obtaining strategic intelligence from the indigenous peoples of northern Brazil. Because of the personal union of the Spanish and Portuguese monarchies in 1580/1581, the Dutch viewed Portuguese Brazil as a legitimate and lucrative target in their ongoing war for independence from Habsburg Spain. After Philip III (1578–1621), the king of Spain and Portugal, enforced the prohibition against Dutch ships visiting Iberian harbors after 1598, the Dutch organized several retaliatory expeditions against Iberian possessions in the Atlantic. As part of the preparation for a Dutch expedition against the rich sugar-growing region of northeastern Brazil, Dutch merchants in Ceará asked the coastal indigenous peoples about Portuguese defenses. This expedition, led by Paulus van Caerden, to damage the Brazilian sugar industry in 1604 likely used some of the intelligence gathered from Ceará Amerindians. The expedition largely failed, however, partly because the mission Amerindians in Bahia offered effective resistance. During the twelve-year truce between Spain and the Dutch Republic from 1609 to 1621, Dutch relations with indigenous Brazilians remained limited to the Amazon delta where merchants from the maritime province of Zeeland had established small tobacco plantations. These Dutch colonists, who rejected the truce and closely collaborated with English and Irish settlers, maintained close anti-Spanish commercial and diplomatic alliances with Carib-speaking native groups.[15]

After the founding of the West India Company (WIC) at the end of the twelve-year truce in 1621, the Dutch trade company made ambitious plans to capture the rich sugar provinces of northeastern Brazil, which included recruiting indigenous allies. Thanks to the earlier contacts between Dutch merchants and Amerindians in Ceará, the WIC rightly concluded that many native groups in Brazil strongly resented the Portuguese. In their search for native allies, the company directors also were influenced by the "black legend," which portrayed the aboriginal Americans as victims of Spanish tyranny. Several pamphlets circulating in the Republic called for establishing alliances with the Amerindians against Spain.[16]

Unfortunately, during the WIC's attempt in 1624 to capture Salvador de Bahia, the capital of colonial Brazil, the *índios aldeados* remained loyal to the Portuguese. The WIC had naively expected that the Portuguese settlers would welcome them as liberators from Spanish tyranny, but instead, the colonial population of Bahia fiercely defended itself against the Protestant invaders. In their resistance, the Portuguese colonists were greatly helped by the local mission Amerindians, who fought an effective guerrilla war against the WIC's invading army. Largely because of the indigenous guerrillas, the company soldiers were afraid to venture outside Salvador. Consequently, when a massive Spanish-Portuguese expedition reached the Bay of All Saints in April 1625, the Dutch garrison at Salvador de Bahia quickly surrendered.[17]

In contrast to the *índios aldeados* of Bahia, the Potiguares in the captaincy of Paraíba were eager to establish an alliance with the WIC. In the spring of 1625, a company fleet arrived too late in Bahia to reinforce the WIC garrison. Realizing that the Iberian forces had recaptured the city, the WIC commanders set sail to the Caribbean, but during an emergency stopover on the coast of Paraíba to care for the many sick sailors and soldiers, the WIC fleet was unexpectedly welcomed by local mission natives of the Potiguar nation. The recently conquered Potiguares exploited the unexpected arrival of more than thirty heavily armed WIC vessels as an opportunity to free themselves from Portuguese rule. To prevent misunderstandings and conflicts between the rowdy company personnel and the Potiguares, the senior commanders instructed all soldiers and sailors to maintain the friendship with the "Brazilians, our friends." Despite the huge cultural and linguistic differences, the WIC army and the Potiguares closely collaborated in several attacks on the Portuguese in Paraíba.[18]

The alliance between the Potiguares of Paraíba and the WIC fleet was nonetheless short lived. After a stay of only one month, the WIC fleet departed to attack Iberian targets in the Caribbean and West Africa. Although the commanders realized that their decision would expose the Potiguares to revenge attacks by the Portuguese, they cynically resolved to let "the Brazilians take care of themselves as much as possible." The Potiguares were shocked when they learned of the WIC commanders' decision to abandon them and pleaded with the company officers to allow them all to board the Dutch ships. But since the WIC fleet had only limited supplies and room, only a few Potiguares were taken on. The company officers simply instructed the rest of their native allies to escape from the Portuguese as best as they could. But shortly after the ships left Paraíba, the Portuguese forces arrived, aided by other Potiguares, who brutally subjugated the rebellious Potiguares. Most of the Amerindians in Paraíba who had aligned themselves with the Dutch were either killed or enslaved. Those Potiguares lucky enough to sail aboard the WIC ships eventually made their way to the Republic, where they were trained as interpreters and informants for a future WIC invasion of Brazil.[19]

After the spectacular WIC capture of the annual Spanish silver fleet in 1628, the company directors again prepared to attack the sugar provinces of northeastern Brazil. But instead of targeting Salvador again, the directors this time chose the province of Pernambuco as their main objective. Pernambuco had even more sugar mills than Bahia and was known to be weakly defended compared with Bahia. But just as during the earlier attack on Bahia, the WIC army occupying the coastal town of Olinda and the nearby harbor of Recife in early 1630 soon found itself confronted by an effective guerrilla force composed of Portuguese soldiers, settlers, and mission Amerindians. [20] The few Potiguar interpreters and informants accompanying the WIC army to Pernambuco were unable to mobilize native support for the Dutch. The first allies of the WIC in Pernambuco thus were not Amerindians but African slaves who offered their military service to the company in return for their liberty. These black auxiliaries were armed with bows and swords, and in addition to military tasks, the company officers used the free black militia to go outside Olinda and Recife to search for necessary food supplies.[21]

As long as the WIC army remained trapped inside Olinda and Recife, most of the mission Amerindians remained loyal to the Portuguese. The Potiguares from Paraíba and nearby Rio Grande also had not forgotten that the WIC had abandoned them in 1625. At the same time, the Potiguares and other Tupis occasionally dispatched messengers to the WIC in Pernambuco to learn more about the Dutch intentions.[22] Even after the WIC capture of the Portuguese Fort Reis Magos in Rio Grande in December 1633, most Potiguares in that captaincy were reluctant to support the Dutch.[23] The only exception was the successful coalition between the WIC and the Tarairius, a Tapuya people from the Sertão of Rio Grande. Led by their main chief,

Nhandui, the Tarairius were eager to join forces with the WIC against the Portuguese, who had often enslaved their people. The WIC officers, however, quickly came to view their the Tarairiu as problematic allies because they gave no quarter to women and children. Consequently, for most of the 1630s, the WIC did not call on the Tarairius to fight against the Portuguese.[24]

The Potiguares and other mission Amerindians accurately read the shift of fortunes and aligned themselves with the WIC after it became clear that the Dutch were likely to win. In December 1634, an amphibious WIC expedition captured the main coastal fort in Paraíba, effectively crippling Portuguese resistance north of Pernambuco. The WIC also established dominance over Brazilian coastal waters, which made it almost impossible for the Portuguese to receive military reinforcements from overseas. Worse yet, without trade goods from overseas, the Portuguese were unable to maintain their support of the mission Amerindians.[25]

Thanks to the mediation of a former Jesuit named Manuel de Morais, a large number of Tupis went over to the WIC's side. In January 1635, around sixteen hundred Tupi-speaking natives from Paraíba aligned themselves with the WIC.[26] In the same period, Potiguares from Rio Grande and the captaincy of Itamaracá also joined forces with the WIC against the Luso-Brazilian settlers. The only mission Amerindians who remained loyal to the Portuguese were several thousand mission natives from Pernambuco, most of whom relocated to Bahia together with the *moradores* in the summer of 1635. After these events, the Tupi allies in the WIC-controlled captaincies of Pernambuco, Itamaracá, Paraíba, and Rio Grande consisted of nearly 8,000 individuals, of whom around 2,500 could be used as military auxiliaries.[27] Since the number of WIC soldiers and sailors in Brazil in 1639 was estimated at 10,000, the number of "Brazilian" allies was clearly not unsubstantial. Moreover, they were less vulnerable than the company soldiers and sailors to the hot climate and the lack of a Western diet, and many of those 10,000 were often serving in the Caribbean or in Brazilian coastal waters. In this environment, the contribution of more than 2,000 experienced Tupi warriors was vital to the WIC's military well-being in Brazil.[28]

The WIC's Motives for Recruiting Tupi Allies

The WIC valued the Tupis as military auxiliaries for various reasons. As we have seen, the Potiguares and other subjugated Tupis of northeastern Brazil already had proved to be effective military forces for the Portuguese. When the first Tupis were deployed by the company in January 1635, the Dutch simply continued previous Portuguese policies. Furthermore, the "Brazilians" were not limited to fighting; they also provided key logistical services. According to Cuthbert Pudsey, an English soldier in company service during the 1630s,

> these Braselians we fynde them very usefull and wyllinge to helpe us, soometymes to make floates of Gyngall wood, to pass rivvers, and to carrie menns armes over drye, as alsoe upon occasion to cast up brest worke for our defence, to cut Pallazadoes, to carry of our hurt, and the like, all which they are ready to due without grudginge.[29]

Furthermore, unlike the Tarairius of the Sertão, who reportedly were fearful of firearms, the Tupis were familiar and considered expert with muskets, swords, and pikes.[30] According to Pudsey, the Tupis were "good musketears, bould and sharpe in execution." Zacharias Wagner, a German company servant, also noted that the "Brazilians" were experienced gunmen.[31] The number of European weapons used by the Tupi units fighting in company service was substantial. For example, on November 9, 1638, a company of 70 "Brazilians" commanded by the Tupi captain Panteleao Correia received 37 muskets, 30 pikes, and 65 swords from the WIC government in Brazil. And in at least one contemporary Dutch engraving, Tupi allies are depicted wearing ammunition belts while on campaign.[32]

Finally, the WIC sought out the "Brazilians" as military allies because of their reputation as fearless fighters. Company officials frequently remarked on the bravery of the Tupi warriors. According to Wagner, the "Brazilians" were loyal soldiers who attacked their enemies with intimidating yells. Although Adriaen van der Dussen, a senior company official in Brazil, was disappointed in the Tupis because they were not accustomed to the rigid discipline common in European armies, the "Brazilians" more than compensated for this by acting ferociously on the battlefield. According to van der Dussen, the "Brazilians" were particularly effective in pursuing an enemy whose ranks had been broken.[33]

"Brazilian" Auxiliaries and WIC Expansion in the South Atlantic, 1635–1642

Almost immediately after the "Brazilians" had aligned themselves with the Dutch, company officials deployed their new allies for military service. In January 1635, a unit of 220 Tupis from the mission village of São Miguel in Pernambuco was formed and utilized during a large-scale attack on enemy positions south of Recife.[34] After the *moradores* and their Tupi allies began a guerrilla war against the WIC in the captaincy of Sergipe and the Pernambuco district of Alagoas in early 1636, the company organized a mobile unit of 600 to 800 soldiers, sailors, and "Brazilians" to intercept the guerrillas.[35]

In 1637, the recently appointed Johan Maurits of Nassau arrived in Brazil as the governor-general of the WIC colony. The energetic German nobleman and experienced military commander had been appointed by WIC directors in the republic to complete the conquest of the sugar-growing provinces of northeastern Brazil. During his tenure in Brazil from 1637 to May 1644, Maurits regularly employed large units of "Brazilians" during company campaigns against the Iberian forces. In early 1637, six hundred Tupis participated in the company's capture of the strategic fort Porto Calvo in southern Pernambuco.[36] After the WIC had driven the guerrillas and Spanish Habsburg troops from Pernambuco and across the strategic São Francisco River, Maurits stationed several units of "Brazilians" along the wide waterway in January 1639 to prevent the Iberian enemy from crossing into company-controlled Brazil.[37] For several years, the São Francisco River functioned as a natural boundary between the Dutch colony and Portuguese Brazil. Around the same time, the Dutch mobilized a large number of Tupis to prevent the landing of a Spanish-Portuguese force in northeastern Brazil. Then after the Iberian fleet had been beaten back by WIC ships, the Tupis were sent back to their *aldeias*.[38]

During Maurits's tenure, the WIC also established military alliances with "Brazilians" in the northern peripheral captaincies of Ceará and Maranhão. After the Potiguares and other Tupi groups from Ceará learned about the WIC conquest of the northeastern captaincies, they sent envoys to Recife to persuade the company officials there to send an expedition against the isolated Portuguese fort São Sebastião in Ceará. After a WIC strike force captured the weakly defended fort in October 1637, the "Brazilians" from Ceará established an anti-Portuguese alliance with the WIC. As part of this coalition, several hundred Potiguares and other Tupi warriors fought on the company side against Iberian forces in Pernambuco in 1638. In April 1639, some 850 Tupi-fighters from Ceará were in the company service.[39]

The WIC also used Tupi auxiliaries during the Dutch conquest of Maranhão Island in November 1641. Because of informants and intercepted correspondence, company officials in Recife knew about the tense relationship between the Portuguese and the indigenous peoples, many of whom had been enslaved by the *moradores*. The WIC hoped that the "Brazilians" of Maranhão would help the company during a future Dutch invasion of the nearby Amazon delta. To persuade the native peoples of Maranhão to join the WIC side, its officers were instructed to ensure that Amerindian slavery was prohibited after the conquest of Maranhão. Following the successful conquest of Maranhão in November 1641, the WIC indeed did prohibit the enslavement of "Brazilians" in that captaincy.[40]

In a fascinating expansion of their usefulness, the native auxiliaries were occasionally deployed for overseas expeditions. In the spring of 1638, around a thousand "Brazilians" accompanied a large-scale amphibious WIC expedition against Salvador.[41] Several years later, in 1641, some 240 Tupis joined a company campaign against the Portuguese slave depot of Luanda in Angola. Gaining access to the West Central African slave trade was essential to the WIC to ensure the shipment of large numbers of forced laborers to Brazil's sugar mills. After the capture of Luanda, the Tupi contingent participated in the successful conquest of the Portuguese island colony São Tomé.[42]

Labor Services and Policing Tasks, 1642–1645

In December 1640, the Portuguese rebelled against Spanish Habsburg rule, reestablished an independent Portuguese monarchy, and concluded a fragile ten-year truce with the Dutch Republic in July 1641. Later the Portuguese even angled successfully for an anti-Spanish alliance with the Dutch. Although the Portuguese were infuriated about the recent WIC conquests in Maranhão, Luanda, and São Tomé—because they had taken place after the Dutch-Portuguese truce had already been agreed upon—the new Portuguese king, João IV, was reluctant to endanger the anti-Spanish alliance with the powerful Dutch Republic.[43]

When the truce went into effect in Brazil, the WIC quickly ended the deployment of the Tupi auxiliaries. Starting in 1641, a growing number of "Brazilians" were recruited for labor services in the sugar economy. Whereas the African slaves were used primarily to harvest and process sugarcane, the Tupis were commonly employed as cutters of firewood and dyewood, cattle drivers, and suppliers of food. In Ceará, the Dutch also recruited Amerindians as workers in the coastal salt pans.[44] The WIC government also encouraged the "Brazilians" to grow manioc, a traditional staple, as a cheap food crop for both the African slaves and the rest of the colonial population.[45] Because the company government worried that the growing use of indigenous workers could result in the exploitation and abuse of its Tupi allies, the WIC frequently issued ordinances prohibiting the enslavement of "Brazilians."[46] But the company government in Brazil occasionally fired servants who had abused their position as overseers in the *aldeias*, suggesting that the antislavery ordinances were ineffective. Corrupt WIC servants often hired out the Tupis under their command to colonists without compensating the Amerindians for their labor. Instead, the company officers kept for themselves the money intended for the "Brazilian" workers, and sometimes even the mission Amerindian leaders were accused of this practice.[47]

In the chaos brought about by the WIC's invasion of Brazil, the number of runaway African slaves had greatly increased. Because the African slaves were indispensable to the sugar economy, the WIC government was eager to track them down. Like the Portuguese, the Dutch relied on indigenous scouts to locate the runaway slave communities that had been established in various places in the hinterland of Pernambuco. In February 1638, the WIC government in Recife ordered that Tupis be armed with firearms to help find the *quilombos*, the runaway slave communities in southern Pernambuco.[48] The use of "Brazilians" as a police force intensified after the cessation of hostilities between the Portuguese and the Dutch in Brazil in 1641. In June 1641, "six qualified Brazilians" were hired by the *schout*, or chief law enforcement officer, in Paraíba to clear that captaincy of "all scoundrels, woodsmen, and negroes," a typical reference to runaway slaves.[49] A larger number of Tupis was used to attack and destroy the Palmares, the largest *quilombo* located in the hinterland of Pernambuco. The Palmares consisted largely of Angolan slaves as well as a number of former indigenous American slaves. In February 1644, at least fifty Tupi fighters participated in an expedition against the largest town of the Palmares, during which more than one hundred Africans were killed and seven "Brazilians" were captured. The presence of Tupis at the Palmares thus indicates that the relationship between the Tupis and Africans was not always antagonistic.[50]

Reasons for the Tupis to Serve as the WIC's Military Allies

The principal reason for the Tupi-speaking peoples to participate as the WIC's military allies was the importance of warfare in the Tupi culture. As we have seen, Tupi communities frequently fought with many of their neighbors before the European contact, and the Portuguese and French shrewdly exploited the Tupis' willingness to wage war. In this colonial context, participating in the WIC's campaigns was therefore a continuation of Tupi martial culture. Many of the Potiguares and other Tupis who sided with the Dutch most likely had previously fought on the side of the French. Furthermore, the Tupis may have been persuaded to support the Dutch after learning of the WIC policy to prohibit the enslavement of "Brazilians." In addition, the firing of corrupt company servants by the WIC government may have convinced many Tupis that the Dutch were different from the Portuguese.

At the same time, the "Brazilians" were willing to serve the WIC only if they received the same privileges they had while living under Portuguese rule. With the help of Portuguese defectors such as the Jesuit Manuel de Morais, the WIC quickly learned how to keep the Tupi leaders loyal. While the company ruled in Brazil, the WIC usually distributed prestigious gifts such as hats, swords, and shoes to the chiefs, whereas "ordinary" Tupis received *lijnwaet*, a type of linen very popular among the "Brazilians."[51] Based on advice from de Morais, WIC officials also relied on the observations of company servants who worked among the Tupis. In an official report about the situation in the recently conquered captaincy of Paraíba in 1635, the WIC official Servaes Carpentier described the ways in which the Portuguese used the Tupis as laborers. According to Carpentier, the Portuguese stationed a "Portuguese captain" in each *aldeia* to distribute the native workers to *moradores* and to ensure that the Tupis were adequately compensated. However, Carpentier noted that many of the Portuguese officers had angered the Tupis for withholding their income.[52]

By adequately compensating the "Brazilians" in both goods and Dutch money, the WIC were able to maintain the Tupis' support. Payment in money was apparently novel for the Tupis. According to the English soldier Pudsey, "the Portigezes never lett them [the Tupis] knowe mooney, which at our arrival heare they weere altogeather Ignorant of the knowledge of yt. But now they know yt very well, and also the use of yt."[53] Tupi officers also earned more than "ordinary" Tupis. The payments for the 240 Tupis who participated in the WIC expedition to Luanda in 1641 reveal the different levels of compensation. In total, three companies of "Brazilians" participated in the transatlantic campaign. The three Tupi army captains earned thirty Dutch guilders per month of service, and the three Tupi sergeants received ten guilders each per month. Each company had one lieutenant and one ensign who, respectively, earned twenty and fifteen guilders. Foot soldiers received only four guilders per month.[54]

Indigenous women who participated in the WIC campaigns were compensated for their services as well. Tupi women often joined their husbands to carry supplies and to prepare food, a long-standing practice that was continued by the "Brazilians" fighting with the WIC. For example, of the one thousand Tupis who participated in the WIC attack on Salvador in 1638, three hundred to four hundred were women. During this campaign, the "Brazilian" women carried hammocks and other materials deemed essential by the Tupis.[55] Another reason that many women and children often accompanied their men was the inherently dangerous situation in northeastern Brazil during the 1630s and 1640s. That is, the Portuguese and indigenous guerrillas threatened not only the WIC but also the mission Amerindians who had allied with the company. Indeed, Wagner, the German company servant, observed that many mission villages were completely abandoned during the WIC expeditions.[56]

Although the company consistently compensated the Tupi women for their services, they always were paid less than the men. In June 1637, male warriors from an *aldeia* in Pernambuco received five *ellen* of *lijnwaet* per person (about 3.5 meters). In contrast, Tupi women from the same *aldeia* were paid only four *ellen* of the same linen.[57] Sometimes "Brazilian" women received their salary through their husbands, though the WIC government distinguished between married and single Tupis. Married couples received a higher salary than single Tupis, and women whose husbands had died while on campaign often were paid the salary of their deceased spouses.[58] Finally, indigenous auxiliaries received about half what European soldiers were paid,[59] which was typical for the lower social status assigned to non-Europeans in a European colony.

The Tupis were willing not only to fight on behalf of the WIC for material benefit but also to maintain and expand their political autonomy. The WIC accommodated the Tupis by keeping intact the system of *aldeia* chiefs. These individuals had been the spokesmen for their people during the period of Portuguese rule. Like the Portuguese, the WIC also appointed individual company servants who functioned as overseers of the mission villages. Then when an *aldeia* was mobilized for military service, the indigenous chief and the company official acted as military commanders.[60] The company government in Brazil tried to bind the *aldeia* chiefs to them by frequently distributing prestigious gifts such as hats and shoes. Johan Maurits also occasionally assembled all the indigenous mission village chiefs to strengthen the alliance between the company and the Tupi peoples. In July 1639, one such council took place during which Maurits succeeded in getting the chiefs to swear an oath of loyalty to the company. After Maurits's speech, the Tupi spokesmen declared themselves as Maurits's "brothers" who were willing to live and die for the company. The kinship analogy used by the Tupi leaders clearly indicated that they viewed themselves as equals in the relationship with the Dutch. As a reward for their obvious loyalty, Maurits presented each chief with a set of clothes.[61]

Because the Tupi leaders clearly felt themselves equal to the Dutch colonial officials, the "Brazilian" captains were not afraid to openly criticize Maurits and the WIC government. In turn, the Dutch colonial officials took the complaints seriously because they were rightly concerned that the Tupis would end the alliance. For example, in October 1638, Maurits and the WIC government fired a certain James Wouts from his position as liaison officer at the mission village of Japipe in Rio Grande. The main motive for the firing of Wouts was an unspecified number of complaints from the "Brazilians" that the WIC government had received. Most likely, Wouts had abused his position by withholding the salaries of Tupi workers who had been hired out to *moradores*.[62] Moreover, in late June 1641, all company agents stationed in the *aldeias* of Rio Grande were replaced by "persons of their own nation, who will serve better" than the European liaison officers, who "are only interested in exploiting the Brazilians for their private purposes."[63]

The WIC government also intervened to assert control over the indigenous leaders. In February 1642, when the Tupi chiefs in Rio Grande revived communal feasts and celebrations during which the "Brazilians" drank large amounts of alcohol made from fermented cashew nuts, Dutch colonial officials restored the presence of company officials in the mission villages of Rio Grande. In addition, Tupi leaders suspected of collaborating with the Portuguese were ruthlessly and swiftly dealt with. In 1639, Maurits banished and then had the Tupi chief Pantaleão Correia drowned after he refused to mobilize his followers when Pernambuco was threatened by the landing of a large Iberian fleet.[64]

The occasionally tense relationship between the Tupis and the WIC deteriorated when the "Brazilians" were struck by a deadly smallpox epidemic during the winter of 1641/1642. In 1635, the Tupi population of the Pernambuco, Itamaracá, Paraíba, and Rio Grande captaincies had been 8,000, but by 1645, their number had fallen to 3,500.[65] Moreover, the Tupis' participation in the WIC campaign against Luanda and São Tomé in 1641 had been a disaster for the "Brazilians." Of the 250 Tupis who began the transatlantic expedition, only 100 returned alive. Most of the others had died of tropical diseases in West Africa. When the surviving Tupis returned to Recife in January 1642, Tupi leaders complained to the WIC government about the heavy losses. Alarmed by both the high mortality and the complaint, Maurits convened an emergency meeting with forty-two "Brazilian" chiefs in March 1642 to assuage their grief and concerns, and at the end of the meeting, Maurits distributed shirts for the chiefs and linen for their wives.[66]

When the Portuguese-Dutch truce of the early 1640s appeared to take hold, the WIC decided to grant more political autonomy to their Tupi allies. This decision also was shaped by a fear of losing the Amerindians' vital support. In October 1642, however, a rebellion broke out among the *moradores* and the mission Amerindians of Maranhão against the WIC's rule. After local company officials failed to improve the situation, the Tupis from Maranhão realigned themselves with the Portuguese. Although the WIC garrison of Maranhão was able to defend itself for more than two years, in January 1644 the beleaguered and isolated company soldiers evacuated their coastal fort. Likewise, in the winter of 1643/1644, the Tupis and Tapuyas of Ceará rose up against the WIC. Dutch officials were initially bewildered by the uprising, but most likely, WIC personnel in Ceará had violated the WIC policy to not enslave Amerindians.

Because of the Amerindian revolts in Ceará and Maranhão, the directors of the WIC in the republic granted significant political and legal autonomy to the "Brazilians" in November 1644. A delegation of Tupi chiefs visited the Republic to receive a formal letter from the company directors, outlining their privileges and rights in the Dutch colony. The letter emphasized that all "Brazilians" were free subjects of the WIC. In a special meeting held in Pernambuco in the spring of 1645, Tupi delegates selected from a previously submitted list to the WIC government their own officials to serve as *regidores* (magistrates) and judicial officers.[67]

Abandoned Allies, 1645–1656

The WIC government's hope for a stable relationship with the Tupis after granting them more autonomy in April 1645 never materialized. Instead, the government faced a rebellion by *moradores* three months later in Pernambuco and the rest of the territories under company rule. Many Portuguese sugar planters had accumulated large debts by buying imported African slaves on credit from the WIC, and by seeking to liberate themselves from the company through force, the indebted settlers hoped to pay off their debts. Moreover, most Catholic settlers resented the Protestant Dutch invaders. The *moradores* were encouraged and aided by Antonio Telles da Silva, the governor of Portuguese Brazil based in Salvador. Da Silva supplied the *moradores* with weapons and fighters, including an effective contingent of Potiguar warriors led by Filipe Camarão, as well as a group of free blacks commanded by the Angolan leader Henrique Diaz.

Soon after Johan Maurits had departed for the republic in May 1644, plans for the revolt began. The rebels also were inspired by the successful uprising against the WIC in Maranhão, which had ended with the withdrawal of the company garrison from that captaincy in January 1644. The Portuguese king,

João IV, approved the rebellion, although he was careful to avoid a war with the Dutch in Europe. At any rate, as they still were involved in a serious war for independence against Spain, Portugal lacked the military and financial resources to actively assist the rebels in Pernambuco. Despite these weaknesses, however, the rebellion quickly proved successful because the WIC government had drastically reduced the company army after 1642 in order to cut expenses. Moreover, the company soldiers' morale suffered, as the financially struggling WIC was often unable and unwilling to pay their salaries, and the WIC garrisons already were seriously undermanned when the rebellion broke out in the summer of 1645.[68]

In this desperate situation, the Tupi allies became indispensable to the WIC in its fight against the rebels. The Dutch even called on the Tarairius from Rio Grande. But the Tarairius embarrassed the company government by massacring almost the entire population, including the local priest, of the village of Cunhaú in Rio Grande. The massacre at Cunhaú angered the *moradores* and resulted in revenge killings by the rebels. In August 1645, one month after the bloodbath at Cunhaú, rebels led by Andre Vidal de Negreiros forced the surrender of a WIC fort at Serinhaem in Pernambuco. Although the company soldiers were spared, Vidal ordered the hanging of thirty-three Tupi auxiliaries also stationed at the fort. As a public warning to other "Brazilian" allies of the WIC, the thirty-three bodies were strung up on the fort's palisades. In addition, the Portuguese rebels divided up the spouses and children of the Tupi men as slaves for themselves. Although WIC officials later protested the treatment of their Tupi allies, Vidal responded that the Tupis were treated harshly because they had rebelled against the Portuguese crown. To retaliate for the mass hanging of their kinsmen at Serinhaem, Potiguares, led by the Tupi *regidor* Anthonio Paraupaba, joined forces with the Tarairius to kill *moradores*. In early October 1645, this multiethnic indigenous force, supported by some WIC soldiers, executed around fifteen unarmed settlers in Uruacu in Rio Grande. Paraupaba even proposed forming a permanent anti-Portuguese alliance with the Tarairius, but the latter retreated into the backcountry where they continued their nomadic subsistence pattern.[69]

For the "Brazilians," the rebellion of the Portuguese settlers had now become a struggle to preserve Amerindian rights and freedoms. After the massacre at Serinhaem, the Tupis not surprisingly fought fiercely and loyally alongside WIC soldiers. The desperate Tupis were good fighters. For example, in the winter of 1645/1646, one "Brazilian" company, under the command of the *regidor* Pieter Poty, defeated a larger force of rebels at an abandoned mission village in Paraíba. Poty and his men reportedly killed twenty rebels without suffering any fatalities themselves. The Tupis also sheltered their women, children, and elders in the vicinity of or inside the coastal WIC forts to better protect them from the rebels. Other Tupis sought a safe haven on the small island of Itamaracá, and by the fall of 1645, around 1,500 "Brazilians" were living on the island, and food soon was running short.

Despite the dire circumstances for the Tupi allies of the Dutch, attempts by the pro-Portuguese Potiguar leader Filipe Camarão to persuade the Potiguares fighting on the side of the WIC to switch sides were counterproductive. Between March 1645 and August 1646, Camarão and some other chiefs tried to convince Pieter Poty, a cousin of Camarão, to go over to the rebels' side. Camarão and the other natives sent a large number of letters written in the Tupi language to Poty. Despite the literary offensive, Poty refused all offers. On October 31, 1645, Poty finally wrote back a lengthy letter to Camarão, in which he reminded Camarão of the recent atrocity committed by the Portuguese at Serinhaem. Poty also expressed confidence that the WIC would eventually prevail because he had been to the republic as a young man, where he had seen for himself the naval power of the Dutch.[70]

Despite Poty's optimism, the situation in northeastern Brazil deteriorated for the WIC and their Tupi allies, and by December 1645, the rebels firmly controlled the countryside of the four northeastern captaincies. The WIC and the Tupis were able to hold on to only a few coastal areas, including Recife and several other fortified harbors. Many other company forts had been surrendered by WIC officers who had deserted to the Portuguese side. To make matters worse, the WIC was unable to send adequate reinforcements to Brazil. The inability to supply military aid to the beleaguered Brazilian colony was caused partly caused by the company's dismal financial situation and partly by a conflict among the States General, Dutch investors, and the WIC over the renewal of the company's charter in 1645. Only with the financial assistance of the States General did small military reinforcements reach Recife in 1646. Between 1646 and 1648, to alleviate the impoverished conditions among the Tupis and to bind the "Brazilians" closer to them, company officials sometimes distributed cloth to destitute Tupis. The textiles had been collected by Reformed Church organizations in the Dutch Republic as a form of Christian charity for the "poor Brazilians." Most of the recipients were Tupi women and children, many of whom had lost their husbands and fathers in the rebellion.[71]

The WIC's position appeared to improve with the arrival of a large fleet and army in Recife in early 1648. This task force had been sent out by the States General and partially financed by the prosperous Dutch East India

Company to stave off a merger with the bankrupt WIC. In March 1648, most of the ships of the relief expedition, led by Admiral Witte de With, finally reached Recife. They quickly decided to attack the rebel army outside the city. But this was an unwise decision, since many of the recently arrived soldiers were weakened from the Atlantic crossing and were unaccustomed to the hot Brazilian climate. To make matters worse, morale was low because the WIC government still was unable to pay the soldiers' salaries.[72]

Despite these serious problems, the WIC army marched out of Recife in mid-April 1648. The army consisted of 4,500 soldiers, including 150 Tarairius and an unidentified number of "Brazilians." The expedition began fortuitously as the Tarairius, fighting as a separate unit, annihilated a forward rebel position. On April 19, the WIC army finally confronted some 2,500 rebels, including Camarão and his Potiguares. The company then lost an opportunity to deliver a decisive blow against the numerically inferior rebels. But the battle-hardened rebels stood their ground and forced the inexperienced company force to retreat to Recife. A major blow to the rebels, however, was the sudden death of the loyal Potiguar chief Camarão several days after this First Battle of Guararapes, presumably from an illness. The rebels gave the Potiguar chief a solemn Catholic burial and financial support for his immediate family.[73]

Despite the inconclusive battle at Guararapes, the WIC army and its "Brazilian" allies remained confident of a military victory. Dutch privateers crippled Portuguese shipping in the Southern Atlantic, preventing the rebels from receiving much needed reinforcements. The privateers also intercepted most of the sugar ships sent from Brazil to Portugal, effectively undermining the financing of the rebellion. On the winter of 1648/1649, however, the WIC soldiers' morale rose after a successful Dutch raid against the *reconcavo*, the sugar-growing district in the Bay of All Saints. By February 1649 the High Council and the senior army commanders were so confident that they launched a new attack against the main rebel army outside Recife. However, the Second Battle of Guararapes, on February 18, 1649, was a disaster for the Dutch. Out of an army of 3,500 men, the WIC suffered more than 950 casualties, including many officers. The battle also proved catastrophic for the Tupis, because their leader Poty was captured. The rebels had hoped to persuade Poty to switch to the Portuguese side, but Poty refused and the frustrated rebels exiled him to Portugal. During the Atlantic crossing, Poty died, most likely from torture.[74]

In the deteriorating military situation, relations between the WIC and the Tupis grew tense. In March 1648, Paraupaba, one of the two surviving Brazilian *regidores*, clashed with the colonial government in March 1648 over whether to contact the Tupis in Ceará. When Paraupaba met Michiel van Goch, a member of the colonial government, in Paraíba in March 1648, the Potiguar chief offered to travel to Ceará and bring with him a large number of Potiguares to help fight the rebels. Paraupaba asked Van Goch to supply him with diplomatic presents so that he could show the Potiguares in Ceará that the WIC had good intentions. Although the WIC was sorely in need of military support, Van Goch rejected Paraupaba's proposal. Company officials apparently still distrusted the indigenous people in Ceará because of the native uprising against the WIC in that frontier province in 1644.[75]

The alliance became more strained after WIC officials openly conflicted with two of the most senior Brazilian leaders. In the fall of 1649, Johannes Listrij, the "director of Brazilians" who was responsible for overseeing the "Brazilians," reported the murder of a junior Tupi officer by Domingos Fernandes Carapeba. Like Poty and Paraupaba, Carapeba had been appointed by Listrij in April 1645 as one of the three Tupi *regidores*. Because the murder caused unrest among the Tupis under Carapeba's command, the colonial government ordered Carapeba to be tried by the company army's military court. The military court found Carapeba guilty of homicide and formally sentenced him to death. But since the Dutch officials were rightfully concerned about the reaction of the "Brazilians" to the execution of one of their leaders by the company, the Recife councillors instead banished Carapeba to the islands of Fernando de Noronha off the coast of Rio Grande.[76]

Three years later, another incident between the WIC and the Brazilian leaders laid bare the alliance's weakness. In July 1652, Paraupaba openly challenged the WIC's authority when company officials attempted to execute three Potiguares from Rio Grande for the murder of several "Tapuyas." Company officials viewed the killing of the Tapuyas as a serious crime because these natives were also allied with the Dutch. Since the High Council attempted to maintain alliances with as many indigenous peoples as possible in the war against the rebels, the murder of several Tapuyas by the Potiguares threatened the system of strategic alliances that the WIC had carefully built in Brazil. The Recife councillors viewed the Potiguares suspects as subservient auxiliaries subject to Dutch colonial law. Paraupaba, however, considered the Dutch attempts to sentence his kinsmen as an infringement on Potiguares autonomy. To emphasize the seriousness of the crime, company officials sentenced the three suspects to death. But right before the public execution was to take place at fort Ceulen, Paraupaba protested. He threatened colonial officials by saying that "a state of hostility would exist between them [the

Potiguares] and our nation" if the Dutch proceeded with the execution. After intervention by a colonial interpreter who personally knew Paraupaba, the indigenous leader backed down. Paraupaba ultimately did not want to disrupt the alliance with the WIC during the life-and-death struggle against the Portuguese.[77]

After the disastrous Second Battle of Guararapes in 1649, people in the Dutch Republic realized that the WIC's colony in Brazil was doomed. Only a minority in the States General still wanted to send more troops and ships to Brazil. When the first Anglo-Dutch War (1652–1654) broke out, the States General shifted most of its attention to the war against the English. While the Dutch were preoccupied in the North Sea, the Portuguese king João IV quickly assembled a fleet and an army to capture Recife. After a month-long siege, the demoralized WIC government in Recife formally capitulated to the Portuguese on January 26, 1654. In the treaty of surrender, the Dutch officially handed over to the Portuguese all their remaining company possessions in Brazil.

The "Brazilians" did not trust the Portuguese promise made to Dutch officials to treat the indigenous allies of the WIC with respect. As the news of the WIC capitulation spread across northeastern Brazil, the Tupi auxiliaries of the Dutch sought refuge from the Portuguese in the northern province of Ceará. In the spring of 1654, Paraupaba and Carapeba, the two surviving Tupi *regidores*, traveled to the republic in WIC ships in order to convince Dutch officials to send military aid to their people in Ceará. The two indigenous leaders received a formal welcome from Dutch officials. With the help of WIC officials who had served in Brazil, Paraupaba petitioned the States General for military aid in 1654 and 1656, but it did not grant either of his requests. The WIC was no longer financially able to afford any support, and not many people in the republic were interested in reviving the costly and failed adventure in Brazil. Although a few Dutch vessels may have reached Ceará with supplies after 1654, the Dutch state was unwilling to provide any substantial aid to the beleaguered Tupis. With the WIC gone from Brazil, the Portuguese unleashed a war of revenge against the indigenous peoples who had sided with the Dutch. It nevertheless took the Portuguese several decades to bring northern Brazil under control, owing to the effective indigenous resistance and the Portuguese lack of resources. After Paraupaba died in exile in the republic in 1656, Carapeba was hired by the WIC in 1657 to travel to Tobago where the company was attempting to establish an island colony. It is unknown whether Carapeba ever reached his destination.[78]

Conclusion

From 1635 to 1654 the Tupis functioned as loyal and valuable military allies of the WIC in northeastern Brazil. In one sense, the Tupis did not serve as "ethnic soldiers" recruited by the WIC because of their specialized military skills. Instead, the colonized Tupis were sought out as allies because of their numerical strength and their familiarity with European weapons. The "wild" Tarairius functioned more as traditional ethnic soldiers owing to their perceived savagery. Since the Tupis had already been partially integrated in colonial society by the time of the Dutch invasion of Brazil, they can be more properly defined as hybrid military allies, combining the exotic identity of ethnic soldiers with the regulated character of colonial auxiliaries. The hybrid nature of the Tupi allies was also reflected in the Tupis' motives to serve as fighters for the Dutch. On the one hand, by aligning themselves with the WIC, Tupi men were able to preserve the indigenous culture of warfare, which played a central role in Tupi manhood. At the same time, the Tupis were already accustomed to serve in colonial wars by the time of the Dutch invasion of northeastern Brazil in 1630. Moreover, the "Brazilians" were willing to fight for the WIC as long as they were adequately paid and received political autonomy. Because the Tupis could provide a large number of effective warriors, the WIC was willing to accede to their demands.

The WIC's fear of losing their "Brazilian" allies gave the Tupis an opportunity to strengthen their position in the colonial society. During Dutch colonial rule in Brazil, the Tupis' political autonomy *increased* rather than decreased. The most dramatic evidence for this assertion is the company's policy of granting formal political and legal autonomy to the "Brazilians" in 1644/1645. In the case of the Tupis of seventeenth-century Brazil, "ethnic soldiering" did not result in the indigenous people's decline.

At the same time, the relatively privileged status of the Tupis in Dutch colonial society was dependent on the WIC's willingness to maintain its colony in Brazil. After the States General no longer was willing to support the bankrupt company, it was only a matter of time before the WIC would withdraw from Brazil. Following the WIC's surrender of Brazil in January 1654, the Tupi allies were suddenly abandoned by their Dutch allies. The rise and fall of the Tupis as Dutch allies demonstrates the limited role of indigenous peoples in European imperial rivalries. While European colonizers could always withdraw from overseas adventures without facing major consequences, indigenous peoples caught up in an imperial conflict did not have this choice.

1. John M. Monteiro, "The Crises and Transformations of Invaded Societies: Coastal Brazil in the Sixteenth Century," in *The Cambridge History of the Native Peoples of the Americas*, vol. 3, part 1, *South America*, ed. Frank Salomon and Stuart B. Schwartz (New York: Cambridge University Press, 1999), 974.

2. Ernst van den Boogaart, "Infernal Allies: The Dutch West India Company and the Tarairiu, 1630–1654," in *Johan Maurits van Nassau-Siegen: A Humanist Prince in Europe and Brazil*, ed. Van den Boogaart (The Hague: Johan Maurits van Nassau Stichting, 1979), 519–38.

3. Alida Metcalf, *Go-Betweens and the Colonization of Brazil, 1500–1600* (Austin: University of Texas Press, 2005); F. L. Schalkwijk, *The Dutch Reformed Church in Brazil (1630–1654)* (Zoetermeer: Boekencentrum, 1998), 48.

4. Eval Cabral de Mello, *Olinda Restaurada: Guerra e açucar no nordeste, 1630–1654* (São Paulo: Editoria 34, 1975).

5. Neil L. Whitehead, "Carib Ethnic Soldiering in Venezuela, the Guianas, and Antilles, 1492–1820," *Ethnohistory* 37 (1990): 357–85. See also Stuart B. Schwartz and Frank Salomon, "New Peoples and New Kinds of People: Adaptation, Readjustment, and Ethnogenesis in South American Indigenous Societies (Colonial Era)," in *The Cambridge History of the Native Peoples of the Americas*, vol. 3, part 2, *South America* (New York: Cambridge University Press, 1999), 448–52; Stuart B. Schwartz and Hal Langfur, "*Tapanhuns, Negros da Terra*, and *Curibocas*; Common Cause and Confrontation between Blacks and Natives in Colonial Brazil," in *Beyond Black and Red: African-Native Relations in Colonial Latin America*, ed. Matthew Restall (Albuquerque: University of New Mexico Press, 2005), 85–93. A further discussion of "ethnic soldiering" appears in the introduction to this volume.

6. William Balee, "The Ecology of Ancient Tupi Warfare," in *Warfare, Culture, and Environment*, ed. R. Brian Ferguson (Orlando, FL: Academic Press, 1984), 241–65; Monteiro, "The Crises and Transformations of Invaded Societies," 986–88.

7. Alfred Métraux, "The Tupinamba," in *Handbook of South American Indians*, vol. 3, *The Tropical Forest Tribes*, ed. Julian H. Steward (Washington, DC: Smithsonian Institution Press, 1946), 119–26; Balee, "The Ecology of Ancient Tupi Warfare," 253–55.

8. Monteiro, "The Crises and Transformations of Invaded Societies," 986–99; Metcalf, *Go-Betweens*, 72–73.

9. Metcalf, *Go-Betweens*, 119–55.

10. Monteiro, "The Crises and Transformations of Invaded Societies," 990–95; Metcalf, *Go-Betweens*, 55–88. On the French in Brazil, see Olive Patricia Dickason, "The Brazilian Connection: A Look at the Origin of French Techniques for Trading with Amerindians," in *Rendezvous: Selected Papers of the Fourth North American Fur Trade Conference, 1981*, ed. Thomas C. Buckley (St. Paul: North American Fur Trade Conference, 1984), 27–42.

11. Monteiro, "The Crises and Transformations of Invaded Societies," 996–1009.

12. John Hemming, *Red Gold: The Conquest of the Brazilian Indians, 1500–1760* (Cambridge, MA: Harvard University Press, 1978), 161–82, esp. 164; João Capistrano de Abreu, *Chapters of Brazil's Colonial History, 1500–1800*, trans. Arthur Brakel (New York: Oxford University Press, 1997), 52–57; *Dialogues of the Great Things of Brazil*, attributed to Ambrósio Fernandes Brandão (1618), trans. and ed. Frederick Arthur Holden Hall, William F. Harrison, and Dorothy Winters Welker (Albuquerque: University of New Mexico

Press, 1987), 31–33. For the use of subjugated Potiguares against hostile natives and runaway slaves, see Schwartz and Langfur, "*Tapanhuns, Negros da Terra*, and *Curibocas*," 91. For Amerindian attacks against Dutch privateers in Bahia in 1604, see J. W. IJzerman, ed., *Journael van de reis naar Zuid-Amerika (1598–1601) door Hendrik Ottsen*, LV 16 (The Hague: Nijhoff, 1918), app. 12 ("De expeditie naar het westen onder Paulus van Caerden,"), 204–7.

13. Monteiro, "The Crises and Transformations of Invaded Societies," 1010–11; Capistrano de Abreu, *Chapters of Brazil's Colonial History*, 57–58; Rita Krommen, *Mathias Beck und die Westindischen Kompagnie. Zur Herrschaft der Niederländer im Kolonialen Ceará*, Arbeitspapiere zur Lateinamerikaforschung II-01 (Cologne: University of Cologne Press, 2001), available at http: //www.uni.-koeln.de/phil-fak/aspla, 16–17; Mathias C. Kienen, "The Indian Policy of Portugal in the Amazon Region, 1614–1693" (PhD diss., Catholic University of America, 1954), 9–10.

14. For the Dutch in sugar trade, see Christopher Ebert, "Dutch trade with Brazil before the Dutch West India Company, 1587–1621," in *Riches from Atlantic Commerce: Dutch Transatlantic Trade and Shipping, 1585–1817*, ed. Johannes Postma and Victor Enthoven (Leiden: Brill, 2004), 59–75. For the Dutch expeditions to Ceará around 1600, see Hessel Gerritsz, "Journeaux et nouvelles tirées de la bouche de marins holandais et portugais de la navigation aux Antilles et sur les côtes du Brésil," trans. E. J. Bondam, *Annais da bibliotheca nacional do Rio de Janeiro* 29 (1907): 158–70; Ernst van den Boogaart and Rebecca Parker Brienen, *Information from Ceará from Georg Marcgraf (June–August 1639)*, vol. 1, *Dutch Brazil* (Petropolis: Editoria Index, 2002), 33–38.

15. Henk den Heijer, *De geschiedenis van de WIC* (Zutphen: Walburg, 1994), 23; Ivo van Loo, "For Freedom and Fortune: The Rise of Dutch Privateering in the First Half of the Dutch Revolt, 1568–1609," in *Exercise of Arms: Warfare in the Netherlands, 1568–1648*, ed. Marco van der Hoeven (Leiden: Brill, 1997), 172–95; Joyce Lorimer, *English and Irish Settlements on the River Amazon, 1550–1646* (London: Hakluyt Society, 1989), 50–59.

16. For the role of anti-Spanish propaganda and the link between the Dutch rebels against Spain and the indigenous Americans, see Benjamin Schmidt, *Innocence Abroad: The Dutch Imagination and the New World, 1570–1670* (New York: Cambridge University Press, 2001), 68–122.

17. Henk den Heijer, "Bewindhebbers, gouverneurs en raden van bestuur (het bestuur van de West-Indische Compagnie in de Republiek en Brazilië)," in *Brazilië in de Nederlandse archieven (1624–1654): De West-Indische Compagnie; overgekomen brieven en papieren uit Brazilië en Curaçao*, ed. Marianne L. Wiessebron (Leiden: Research School CNWS, 2005), 29–30.

18. S. P. L'Honoré Naber, ed., *Het Iaerlyck verhael van Joannes de Laet, 1624–1636*, Linschoten-Vereeniging 34) (The Hague: Nijhoff, 1931), vol. 1, 85–92 (including quotation).

19. Den Heijer, *De geschiedenis van de WIC*, 57–59; L'Honoré Naber, *Iaerlyck verhael van Joannes de Laet*, vol. 1, 92 (quotation), Schalkwijk, *The Dutch Reformed Church in Brazil*, 37; Marcus P. Meuwese, "For the Peace and Well-Being of the Country: Intercultural Mediators and Dutch-Indian Relations in New Netherland and Dutch Brazil, 1600–1664" (PhD diss., University of Notre Dame, 2003), 83–92.

20. Den Heijer, *De geschiedenis van de WIC*, 39; Charles R. Boxer, *Nederlanders in Brazilië, 1624–1654*. [Dutch translation of the original English study, *The Dutch in Brazil, 1624–1654*, published in 1957] (Alphen aan den Rijn: A. W. Sijthoff, 1977), chap. 2.

21. Ambrosius Richshoffer, "Reise nach Brasilien, 1629–1632," in *Reisebeschreibungen von Deutschen beambten und kriegsleuten im dienst der Niederländischen West- und Ost-Indischen kompagnien, 1602–1797*, ed. S. P. L'Honore Naber (The Hague: Nijhoff, 1930), vol. 1, 55–59.

22. Ibid., 62, 69, 72–75, 88.

23. Dutch National Archives (DNA), Archive of the Old West India Company (OWIC), inv. nr. 50, item 18 (Letters and Papers from Brazil, LPB): "Journal of the Expedition to Rio Grande, 5–21 December 1633."

24. Van den Boogaart, "Infernal Allies," 527.

25. Arnoldus Montanus, *De nieuwe en onbekende wereeld, of beschrijving van America en't Zuid-land* (Amsterdam: Jacob Meurs, 1671), 451.

26. Ernst van den Boogaart, "Nederlandse expansie in het Atlantische Gebied, 1595–1674," in *Overzee: Nederlandse Koloniale Geschidenis, 1595–1975*, ed. Ernst van den Boogaart et al. (Haarlem: Fibula-Dishoeck, 1982), 119–20; Meuwese, "For the Peace and Well-Being of the Country," 63–66.

27. S. P. L'Honoré Naber, ed., *Het Iaerlyck verhael van Joannes de Laet, 1624–1636*, Linschoten-Vereeniging 34) (The Hague: Nijhoff, 1937), vol. 4, 128–31.

28. Boxer, *Nederlanders in Brazilië*, 81–82.

29. Nelson Papavero and Dante Martins Teixeira, eds., *Cuthbert Pudsey. Journal of a Residence in Brazil*, vol. 3 of *Dutch Brazil* (Petropolis: Editora Index, 2000), 23.

30. Elias Herckmans (1639), "Generale beschrijvinge van de capitanie Paraíba," in *Zo wijd de wereld strekt*, ed. Ernst van den Boogaart and F. J. Duparc (The Hague: Stichting Johan Maurits van Nassau, 1979), 254.

31. Papavero and Texeira, *Cuthbert Pudsey*, 23; Dante Martins Texeira, ed., *The "Thierbuch" and "Autobiography" of Zacharias Wagener*, vol. 2 of *Dutch Brazil* (Rio de Janeiro: Editora Index, 1997), 162–63.

32. DNA, OWIC, inv. nr. 68, Daily Minutes of the High and Secret Council in Recife (DM), 9 November 1638. For similar distributions, see OWIC, DM, inv. nr. 50, 10 November 1638. For the engraving, see José Antonio Gonsalves de Mello, *Nederlanders in Brazilië (1624–1654): De invloed van de Hollandse bezetting op het leven en de cultuur in Noord Brazilië*, trans. G. N. Visser and ed. B. N. Teensma (Zutphen: Walburg, 2001), 204.

33. Koninklijk Huisarchief (Dutch Royal Archives), Archive of Johan Maurits, inv. nr. A-4-1454, "Rapport van den Staet van de Geconquesteerde Landen van Brasil, 1639," folio 60; this report is also reprinted in Caspar Barlaeus, *Nederlandsch Brazilië onder het bewind van Johan Maurits, grave van Nassau, 1637–1644*, ed. S. P. L'Honore Naber (The Hague: Nijhoff, 1923), 150–99.

34. L'Honoré Naber, *Iaerlyck verhael van Joannes de Laet*, vol. 4, 139.

35. NA, OWIC 68, DM, 20 August 1636.

36. Barlaeus, *Nederlandsch Brazilie*, 44–46.

37. DNA, OWIC 68, DM, 29 January 1639; Barlaeus, *Nederlandsch Brazilie*, 52–54.

38. Barlaeus, *Nederlandsch Brazilie*, 212–13; Boxer, *Nederlanders in Brazilië*, 113–19; OWIC, DM, inv. nr. 68: DM, 7 February and 26 April 1639.

39. Van den Boogaart and Brienen, *Information from Ceará*, 33–38. For the Ceará Tupis in 1639, see DNA, OWIC, inv. nr. 54, item 79 (LPB), Johan Maurits to the Lords XIX, 10 April 1639.

40. DNA, OWIC, inv. nr. 56-243 (LPB), Secret instructions, 28 October 1641.

41. DNA, OWIC, 53-61 (LPB), Letter from Adriaen van der Dussen, 23 May 1638; OWIC, 68, DM, 7 and 8 June 1638.

42. Klaas Ratelband, *Nederlanders in West-Afrika, 1600–1650; Angola, Kongo, en São Tomé*, ed. René Baesjou (Zutphen: Walburg, 2000), 103–4.

43. Van den Boogaart, "Nederlandse expansie," 120; Schalkwijk, *The Dutch Reformed Church in Brazil*, 46.

44. OWIC, inv. nr. 70, DM, 18 April 1643; OWIC, inv. nr. 69, DM, 24 September 1641. See also Van den Boogaart, "Nederlandse expansie," 125.

45. OWIC, 69, DM, 3 December 1642.

46. OWIC, 69, DM, 21 November 1641.

47. Mello, *Nederlanders in Brazilië*, 211–15.

48. OWIC, 69, DM, 26 February 1638.

49. OWIC, 69, DM 29 June 1641.

50. OWIC 59-item 143 (LPB), missive of Johan Maurits, 5 April 1644. For the fifty Tupis, see OWIC, 70, DM, 29 February 1644; see also Schwartz and Langfur, "*Tapanhuns, Negros da Terra*, and *Curibocas*," 101–2.

51. OWIC 8, letter from the Lords XIX to the WIC government in Recife, 1 August 1635.

52. L'Honoré Naber, *Iaerlyck verhael van Joannes de Laet*, vol. 4, 123–24.

53. Papavero and Teixeira, *Cuthbert Pudsey*, 23.

54. OWIC 69, DM, 20 February 1642.

55. OWIC, 53, item 78 (LPB), letter from WIC officials Van Ceulen and Van der Dussen to the Lords XIX, 23 May 1638.

56. Teixeira, *The "Thierbuch*," 184–85.

57. OWIC 68, DM, 26 June 1637.

58. OWIC 68, DM, 5, 11, 15 May 1637; OWIC 69, DM, 20 February 1642.

59. Van den Boogaart, "Nederlandse expansie, " 125; Meuwese, "For the Peace and Well-Being," 162.

60. Van den Boogaart, "Nederlandse expansie," 124–25; Mello, *Nederlanders in Brazilie*, 213–15.

61. OWIC 68, DM, 15 July 1639.

62. OWIC 68, DM, 12 October 1638.

63. OWIC 59, DM, 26 June 1641.

64. Meuwese, "For the Peace and Well-Being," 165–67; B. N. Teensma, "The Brazilian Letters of Vicent Joachim Soler," in *Documents in the Leiden University Library*, ed. Cristina Ferrão and José Paulo Monteiro Soares, vol. 1 of *Dutch Brazil* (Rio de Janeiro: Editoria Index, 1997), 13.

65. Schalkwijk, *The Dutch Reformed Church in Brazil*, 170–71.

66. OWIC 69, DM, 10 and 25 March 1642.

67. NA, SG 5757 II (WIC files) folios 941–42: copy of the letter of Freedoms for the Brazilians, 24 November 1644; Meuwese, "For the Peace and Well-Being," 171–83.

68. Van den Boogaart, "Nederlandse expansie," 130–31; Boxer, *Nederlanders in Brazilië*, 197–204.

69. For the Serinhaem massacre, see Hendrik Hamel, Adriaen van Bullestraten, and Pieter Bas, "Report on Brazil," undated manuscript (fall 1645?), manuscript collection of the Dutch Royal Library, inv. nr. 76 A16, folios 62–63; Johan Nieuhof, *Gedenckweerdige*

Brasiliaaense Zee- en Lant-reize (Amsterdam: Weduwe of Jacob van Meurs, 1682), 119–21; OWIC, LPB 60, item 148: documents relating to the surrender of Serinhaem; LPB 60, item 159: testimony of three Brazilian refugees to the High Council. For the Uruacu massacre, see OWIC, DM 71, October 10, 1645; "Report on Brazil," folios 18–19. For a Portuguese account, published in 1648, see Manuel Calado, *O valeroso Lucideno* (São Paulo: Itaiaia and Editora da Universidade de São Paulo, 1987), vol. 2, 126–30. See also Van den Boogaart, "Infernal Allies," 529. For Paraupaba's proposal to the Tarairius, see OWIC, LPB 60-item 216: report of Councilor Adriaen van Bullestraten in Rio Grande and Paraíba, October 1645.

70. For Brazilian soldiers supporting WIC attacks, see Nieuhof, *Gedenckweerdige Brasiliaaense Zee- en Lant-Reize*, 83, 113, 159 (Poty defeating large rebel force). For the letter exchange, see Schalkwijk, *The Dutch Reformed Church in Brazil*, 204–6. The letter by Poty was translated into Dutch and published as a pamphlet: *Copye, van een Brasiliaensen Brieff gheschreven van Pietter Potty, Brasiliaen, en Commanderende over't Regiment Brasilianen van Paraíba, . . . dato 31 October 1645* (Amsterdam: Lieshout, 1646). The original manuscript letter, in Tupi and translated into Dutch, can be found in OWIC, LPB 61, item 59. For Camarão's letters, see also José Antonio Gonsalves de Mello, *D. Antônio Filipe Camarão. Capitão-Mor dos índios da costa do nordeste do Brasil* (Recife: Universidade do Recife, 1954), 38–43.

71. Boxer, *Nederlanders in Brazilië*, 209–25; Van den Boogaart, "Nederlandse expansie," 133. For the distribution of cloth to the Brazilians, see Schalkwijk, *The Dutch Reformed Church in Brazil*, 208–10.

72. Henk den Heijer, "Het recht van de sterkste in de polder: Politieke en economische strijd tussen Amsterdam en Zeeland over de kwestie Brazilië, 1630–1654," in *Harmonie in Nederland: Het poldermodel van 1500 tot nu*, ed. Dennis Bos, Maurits Ebben, and Henk te Velde (Amsterdam: Bert Bakker, 2007), 84–88; Boxer, *Nederlanders in Brazilië*, 226–34; W. J. van Hoboken, *Witte de With in Brazilië, 1648–1649*, Koninklijke Nederlandse Akademie van Wetenschappen, Werken uitgegeven door de Commissie voor Zeegeschiedenis XIII (Amsterdam: Noord-Hollandsche Uitgevers Maatschappij, 1955), 21–85.

73. Boxer, *Nederlanders in Brazilië*, 236–38 ; Van Hoboken, *Witte de With*, 85–93. For the Tarairius at Guararapes, see OWIC, DM 72, 18 and 31 March, 24 April 1648. For the death and burial of Camarão, see Mello, *D. Antônio Filipe Camarão*, 47–48.

74. For Dutch privateering and the Second Battle of Guararapes, see Van Hoboken, *Witte de With*, 128–50; Boxer, *Nederlanders in Brazilië*, 240–43, 258–60. For Poty's fate, see Schalkwijk, *The Dutch Reformed Church in Brazil*, 210–11.

75. OWIC, DM 72, 4 March 1648.

76. Lodewijk Hulsman, "Brazilian Indians in the Dutch Republic: The Remonstrances of Antonio Paraupaba to the States General in 1654 and 1656," *Itinerario* 29, no. 1 (2005): 55. Apparently the murder was over a native slave kept by Carapeba.

77. Frank Ibold, Jens Jaeger, and Detlev Kraack, eds., *Das Memorial und Jurenal des Peter Hansen Hajstrup (1624–1672)* (Neumuenster: Wachholtz Verlag, 1995), 98–99.

78. Meuwese, "For the Peace and Well-Being of the Country," 203–13; Hulsman, "Brazilian Indians," 51–78; Schalkwijk, *The Dutch Reformed Church in Brazil*, 212–16. For Carapeba's request, see NA, SG, Secret Resolutions, inv. nr. 4846: January 5, 1657. For the Dutch colony of Tobago, see Cornelis Ch. Goslinga, *The Dutch in the Caribbean and the Wild Coast, 1580–1680* (Gainesville: University Press of Florida, 1971), chap. 17.

9

Deploying Tribes and Clans

Mohawks in Nova Scotia and
Scottish Highlanders in Georgia

GEOFFREY PLANK

Along the Atlantic coasts of North America in the seventeenth and eighteenth centuries, French, Spanish, Dutch, and British colonists sought out Amerindian warriors to fight with them as allies or as individual recruits in times of war. Not all the colonists understood the imperial project as a civilizing mission, but for those who did, encouraging "Indians" to fight in their distinctive way involved an agonizing ideological compromise. Writing in 1977, Richard Johnson used language that may seem dated today, but he described the problem succinctly: "In seeking Indian aid, the whites were requiring the Indian to be precisely what they most detested in him—savage, bloodthirsty, relentless, skulking, terrorizing and tearing the scalp from his opponents."[1]

Despite many colonists' misgivings, there was a powerful logic to justify the enlistment of local, indigenous military aid. During the early years of most colonial settlements, the colonists constituted only a minority of the population in the region they intended to occupy. Furthermore, they knew that in the case of hostilities, they would be operating on unfamiliar terrain. They feared that they would be facing adversaries who not only knew the land better than they did but also fought in ways more appropriate to the peculiar challenges of the local environment. Indeed, the colonists continually worried that their clothes were all wrong, their muskets were too heavy, and, when they marched, they moved too slowly, made too much noise, and were likely to walk into ambushes. The problem of navigating unfamiliar swamps and woods seemed almost to dictate the adoption of distinctively North American military tactics. Amerindian military culture changed after the introduction of metal weapons. By the late seventeenth century, especially when they were fighting in the vicinity of European or colonial armies, they usually refused to mass their forces. Instead, they fought in a loosely

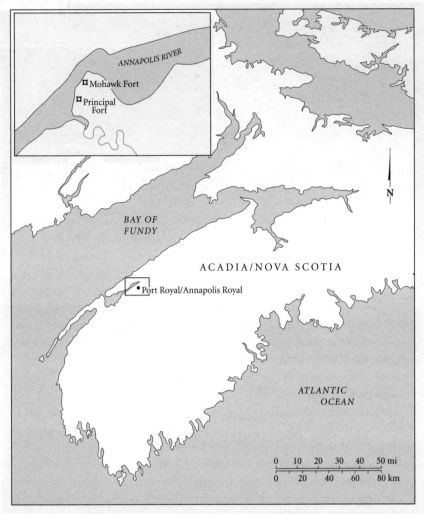

ANNAPOLIS RIVER

□ Mohawk Fort

□ Principal
Fort

N

BAY OF
FUNDY

ACADIA/NOVA SCOTIA

• Port Royal/Annapolis Royal

ATLANTIC
OCEAN

| 0 | 10 | 20 | 30 | 40 | 50 mi |
| 0 | 20 | 40 | 60 | 80 km |

Acadia / Nova Scotia, 1713.

coordinated fashion, targeting individuals or small groups. They conducted deadly ambushes, took captives, and also engaged in ritualized, demonstrative displays of violence.[2]

Even though the colonists hoped to tame the wilderness, as long as the land around them continued to seem wild, they recognized the tactical utility of fighting "like an Indian." Nonetheless, even in the short run, virtually no one in any of the colonial empires thought that their armies should abandon the advantages that they held as a consequence of capital accumulation, European technological development, and military discipline. As the indigenous peoples of Mexico realized from the moment they first met Cortez, the European invaders benefited from the deployment of ships and horses, the construction of roads, and the maintenance of supply lines.[3] From the time of the conquest of Mexico onward, the military ascendancy of all the colonial powers in North America depended on the colonists' ability to transport and deploy large numbers of soldiers while keeping the men clothed, fed, healthy, and well armed. In his study of warfare in northeastern North America, Guy Chet demonstrated that the New Englanders consistently sought to maintain fortified strongholds with reliable, defensible lines of supply.[4]

By the late seventeenth century, in New England and elsewhere across English North America, military leaders believed that the successful prosecution of warfare on the continent required the tandem deployment of regular military units and rangers. The regulars would fight in ranks and live in forts or large encampments, while the rangers would "lie not in any town or garrison . . . but would lie in the woods as enemy did."[5] The ideal rangers were men with talents peculiarly suited to frontier warfare. Even though Amerindian warriors often made good rangers, the distinction was understood to be more a product of custom than heredity, and rangers could belong to any race. The New Englanders recruited rangers from nearby indigenous tribes, and the colonists in Virginia and South Carolina manned their own ranger companies. In New England, in and around New York, and in the south, colonial military leaders also sought alliances with autonomous Amerindian groups. By the end of the seventeenth century, regular soldiers, ranger companies, and indigenous warrior bands thus worked together to prosecute campaigns in the peculiar manner that John Grenier described as a distinctively American "way of war."[6]

By the start of the eighteenth century, British imperial promoters were accustomed to believing that warfare in America required the deployment of a combination of units with specialized skills. They always preferred having Amerindian allies, and many sought to field their ranger companies with recruits from the local indigenous peoples. They wanted the aid of warriors familiar with the peculiar demands of the local landscape, but they knew that such assistance would not always be available. In some instances in both the north and the south, when the British attempted to establish new settlements in regions where their alliances with the indigenous peoples were weak or nonexistent and where it was difficult for them to raise an effective ranger force from the local population, they decided to bring in warriors from afar. To aid their colonizing (and supposedly civilizing) ventures, they sought to introduce new cohorts of fighting men accustomed to uncivilized, ruthless warfare.

From the perspective of the Scottish, English, and Anglo-American men who made these decisions, there seemed to be no shortage of places where such warriors could be found. The English-speaking leaders of the British Empire believed that barbaric customs influenced the practice of warfare in nearly every margin of the imperial domain, in North and South America, the Caribbean, Africa, Ireland, and northern Scotland. Imperial propagandists publicized the brutality of warriors from all of these regions and, in the process, bestowed on them fearsome, ocean-spanning reputations. To be sure, initially at least, the imported men were unfamiliar with the local terrain, but there were countervailing advantages. The mere threat of transporting alien warriors into new military arenas could terrify Britain's adversaries. In addition, moving such men out of their home countries made it easier for the British army to control them.

This chapter examines two experiments conducted by British commanders in which they deployed reputedly uncivilized fighting men in colonial outposts far from the warriors' homes. In 1712 the British army stationed a company of Mohawk warriors in Nova Scotia (the formerly French colony of Acadia), and in 1736 the colonial authorities in Georgia placed Scottish Highlanders near that colony's frontier with Spanish Florida, in a town that came to be known as Darien.[7] The Mohawk warriors arrived in Nova Scotia as a formal company and were stationed together in a small fort. Darien, by contrast, was a complete frontier settlement, with farmers, merchants, women, and children as well as men of fighting age. While the experiments differed in significant ways, the outposts were established with similar strategic purposes in mind, and they therefore shared many characteristics. In Scotland and in Iroquois country, the recruiting officers representing Nova Scotia and Georgia deferred to traditional tribal and clan leaders when seeking volunteers. Men described in the English documents as "chiefs" traveled with the recruits and helped direct both the Highlanders and the Iroquois in combat.

Both experiments foundered in the end, in part because they were designed with contradictory purposes in mind. Although the Mohawk fort and Darien were intended to serve as staging grounds for savage warfare, they also were meant to function as bastions defending colonial settlements, thereby protecting the advance of civilization. This contradiction confused the administration of the outposts. Military commanders tried to incorporate the fighting men into a coherent military command structure while at the same time making the best use of their distinctive warrior customs and reputation for savagery. The Iroquois stationed in the Mohawk fort and the Highland soldiers operating out of Darien were instructed to range away from the hierarchically ordered lines of the battlefield. They were expected to fight in ways that horrified many observers in the age of gunpowder, stabbing and hacking at their opponents with hatchets, knives, bayonets, and broadswords. Almost nothing about the Darien experience would have led anyone to predict that the Highlanders would eventually provide essential military manpower for British imperialism around the globe. In the eyes of the world, however, the Highlanders changed, and this mid-eighteenth-century transformation tells us much about the contrasting geopolitical position of the Gaels and the Amerindians in the British Empire and about the shifts in the way most people viewed the process of civilization.

The Mohawk Fort

The Mohawk fort was the brainchild of Samuel Vetch, a man with a peculiar vision for the transformation of North America. He led the invasion force that took Acadia from the French in 1710, but his ambitions reached far beyond that colony. For at least a decade, he tried to orchestrate the incorporation of all of France's North American possessions into the British Empire. In 1701, with his brother-in-law John Livingston, Vetch sailed up the St. Lawrence River to trade with the French Canadians. After his return, he composed an essay entitled "Canada Survey'd," which argued that the acquisition of France's North American empire would provide Queen Anne with "hundreds of nations of new subjects, who will become intirely obedient to her laws."[8] The essay made such a strong impression on the Board of Trade that in 1709 Vetch received a commission as a colonel in the British army and instructions to lead a military expedition against the French in Canada. Vetch expected North America's aboriginal peoples to take an active role in building a new and more expansive British Empire, and he sought their help in carrying out the conquest. In preparation for the projected 1709 invasion of Canada, he worked closely with the governor of New York and arranged for the recruitment of 450 Iroquois warriors who were to march north in support of the attack.[9] He also enlisted help from his brother-in-law Livingston, who commanded a ranger company in Connecticut composed of "Volunteers English & Indians."[10]

The 1709 campaign was canceled, however, for lack of naval support, and in the aftermath of that disappointment, Vetch helped send a delegation of Iroquois to London to plead for the expulsion of the French from North America. Vetch met the Iroquois men in Boston before they crossed the Atlantic and gave them "fine clothes laced with true gold and silver lace."[11] Upon their arrival in England, the men were hailed as "Four Indian Kings." Dressed in their finery, they went to the theater to see a performance of *Macbeth*. They also had an audience with the queen. Their visit created a public sensation and earned Vetch and his allies the political backing they needed to secure British naval support for the 1710 Acadia campaign.[12]

As he prepared for the conquest of Acadia, Vetch did not anticipate receiving any military assistance from the local indigenous people, the Mi'kmaq. The Mi'kmaq were loosely allied with the Wulstukwiuk and the eastern Abenaki, all Algonquian peoples who inhabited much of present-day New Brunswick and Maine. The Wulstukwiuk and Abenaki had effectively defended their autonomy for decades, in part by resisting incursions from the New Englanders to their south and west.[13] Over the years, the New Englanders may have overestimated the extent of Mi'kmaq complicity in various actions taken by Abenaki warriors, but in conflicts at least since 1675, the colonists' reprisals could be harsh. In 1676 a New England ship captain seized a group of Mi'kmaq and sold them to the Portuguese as slaves, and a low point was reached in 1696 when the government of Massachusetts offered bounties for the scalps of Mi'kmaw men, women, and children.[14] Despite these provocations, the Mi'kmaq, in general, had avoided direct confrontations with the New Englanders and the British, but Vetch could hardly expect them to join him in a military alliance.[15] Although he believed that he would need Amerindian warriors to assist him in his upcoming campaigns, he knew he would have to find them elsewhere.

In 1710, Vetch sought assistance from his brother-in-law Livingston, who continued to hold nominal command of a troop that Vetch described as a company of "New England Indians."[16] Livingston and his company sailed with Vetch to Acadia, and they ranged on the flanks of the regular forces during the siege of Port Royal. After the French commander of the fort surrendered, Livingston left, but the Algonquian warriors stayed behind in the renamed colony of Nova Scotia as part of Vetch's garrison.[17] Vetch kept them employed "scowring the woods" until the late autumn of 1711, but he was not fully satisfied with their performance.[18] By the spring of 1711, he was complaining that the countryside around Annapolis Royal had become "troubled and infested by small skulking parties of [enemy] Indians." The Acadians had sensed the weakness of the British garrison and had grown "uppish," and Vetch's soldiers were too frightened to travel more than "half a mile from the garrison without a guard." Vetch believed that he needed a different set of warriors with greater power to intimidate, and by June he had begun to develop his scheme for the Mohawk fort. He determined that his first step should be to plant kisses on the hands of Robert Hunter, the governor of New York.[19]

Given his situation, Vetch knew that the gesture would have to be carried out from a distance, and to achieve his goal he required assistance from Livingston. Early in June, Vetch sent a letter to Livingston addressed to Governor Hunter, which began: "This is to introduce my brother Major Livingston." He went on to explain that he had directed Livingston "to kiss your hands." Upon receiving the letter, Livingston took it to the governor's office in New York, bowed, and kissed Hunter's hands.[20]

Livingston and Vetch intended this to be more than a mere formal courtesy. As Vetch explained in the body of his letter, the two men hoped that this quick, deferential ritual would mark the formation of a partnership that would eventually include military officers in the palace of Westminster and leaders of the Iroquois League. Hunter was new to the region and had never met either Livingston or Vetch. Although Vetch felt uneasy about proposing his scheme to him without first receiving authorization from London, he was in a hurry and considered Hunter's assistance indispensable. Since the 1670s, New York's governors had served as the principal spokesmen for the British Empire in its relations with the nations of the Iroquois League. In keeping with this tradition, the lieutenant governor of New York had helped prepare the Iroquois for war against Canada in 1709, and in 1711 Hunter himself would participate in the gathering of hundreds of Iroquois warriors in anticipation of that year's intended invasion of the northern French colony. Vetch assumed that the Iroquois League would comply with Hunter's orders. The "Five Nations," he declared, are "under the government of New York."[21]

Vetch complained that the Amerindian warriors who opposed him in Nova Scotia appeared to be operating with impunity because they enjoyed protection within "their impregnable fortress the woods." He hoped to find a way to penetrate their defenses. The only solution he could see was to fight the warriors with "other Indians." The Algonquians from New England in his garrison had not proved effective, however, and of all the indigenous peoples of North America, he imagined that none could serve him better than the Iroquois. As he described the situation to Hunter, the Acadians and the Mi'kmaq were "more in fear of your Iroquois than any other sort."[22] The "Five Nations Indians," he insisted, were "a terror to the Indians and French in these parts of Nova Scotia."[23] As a consequence, they would be "of greater use and service than double their number of British troops."[24]

Vetch's circumstances went from bad to worse in the weeks after he sent that first letter to Hunter. As he described the situation to General John Hill, "the skulking Indians and French" lay in wait in the forest within a few miles of his fort and "often shot down our men without being seen."[25] In late June, a party of his soldiers who had left the garrison to forage for firewood walked into an ambush. Eighteen of the men were killed, eleven more wounded, and as many as thirty-five taken captive. These losses were particularly difficult to absorb, because disease had struck the garrison that month and would kill more than three hundred soldiers by the end of July.

That summer Vetch briefly left Annapolis Royal to sail for Canada with Admiral Hovenden Walker's fleet, but much of the flotilla foundered in the Gulf of St. Lawrence and the expedition was canceled. From that time on, the conquest of Acadia could no longer be interpreted as part of a grand imperial project to evict the French from North America. Instead, it appeared that Nova Scotia had joined territories like Newfoundland, Cape Breton Island, Gibraltar, Minorca, and St. Kitts, as an outpost that Britain might easily retain or trade away in the ongoing, tortuous negotiations for a comprehensive peace. Vetch was unsure whether he could hold Nova Scotia; he wondered whether anyone in the British Empire valued the colony; and the men under his command defiantly questioned why they were there. In November 1711, more than 150 men deserted the garrison and sailed for Boston. Livingston's erstwhile "company of Indians" also joined the deserters, leaving Vetch without any Amerindian warriors to assist him in Annapolis Royal's defense.[26]

Vetch himself sailed to Boston in November 1711, carrying with him orders from General John Hill authorizing him to raise a company of Mohawk warriors to serve in the garrison of Nova Scotia. According to Hill's instructions, the men would be "upon the establishment" of the garrison and "subjected in the same manner as H.M. regular troops."[27] Vetch met Livingston in Boston, where the two men consulted, and once they had assured themselves that they possessed a workable plan and had secured the necessary authorizations, Livingston left for New York to recruit a "company of Mohawk."[28] Livingston offered presents to a number of Mohawk "sachems or chiefs," who agreed to sail with a company of several dozen warriors to Nova Scotia.[29] He promised to feed and clothe all the men and vowed that each warrior would be "punctually paid."[30] During the process of recruitment, Livingston assigned ranks to the men, and those he identified as officers began receiving their pay immediately, retroactive to the beginning of November.[31] None of the men Livingston recruited are named in the surviving documents, but it is likely they were drawn from the group that Vetch had described as "sachems or chiefs." The private men in the Mohawk company would not get paid until they reached Nova Scotia. According to Vetch's calculations, the total expense would be "little more" than what it would have cost to maintain "the other soldiers who are now dead or deserted."[32] The Mohawk warriors would simply "complete the garrison."[33]

The strategy that Vetch and Livingston devised for recruiting Iroquois warriors drew on customs that were familiar to Livingston, recruitment practices that had been developed in New England in the last quarter of the seventeenth century. Beginning with King Philip's War, New England's colonial governments had appointed emissaries to raise Amerindian troops to serve in companies of rangers. These agents took their commissions to tribal gatherings, where they participated in a mixture of ritual observances, dances, and drinking bouts and distributed gifts before enlisting volunteers. Vetch calculated that Livingston must have been "considerably out of pocket" raising his company.[34] It was widely assumed that raising an Amerindian ranger company required special skills, and therefore the recruitment process was entrusted to only a select group of New Englanders,[35] which included Livingston. Vetch boasted that there was no person alive "more capable to procure" Iroquois warriors than Livingston "or [to] command them."[36]

Even though Livingston may have used tactics similar to those he had previously employed recruiting Algonquian men in New England, after the Mohawk warriors enlisted, they would not be treated like New England's Amerindian rangers. Algonquian men serving in ranger companies were never paid in the same way as regular colonial soldiers were. On the contrary, the New England governments experimented with compensation schemes they deemed more appropriate to the warriors' status and interests as "Indians." Amerindian rangers received presents at the time of their enlistment, small provisions during their time of service, and low pay. In the early eighteenth century, Connecticut paid its Amerindian volunteers six shillings a week instead of the ten shillings it offered to every colonist who enlisted. In partial compensation for this inequity, New England's indigenous warriors were often given performance bonuses in the form of bounties for taking prisoners or scalps, and shares of plunder seized in combat. The prizes could be substantial, ranging as high as fifty pounds for a scalp, and on occasion the bounties would be doubled if the warriors had outfitted and fed themselves and fought without demanding provisions or pay. In addition, at the conclusion of hostilities Massachusetts sometimes offered veteran warriors land, including at least one elusive offer to allow them to "repossess" previously confiscated plots "not formerly disposed of."[37] By contrast, the warriors that Livingston recruited to man the Mohawk fort would not be offered any exotic kind of compensation. They would serve in their own specialized unit, but in accordance with General Hill's orders, in other respects they would be treated the same as regularly enlisted soldiers.

Battling severe weather, the recruits made their way overland to Boston in November and December 1711. They did not travel as a group, and the full company was not assembled until early January. On January 3, 1712, still in Boston, Vetch counted fifty-eight officers and men.[38] The Mohawk boarded a ship bound for Nova Scotia in early February, but the threat of high winds and ice kept them moored in Boston Harbor until March 1, when they sailed.[39] Upon their arrival in Nova Scotia, they initially were quartered in houses owned by Acadians. The weapons they were issued had been seized from the former French garrison because, as Vetch explained it, "our muskets are too heavy for them." They also were given axes, and their first assignment was to collect firewood for the garrison. Gathering wood became part of their daily routine.[40] Vetch thought that the Mohawk were terrifying, and at first he was frightened of them himself. Accordingly, he issued orders that they were not to go hunting unless accompanied by a British officer, and he commented that it would be best "to keep them always employed" because "otherwise they will be drunk and troublesome."[41]

For the first few weeks, the men spent much of their time on construction duty. By June they had built their own fort a quarter mile upstream from the old French fort that Vetch and the rest of the garrison occupied.[42] The Mohawk fort was a square enclosure of dry stone walls, six feet high, and surrounded by a five-foot-wide, four-foot-deep ditch. There were bastions at three of the corners. Behind the walls there was one house for the officers and two barracks for the men. The wall facing the river had an opening for a cannon, and it was reported that the battery "commands the river very well thereabouts."[43] Vetch believed that the mere presence of the Mohawk "struck a terror" into the Mi'kmaq, and he predicted that the deployment would induce the Mi'kmaq, as a group, either to leave Nova Scotia or to "submit themselves" to British rule.[44]

In late June Vetch received a report that a contingent of Mi'kmaq and Abenaki warriors were gathering to the east somewhere by the shore of the Bay of Fundy, where they were expected to meet French soldiers arriving from Quebec. Vetch ordered fifty of the Mohawk company to board a sloop and sail up the bay. He wanted them to "surprise" the Mi'kmaq and Abenaki, and he specifically instructed the Mohawk warriors to proceed cautiously and stealthily. He did not want them to open fire until fired upon, and he suggested that instead of attacking their foes directly, they might simply destroy or seize their canoes.[45] Vetch valued the Mohawks enormously, and he did not want to lose any of them. Before they arrived, he had predicted that they would be twice as valuable as British soldiers. In June he asserted that they were "better than three times their number of white men."[46] He made a slightly more extravagant claim to the earl of Dartmouth, telling him that the Mohawks were "worth four times their number of British troops."[47]

Nonetheless, shortly after Vetch made these statements, his project began to unravel. Nova Scotia's financial accounts were not in order, and after the summer of 1712 no one in the garrison, Mohawk or British, was reliably supplied or paid.[48] Livingston left for Connecticut in the winter of 1712, and the officer who replaced him at the Mohawk fort, Peter Mason, did not command the same respect.[49] In the spring of 1713, Vetch complained that the Mohawks were hunting hogs and sheep in the woods, much to the consternation of the Acadians. In May, two dozen of the Mohawks deserted, striking out overland and reportedly seizing cattle along the way to provision themselves for the journey home. Vetch then disbanded the remainder of the Mohawk company. He explained that they were irritating the Acadians, and he did not believe that he needed them any longer, with "the prospect of war's being at an end." He arranged for the remaining men to sail to Boston and promised to compensate them for the cost of their travel at least as far as Hartford or New London.[50]

Several factors contributed to the abandonment of the Mohawk fort. The men were kept segregated, but only a short distance from the main garrison, and relations between the two contingents were tense. After provisions ran short in 1712 and 1713, the Mohawk warriors had been left to fend for themselves. Isolated in Nova Scotia with inadequate resources, they had no way to buy supplies from the Acadians and no local community willing to support them. They went hunting, but in doing so they further alienated the people around them. The sight of armed parties of Mohawk warriors frightened even the officers of the British garrison, and there is every reason to believe that the Acadians were even more worried. From Vetch's perspective, after the threat of counterattacks from the French, Abenaki, and Mi'kmaq diminished in 1713, the Mohawks' presence seemed unnecessarily disruptive, and when they began raiding the Acadians' farms, he concluded that their deployment was doing more harm than good. Recognizing the difficulty of the situation, he made no effort to punish any of the warriors, but he hastened to send them all away.

Many of the problems associated with the Mohawk fort might have been avoided if the warriors had been brought into Nova Scotia with their families and given space to establish a self-supporting community away from both the Acadians and the British garrison. But that strategy might have had its own problems, some of which the trustees of Georgia found when they decided to import Scottish Highlanders to help defend that colony's southern frontier.

Darien

On June 26, 1734, Tomochichi, the headman of a small town inhabited by Lower Creeks, arrived in London. He was accompanied by his nephew Tooanaway and the largest group of Amerindians to visit England since 1616, and they traveled with James Oglethorpe, the governor of the newly established British colony of Georgia. Oglethorpe had organized the visitors' itinerary, which included performances of *Hamlet*, *Henry VIII*, and *Henry IV*, *part 1*, as well as an audience with George II and Queen Caroline. Oglethorpe grandly introduced Tomochichi as the leader of the Creek nation and announced that the Creeks had ceded the lands that Oglethorpe needed to settle Georgia. The purpose of Tomochichi's visit was to declare his gratitude and support for the ongoing project of colonization. Many Londoners were enthralled, and the British press referred to Tomochichi and Tooanaway as a king and a prince.[51]

Tomochichi's trip to London bears some resemblance to the earlier visit of the Iroquois delegation that came to be known as the "Four Indian Kings." Both events were pageants designed to publicize and promote imperial expansion, and in both instances, in the pursuit of that agenda, the British inflated the visitors' status and authority. The "Four Indian Kings" were hardly royalty, and neither was Tomochichi. On the contrary, he occupied a tenuous position among the Creeks, and it may have been his political weakness among them that inspired him to seek an alliance with Britain. In any case, Tomochichi's actions had strategic ramifications, and like the earlier visit of the Iroquois, they helped lay the groundwork for an unusual military deployment. In 1739, when Oglethorpe mustered Georgian troops for an invasion of Spanish Florida, Tooanaway joined approximately forty other Creek warriors to serve in the expedition. This was hardly out of line with well-established military customs in the colonial Southeast, except that by 1739 there were new players on the scene: Tooanaway would fight as a ranger alongside men drawn from the Gaelic Scottish settlement at Darien.

The new colony of Georgia had been established on land that had lost much of its population over the previous fifty years. A combination of Spanish missionary work, warfare, slave raiding, and epidemic disease had uprooted or destroyed nearly every Amerindian community that had occupied the region since the 1670s.[52] Tomochichi and his band were new to the area and were far too small in number to control it. Tomochichi's support of the Georgia colony may have strengthened Oglethorpe politically in London, but militarily Tomochichi had very little to offer in the event of a confrontation with Spain. Oglethorpe believed that his colony needed a larger body of warriors ready to withstand the rigors of frontier warfare, and therefore even before he brought Tomochichi to London, he sent recruiters to the Scottish Highlands.

The Scottish Highlanders' settlement would be a small experiment within a much larger one. Georgia was designed to function as a huge strategic barrier helping protect South Carolina from possible Spanish attack. The colony also was founded with the purpose of changing the character of the colonists who came there.[53] Georgia's trustees crafted the colony's land laws with the aim of keeping the farms small and discouraging social stratification.[54] They prohibited slavery, in part for tactical, military reasons but also to foster self-reliance among the colony's "English and Christian inhabitants," a category of settlers that, according to the trustees' understanding of the world, could not include black slaves.[55] The trustees also banned alcohol, out of a professed desire to advance the king's "fatherly intentions" toward the settlers.[56] Overall, the trustees governed the colony in its early years with the goal of creating a sober, industrious, and egalitarian society, and they touted Georgia as a place of refuge and reform for those who needed a new start in life, including individuals and families from among the "deserving poor" of England.

Under the terms of its charter, Georgia was open not only to the English poor but also to "foreigners," and the children of immigrants were granted full legal status as subjects or denizens of the British realm. As part of the effort to make large groups of foreigners feel welcome, liberty of conscience was guaranteed to Jews, Protestant Christians, and members of every other religious group except "Papists."[57] Hoping that their colony would work to create new subjects for George II, the leaders of Georgia actively recruited colonists from the continent of Europe, especially German and Swiss Protestants.[58]

In September 1733, Oglethorpe recommended to the Common Council of Georgia that it sponsor a venture by George Dunbar of Inverness to recruit Scottish Highlanders for the colony.[59] Word of his intentions spread fast, and the first reports to reach Scotland were extravagant.[60] Hugh Mackay, an associate of Dunbar's involved in recruiting settlers from the Highlands, discovered that many potential settlers were disappointed with his account of what Oglethorpe had to offer, because the advance notice that the Georgia project had received in Scotland, in the press and by word of mouth, had exaggerated the governor's promises.[61]

Supporters of the colonial endeavor argued that sending Highlanders to America would enhance security and stability in the Highlands and would "effectually civilize our Highlanders and divert that boisterous humour, which used, upon the least commotion, to fly out in the face of their sovereign."[62] The "Highland problem" had been the subject of intense debate for years, but the promotion of emigration to Georgia as a strategy for civilizing the Highlanders created a conflict of interest between the colony and the home country. As one writer expressed the difficulty in relation to the poor of England, "many of the poor who had been useless in England, were inclined to be likewise in Georgia."[63] It could equally easily be argued that those Highlanders most needing reform were not those most likely to serve the interests of the colony. As a result, those employed in recruiting settlers often contradicted themselves. The same recruiter who argued that Georgia would "effectually civilize our Highlanders" also vowed *not* to enlist "vagabonds that go about, a pilfering, robbing, and doing mischief." Instead, he promised to choose "honest, industrious farmers"—not the individuals most in need of civilization.[64] Dunbar reported that he selected only the smartest applicants for emigration. "I'll venture to say they do not leave cleverer people behind them."[65]

The recruiters sought to reconcile the interests of the Highlands with those of the colony by emphasizing the settlers' military potential. Dunbar and Mackay concentrated their recruitment efforts on areas that had supported the Jacobite Rising of 1715, and Mackay promised Oglethorpe that they would recruit "active young fellows and soldiers."[66] Most of the men they enlisted were affiliated with Clan Chattan, which had turned out almost uniformly in

1715 in support of the exiled Stuart dynasty, and it is likely that many of the older recruits had gained military experience fighting in the Jacobite army against the forces of George I.[67] Oglethorpe and his emissaries assumed that once relocated in America, these men would fight to defend their new homes.

The 166 Highlanders that Dunbar and Mackay recruited left Inverness for Georgia on October 21, 1735, with Dunbar reporting that when he disembarked from Scotland, he left several eager would-be emigrants behind.[68] The settlers arrived in Georgia the following January, and in accordance with promises made to them at the time of enlistment, upon their arrival each man received a new flintlock, an ax, and a broadsword.[69] They established a settlement near the border with Florida, which had been provisionally named "New Inverness" but which the settlers quickly renamed "Darien" in reference to Scotland's earlier ambitious, ill-fated colonial project on the isthmus of Panama.[70] A delegation of Creek hunters affiliated with Tomochichi visited them shortly after their arrival and provided them venison.[71]

In contrast to other immigrant communities in Georgia, the settlers in Darien were discouraged from assimilating into Anglo-American society. The colony's trustees stipulated that all landholders at the new settlement had to speak "the Highland language."[72] The trustees also expected the Highlanders to retain their distinctive style of clothing. When he visited Darien in 1736, Oglethorpe came dressed in the "Highland habit," which included, according to the *South Carolina Gazette*, "a Highland dress, with a bonnet, target, plaid, broad sword, pistols," and more.[73] One witness of the event reported that "several of the people (hearing that he was come) cried out, 'Mr. Oglethorpe, where's Mr. Oglethorpe?' Not knowing him from the rest of their brethren."[74] The story was probably embellished, but other sources confirm its gist: the men of Darien wore plaids.[75]

Once the settlement had been established, colonists returned intermittently to the Highlands with reports of developments in Georgia.[76] According to one published account, in the late 1730s the buildings in Darien were "mostly huts, but tight and warm." The settlers had a "little fort," and they had been "industrious in planting, and have got into driving of cattle, for the supply of the regiment."[77] Another writer similarly claimed that the Highlanders,

> being accustomed to hardship, and labor, were not afraid of it in Georgia, and they live by it very comfortably. . . . They at first applied themselves, with success, to the raising of corn, and have since taken to feeding of cattle, as yielding a more immediate profit, on account of supplying General Oglethorpe's regiment and the shipping with fresh beef.[78]

Although on one occasion Oglethorpe had disguised himself as a Highlander, he did not believe that they were like him. Sometimes he grouped the settlers among the "foreigners" he hoped to draw into his colony, a category that included Germans and Welsh, but on other occasions, as Colin Calloway emphasized, he declined to count them among the colony's "white people."[79] In the colonial American South, even more than in other places, racial categories mattered. Nonwhite status implied marginalization, and there was no consensus concerning the race of the Scottish Highlanders. In 1716, when South Carolina was recovering from the Yamasee War, its colonial assembly successfully petitioned the Board of Trade to send them prisoners seized during the 1715 Jacobite Rising, almost all of whom would have been Scottish Highlanders. The assemblymen explained that they wanted to augment "the small number of white men (fit to bear arms) remaining in the colony."[80] A similar calculus had contributed to the decision to bring Highlanders to Georgia. Georgia originally had been conceived as an all-white colony, with black settlers outlawed in order to make it more difficult for runaway slaves from South Carolina to cross over and make their way to Spanish Florida. The racial exclusion also was designed to create a more egalitarian environment for the colonists, and the Highlanders at Darien were among the staunchest defenders of the policy of barring blacks. In a celebrated statement on the issue in 1739, they declared, "We are laborious and know a white man may be, by the year, more usefully employed than a Negro."[81]

Nonetheless, among the Georgia colonists, the Highlanders stood out. Along with the Gaelic language and plaids, clanship—the kinship-based, hierarchical social structure of the Highlands—was another feature that set them apart. British commentators and their counterparts in the colonies may have exaggerated the power of clanship, but when war broke out with Spain in 1739, Oglethorpe tried to take advantage of the distinctive social customs that seemed to prevail in Darien.[82] Some among the trustees doubted the wisdom of his strategy, but Oglethorpe was adamant that the Highlanders' own leaders be recognized and used, especially in wartime. He wrote that they would not take direction from "anyone that does not understand the Highland language. . . . They are useful under their own chiefs and nowhere else."[83]

When the war with Spain began, Oglethorpe called on John Mohr Mackintosh, a man who identified himself as the settlement's "commander," to mobilize the fighting-age men and ready them for combat.[84] As a young man, Mohr Mackintosh had served under his uncle, Brigadier Lachlan Mackintosh, in the 1715 Jacobite Rising, and his unit had fought with famous effectiveness. In one engagement, the Mackintoshes killed approximately 180 government troops while losing only 35. In an uncomfortable exchange of messages after that battle, the commander of the government's troops promised Lachlan Mackintosh that he would regroup and fight back mercilessly; "I will not spare one man of you."[85] Despite this pledge, Mohr Mackintosh had lived to fight another day.

He repaid the trust Oglethorpe placed in him. Within four days of receiving a commission, he raised seventy men and marched them south toward Spanish Florida. Oglethorpe kept Mohr Mackintosh's troops separate from the rest of the colonial military establishment. The Highlanders entered combat dressed in plaids and bearing swords.[86] Near St. Augustine they were assigned to a unit that, according to Mohr Mackintosh, consisted of "eighty-five white men and forty Indians." Deployed as rangers, the men were ordered to patrol the inland side of the fortress and harass the Spanish with hit-and-run tactics.[87] When the time came to fight, they used their muskets first but quickly set aside their firearms and opted instead for swordplay, "cutting and slashing as fast as they could." It was a tactic dictated in part by circumstances but also close to the traditions of the Highlands.[88]

The Highlanders had been sent into Florida on a military campaign that served the purpose of defending the slave system in the British colonies north of Georgia. This aspect of their role became dramatically evident when the men were sent to occupy Mose, a settlement in Florida established years earlier by runaway slaves who had fled British masters.[89] Mohr Mackintosh described Mose as "a demolished Negro fort made of mud within canon shot of St. Augustine."[90] He and his fellow rangers spent nine days in the fort before a contingent of fighting men under Spanish command, including, in the words of one dismissive report, "convicts, Negroes and Indians," surrounded and defeated them. The Spanish-led force killed thirty-six men and took forty prisoners.[91] Together, the prisoners and the fallen constituted a large share of Darien's adult male population. Mohr Mackintosh was taken captive, leaving behind a wife and seven sons and daughters. Overall, according to a one account, Darien was left with "not one quarter part the number who settled there at first, and that is made up chiefly of women and children."[92]

The Spanish held Mohr Mackintosh and his fellow prisoners for four months in St. Augustine before transporting them to Havana. Three months later, they were shipped across the Atlantic to Spain and confined in a jail in the Basque country.[93] During his captivity, Mohr Mackintosh received a stipend of six pence a day from the British government, but he complained bitterly that he had been neglected by the authorities of Georgia and the secretary of war.[94] He wanted someone to arrange a prisoner exchange, but he could not gain the attention of anyone in the colony, the army, or the ministry. "What completes my misfortune and makes it really worse than any other of his Britannic majesty's subjects is that there was no inquiry made concerning me whether dead or alive."[95] Mohr Mackintosh's experience was in many ways unique, but he articulated a sense of alienation from the leaders of Georgia that afflicted nearly all the settlers at Darien.

Even before this catastrophe, many of the townspeople had started to cool toward Darien. They complained of poor soil conditions and chronic difficulties in securing markets for their produce.[96] As early as 1737, news of their unhappiness had reached Scotland, and in the summer of that year, colonial recruiters seeking new Gaelic-speaking settlers struggled to enlist thirty-three.[97] No others would come before the outbreak of the war with Spain. After the war started, most of the settlers at Darien left, and by the end of 1740, the town's population may have dropped to as low as fifty-three.[98] Forty-five new Highlanders were recruited for the settlement in the summer of 1741, but when they arrived in Georgia, the colonial authorities did not trust them to settle as a group in the outpost, and the newcomers were brought to the town under guard.[99] Darien's reputation had suffered a blow. Indeed, the threat of a posting there served as a way to discipline the government's Highland troops.

In London in 1743, 120 members of the Forty-third Highland Regiment deserted.[100] The soldiers had been told that they were coming to the capital in order to be reviewed by the king, when in fact the intention was to ship them to Flanders. Before the soldiers learned that news, a rumor spread among them that they were to be sent to the West Indies and subsequently "broke, or divided, amongst the colonies."[101] Even after they were told they were headed to Flanders, they still believed they were bound across the ocean. The idea shocked the men, who had joined the regiment in the expectation that it would stay—as had all previous Highland units in the army—in Scotland. As one observer put it, "They had been so long settled in that country that it amounted to as great a hardship on them (comparatively speaking) as it would be to the militia of London to be shipped to the Indies on an hour's warning."[102] The soldiers objected because they had never been told they would be stationed abroad, and they had not settled their affairs at home before leaving Scotland. They were poorly prepared for a transatlantic voyage, and the possibility that they might be sent overseas brought other complaints—overdue pay, inadequate shoes—to a crisis. With reason, the men worried that a posting in the West Indies would be "destructive to their health."[103] Most of the deserters faced trial, and upon conviction, three of the men were executed by firing squad in the Tower of London. Twenty-six had their sentences commuted and were sent to join the garrison on Gibraltar. Thirty-eight were similarly deployed to the West Indies, and thirty-eight to Darien.[104]

Although Darien had not lived up to its promise, the experiment was not a complete failure. On two occasions in 1742, soldiers serving in the rump of Mohr Mackintosh's company performed exactly as Oglethorpe had originally intended them to, fighting back Spanish incursions into Georgia near their homes.[105] But to the extent that anything had gone right in Darien, the accomplishment had been purchased at such a great cost that it diminished the apparent likelihood that anyone would be able to establish similar outposts in the future.

In the long run, some survivors of the Darien settlement made a significant mark on the landscape. By the 1770s some had grown wealthy and risen to prominence. A few of the most successful among them had entered the fur trade and established families while living among the Amerindians. By late in the century, some of their descendants were leaders among the Creeks.[106] Historian A. W. Parker had reason to claim that the Darien experiment was a success,[107] but the verdict in the 1740s was decidedly more mixed. As the story of the 1743 mutiny indicates, after the defeat of the Highland company at Mose, the British army was forced to resort to duplicity and coercion in order to recruit Highlanders for service overseas. Partly as a consequence, in the years leading up to 1745, the fighting men of the Scottish Highlands were increasingly, sometimes even violently, opposed to being posted on the British Empire's North American frontiers.

Mid-Eighteenth-Century Transformations

Late in August 1757, a regiment of Highlanders arrived in Nova Scotia. On a misty day near Halifax less than a month later, one of the men took a dangerous hike. He had left his regiment wearing his hair "hanging loose" and was "wrapped up in a dark-colored plaid." A sentry from another British regiment saw him emerging from the woods and shouted questions to him in English, but the Highlander spoke only Gaelic. The sentry "challenged him repeatedly" and, "receiving no answer," took aim and shot the man dead. The sound of the gunshot attracted other soldiers, including the sentry's sergeant. The sentry greeted his sergeant excitedly, pointing and repeating, "I have killed an Indian, I have killed an Indian, there he lies." He explained that he had killed "an Indian, wearing a blanket." The sergeant walked over to inspect the body and returned to tell the sentry that he had killed "one of our own men, and a Highlander." According to other soldiers in his company, the sentry was "so oppressed with grief and fright" upon hearing this news that he fell physically ill and remained incapacitated for several days.[108]

This incident illustrates a dilemma that had faced Highland soldiers in North America since the beginning of their deployment on the continent in 1756. They were valued as soldiers in part because of their reputation for primitive violence. Their hardiness and way of living, including their loose clothing, was widely assumed to be appropriate for service on the American frontier. In short, they were commonly thought to resemble "Indians." When the first Highland regiment arrived in 1756, the earl of Loudon, as commander of British forces in North America, stationed the unit in Iroquois country. The Highlanders performed well in the company of Amerindians, and Loudon boasted that the Iroquois considered each of them "a kind of Indian."[109] Believing that the Highlanders brought unique skills to America, Loudon struggled to make sure they retained their distinctiveness. He consistently assigned new Gaelic-speaking recruits to segregated Highland regiments, and he sought to purge "low countrymen" from the units.[110] For the duration of the war, and indeed for years thereafter, he and his successors in command repeatedly sent their Highland units to patrol and fight in regions where European rules of warfare did not seem to apply.

Some Highlanders enjoyed their savage reputation, and a few even came to believe that they had learned their distinctive military practices from North America's indigenous peoples. The Highlanders' tradition of entering combat with yells, for example, dated back generations, but some Highland soldiers in North America believed that their units had learned the practice from the local tribes. One soldier called the yell "the Indian Halloo," listed in among the Highlanders' "backwoods acquirements."[111]

Others in the Highland regiments, however, worried about their units' association with savagery. In 1757 Simon Fraser commanded the Highland regiment in Nova Scotia. Although his soldiers generally were too young to have fought in the Jacobite Rising of 1745, Fraser had done so. As one critic in the House of Commons had put it, if Fraser knew anything about military affairs, "he had learnt it in rebellion."[112] With the support of his famous father, the earl of Lovat, Fraser had served in the Jacobite army. After the fighting ended, Lovat was tried, convicted for treason, and beheaded in the Tower of London. Fraser had been spared because he gave evidence against his father, and with Loudon's help he had been gradually rehabilitated.[113] These experiences made Fraser cautious about his reputation. He bristled when his fellow officers called his unit a mere "battalion," and he labored hard to make sure that his men performed well at drill.[114] He wanted his soldiers to gain respect, and the sentry's remorse after killing the Highlander suggests that within a month of his arrival in Nova Scotia, he had made some progress in that regard. Emotionally as well as formally, the sentry recognized the Highlander as "one of our own men."

While this 1757 incident is suggestive of the evolving status of Highlanders within the British army, it is even more telling with respect to the army's relations with the indigenous people of Nova Scotia. Although they had maintained a garrison in the colony for forty-seven years, the British had failed to subdue their Mi'kmaq opponents and had been equally unsuccessful in their intermittent efforts to recruit local indigenous allies.[115] The sentry's readiness to open fire upon the mere sight of an "Indian" and his initial glee at having ended that man's life reflected an outlook that was more widespread in Nova Scotia than elsewhere but was common throughout the British colonies in the early years of the Seven Years' War.[116] Colonial hostility toward the indigenous peoples of North America had never been more virulent, and on the basis of atrocity stories they had heard even before their deployment in the colonies, newly arrived British officers and soldiers came ready to hate "Indians."

The future was not quite as bleak, however, as these circumstances might suggest. In other parts of North America, British soldiers worked effectively with indigenous allies. Indeed, in 1758 Fraser's Highland regiment moved westward to live and fight among Amerindians, and along with other units of Gaelic-speaking soldiers they played an important role in easing animosities between the British army and indigenous peoples in the north, in the lands west of Georgia, and in the trans-Appalachian west. In many military contexts for decades to come, Highland soldiers and Amerindian warriors worked well together, and often they were assigned similar roles, such as working as rangers and guides.[117]

Nonetheless, with the rare exception of Brigadier General Stand Watie's "Indian Cavalry," which fought for the Confederacy in the U.S. Civil War, regular armies in North America did not field segregated companies or battalions composed of indigenous warriors who fought in the uniform style of their recruiter.[118] There would never be an Iroquois regiment comparable to those of the Highlanders. Part of the explanation for the divergent paths taken by Highland soldiers and Iroquois warriors lies in their distinctive military traditions. In the eighteenth century, it was much more common for observers to comment on the similarities, despite the stark differences between Gaelic and American ways of warfare. In eighteenth-century North America, indigenous warriors fought in small groups and avoided massed close combat. As one witness of the Seven Years' War put it, the Amerindians would never "stand cutting, like the Highlanders or other British troops."[119] While the tribal warriors of North America apparently performed poorly in large groups, the Highlanders were vulnerable when they ventured into the woods alone. One commander complained, "I cannot send a Highlander out of my sight without running the risk of losing the man."[120] The Highlanders' long-standing military traditions facilitated their adjustment to regimental discipline, but that hardly explains why there were no Iroquois companies serving in any army.

In order to understand the forces pulling the Highlanders and the Iroquois in different directions, we must take into account the geopolitical and economic positions of their respective homelands during the Seven Years' War. In the aftermath of the 1745 Jacobite Rising, the British government systematically dismantled the customary practices that had given the Highland clans a relatively autonomous power base.[121] Stripped of much of their ancestral power, formerly rebellious clan leaders embraced the new order and began to cooperate with the British army; Simon Fraser was only one of many who chose to collaborate. By the late 1750s, Jacobitism as a political movement had collapsed. As the Highland clans lost their political independence, they also suffered economic deprivation, and the weakness of the Highland economy drove many young men into military service as a way to support their families.[122]

For the nations of the Iroquois League, by contrast, the 1750s and, even more so, the 1760s were a period of power and prosperity. They had not been militarily defeated, nor were they fully integrated into the British-colonial polity. During the Seven Years' War, the Iroquois nations deployed warriors to serve their own interests, and in comparison with the Scottish Highlanders, they had little incentive to hire out their fighting men for service abroad. It made an enormous practical difference that the Iroquois occupied strategically important land. As long as the Iroquois remained militarily significant, that is, at least until 1815, the Europeans and Anglo-Americans who sought Iroquois warriors as allies generally wanted them to fight close to their homes.

Historians should be skeptical of the hierarchical thinking of those British imperial officials who routinely suggested that service in the army was an honor and a way to gain admission into a powerful and privileged elite. The

Highlanders agreed to serve in their regiments out of a position of weakness, and the Iroquois avoided such service because they retained their autonomy and enjoyed a position of strength. Young men in the Highlands frequently resented the coercive pressures that induced them to enlist, and with good reason.[123] Highlanders were assigned dangerous missions. During the Seven Years' War, their units suffered a casualty rate of 32 percent, more than triple the rate experienced by the rest of the army.[124]

Nonetheless, although it is important not to allow Anglo-Saxon ways of thinking to dominate our historical analysis, in order to understand the long-term significance of the Highlanders' record of military service, we must consider its place within the systems of social hierarchy that came to dominate life in the British Empire and North America. Despite Oglethorpe's early misgivings about the Highlanders' racial status, by the second half of the eighteenth century, particularly after they became the empire's heroes, they were increasingly accepted as "white," whereas North America's indigenous peoples continued to be categorized as something else. But racial categories were never rigid, and taking the long view, Stand Watie's service in the Confederate army should remind us to be wary of simplistically employing race as an explanatory variable for understanding the social status of North America's indigenous peoples.

At least through the first three quarters of the nineteenth century, Enlightenment ideas concerning the stages of human progress had as much influence as did racial theories in determining the pattern of relations between Highlanders and Amerindians. It was not until the 1770s that the stadial theory was clearly and systematically articulated, but even in Simon Fraser's time Scotland's philosophers were wrestling with the idea that human societies evolved from savagery through pastoralism toward agriculture and urban life. Most European observers were oblivious to Amerindian agriculture, and therefore the emerging evolutionary theory seemed to suggest that because the Highlanders had traditionally been pastoralists, they had long ago taken a step ahead of the Amerindians. Fraser was aware of the implications of this idea. As commander of a camp stationed among the Iroquois in 1758, he convinced himself that his soldiers could serve as agents of progress. "This is the country for a philosopher," he wrote. "What is most wanted here is persons to think for the people and to put them in motion."[125] Like Samuel Vetch and Oglethorpe, Fraser had become a dreamer. Although he did not consider the Iroquois his equals, he thought that he could serve them as their guide.

1. Richard R. Johnson, "The Search for a Usable Indian: An Aspect of the Defense of Colonial New England," *Journal of American History* 64 (1977): 623–51, 649–50.

2. On the shifts in Amerindian tactics, see Wayne E. Lee's essay in this volume; Craig S. Keener, "An Ethnohistorical Analysis of Iroquois Assault Tactics Used against Fortified Settlements of the Northeast in the Seventeenth Century," *Ethnohistory* 46 (1999): 777–807; and Wayne E. Lee, "Fortify, Fight, or Flee: Tuscarora and Cherokee Defensive Warfare and Military Culture Adaptation," *Journal of Military History* 68 (2004): 713–70.

3. Camilla Townsend, "Burying the White Gods: New Perspectives on the Conquest of Mexico," *American Historical Review* 108 (2003): 659–87.

4. Guy Chet, *Conquering the American Wilderness: The Triumph of European Warfare in the Colonial Northeast* (Amherst: University of Massachusetts Press, 2003).

5. Benjamin Church, *Diary of King Philip's War*, ed. Alan Simpson and Mary Simpson (Chester, CT: Pequot Press, 1975), 106.

6. John Grenier, *The First Way of War: American War Making on the Frontier, 1607–1814* (Cambridge: Cambridge University Press, 2005).

7. See John Grenier, *The Far Reaches of Empire: War in Nova Scotia, 1710–1760* (Norman: University of Oklahoma Press, 2008), 21, 24–25, 30; A. W. Parker, *Scottish Highlanders in Colonial Georgia: The Recruitment, Emigration and Settlement at Darien, 1735–1748* (Athens: University of Georgia Press, 1997); Edward J. Cashin, *Lachlan McGillivray, Indian Trader* (Athens: University of Georgia Press, 1992), 6–33; Harvey H. Jackson, *Lachlan McIntosh and the Politics of Revolutionary Georgia* (Athens: University of Georgia Press, 1979), 1–5.

8. Samuel Vetch, "Canada Survey'd," in *Samuel Vetch Letter-Book*, 55, Museum of the City of New York (hereafter MCNY), reprinted in *Calendar of State Papers, Colonial Series, America and West Indies* (London: Public Record Office, 1860–), 1708–1709, 51 (hereafter *CSP-AWI*). See James D. Alsop, "Canada Survey'd: The Formation of a Colonial Strategy, 1706–1710," *Acadiensis* 12 (1982): 39–58.

9. Daniel K. Richter, *The Ordeal of the Longhouse: The Peoples of the Iroquois League in the Era of European Colonization* (Chapel Hill: University of North Carolina Press, 1992), 226, 367, n. 27.

10. John David Krugler, "Livingston, John," *Dictionary of Canadian Biography* (Toronto: University of Toronto Press, 1966), vol. 2, 436–37.

11. Samuel Vetch to Francis Nicholson, August 12, 1709, in *Samuel Vetch Letter-Book*, 60.

12. Eric Hinderaker, "The 'Four Indian Kings' and the Imaginative Construction of the First British Empire," *William and Mary Quarterly*, 3d ser., 53 (1996) 487–526, 488–89.

13. See Emerson W. Baker and John G. Reid, "Amerindian Power in the Early Modern Northeast: A Reappraisal," *William and Mary Quarterly* 61 (2004): 3–32.

14. William Hubbard, *A Narrative of the Troubles with the Indians* (Boston, 1677), 29–30; Olive Patricia Dickason, "La 'guerre navale' des micmacs contre les britaniques, 1713–1763," in *Les Micmacs et la mer*, ed. Charles A. Martijn (Montreal: Recherche amérindiennes au Québec, 1986), 233–48, 237; Proclamation, May 27, 1696 (Boston, 1696).

15. On the initial Mi'kmaq response to Vetch's 1710 operation, see John G. Reid, "The 'Conquest' of Acadia: Narratives," in John G. Reid et al., *The "Conquest" of Acadia, 1710: Imperial, Colonial and Aboriginal Constructions* (Toronto: University of Toronto Press, 2004), 3–22, 14.

16. Vetch to John Hill, September 11, 1711, Sloane 3706, f. 6, British Library.

17. Krugler, "Livingston, John," 436–37; *Journal of John Livingston*, October 15, 1710–February 23, 1711, CO 217/31, f. 1, National Archives, Kew.

18. *CSP-AWI*, 1711–1712, p. 152.

19. Vetch to Robert Hunter, June 1, 1711, in *Samuel Vetch Letter-book*, 165.

20. Ibid.

21. *CSP-AWI*, 1710–1711, p. 550; Vetch to Board of Trade, June 24, 1711, Sloan 3607, f. 3, British Library; Richter, *The Ordeal of the Longhouse*, 228–29, 369, n. 32.

22. Vetch to Hunter, June 1, 1711, in *Samuel Vetch Letter-book*, p. 165.

23. Vetch to Hill, September 11, 1711, Sloane 3706, f. 6, British Library.

24. *CSP-AWI*, 1711–1712, p. 200.

25. Vetch to Hill, September 11, 1711, Sloane 3607, f. 6, British Library.

26. Reid, "The "Conquest' of Acadia," 16–18; John G. Reid, "Imperialism, Diplomacies, and the Conquest," in *The "Conquest" of Acadia, 1710: Imperial, Colonial and Aboriginal Constructions* (Toronto: University of Toronto Press, 2004), 101–23, 102–6; Vetch to Hunter, June 19, 1711, Sloane 3607, f. 42, British Library; Letter from Christopher Cahonet, July 20, 1711, RG1, vol. 3, f. 51, Nova Scotia Archives and Records Management, *CSP-AWI*, 1711–1712, pp. 148–49.

27. *CSP-AWI*, 1711–1712, pp. 152, 200–201.

28. Vetch to Hill, September 11, 1711, Sloane 3706, f. 6, British Library.

29. Vetch to Board of Trade, June 24, 1711, Sloane 3607, f. 3, British Library.

30. Vetch to Hunter, June 1, 1711, in *Samuel Vetch Letter-book*, p. 165.

31. *CSP-AWI*, 1711–1712, p. 201.

32. Vetch to Board of Trade, June 24, 1711, Sloane 3607, f. 3, British Library.

33. Vetch to Dartmouth, November 6, 1711, Sloane 3607, f. 9, British Library.

34. *CSP-AWI*, 1711–1712, p. 226.

35. Grenier, *The First Way of War*, 33–39; Johnson, "The Search for a Usable Indian," 627–31.

36. Krugler, "Livingston, John," 436–37; *Journal of John Livingston*, October 15, 1710–February 23, 1711, CO 217/31, f. 1, TNA; Vetch to Board of Trade, June 24, 1711, Sloan 3607, f. 3, Vetch to Hill, September 11, 1711, Sloane 3706, f. 6, Vetch to Dartmouth, November 6, 1711, Sloane 3607, f. 9, British Library.

37. Johnson, "The Search for a Usable Indian," 627, 630, 641; Daniel R. Mandell, *Behind the Frontier: Indians in Eighteenth-Century Eastern Massachusetts* (Lincoln: University of Nebraska Press, 1996), 51; Ann Marie Plane, *Colonial Intimacies: Indian Marriage in Early New England* (Ithaca, NY: Cornell University Press, 2000) 87.

38. *CSP-AWI*, 1711–1712, p. 201.

39. *CSP-AWI*, 1711–1712, p. 226; Vetch to William Alden, March 1, 1712, Sloane 3607, f. 16, British Library.

40. Vetch, Letter of introduction for Livingston, March 1, 1712, Sloane 3607, f. 15, British Library.

41. Ibid.

42. *CSP-AWI*, 1711–1712, p. 307.

43. George Vane, Report on Colonel Livingston's Fort, October 27, 1712, Sloane 3607, f. 24; see also Report of Seven Officers, October 31, 1712, Sloane 3607, f. 23, British Library.

44. *CSP-AWI*, 1711–1712, p. 307.

45. Vetch to Livingston, June 20, 1712, Sloane 3607, f. 19; Vetch, Letter of introduction for Livingston, March 1, 1712, Sloane 3607, f. 15, British Library; see also *CSP-AWI*, 1711-1712, p. 308.

46. Vetch to James Douglas, June 24, 1712, Sloane 3607, f. 18, British Library.

47. *CSP-AWI*, 1711-1712, p. 307.

48. Vetch to Dartmouth, August 8, 1712, Sloane 3607, f. 19, British Library.

49. Krugler, "Livingston, John," 437.

50. *CSP-AWI*, 1712-1714, p. 182.

51. Alden Vaughan, *Transatlantic Encounters: American Indians in Britain, 1500-1776* (Cambridge: Cambridge University Press, 2006), 151-62; Nancy Shoemaker, *A Strange Likeness: Becoming Red and White in Eighteenth-Century North America* (Oxford: Oxford University Press, 2006), 35-39; Julie Ann Sweet, *Negotiating for Georgia: British-Creek Relations in the Trustee Era, 1733-1752* (Athens: University of Georgia Press, 2005), 40-60; Steven Hahn, *The Invention of the Creek Nation* (Lincoln: University of Nebraska Press, 2004), 149-85.

52. See generally Paul Keaton, *Epidemics and Enslavement: Biological Catastrophe in the Native Southeast, 1492-1715* (Lincoln: University of Nebraska Press, 2007), 126-224.

53. See Kenneth Coleman, *Colonial Georgia: A History* (New York: Scribner, 1976), 15-54; Harold E. Davis, *The Fledgling Province: Social and Cultural Life in Colonial Georgia, 1733-1776* (Chapel Hill: University of North Carolina Press, 1976), 7-14; Daniel J. Boorstin, *The Americans: The Colonial Experience* (New York: Vintage Books, 1958), 71-96; J. E. Crowley, *This Sheba Self: The Conceptualization of Economic Life in Eighteenth-Century America* (Baltimore: Johns Hopkins University Press, 1974), 16-34; Paul S. Taylor, *Georgia Plan, 1732-1752* (Berkeley, CA: Institute of Business and Economic Research, 1972); Verner W. Crane, "Dr. Thomas Bray and the Charitable Colony Project, 1730," *William and Mary Quarterly*, 3d. ser., 19 (1962): 49-63.

54. See, for example, Instructions for Hugh Mackay, July 16, 1735, *The Colonial Records of the State of Georgia* (Atlanta and Athens, Georgia, 1904-), 32: 141-43 (hereafter *CRG*).

55. *CRG* 1: 49-52.

56. *CRG* 1: 44.

57. *CRG* 1: 21.

58. *CRG* 1: 78.

59. *CRG* 2: 75.

60. A. W. Parker, *Scottish Highlanders in Colonial Georgia: The Recruitment, Emigration and Settlement at Darien, 1735-1748* (Athens: University of Georgia Press, 1997), 38.

61. *CRG* 21: 13.

62. *CRG* 20: 338-40, 339.

63. *An Account Shewing the Progress of the Colony of Georgia in America from Its First Establishment*, reprinted in *The Clamorous Malcontents: Criticisms and Defenses of the Colony of Georgia*, ed. Trevor R. Reese (Savannah, GA: Beehive Press, 1973), 181-258, 204.

64. *CRG* 20: 338-40, 339.

65. *CRG* 21: 26.

66. *CRG* 21: 13.

67. Parker, *Scottish Highlanders in Colonial Georgia*, 25; Cashin, *Lachlan McGillivray*, 13; Daniel Szechi, *1715: The Great Jacobite Rebellion* (New Haven, CT: Yale University Press, 2006), 178.

68. *CRG* 21: 26; Parker, *Scottish Highlanders in Colonial Georgia*, 51.

69. Parker, *Scottish Highlanders in Colonial Georgia*, 20, 39, 54.

70. Cashin, *Lachlan McGillivray*, 1, 53; *CRG*, 2: 135, 164.

71. Parker, *Scottish Highlanders in Colonial Georgia*, 55.

72. *CRG* 32: 142, 29: 83.

73. *South Carolina Gazette*, March 13–20, 1736.

74. Samuel Eveleigh to Verelst, March 24, 1736, in *General Oglethorpe's Georgia: Colonial Letters, 1733–1743*, ed. Mills Lane (Savannah, GA: Beehive Press, 1990), 1: 253–56, 254; see also *CRG* 21: 120; *South Carolina Gazette*, March 13–20, 1736; Parker, *Scottish Highlanders in Colonial Georgia*, 54.

75. Cashin, *Lachlan McGillivray*, 16.

76. See Oglethorpe to Duncan Forbes, February 21, 1740, in *Culloden Papers*, ed. R. H. Duff (London, 1815), 155; Parker, *Scottish Highlanders in Colonial Georgia*, 46.

77. *A State of the Province of Georgia* (London, 1742), reprinted in *The Clamorous Malcontents: Criticisms and Defenses of the Colony of Georgia*, ed. Trevor R. Reese (Savannah, GA: Beehive Press, 1973), 3–22, 8.

78. Benjamin Martyn, *An Impartial Enquiry into the State and Utility of the Province of Georgia* (London, 1741), in *The Clamorous Malcontents: Criticisms and Defenses of the Colony of Georgia*, ed. Trevor R. Reese (Savannah, GA: Beehive Press, 1973), 125–80, 132.

79. Oglethorpe to the Georgia Trustees, June 1736, in *General Oglethorpe's Georgia: Colonial Letters, 1733–1743*, ed. Mills Lane (Savannah, GA: Beehive Press, 1990), 1: 268–78, 274–75; Colin G. Calloway, *White People, Indians and Highlanders: Tribal People and Colonial Encounters in Scotland and America* (Oxford: Oxford University Press, 2008), xi, 94.

80. CSP-AWI, 1716-1717, pp. 130-31. Abbott Emerson Smith, *Colonists in Bondage: White Servitude and Convict Labor in America, 1607-1776* (Chapel Hill: University of North Carolina Press, 1947), 198; see also Margaret Sankey, *Jacobite Prisoners of the 1715 Rebellion: Preventing and Punishing Insurrection in Early Hanoverian Britain* (Aldershot: Ashgate, 2005), 70.

81. Petition to Oglethorpe, January 3, 1738/9, in Parker, *Scottish Highlanders in Colonial Georgia*, 126. See David Brion Davis, *The Problem of Slavery in Western Culture* (Ithaca, N.Y.: Cornell University Press, 1966), 148; Harvey H. Jackson, "The Darien Anti-Slavery Petition of 1739 and the Georgia Plan," *William and Mary Quarterly*, 3d ser., 34 (1977): 618-31.

82. For a contemporary discussion of local politics in Darien emphasizing its hierarchical nature, see *CRG* 4: 555.

83. Oglethorpe to trustees, October 20, 1739, in Lane, ed., *General Oglethorpe's Georgia*, 2: 418–20, 418–19.

84. Colonial Records of Georgia (microfilm continuation, Newberry Library, Chicago) 35: 355; hereafter CRG (microfilm).

85. Major-General Charles Wills, quoted in Szechi, *1715*, 178; see Cashin, *Lachlan McGillivray*, 13.

86. CRG (microfilm), 35: 340.

87. CRG (microfilm), 35: 336, 35: 340–41.

88. South Carolina Assembly, *The Report of the Committee of Both Houses of Assembly* (London, 1743), 49; CRG (microfilm), 35: 341.

89. Coleman, *Colonial Georgia*, 49, 66; Phinizy Spalding, *Oglethorpe in America* (Chicago: University of Chicago Press, 1977), 112; Jane Landers, "Gracia Real de Santa Teresa

de Mose: A Free Black Town in Spanish Colonial Florida," *American Historical Review* 95 (1990): 9–30; Larry E. Ivers, "The Battle of Fort Moosa," *Georgia Historical Quarterly* 51 (1967): 135–53; Albert Sidney Britt Jr., "John Mohr McIntosh, A Prisoner of War in Spain, 1741," *Georgia Historical Quarterly* 51 (1967): 449–53; Parker, *Scottish Highlanders in Colonial Georgia*, 20, 38–51.

90. CRG (microfilm), 35: 336.

91. South Carolina, *Report of Committee of Both Houses*, 50; Coleman, *Colonial Georgia*, 49; Spalding, *Oglethorpe in America*, 112; Larry E. Ivers, "The Battle of Fort Moosa," *Georgia Historical Quarterly* 11 (1967): 135–53; Britt, "John Mohr McIntosh," 449–53.

92. Patrick Tailfer, *A True and Historical Narrative of the Colony of Georgia in America* (London, 1741), reprinted in *The Clamorous Malcontents: Criticisms and Defenses of the Colony of Georgia*, ed. Trevor R. Reese (Savannah, GA: Beehive Press, 1973), 104; Parker, *Scottish Highlanders in Colonial Georgia*, 78–81.

93. CRG (microfilm), 35: 337, 35: 341–42.

94. CRG (microfilm), 35: 342.

95. CRG (microfilm), 35: 345.

96. *CRG* 4: 239–41. See also the depositions of John McLeod and Alexander Monroe, November 1741, in Thomas Stephens, *A Brief Account of the Causes That Have Retarded the Progress of the Colony of Georgia* (London, 1743), reprinted in *The Clamorous Malcontents: Criticisms and Defenses of the Colony of Georgia*, ed. Trevor R. Reese (Savannah, GA: Beehive Press, 1973), 299–304; Cashin, *Lachlan McGillivray*, 26; Parker, *Scottish Highlanders in Colonial Georgia*, 71–72.

97. Parker, *Scottish Highlanders in Colonial Georgia*, 61–67.

98. Cashin, *Lachlan McGillivray*, 82–83.

99. Parker, *Scottish Highlanders in Colonial Georgia*, 84–86.

100. The Forty-third Highland Regiment subsequently became the Forty-second.

101. "The Behaviour and Character of Samuel Macpherson, Malcolm Macpherson and Farquhar Shaw," (London, 1743), reprinted in *Transactions of the Gaelic Society of Inverness* 3–4 (1873–75): 154–66, 157; see also Leah Leneman, *Living in Atholl, 1685–1785* (Edinburgh: Edinburgh University Press, 1986), 140–41.

102. "The Behaviour and Character of Samuel Macpherson," 157.

103. Ibid., 159.

104. Parker, *Scottish Highlanders in Colonial Georgia*, 93; see Letters to John Hay, marquis of Tweeddale, May 19 and July 14, 1743, GD1.609/3, ff. 5 and 8, National Archives of Scotland.

105. Parker, *Scottish Highlanders in Colonial Georgia*, 87–91.

106. See generally Cashin, *Lachlan McGillivray*; Claudio Saunt, *A New Order of Things: Property, Power, and the Transformation of the Creek Indians, 1733–1816* (Cambridge: Cambridge University Press, 2003), 67–89.

107. Parker, *Scottish Highlanders in Colonial Georgia*.

108. Arthur G. Doughty, ed., *An Historical Journal of the Campaigns in North America for the Years 1757, 1758, 159, and 1760, by Captain John Knox*, 3 vols. (Toronto: Champlain Society, 1914), 1 :73–75.

109. John Campbell, 4th earl of Loudon, to William Augustus, duke of Cumberland, November 22, 1756, in *Military Affairs in North America, 1748–1765*, ed. Stanley Pargellis (New York: American Historical Association, 1936), 263–80, 264.

110. Loudon to Henry Bouquet, September 8, 1757, Loudon North America Papers, Huntington Library 4430 (hereafter LO (NA) ms. No, HL); see also Archibald Montgomery, General Return of the 1st Highland Battalion, September 18, 1757, LO (NA) 6695. On the steering of Gaelic speakers to the units, see LO (NA) papers nos. 4239, 4240, 4330, 4431, 4416, 4430, 4469, 4646, 4649, 4693, 4727, 4951, 5050, 5099, 5113, 5129 and 5374, 6873, Huntington Library.

111. Stephen Brumwell, *Redcoats: The British Soldier and War in the Americas, 1755–1763* (Cambridge: Cambridge University Press, 2002), 225.

112. Horace Walpole, *Memoirs of King George II*, ed. John Brooke, 3 vols. (New Haven, CT: Yale University Press, 1985), 207.

113. See Geoffrey Plank, *Rebellion and Savagery: The Jacobite Rising of 1745 and the British Empire* (Philadelphia: University of Pennsylvania Press, 2006), 75–76.

114. Peregrine Thomas Hopson to Loudon, October 16 and 23, 1757, LO (NA) 4646 and 4693, Huntington Library.

115. See Geoffrey Plank, *An Unsettled Conquest: The British Campaign against the Peoples of Acadia* (Philadelphia: University of Pennsylvania Press, 2001).

116. See Peter Silver, *Our Savage Neighbors: How Indian War Transformed Early America* (New York: Norton, 2008), 33–53.

117. Calloway, *White People, Indians and Highlanders*, 88–116.

118. Frank Cunningham, *General Stand Watie's Confederate Indians* (Norman: University of Oklahoma Press, 1998). Another possible exception is the Stockbridge companies that fought with the Continental army during the American Revolution. See Colin Calloway, *The American Revolution in Indian Country* (Cambridge: Cambridge University Press, 1995), 85–107.

119. James Smith, quoted in Brumwell, *Redcoats*, 205.

120. Brumwell, *Redcoats*, 225.

121. Bruce Lenman, *The Jacobite Risings in Britain, 1689–1746* (Aberdeen: Scottish Cultural Press, 1995), 278–79.

122. See generally Andrew Mackillop, *"More Fruitful Than the Soil": Army, Empire and the Scottish Highlands, 1715–1815* (East Linton: Tuckwell Press, 2000).

123. See Brumwell, *Redcoats*, 273–74; James Grant to Robert Grant, March 2, 1757, Add. Ms. 25,411, f. 240, British Library.

124. Calloway, *White People, Indians and Highlanders*, 96.

125. Simon Fraser to Sir William Johnson, February 23, 1759, PU 1790, Huntington Library.

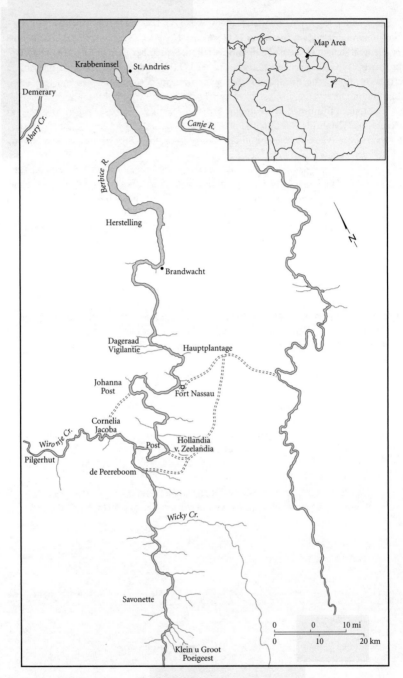

Berbice and Canje rivers, Dutch Berbice, 1763.

10

"Cleansing the Land"

Dutch-Amerindian Cooperation in the Suppression
of the 1763 Slave Rebellion in Dutch Guiana

MARJOLEINE KARS

In 1763, the biggest and longest-lasting slave rebellion in the Caribbean before the St. Domingue revolution erupted in the Dutch colony of Berbice in northern South America.[1] The great majority of the colony's enslaved
people were caught up in the rebellion, as either rebels or fugitives. The Dutch
had an exceedingly hard time saving themselves and their colony; in fact, it
took them almost two years to do so. The rebels were determined and their
numerical preponderance overwhelming, so the Europeans could not readily defend themselves against their hit-and-run tactics. Moreover, at first, the
Dutch lacked a clear counterinsurgency effort. Their soldiers were helpless
in the thick, unmapped jungle, where western cannon and guns were of little
use. Most of the planters had no stomach for fighting, and the frustrated and
unhappy soldiers and sailors absconded and mutinied. Reinforcements from
Holland were slow to arrive, and when they did, they succumbed to tropical
disease at an alarming rate. Eight months after the start of the rebellion, Governor Simon Wolfert van Hoogenheim lamented that he feared a "sad ending," predicting that "Christendom" would fall sacrifice to its "angry barbaric
enemies" because the "way things are going, we cannot hold out long."[2]

In the end, though, "Christendom" was not defeated, and the Dutch
restored their authority. In part, this was thanks to Dutch reinforcements
who forced the rebels deeper into the jungle. There they found it harder to
obtain food and weapons, which intensified internal divisions. But just as
important, the restoration of Dutch authority and the plantation economy
depended on Amerindians, for they possessed the strength, local knowledge,
and military skills for jungle fighting that the Dutch lacked. Without the
assistance of its longtime indigenous allies, the Dutch colonial power likely
would have failed, and the former slaves would have set up Maroon settlements, much as they had in neighboring Suriname.

Throughout the early modern world, Amerindian allies helped Europeans militarily in creating and maintaining their colonies. They fought against not only their fellow indigenes but also rebelling slaves and European colonial rivals, having been forced or seduced into such service with promises of political, military, or economic advantages or their own shrewd calculations of self-interest. The balance of power between the indigenous peoples and the colonists thus determined the degree of control the colonial authorities could exercise over these soldiers.[3] On the "Wild Coast" of South America, as elsewhere, however, Europeans were not able to force Amerindians to fight, notwithstanding any treaties. Rather, because they had to persuade them to do so, personal relationships between Amerindians and colonists were crucial to mobilizing indigenous fighters.

This chapter sketches the unfolding of the Berbice slave rebellion and describes the role of Amerindians in its suppression. What did the alliance of natives and colonists consist of? How was it organized? What held it together? How did Amerindian assistance help the Dutch project power and establish its coercive authority?

Berbice

In the seventeenth and eighteenth centuries, the Dutch established a number of colonies between the Amazon and the Orinoco rivers in northeastern South America. The Dutch called the area the "Wild Coast" because it was controlled by *wilden*, as they called the Amerindians. Moving from east to west, Dutch Guiana comprised the colonies of Suriname, Berbice, Demerara, and Essequibo, all named after the main rivers of settlement. Of these four, Suriname was the largest and the most profitable. Whereas the Dutch West India Company (WIC) and, more particularly, the Zeeland Chamber, governed Essequibo and Demerara, private companies ran Berbice and Suriname.

A Dutch "patroon" first settled the Berbice River early in the seventeenth century. His descendants ran the colony for a century before selling it in 1714 to private investors from Amsterdam, who organized the Society of Berbice in 1720. This society, chartered by the Dutch government in 1732, governed the colony until 1791 when the States General, the Dutch general decision-making body in which each of the seven provinces (or "states") had one vote, took over all four Guiana colonies. Early in the nineteenth century, Berbice, along with Essequibo and Demerara, passed into British hands, and the area became known as British Guiana. Independent since 1966, it is now the Republic of Guyana.[4]

Under the direction of the Society of Berbice, the colony grew, but slowly, as the economy of the Dutch Republic was geared toward trade, not the production of tropical cash crops. Unlike the British, the Dutch had no protective tariffs for products such as sugar, cacao, cotton, and coffee, and slaves were expensive to buy, especially given the prices that planters could expect for their crops. Consequently, the number of people willing to invest in new plantations in Berbice was never large, and even fewer were willing to move to the colony. Instead, investors hired local directors to establish new coffee, cacao, and cotton plantations along the Berbice and its tributary, the Canje. Because few private individuals could afford the high start-up costs involved in growing sugar, they left that business to the more financially robust Society.[5]

By the time the slaves revolted in 1763, the society was operating eleven large sugar plantations on the Berbice River, employing close to 1,500 slaves. In addition, some eighty to ninety smaller plantations were in private hands on the Berbice River, and another forty to fifty on the Canje River. Around 350 Europeans, a total of 4,000 to 5,000 enslaved Africans and creoles, some 300 native slaves, and an unknown number of free Amerindians lived in the colony at that time.[6]

Beyond the ribbon of riverside plantations stretched vast savannas and uncharted rainforest, which was frightening to Europeans. During the year's two rainy seasons, much of the savannas and forests flooded, making overland travel difficult. Instead, as they do today, people and goods in dugouts and tent boats moved up and down the two main rivers and numerous creeks. Strong tides made it possible for smaller sailing ships to float up and down the Berbice River for more than a hundred miles with the rising and falling water.[7]

The Dutch maintained close military and trade relations with Amerindians in the area. The Arawaks and Waraos, known to the Dutch as "our Indians," lived closest to the plantations, and they performed a great many services for the Dutch, such as hunting and fishing. Beyond the Dutch settlement, the Caribs and Akawaios maintained much greater independence, although they traded with the Dutch and had obligated themselves via treaties to provide military aid to them in case of foreign attack or slave uprisings.[8] Amerindians also prevented the establishment of Maroon communities in Berbice that, as far as we know, did not exist before 1763. This indigenous military help was badly needed because neither the planters nor the Society was willing to spend much on defense. The three small forts, two near the ocean and a third, Fort Nassau, near the hamlet of New Amsterdam in the heart of the colony, were sadly neglected and in a poor state of repair. Fewer than fifty soldiers were stationed in Berbice at any given time. Many were ill or old, and all of them were spread out among the forts and a number of small inland posts intended for both defense and trade with the Amerindians.[9] These soldiers, their numbers even further reduced by a series of epidemics that hit both the black and white populations hard in the five years before the rebellion, were of little help at the start of the 1763 uprising.

Rebellion

Small slave rebellions on individual plantations had broken out in Berbice every decade since 1730 and were usually quickly suppressed. In July 1762, twenty-six slaves on a plantation high up the Berbice River rebelled, fled into the woods, and proved difficult to subdue. On the eve of his execution, one of the leaders predicted that what the rebels had not succeeded in doing this time, "others would soon carry out."[10] Later that year, unrest broke out among enslaved workers at the fort and on the Savonette, the outermost company plantation farthest upriver. A rattled Governor van Hoogenheim sent urgent letters to the society requesting more soldiers and supplies, but his missives brought no result.[11] Frightened whites, reduced by epidemics to fewer than one for every twenty-five enslaved workers, became more violent and repressive, thereby encouraging further rebelliousness.

On February 23, 1763, more than seventy slaves on Magdalenenburg and Providence plantations on the Canje River revolted and, armed with guns, took off in the direction of the Courantyne River, on the border with Suriname. Two days later, thirty of them attacked a small Suriname trading post on the Courantyne River. The postholder, his assistants, and the Amerindians living around the post fled in panic. The rebels helped themselves to axes and knives intended for trade with Amerindians. After attacking an Amerindian village, the insurgents settled higher up the Courantyne, and for more than a month, local Amerindians were afraid to attack them. Finally, in mid-April, Caribs arrived in several canoes from the Waijombo River, in Suriname, and together with the Arawaks and Waraos, they attacked the rebel village, killing at least ten people.[12] Meanwhile, fearful whites had begun to desert the Canje en masse, many leaving their enslaved workers behind, most of whom stayed on their plantations.

Four days after the start of the Canje rebellion, on Sunday, February 27, while the Dutch were at church, the slaves started a "revolution," as the Europeans referred to it, on a number of private plantations just north of New Amsterdam on the Berbice River.[13] Unlikely as it seems, we have no evidence that the Canje and Berbice uprisings were connected. The leader on the Berbice, who took the title of governor, was a man named Coffy who was brought to the colony as a child. He was a skilled slave on the plantation Lelienburg, where he worked as a cooper and *bomba*, or driver. His second in command, Accarra, lived on the same plantation. The male rebels organized themselves along military and civilian lines: some were captains, lieutenants, or soldiers, and others became councillors or held offices such as that of prosecutor. The rebels divided their supreme authority in the same way: Governor Coffy was the head of the civil administration, and Captain Accarra was the head of the military force.[14]

The well-organized rebellion rapidly spread from the center of the colony. Within a day, twenty plantations were involved, and that number rose quickly. The rebels moved from plantation to plantation, urging or forcing people to join, confiscating crucial resources such as weapons, boats, and food, and setting plantations on fire. The evidence strongly suggests that the initial plans and execution involved a broad partnership of people from different backgrounds, uniting creoles and Africans in a common cause. The majority of rebels came from private plantations. The slaves on Society plantations known as *Colonie volk* were the most reluctant to join, and they were also the first to return to the Dutch at the end of the rebellion.[15] Some forty Europeans were killed in the first few weeks, many of them on the society plantation Peereboom, where a large number of frightened whites had taken refuge and others were taken hostage. In a series of letters the rebels sent to the governor at the start of the rebellion, Coffy and Accara explained that certain plantation owners' and managers' cruel treatment, low rations, and denial of customary rights had forced the slaves to rebel.[16]

At the first signs of rebellion, Dutch authority utterly collapsed. Only ten healthy soldiers were stationed at Fort Nassau, and a mere forty-five were available in the colony as a whole. The ten soldiers stationed at the "Accoway" trading post high up the Berbice River immediately took off for Demerara,[17] along with most of the planters and government officials living upriver from the rebellion. Some went east to Demerara and Essequibo. Others scrambled to secure themselves and their possessions on the merchant ships and the one slaver that happened to be in port, thereby preventing these ships from participating in the defense of the colony.[18] Local Amerindians left their villages and rushed further into the bush. Early in March, Governor van Hoogenheim, along with a few remaining officials and a handful of militiamen, soldiers, and burghers retreated to Fort St. Andries on the coast, effectively turning the entire colony over to the insurgents.[19]

The situation at Fort St. Andries was little better. The fort lay in plain sight in the middle of the savanna, lacked breastworks or entrenchments, and boasted only two old cannon. There were a mere twenty-four soldiers, a handful of officers, large numbers of refugees, and no supply of fresh water. Panicked planters from the Canje had flocked to the fort with their families and slaves; others had left their laborers behind. Van Hoogenheim immediately ordered the slaves to build huts for everyone. Only twelve planters had a stomach for fighting; the others demanded to be given leave to board the ships and go home. Despite these precarious circumstances, however, Van Hoogenheim was determined not to abandon the colony.[20]

At the end of March, valuable help arrived from neighboring Suriname, a colony that had been fighting its own rebellious slaves for decades. Governor Wigbold Crommelin was determined to prevent the Berbice rebels from crossing into Suriname where, it was feared, they might try to join the newly pacified Saramaka Maroons. The soldiers he now sent to Berbice from Suriname had learned jungle warfare while fighting runaway slaves and, Crommelin boasted, "the habits of the blacks are familiar to them."[21] Van Hoogenheim immediately sent twenty-five soldiers and six colonists to the Canje to the Fredriksburg plantation from where they were to patrol the river. Two ships full of refugees remained at St. Andries. The other two ships and the slaver, loaded with the rest of the soldiers, the governor, a handful of colonists, and an unknown number of slaves and Amerindians, sailed back upriver for some twenty miles. On April 1, Van Hoogenheim set up headquarters on a large society plantation, Dageraad, determined to stay in the colony. Here the Dutch maintained a tenuous hold while waiting for reinforcements from the republic, who did not arrive until year's end.[22]

A major rebel force, meanwhile, had dug in upstream from the Dageraad at the neighboring Vigilantie plantation, and a larger force occupied the now-burned Fort Nassau. On April 2, around three hundred to four hundred rebels attacked the Dageraad, but the Dutch succeeded in beating back three successive attacks using the cannon on their ships. One colonist and at least seven rebels were killed.[23] The next day, two Amerindians and a male hostage brought a letter from the rebel leader Coffy. Coffy apologized for the attack, which had been carried out, he claimed, without his knowledge or permission by his right-hand man, Captain Accarra. Coffy assured Van Hoogenheim that he wanted to negotiate, not fight, and he proposed dividing the colony in two. It seems likely that this proposal was partly inspired by recent peace negotiations in Suriname with the Saramaka and Ndjuka Maroons.[24] To gain time, Van Hoogenheim began a cautious correspondence with the rebel leader. Local Amerindians and slaves loyal to the Dutch carried the letters back and forth, just as they also handled written communications with other posts and neighboring colonies. Meanwhile, Van Hoogenheim ordered defenses built and a battery on the river's edge. Each day, he sent out patrols of indigenous and enslaved men to reconnoiter and keep track of rebel locations.[25]

The situation of the Dutch deteriorated rapidly. On April 6, about four hundred well-armed rebels attacked the Fredericksburg plantation on the Canje. The twenty-five soldiers, six citizens, and handful of Amerindians and slaves there were forced to retreat to Fort St. Andries, carrying along nine injured men and leaving behind three casualties. The rebels, who may have lost as many as thirty men, then set fire to Fredericksburg.[26] Again, the Dutch found themselves in dire straits, as once more the rebels were in charge of the Canje. The slaver and one of the merchant ships refused to remain in Berbice any longer and left for home, and more soldiers fell ill every day. Then, yet again, help arrived from abroad. At the end of May, two ships from St. Eustatius entered the Berbice with 150 fighters. Even with these reinforcements, however, the Dutch considered themselves too weak to undertake a campaign against the rebels. They needed more soldiers, but more important, they needed the help of the Amerindians.[27]

Up to this point, the assistance of the Amerindians had been limited. Much as the Europeans had, the indigenous peoples living near plantations had scattered in fear as soon as the rebellion began. The Amerindians near the post on the Courantyne, too, had fled when the rebels appeared. But a small force of Suriname Caribs had attacked a rebel stronghold high up the Courantyne River in mid-April, killing about ten rebels.[28] By and large, however, the local Amerindians had been reluctant to resist the insurgents. At the end of May, Van Hoogenheim called together a number of their leaders to impress upon them the danger they were in from the rebels. Assisting the Dutch was not only their duty, he reminded them, but in fact was in their own interest. Thereupon, they promised assistance and agreed to carry out nightly patrols.[29]

While local Amerindian patrols, scouts, guides, and messengers were important, their ability to cordon off the colony to prevent the rebels' retreating into the trackless highlands was indispensable. For this, the Dutch had to rely on the powerful and numerous Caribs living higher up the Essequibo River. Because the governor of Essequibo had close relations with these Caribs, it fell to him to mobilize them as soon as he heard about the rebellion. He urged them to occupy the upper Berbice, close off all escape routes, and catch or kill any and all rebels. The start of the long rainy season in early May, however, prevented the Caribs from taking the field as quickly as the Dutch had hoped.[30]

Meanwhile, the soldiers from St. Eustatius arrived just in time. On May 12, a patrol discovered that the rebels were cutting paths toward Dageraad. The next morning a large rebel force—Van Hoogenheim's estimate of two thousand seems high—attacked the plantation from three different sides, drums beating. Initially they put the Europeans on the defensive. The artillery of the two ships and the battery at the water's edge, however, forced the rebels back, and faced with a counterattack of some 280 soldiers, they retreated. One of the Dutch ships tried to prevent the rebels' sixty canoes from crossing the river but failed because of a lack of wind. The sailors did, however, succeed in using their cannon to sink several canoes "filled to the brim with goods and blacks," forcing those aboard to save themselves by swimming.[31]

Despite the size of this battle, there were few deaths. The Europeans found eight dead rebels, whose heads they put on poles at the river's edge. The other casualties and wounded the insurgents had taken with them. The Dutch lost one man and sustained ten wounded, one of whom later died. However, the soldiers from St. Eustatius now declared that they would "not step off their ships or pick up a gun again" unless they were given generous premiums for killing or capturing rebels. The embattled governor thus had no choice but to accede to their demands.[32]

During the summer and fall, the rebels and Europeans kept a close eye on each other. The Dutch relied almost exclusively on local Amerindians and enslaved creoles to carry out spy missions. After all, these men were familiar with the terrain and knew how to survive in the woods. But neither the rebels nor the Europeans undertook a great offensive. The rainy season had started in May, causing European soldiers and sailors to fall ill and die in large numbers. On one ship alone, for instance, 80 of the 110 sailors were either sick or had died, and the remainder refused to serve. Having only 400 men, many unwell, the Dutch did not dare attack, and moreover, the woods were flooded.[33]

The rebels had their own problems, as they were short on food, shot, and powder. The Amerindian spies also discovered that rebels were making bows and arrows to arm those without guns.[34] Moreover, the African and creole rebels, initially allied, were increasingly disagreeing over strategy. Coffy and his supporters wanted to continue negotiating with Van Hoogenheim about dividing the colony, and he briefly reopened written negotiations with the Dutch in early August. The more radical Africans, however, wanted to fight and drive the Europeans into the sea. Some wanted to join the Maroons in Suriname, and others wanted to free the slaves in neighboring Demerara in order to increase their total strength. The rebels likely also had different goals. Some wanted to keep the plantation system, but with black rather than white planters, while others imagined a community of smallholders.[35]

By early fall, internal divisions over strategy, along with disease, hunger, and a shortage of weapons, began to take their toll on the rebels. An Amina named Atta, who disapproved of Coffy's attempts at negotiation and wanted to fight the Dutch instead, increasingly challenged Coffy's leadership.[36] As a result of this power struggle, sometime before October, Coffy committed suicide and Atta took over.[37] Despite these difficulties, the rebels kept the initiative. They moved about the colony with relative freedom, while the Dutch, their main force pinned down on the Dageraad, dared send out only small patrols over short distances. The rebels regularly carried out small hit-and-run attacks on various Dutch posts, keeping the Dutch on the alert, and on several occasions they battled Amerindians allied with the Dutch.[38]

The Dutch, meanwhile, feared not only the rebels but also, increasingly, their own rank and file. A regiment of some seventy soldiers from Suriname stationed on the border between the two colonies mutinied in early July, and fifteen of them ended up joining the rebels. The Dutch were convinced that the assistance of these white soldiers would be what would allow the rebels to win the war.[39] Soldiers and sailors on the Dageraad, too, were unhappy with their working conditions, and by September their officers declared that they could no longer count on their men. They also feared that any deserters might convey valuable information to the rebels, as they knew several slave runaways had already done. "So at all moments we have to fear," the governor informed the authorities in Holland, "disloyalty and treason within, as much as attacks from without."[40]

By the end of summer, the situation for the Europeans was critical. The "raging illness" claimed many victims; between mid-June and mid-August, more than a third of the entire military force died and another third was sick. In addition, the rainy season was about to end, making a rebel attack more likely. The only bright spot was the assistance of the Amerindians. On July 27, Akawaio Amerindians from Demerara, prompted by the Essequibo governor, Laurens Storm van 's Gravesande, had attacked Savonette, the outermost plantation on the Berbice, where a large group of rebels had congregated to plant provision grounds. In a nighttime raid, the indigenous fighters reportedly killed fifty-five slave men, women, and children.[41] The Akawaios then retreated when a rebel force, accompanied by some of the mutinied soldiers, came to the aid of their comrades. Storm van s' Gravesande then rearmed the Akowaoi so they could join a large group of Caribs on their way to Berbice.[42] In September, Van Hoogenheim received word that Caribs living near the Courantyne, on the eastern border of the colony, were willing to ally with the Akowaio to jointly attack a band of rebels stationed in the Wikki Creek.[43] In addition, local Amerindians patrolled most of the larger creeks, preventing rebels from setting up camps.[44] Despite the Amerindians' assistance, in early October, Van Hoogenheim's military advisers again advocated abandoning the Dageraad and retreating once more to burned-out St. Andries on the coast. The governor refused.[45] He kept hoping that the military assistance he had requested from the republic as soon as the rebellion started would arrive momentarily.[46]

Turning of the Tide

That fall, as the situation worsened for the rebels, the tide began to turn for the Dutch, thanks to an important advantage: they could be reinforced with men and matériel from Europe. At the end of October, at long last, a twenty-gun warship from the republic sailed up the Berbice with 150 soldiers. Fearful that the newly arrived soldiers would fall ill and become useless, the Dutch decided that they would deploy them immediately in gaining back the Canje. Controlling that river would improve communication with the Courantyne River and the Suriname government and would command the crucial trail between the Canje and New Amsterdam. In November, the Canje expedition was launched, with two armed ships and 180 soldiers, officers, and sailors, and it was carried out without a major battle. Instead, the rebels retreated upriver without a fight, employing a "scorched earth" technique, setting fire to any plantations that had been spared earlier. Those slaves still living on abandoned plantations were forced out by the rebels. The advancing Dutch thus found few prisoners to take, as most of the former slaves had escaped. The Europeans did succeed, though, in retaking the river and securing the trail from Canje to the fort. Now they waited for the rest of the force from home.[47]

At the end of November 1763, a second warship arrived with twenty-four guns and 150 men, along with two merchant ships sent by the society with 50 soldiers. Early in December, a twelve-gun man-of-war with 110 soldiers sailed up the Berbice. With these reinforcements, the Dutch finally felt strong enough to undertake a large expedition up the Berbice in mid-December, involving five ships with three hundred to four hundred soldiers, accompanied by Amerindian and enslaved support personnel. No one believed it possible to conquer the rebels, but they hoped to drive them away from the plantations and thus away from their provisions. In addition, the Dutch planned to persuade as many slaves as possible to return to them or, failing that, to take them prisoner. A detachment of thirty soldiers was sent to Demerara where they would be reinforced with another thirty.[48] These sixty men were to make their way to the southernmost Berbice plantation, Savonette. This maneuver, it was hoped, would cut off the rebels and prevent them from fleeing higher upstream.

As the ships slowly made their way south, the rebels retreated higher upriver, as they had done on the Canje, abandoning plantations and their provisioning grounds, as the Dutch had hoped they would. What did not fit into Dutch plans, however, was the fact that the rebels forced any slaves still living peacefully on the plantations along the route to accompany them, and they torched whatever Dutch property had escaped destruction at the start of the rebellion. Moreover, at various locations, the rebels and Europeans exchanged gunfire. Soldiers fell on both sides. Amerindians and rebels repeatedly clashed high up the river, increasing mutual hostility.[49] Just before Christmas, all converged on Savonette, where rebels, Amerindians, and Europeans fought bitterly. This was the last settled spot where the rebels could congregate. After the battle, the insurgents dispersed, fading into the bush and jungle.[50] The Dutch could do little but set up small posts in strategic places from which local Amerindians and slaves, at times accompanied by soldiers, tried to discover the rebels' whereabouts. Indigenous fighters also stationed themselves on major creeks to prevent the insurgents from planting provision grounds or escaping from the colony.

In January, the long-awaited regiment of some six hundred "State troops," hired by the Dutch Estates General and commanded by Colonel Jan Marius de Salve, finally arrived from Holland. These troops were stationed in the ruins of New Amsterdam. De Salve made his headquarters in the parsonage, and he turned the church, the only other building still standing, into a military hospital. The new arrivals, however, could do little besides relieve the exhausted soldiers stationed on the various posts. Given that the rebels were now scattered inland and were moving around the colony in ever-smaller bands at war with one another as well as with the Dutch, it was difficult to mount a large expedition against them. Besides, European soldiers were singularly ineffective in the thick forest, where they became bogged down in morasses and creeks and repeatedly lost their way. Nor were there enough slaves available to carry the ammunition and food for the soldiers. Although operations on water could be supplied by ship, for land expeditions, porters were indispensable. Moreover, a large expedition against the highly mobile rebels would be exhausting and unlikely to succeed. Van Hoogenheim and De Salve also were afraid that such an expedition would scare off any slaves who might want to return on their own accord to the Dutch. De Salve therefore was reduced to sending out small reaction patrols whenever native and black scouts reported having spotted rebels, but his men did not always arrive on time.[51] As one of De Salve's officers, a Briton, put it, "but to get att them is impossible, they are now here, now there, & every Intelligence we get say they have Jump'd from where they were last."[52]

By now, the rebels were fighting one another as much as they were fighting, or hiding from, the Amerindians and the Dutch. Atta's Amina forces fought the "Gangoe" and small groups of Louango. Africans and creoles, too, had become enemies.[53] Increasingly short of weapons and ammunition, the rebel bands broke up as people deserted their erstwhile leaders and formed new, smaller bands or deserted to the Dutch. Prevented by the Amerindians from settling outside the colony, others moved back to live near plantations, where they hoped to find food. Every day, more and more former slaves began to turn themselves in to the Europeans, with their number mounting to several thousand by spring. But even as the rebellion fell apart, it took De Salve's forces until September to subdue the last determined fighters.[54]

For this last phase of the war, the Dutch once again relied heavily on the Amerindians. By July 1764, of the six hundred soldiers who had arrived in January, only twenty were still healthy. A month later, all the officers were ill except De Salve himself. Meanwhile, catching those rebels who refused to return of their own accord turned out to be an exhausting affair. During the summer, Amerindians, slaves, and soldiers on the various posts hunted down the last intrepid rebels. Almost daily, the Europeans received intelligence of one or another band of rebels. But the military units sent out to catch them usually found out, to their peril, that much of the news was incorrect or outdated by the time they arrived. In the end, it was patrols of Amerindians and slaves, who ignored rumors and instead followed tracks, who succeeded in taking prisoners or killing rebels. Especially upriver, rebels and indigenes regularly fought. To obtain payment from the Dutch for their services, the Amerindians either brought back rebel prisoners from such encounters, or they killed them and hacked off their right hand to be turned in to the colonial authorities.[55]

In March 1764, the Dutch began to investigate and try the growing number of suspected rebels in their custody. Their investigations were remarkably thorough, including interviews and confronting suspects with witnesses. In the end, some were released to plantation owners, and others, deemed guilty, were sentenced. Some 140 men and women were executed on the wheel, at the stake, and on the gallows. After the last executions in December 1764, a general amnesty was declared, but just a few Society slaves were set free as a reward for aiding the Dutch.[56]

The Dutch suffered massive losses as a result of the rebellion. More than 1,200 slaves had been killed in battle or had died of illness, hunger, and exposure. More than half the European inhabitants went home or were killed. Five of the eleven company plantations were destroyed. More than a third of the private plantations were abandoned after the revolt, and many others had to be rebuilt from the ground. The Estates General spent close to 800,000 guilders to help regain and rebuild the colony, money it never recouped from the Society of Berbice. But in the end, the Dutch regained their grip and restored both colonial authority and the institution of slavery.[57]

Amerindian-Dutch Relations

The narrative of the suppression of this rebellion indicates how difficult it was for the Dutch to retain their colony in the face of a massive slave uprising. The rebels and runaways hugely outnumbered them. The Dutch were short of men and matériel and faced a challenging climate and a demanding landscape. They struggled against crippling internal divisions, catastrophic tropical diseases, and slow support from home. Their supposed technological advantages appeared only when they could use ships and artillery but disappeared in the face of the irregular warfare that broke out as soon as the rebels left the plantations and retreated into the forest and savannas. The Dutch capacity to project power into the interior depended in great measure on their Amerindian allies and loyal slaves, who had the indispensable local knowledge and skills that the Europeans lacked. They provided communication, intelligence, reconnaissance, and orientation, and they could track down the insurgents. In this sense, the Amerindians were "ethnic soldiers," warriors recruited for military skills specifically associated with their local knowledge and lifestyle. More generally, however, they also provided essential support tasks, such as hauling, rowing, and foraging. Finally, acting as "secondary" agents of the Dutch, at their instigation but not under their direction, it was only the Amerindians who could provide a cordon to close off the southern reaches of the colony to prevent the insurgents from disappearing into the jungle for good. Clearly, Amerindians were crucial to Dutch power and the success of slavery. How did the Dutch-native alliance work?

By the time of the rebellion, Amerindians and Dutch colonists had been military allies for 150 years. The Dutch first became involved in the area in the late sixteenth century. At that time, Spain claimed the Orinoco area and Portugal the lower Amazon, but the land between remained in Amerindian hands, untouched by Europeans, owing to a forbidding coast of mangrove thickets, soggy soil, and sandy river-mouths. A large, multiethnic and multilingual indigenous population inhabited the region, including Arawaks (Lokono), Caribs (Kari'na), and Waraos, hence the name, the "wild coast," after the Dutch term for indigenous peoples, *wilden*. Extensive trade networks in foodstuffs, slaves, and handicrafts connected Amerindians for hundreds of miles inland.[58]

Starting in the early seventeenth century, competing European trading settlements began to dot the area. Their success or failure depended entirely on the goodwill of Amerindians interested in helping the newcomers because, unlike the Spanish, the Dutch came to trade, rather than to conquer or Christianize. In time, a few Dutch posts developed into permanent colonies.[59] Essequibo (1616) and Berbice (1627) survived because powerful natives were eager to aid them against the Spanish and to secure monopoly access to European goods, thereby enhancing their own political significance in the region. The Dutch brought knives, axes, beads, and fishhooks (all made to exacting Amerindian specifications), which they traded for food, tobacco, dyes, wood, and Amerindian slaves. Trade relations were sealed with marriages to Amerindian women, in keeping with indigenous notions of the interrelation between trade and kinship. "Several of the most considerable families, in rank and fortune," one traveler to the area reported in the 1760s, "derive their origin from these alliances."[60] At times, the trading partners fought with the Dutch against European rivals, and they protected the Dutch from hostile natives.

In the latter third of the seventeenth century, slavery increasingly affected the relationship between the Dutch and Amerindians. While the trade in indigenous slaves had bound them together for decades, the mistreatment and indiscriminate enslavement of native allies led to Amerindian uprisings in the late 1670s, not only in Suriname, but, albeit on a smaller scale, in Berbice and Essequibo as well. Eager to avoid bloody and costly attacks and the interruption of trade, Dutch colonial authorities tried to regulate the enslavement of Amerindians, protecting their allies from sale. The steady republication of such regulations over the next century suggests that labor-hungry colonists and eager traders regularly circumvented them. Moreover, of course, the inland Indians remained fair game; in fact, slaving provided much of the incentive for Amerindian military aid to the colonists. In addition, as the plantation economy and, with it, the enslaved African population grew, Amerindians increasingly profited from serving as slave catchers. Arawaks, Caribs, and others signed peace treaties in the 1680s obligating themselves to return runaway slaves, a duty they carried out, or not, as it suited them over the next one hundred years. Such agreements had the additional benefit of discouraging any future coalitions between Amerindians and enslaved Africans, who had joined in the Amerindian attacks in large numbers.[61]

To manage relations and trade with their Amerindian allies living beyond colonial settlements, the Dutch set up posts on the edges of their territories. Their locations shifted as native politics dictated. On each post, a "postholder" and several assistants managed trade and diplomacy: they urged Amerindians to keep up the supply and production of trade goods; they negotiated their help in returning runaway slaves; and they diffused local disputes that might hamper trade or imperil the colony. Just as English colonies competed with one another for Amerindian alliances in North America, so did Dutch settlements on the Wild Coast. Thus the postholders were also charged with preventing Amerindians from trading with neighboring colonies or rival Europeans. Some posts were more heavily engaged in slave trading, and others focused more on trade in dyes, balsam, hammocks, or canoes.[62] In Essequibo, most of the traders employed by the West India Company (WIC) were of African or mixed African and Amerindian descent, and most, but not all, were enslaved. These men, accompanied by native carriers and rowers, traveled the interior for months on end, trading for wood, dyes, horses, food, and slaves.[63] They married Amerindian women, and their sons followed in their father's footsteps.[64] We know little about the identities of these private traders, that is, those not employed by the authorities, who similarly may have had Amerindian mothers, as was common among traders in North America as well.

Of the four Dutch colonies on the Wild Coast, Essequibo was, and remained, the most deeply involved in Amerindian trade.[65] Although the other colonies turned from trade to plantation agriculture in the eighteenth century, Essequibo continued to depend on native-produced dyes, which were used to color butter and cheese in the Netherlands. The Caribs' dominance of this trade and a shared interest in containing the Spanish on the Orinoco formed the basis of a continued strong partnership. It was therefore the governor of Essequibo, rather than of Berbice, who negotiated the aid of allied Caribs in the suppression of the 1763 slave rebellion. As soon as Storm van 's Gravesande heard about the Berbice rebellion, he sent upriver Joseph de Meijer, a man who had "criss-crossed the highlands and speaks the Indian languages fluently."[66] De Meijer's mission was to persuade the Caribs to go fight in Berbice and, once he had done so, to accompany them. Storm agreed to arm any Carib willing to go to Berbice because, as he explained, they "cannot or will not fight without guns."[67] Confirming the long-standing conflation of commercial and military alliances, the Amerindians received trade goods for any prisoners they took or any rebels they killed, bringing along the right hands of their victims as proof.

Although Van Hoogenheim in Berbice had to leave the recruitment of Caribs to his Essequibo counterpart, he did personally work to obtain the aid of local Indians. Usually designated "free Indians" or "our Indians," they lived behind the Dutch plantations and formed the first line of defense against rebelling or absconding slaves and soldiers. In addition to catching runaways (or, sometimes, concealing them), they fished and hunted game for the colonists. Some local Indians lived in villages under chiefs or "captains" whose authority the Dutch strengthened as much as possible. Others lived scattered about, in which case they really were under no one's immediate direction. Van Hoogenheim regularly met with Amerindian captains to persuade them to aid the Dutch.

To ensure that the local Amerindians carried out his wishes while on their expeditions, Van Hoogenheim relied on go-betweens, men who were trusted by the indigenes, spoke their languages, and were familiar with their culture. So it was that free men of mixed descent were hired by the governor to guide most of the Amerindian patrols. In particular, Van Hoogenheim turned time and again to the male members of the free "Christian mulatto" Broer family.[68] The Broer men patrolled with Amerindians who lived near their plantations and with whom they evidently maintained a patron-client relationship. They used their language skills and positions of trust to mediate between them and the colonial authorities.[69] When Jan Broer Sr. died after a lingering illness in September 1763, Van Hoogenheim lamented the great loss of this man so valued "for his skills with the Indians, whom he knew how to keep on task and with whom he interacted so well."[70] In the spring of 1764, the Broer men expanded their activities by leading Essequibo Caribs on expeditions to catch outlying rebels. Evidently, the Caribs had refused to work with black guides, which made the mixed-descent Broer men even more valuable.[71] Another acceptable mediator was a *mulat neger*, a company slave named Frederik, "known to all Indians."[72] Like the Broers, Frederik communicated the governor's wishes to the local indigenes, and he guided them on patrols and expeditions.

Despite these strong and long-standing alliances and treaties, the Amerindians' cooperation in the Berbice rebellion was by no means a forgone conclusion. The Amerindians' willingness to provide aid depended on their own interests, their relationships with other native communities, and their connections with individual colonial representatives such as local postholders or colonial governors. Just as the Six Nations Iroquois in North America, for instance, did not act as a body but as individual villages or nations, so not all Caribs, Arawaks, or Akawaios supported the Dutch. Individual bands made their own determination of whether or not to fight. And although those who did so were paid for their services, they did not fight just to obtain goods. Rather, the Caribs and Akawaios wanted to retain their positions as favored trading partners. Perhaps, too, they wanted to ensure their access to guns. Moreover, most Amerindians resented the Maroons, whom they saw as competitors for natural resources and indigenous women, even if they sometimes took in runaway slaves. Furthermore, local Amerindians wanted revenge on those rebels who had attacked their villages or killed their family members. Yet despite their shared interests, natives fought on their own terms. They came and went as they pleased, and they refused to fight when they felt badly treated or when they judged the risks to be too high. Even "our" Amerindians, who were most dependent on the Dutch, retained enough autonomy to refuse to carry out requests they deemed too dangerous. Only appeals to their pride and larger economic incentives could persuade them to resume their tasks.[73]

The Dutch, in a pattern seemingly common to the European colonial world, depended heavily on Amerindian aid but simultaneously resented that dependence. They frequently complained about the natives' cowardice and unreliability, especially that of the local Indians, but they nonetheless depended on them and accommodated them. Storm van 's Gravesande complained that his house was overrun with Amerindians. "Its looks nowadays," he reported, "as if it rained Indians." While they were highly troublesome, they had "to be treated with consideration and kindness."[74] Van Hoogenheim urged everyone to behave toward all Amerindians with the utmost circumspection and to reward them generously for any assistance. But such conduct did not always sit well with European soldiers. Indeed, anger at what they perceived as preferential treatment of native forces played a large part in the mutiny of a Suriname regiment in the midst of the rebellion.[75]

The Dutch authorities were well aware of the crucial role of the Amerindians in their counterinsurgency, even if they regarded the Europeans as the main actors. They realized that the additional 1,100 soldiers from Europe could not do the job without native assistance. Indeed, in February 1764, Van Hoogenheim noted that "if we are lucky enough not to lose too many soldiers to illness, we will, with the help of the Indians, be able to suppress the entire rebellion and restore the colony to its former safety."[76] So he was pleased with the arrival of several hundred Caribs from Essequibo in the spring of 1764, even if he had to feed them, no mean task given the circumstances. These Caribs were instrumental in hunting down rebels remaining in the bush.

At the same time, the Dutch understood perfectly well that native assistance encouraged animosity between Amerindians and slaves, and they were eager to promote enmity between the two groups to help prevent slave rebellions and marronage in the future. Storm van 's Gravesande remarked that the actions of the Amerindians "caused a great embitterment between the blacks and them, which, if well and reasonably stimulated, can not fail to be of much use and service in the future to the Colonies."[77] The formidable force that the indigenous fighters displayed in the suppression of the rebellion also gave the colonists pause. Their assistance in Berbice provided, as one official put it, "convincing proofs of what advantage their friendship, and how injurious their enmity, might be to the Colonies."[78]

Without the help of Amerindians, the Dutch might not have reconquered Berbice, and they most certainly would have had to battle Maroons for decades to come. The Dutch lacked sufficient political will, logistical capacity, local knowledge and skills, and immunity against tropical diseases to overcome domestic insurrection without Amerindian help. Van Hoogenheim was right when he characterized the aid of the Amerindians as "truly, the means of cleansing the land."[79] The slave rebellion in Berbice thus is yet another illustration of the limits of early modern colonial power. Given the small size of Berbice, Essequibo, and Demerara, these colonies relied on native military aid for two centuries not merely for defense against outside attack but, more important, to exercise the power allowing for the large-scale exploitation of enslaved laborers. Accordingly, "ethnic soldiering" might more aptly be called "ethnic shouldering."

NOTES

1. I would like to thank Victor Enthoven and Han Jordaan, who helped with an earlier Dutch version of this chapter, as well as Kate Brown, Lee Gould, and Wayne Lee.

2. Dagregister van Gouverneur-Generaal W. S. van Hoogenheim (hereafter DH), 27 September 1763, Archief van de Sociëteit van Berbice (hereafter SvB) 226, Dutch National Archives in The Hague (hereafter NA). This journal contains lengthy daily entries by the governor for the entire period of the rebellion.

3. Neil L. Whitehead, "Carib Ethnic Soldiering in Venezuela, the Guianas, and the Antilles, 1492–1820," Ethnohistory 37, no. 4 (1990): 357–85. For similar "ethnic soldiering" on the part of enslaved people, see Christopher Leslie Brown and Philip D. Morgan, eds., Arming Slaves: From Classical Times to the Modern Age (New Haven, CT: Yale University Press, 2006).

4. Suriname remained Dutch until 1975 when it became an independent republic. Demerara, incidentally, was not settled by Europeans until the 1740s. Almost nothing is known about Berbice before 1720 because the German bombing of Middelburg in World War II destroyed many Zeeland records. Nor is there much secondary literature on eighteenth-century Berbice or, for that matter, on the 1763/1764 slave rebellion. There are only two books on the rebellion, both in Dutch, written in 1770 and 1888, respectively: Jan Jacob Hartsinck, *Beschryving van Guiana, of de Wilde Kust in Zuid-America . . .* (1770; repr., Amsterdam: S. Emmering, 1974); and P. M. Netscher, *Geschiedenis van de koloniën Essequebo, Demerara en Berbice, van de vestiging der Nederlanders aldaar tot op onzen tijd* ('s Gravenhage: Nijhoff, 1888). See also Ineke Velzing, "The Berbice Slavenopstand, 1763" (master's thesis, University of Amsterdam, 1979), an excellent study that makes extensive use of primary sources; and Cornelis Ch. Goslinga, *The Dutch in the Caribbean and in the Guianas, 1680–1791* (Assen/Maastricht: Van Gorcum, 1985), which is less reliable and relies heavily on Hartsinck.

5. Hartsinck, *Beschryving van Guiana*; Netscher, *Geschiedenis van de koloniën Essequebo*; Pieter C. Emmer and Willem Klooster, "The Dutch Atlantic, 1600–1800: Expansion without Empire," *Itinerario* 23, no. 2 (1999): 48–69.

6. Missieve van de Directeuren der Geoctroijeerde Colonie de Berbice, Amsterdam, 17 August 1763, SvB 49. Compare the size of the Berbice slave population with that of neighboring Suriname, which reached 50,000 by 1770. There is no way to know the proportions of creoles and Africans in the enslaved Berbice population, nor do we have anything more than a general picture about origins. According to David Eltis, "in the Guianas, two-thirds of all arrivals before 1750 came from the adjacent Gold Coast and Bight of Benin. A switch to West Central Africa in the third quarter was followed by a Cuban-style provenance pattern after 1775." See David Eltis, "The Volume and Structure of the Transatlantic Slave Trade: A Reassessment," *William and Mary Quarterly* 58, no. 1 (January 2001): 39. See also Rik van Welie, "Slave Trading and Slavery in the Dutch Colonial Empire," *New West Indian Guide* 82, nos. 1–2 (2008): 55, 65–67.

7. For an impression of what Guyana is like today, see Marjoleine Kars, "Adventures in Research: Chasing the Past in Guyana," *Uncommon Sense* 124 (fall 2007): 17–20.

8. Whitehead, "Carib Ethnic Soldiering," esp. 370–75; and Neil L. Whitehead, "Native Peoples Confront Colonial Regimes in Northeastern South America, c. 1500–1900," in *The Cambridge History of the Native Peoples of the Americas*, vol. 3, *South America*, part 2, ed. F. Salomon and S. B. Schwartz (Cambridge: Cambridge University Press, 1999); Gerrit Bos, *Some Recoveries in Guiana Indian Ethnohistory* (Amsterdam: VU Uitgeverij, 1998); Edward Bancroft, *An Essay on the Natural History of Guiana . . .* (London: printed for T. Becket and P. A. De Hondt in the Strand, 1769); Philip Fermin, *Nieuwe Algemeene Beschryving van de Colonie van Suriname . . .* (Harlingen: Ter Drukkery van V. Van der Plaats Junior, 1770); Christlieb Quandt, *Nachricht von Suriname und seinen Einwohnern . . .* (Leipzig: Publisher Görlitz: Gedruckt bey J. G. Burghart; zu finden bey dem Verfasser . . . in Leipzig, 1807); and J. Colier, "Korte Memorie wegens de tegenwoordige toestand der Colonie de Berbice . . . ," 8 January 1757, SvB 223.

9. Netscher, *Geschiedenis van de koloniën Essequebo*, 179.

10. Collectie Bentinck, G2-54 I, Hr. George aan Bentinck, 8 February 1763, Koninklijk Huisarchief, The Hague (hereafter CB); J. P. Wyland, *Journaal van dags-aantekening van het voorgevallene in de colonie van Rio Berbiecie: Beginnende met de Revolte der Negers van den 6*

july 1762 en Eyndende met des Schrijvers Arriviment in Texel op den 11 July 1763 (Amsterdam: Gedrukt voor rekening van de auteur; 1763), 1–5; Netscher, *Geschiedenis van de koloniën Essequebo*, 191–92.

11. Van Hoogenheim aan Directie, 3 July 1762, 25 January 1763, SvB 132. Velzing, "The Berbice Slavenopstand," 91–93.

12. Journael Albert Heuer, Posthouder aan de Courantijn, 25 February–5 March 1763, Archief van de Society of Suriname (hereafter SvS) 317, NA; Heuer aan Gov. Crommelin, 5 March 1763, SvB 134; Heuer aan Gov. Crommelin, 14 April 1763, Collectie Fagel (hereafter CF) 1824, NA; Notulen Hof van Politie, 5 April 1763, SvB 134; Wyland, *Journael*, 8–9; Netscher, *Geschiedenis van de koloniën Essequebo*, 194–95.

13. It is interesting that the Dutch governor frequently refers to "the revolution" and that the enslaved more often speak of "the war."

14. Velzing, "The Berbice Slavenopstand," 116; DH, 9 May 1764. For a similar division of labor among Suriname Maroons in the eighteenth century, see Bonno Thoden van Velzen, "De wijze raadslieden en de kapotmakers: Een probleem met mondelinge overleveringen," in *Ik ben een haan met een kroon op mijn hoofd; Pacificatie en verzet in koloniaal en postkoloniaal Suriname*, ed. Peter Meel and Hans Ramsoedh (Amsterdam: Bert Bakker, 2007), 79. For relevant African military organization, see John K. Thornton, "African Soldiers in the Haitian Revolution," *Journal of Caribbean History* 25, no. 1 (1991): 58–80.

15. DH, 26 May, 3 August, 19 October, and 13 and 22 November, 1763; Van Hoogenheim aan de Directeuren, 26 February 1764, SvB 135. For references to colony people, see DH 26 February 1764, 31 August 1763, 27 December 1763; on creole-African divisions, see DH 19 and 29 June 1763; Zevende Verbael gehouden bij den Collonel Desalve van den 26 April 1764 tot den 11 Junij 1764, 23 March 1764, Archief Staten Generaal, 1.01.05, inv. 9219, Nationaal Archief, Den Haag (hereafter ASG), and the examination of slaves, passim, in SvB 135.

16. Coffy en Akkarra aan Van Hoogenheim, 8 March 1763 and Coffy aan Van Hoogenheim, 2 August 1763, SvB 227. Both letters are also printed in Ursy M. Lichtveld and Jan Voorhoeve, eds., *Suriname: Spiegel der Vaderlandse Kooplieden: Een Historisch Leesboek* (Zwolle: W. E. J. Tjeenk Willink, 1958), 85. See also Schrijven aan Brunswick, 19 July 1763, CB.

17. Monsterlijst der militie, 26 March 1763, CF. These soldiers returned to Berbice in May, see DH, 10 May 1763.

18. Resoluties Hof van Politie, 6 March 1763, SvB 134; DH, 28 February–7 March 1763; Van Hoogenheim aan Directeuren, 6 April 1763, SvB 134.

19. DH, 8–16 March 1763; Netscher, *Geschiedenis van de koloniën Essequebo*, 203–4.

20. DH, 17 March 1763.

21. Crommelin aan Van Hoogenheim, 26 March 1763, SvB 134. On the Saramaka, see Richard Price, *Alabi's World* (Baltimore: Johns Hopkins University Press, 1990). For other works on Suriname Maroons in this period, see Harry van den Bouwhuijsen, Ron de Bruin, and Georg Horeweg, eds., *Opstand in Tempati, 1757–1760: Bronnen voor de studie van Afro-Amerikaanse samenlevingen in de Guyana's*; dl. 12. (Utrecht: Centrum voor Caraïbische Studies, 1988). See also Wim Hoogbergen, *De Boni-oorlogen, 1757–1860. Marronage en guerilla in Oost-Suriname*. Bronnen voor de studie van Afro-Amerikaanse samenlevingen in de Guyana's, dl. 11 (Utrecht: Centrum voor Caraïbische Studies, 1985); and Wim Hoogbergen, "The History of the Suriname Maroons," in *Resistance and Rebellion in Suriname: Old and New*, ed. Gary Brana-Shute, Studies in Third World Series (Williamsburg, VA: College of William and Mary Press, 1990), 65–102. For a well-known

account of a European officer fighting such Maroons, see John Gabriel Stedman, *Narrative of a Five Years Expedition against the Revolted Negroes of Suriname. Transcribed for the First Time from the Original 1790 Manuscript.* Edited and with an introduction and notes by Richard Price and Sally Price (Baltimore: Johns Hopkins University Press, 1988).

22. DH, 29–31 March 1763; Netscher, *Geschiedenis van de koloniën Essequebo*, 207; Rapport van G. Knollard and W. W. Hattinga, 1 April 1763, SvB 135, Notulen, 2 April 1763, SvB 135. The number of slaves on Dageraad is an estimate. See Inventaris van de Dageraad, 10 October 1762, SvB 133; DH, 31 October 1764.

23. DH, 2 and 3 April 1763. Notulen Hof van Politie, 2 April 1763, SvB 134. In his journal, the governor estimates the attacking force at 300 to 400, and the Council mentions 700. See Coffy's letters in Lichtveld and Voorhoeve, *Suriname*, 71–97.

24. DH, 2 April 1763.

25. DH, 4 and 6 April 1763.

26. "Rapport van G. Knollart aan Capit. D. W. C. Hattinga, Commandant aan 't fort St. Andries, gedaan op den 6e April 1763, van de Plant. Frederiksburg," SvB 134.

27. DH, 3 and 6 May 1763; Netscher, *Geschiedenis van de koloniën Essequebo*, 212–13.

28. Albert Heuer aan Crommelin, 10 April 1763; Heuer aan zijne Ecellentie, 24 April 1763, SvB 134.

29. DH, 26 May 1763.

30. Storm van 's Gravesande to Hoogenheim, 12 April 1763, SvB 134; Storm van 's Gravesande to the UEGA Heeren [WIC directors], 2 May 1763, in C. A. Harris and J. A. J. de Villiers, *Storm van 's Gravesande: The Rise of British Guiana, Compiled from His Despatches* (London: Printed for the Hakluyt Society, 1911), vol. 2, 424; DH, 18 April, 10 May, 14 May 1763.

31. Notulen, 14 May 1763, SvB 134; DH, 13 May 1763.

32. DH, 13 May and 4 June 1763.

33. DH, 13 May, 4 June 1763; DH, 25, 28 May and 26 August 1763; Goeverneur en Raad and de YY.HH [Society of Berbice], 24 August 1763, SvB 134.

34. DH, 30 September 1763.

35. For a similar disagreement among slave rebels in St. Domingue, see John Thornton, "'I am the Subject of the King of Congo': African Political Ideology and the Haitian Revolution," *Journal of World History* 4, no. 2 (1993): 199–200, 206. For a similar dispute on St. John, see also Jon Sensbach, *Rebecca's Revival: Creating Black Christianity in the Atlantic World* (Cambridge, MA: Harvard University Press, 2005), 18–20.

36. Examination no. 181 Brutos off Accabiré van Stevensburg, 4/11/1764 and Confrontagie van de negers Arrabiré van Stevensburg & Atta van Altenklingen, 4/18/1764; Examination no. 236 Mars alias Atta van Altenklingen, 4/16/1764 and Nader geExamineert den Neger Mars off Atta van Altenklingen," 4/18/1764. All examinations of returned slaves may be found in SvB 135. On Atta's being a "nieuwe neger," that is, African born, see DH, 15 November 1763.

37. Capt. Texier and Suriname Directeuren, 14 November 1763, SvS 320.

38. DH, 11, 19, 20, 21 June; 9 October; 19 and 23 November 1763.

39. For this mutiny, see Marjoleine Kars, "Policing and Transgressing Borders: Soldiers, Slave Rebels, and the Early Modern Atlantic," *New West Indian Guide / Nieuwe West Indische Gids* 83, nos. 3 and 4 (2009): 187–213.

40. Goeverneur en Raad and [SvB Directors], 29 September 1763, SvB 134.

41. DH, 25 September 1763 and 1822.

42. Storm van 's Gravesande, 27 September 1763, in Harris and Villiers, *Storm van 's Gravesande*, vol. 2, 436; DH, 27 July and 20 September 1763.

43. DH, 10 September and 9 October 1763.

44. Cf. DH, 14 September 1763.

45. DH, 4 October 1763.

46. In late May 1763, the society decided to send two ships with 50 soldiers. A month later, the Estates General allocated three warships and 400 soldiers. These ships were not ready to leave, however, until late July and August. Moreover, the Estates General decided to create a regiment of 600 volunteers from the Staatse Leger (the standing army of the Republic) and send it over under the command of Colonel Jan Marius de Salve. It took three months to form this regiment, which would not arrive in Berbice until January 1764. See C. J. O. Dorren, *De Geschiedenis van het Nederlandsche Korps Mariniers van 1665–1945* (The Hague: Ad. M. C. Stok, Zuid-Hollandsche Uitgevers Maatschappij, 1948), 302–5; Douglas to Brunswijk, 21 December 1763, CF, NA.

47. DH, 9–19 November 1763; Haringman and Staten Generaal, 20 November 1763, CF.

48. Storm van 's Gravesande to the WIC, 21 December 1763, Harris and Villiers, *Storm van 's Gravesande*, vol. 2, 440–44.

49. See, for instance, Scheepsjournaal van de Zephyr, 2 January 1764, Admiraliteits College, 1586–1785, no. 1161, NA; DH, 10 and 25 September 1763; Texier aan de Suriname Directeuren, 14 November 1763, SvB 320.

50. DH, 29 December 1763.

51. DH, 23 to 26 January 1764, and 17 February 1764; Vierde verbael De Salve, 13 to 17 February 1764, SG 9219. Stedman, *Narrative*, provides multiple examples of the ineffectiveness of European soldiers in the bush.

52. Robert Douglas to Lodewijk Ernst, duke of Brunswijk-Wolfenbuttel, 26 February 1764, CB.

53. The "Gangoe" are also referred to as Cango or Guango. It is possible that what is meant are the Kanga, people from Liberia/Sierra Leone. See Christian Georg Andreas Oldendorp, *Historie der caribischen Inseln Sanct Thoams, Sanct Crux und Sanct Jan. Kommentierte Edition des Originalmanuskriptes*, ed. Erster Teil, Gudrun Meier, Stephan Palmié, Peter Stein, and Horst Ulbircht (Berlin: Verlag für Wissenschaft und Bildung, 2000), 378–81. See also DH, 29 March 1764, where he refers to Accabiré's forces as "Kangas."

54. Douglas to Bentinck, 12 and 26 February 1764, CB; DH passim, esp. 25 January 1764 and 8 February 1764; Van Hoogenheim aan de Directeuren, 29 March 1764, SvB 135; Verbaelen gehouden bij den Collonel DeSalve, ASG 9219, NA.

55. For a similar practice in New England, see Andrew Lipman, "'A Meanes to knit them togeather': The Exchange of Body Parts in the Pequot War," *William and Mary Quarterly* 65, no. 1 (2008): 3–28, esp. 22–24.

56. It appears that the procedures in judging the enslaved in Berbice followed, in broad strokes, those procedures common in the Netherlands in the eighteenth century, which, by the way, were not uniform throughout the United Provinces until the early nineteenth century. See Sjoerd Faber, *Strafrechtspleging en criminaliteit te Amsterdam, 1680–1811* (Arnhem: Gouda Quint, 1983), chap. 1; and Frans Thuijs, *De Ware Jaco: Jacob Frederik Muller, alias Jaco (1690–1718), zijn criminele wereld, zijn berechting en zijn leven na de dood* (Hilversum: Verloren, 2008).

57. Klaas Kramer, "Plantation Development in Berbice from 1753 to 1779: The Shift from the Interior to the Coast," *New West Indian Guide / Nieuwe West-Indische Gids* 65, nos. 1–2 (1991): 53; Netscher, *Geschiedenis van de koloniën Essequebo*, 247, 256; Vervolg Verhaal De Salve, 14 September 1764, ASG 9220; "Opgaave van Slaaven en Slaavinnen behoorende Aan de Wel Ed. Agtb. Heeren Directeuren deezer Colonie Inhoudende het getal Slaaven voor der Revolte . . . ," 14 June 1764, SvB 135, indicates that by June 1764, 395 of the original 1,451 company slaves had died or had not (yet) returned.

58. The Warao inhabited the Orinoco delta and swampy areas in Western Guiana, and the Arawak lived on the lower reaches of the rivers but stretched farther east, perhaps to the Marowijne River in Suriname. Carib lived upstream from the Arawak in the western part of the region and east of the Courantyne, closer to the coast. See Arie Boomert, "The Arawak Indians of Trinidad and Coastal Guiana, ca. 1500–1650," *Journal of Caribbean History* 19 (1984): 127–29; and H. Dieter Heinen and Alvaro García-Castro, "The Multiethnic Network of the Lower Orinoco in Early Colonial Times," *Ethnohistory* 47, nos. 3–4 (2000): 561–79. See also Neil L. Whitehead, "Ethnic Transformation and Historical Discontinuity in Native Amazonia and Guyana, 1500–1900," *L'Homme* 126–28 (1993): 292–93.

59. For a detailed overview of Dutch activities on the Wild Coast in this early period, see L. A. C. Hulsman, "Nederlands Amazonia: Handel met indiaanen tussen 1580 en 1680" (PhD diss., University of Amsterdam, 2009).

60. Edward Bancroft, *An Essay on the Natural History of Guiana . . .* (London: Printed for T. Becket and P. A. De Hondt in the Strand, 1769), 376; and Netscher, *Geschiedenis van de koloniën Essequebo*, 59. For a similar practice in Suriname, see Whitehead, "Carib Ethnic Soldiering," 366.

61. For the Indian war in Suriname, see F. E. Baron Mulert, "Eene Episode uit den Indianen-Oorlog in Suriname in den Zeeuwschen Tijd," *De West-Indische Gids* 1 (1919): 221–25; Justus B. Ch. Wekker, "Indianen en Pacificatie," *OSO: Tijdschrift voor Surinamistiek en het Caraïbisch gebied* 12, no. 2 (1993): 175–87; R. A. J. van Lier, *Frontier Society: A Social Analysis of the History of Suriname* (The Hague: Nijhoff, 1971), 76. On the events in Berbice and Essequibo, see the documents in F. van der Doe et. al., eds., *Indianen in Zeeuwse Bronnen: Brieven over Indianen in Suriname tijdens het Zeeuwse bewind gedurende de periode 1667–1682* (Paramaribo: Stichting, 12 October 1992). (I would like to thank Blanche T. Ebeling-Koning, then of the John Carter Brown Library in Providence, RI, for bringing this publication to my attention.) Also see Mathijs de Feer aan Abraham Beekman, 4 November 1687, Tweede West Indische Compagnie, 1.05.01.02, no. 1025, NA; "Ordonnantie of placaet nopende den handel ent coopen van roô Indiaense slave gedaen den 23 Augustij 1686 [Essequibo]," in Netscher, *Geschiedenis van de koloniën Essequebo*, 367–69, see also 91–92 and 372–73; Abram Beekman aan Zeeland Kamer, 4 November 1687 in Netscher, *Geschiedenis van de koloniën Essequebo*, 375–77; Verklarring van Oorlog en Invasie die de Caribiese in issekepe gedaen haebben waar door wijnige off geen verve sal koomen, 20 October 1686, Tweede WestIndische Compagnie,1.05.01.02, no. 1025, NA; and Hulsman, "Nederlands Amazonia," 177–79, 204, 205, 223. On evasions of the laws, see, for instance, Commander Essequibo to WIC, 19 April 1713, in *British Guiana Boundary: Arbitration with the United States of Venezuela, Appendix to the Case on Behalf of the Government of Her Britannic Majesty* (London: Foreign Office, 1898), 1: 211, and passim. On Carib slave catching and relations with Maroons, see also Whitehead, "Carib Ethnic Soldiering," 372–74.

62. See, for instance, Storm van 's Gravesande to WIC, 27 September 1763, in Harris and Villiers, *Storm van 's Gravesande*, 2: 430–31.

63. Extracts from an official journal kept at Fort Kijkoveral (1699–1701), *British Guiana Boundary*, 1: 214.

64. Commander Essequibo to the WIC, 1706, in *British Guiana Boundary*, 1: 228–29, also 183–84; Neil L. Whitehead, *Lords of the Tiger Spirit: A History of the Carib in Colonial Venezuela and Guyana, 1498–1820* (Dordrecht: Floris Publications, 1988), 161–64. For an example, from Berbice, see DH 10 October 1763.

65. Whitehead, "Carib Ethnic Soldiering," 365, Hulsman, "Nederlands Amazonia," 225–26.

66. Storm van 's Gravesande to the WIC, 2 May 1763, in Harris and Villiers, *Storm van 's Gravesande*, 2: 424.

67. Storm van 's Gravesande to the WIC, 28 August 1762, in Harris and Villiers, *Storm van 's Gravesande*, 2: 404; and Storm van 's Gravesande to Van Hoogenheim (?), 6 June 1763, SvB 135. Storm van 's Gravesande was not especially eager to arm Carib Indians with guns. On one occasion he asked the Indian chief who requested guns whether he was short on poisonous arrows. The man replied that he had plenty but that "the rebels in Berbice had fortified themselves in the houses of the Christians and arrows could not penetrate walls and windows." Storm van 's Gravesande, 6 June 1763, to Van Hoogenheim (?), SvB 135.

68. For the designation "Christen mulat," see DH, 5 May 1763.

69. All the Broer men were plantation owners and suffered in the rebellion along with white planters. Philip Broer, for instance, was killed by rebels in the first weeks of the uprising. Jan Broer Jr. was killed by the rebels while on a mission to convince slave drivers loyal to the Dutch to remain so. The rebels put his head on a stake. His murderer turned out to have been the driver on his father's plantation.

70. DH, 9 September 1763.

71. The governor noted in his journal that the Carib Indians from Essequibo did not want black guides, "so we will only employ in that capacity the two free mulatto Hendrik Broer and Jeremias Broer and our mulat negro Fredrik . . . ," DH, 15 April 1764.

72. Frederik is mentioned throughout Van Hoogenheim's journal. For the quotation, see DH, September 13, 1764. For a report on local Indians, see "Korte Memorie wegens de tegenwoordige toestand der Colonie de Berbice . . . ," J. Colier, Amsterdam, 8 January 1757, SvB 223.

73. See, for instance, DH, 9 September 1763. Indians were compensated in various ways: with liquor, cloth from India, beads, mirrors, scissors, knives, and guns. It appears that some of these guns had to be returned at the end of the expeditions when the Indians went home.

74. Storm van 's Gravesande to WIC, August 1764, in Harris and Villiers, *Storm van 's Gravesande*, 458.

75. See Kars, "Policing and Transgressing Borders."

76. DH, 14 February 1764.

77. Storm van 's Gravesande to WIC, 4 April 1764, in Harris and Villiers, *Storm van 's Gravesande*, 2: 447.

78. Storm van 's Gravesande to WIC, 3 February 1765, in Harris and Villiers, *Storm van 's Gravesande*, 2: 478.

79. Van Hoogenheim to Storm van 's Gravesande, 25 February 1764, quoted in Harris and Villiers, *Storm van 's Gravesande*, 2: 445–46, n. 3. Their translation of the Dutch original (Waarlijk het is het middel om het land regt te suijvere) is less literal than mine. They render it as "This is really the means by which the country may be kept in order," which means more or less the same as my translation.

Contributors

VIRGINIA AKSAN is a professor at McMaster University, the author of *An Ottoman Statesman in War and Peace: Ahmed Resmi Efendi 1700–1783*; *Ottomans and Europeans: Contacts and Conflicts*; and *Ottoman Wars, 1700–1870: An Empire Besieged*, as well as the coeditor, with Daniel Goffman, of *The Early Modern Ottomans: Remapping an Empire*.

DAVID R. JONES is an adjunct professor at Dalhousie University and the author of *The Advanced Guard and Mobility in Russian and Soviet Military Thought and Practice*. He also is the founding editor of the *Military-Naval Encyclopedia of Russia and the Soviet Union*.

MARJOLEINE KARS is an associate professor at the University of Maryland, Baltimore County, and the author of *Breaking Loose Together: The Regulator Rebellion in Pre-Revolutionary North Carolina*.

WAYNE E. LEE is a professor at the University of North Carolina, Chapel Hill, and the author of *Barbarians and Brothers: Anglo-American Warfare, 1500–1865* and *Crowds and Soldiers in Revolutionary North Carolina: The Culture of Violence in Riot and War*.

MARK MEUWESE is an associate professor at the University of Winnipeg.

DOUGLAS M. PEERS is a professor of history and the dean of graduate studies at York University and the author of several books, including *Negotiating India in the Nineteenth Century and India and the British Empire*, for the Oxford History of the British Empire companion series.

GEOFFREY PLANK is a professor of American studies at the University of East Anglia and the author of *Rebellion and Savagery: The Jacobite Rising of 1745 and the British Empire* and *An Unsettled Conquest: The British Campaign against the Peoples of Acadia*.

JENNY HALE PULSIPHER is an associate professor at Brigham Young University and the author of *Subjects unto the Same King: Indians, English, and the Contest for Authority in Colonial New England.*

JOHN K. THORNTON is a professor at Boston University and the author of many books, including *Warfare in Atlantic Africa, 1500–1800.*

Index

Abdülhamit II (Sultan) (1876-1909), 144
Abenakis, 31, 226; threatening counteracts from, 231–32
Absolutism, 90
Abulkhair (Khan) (1693-1748), 128
Acadia, 30–31, 36; campaign of 1710, 226; 1713, 222. *See also* Nova Scotia
Acadia Trading Company, 46n114
Accarra (Captain), 255–56
Adaptation, 13; Amerindian polity, 65–70; Muscovite-Nomad, 12; in North America and, 63–64; Portuguese-West African, 12; process of, 7. *See also* Warfare adaptation
Adargueiros (shield bearers), 171
Afghanistan, 88, 96
Afonso I (King), 173, 175
Africa, West Central: adaptations, 12; campaigns of conquest in, 11; Dutch departure from, 185; foundations of warfare, 171–72; mobility in, 172; Portugal's arrival, 172–87; 1650, 166. *See also* Angola; *specific places and rulers*
African slaves: as allies of WIC, 200; in Brazil, 197, 204, 209; disease and, 195; growing population, 265; as military auxiliaries, 16n26; runaways, 197, 205; trade, 167–68, 179–80, 187–88. *See also* Berbice slave rebellion
de Aguilar, Nicolás, 7
Akowaios, 253–54, 259; Caribs ally with, 260
Aksan, Virginia H., 3, 10
Albania, 144–46, 157
Aldeias, 194, 204–7
Algonquians, 23, 31, 77n71, 227–28; firearm supply to, 34; serving in ranger companies, 229. *See also specific groups*

Ali, Haider, 83, 92, 96–97, 99, 101
Ali, Mehmed, 163n40
Alliance, 69; between Amerindian groups, 20–22; Caddo-French, 28; ceremonial support for, 20–21; Covenant Chain, 26; disappointments in, 31; Indian politics in, 100; intercultural, 9–13; intermarriage and formation of, 27–29; Iroquois-French, 23, 25–26; military assistance and, 31; Portugal-Imbangala, 180–81; Portugal-Ndongo, 175; Russian negotiations for, 120; trade and, 24, 31; Wabanakis favored, 32–33; Wampanoags-English, 19–20, 25; war and, 33, 37. *See also* Amerindian-European alliances; *specific examples between groups*
Álvaro I (King), 173–74
Álvaro II (King), 176
Álvaro III (King), 182
Ambrósio I (King) (1626-1631), 174
Ambush, 52–53, 60
American Revolution, 58, 67
Amerindian allies: in Berbice, 252; "Brazilian," 201–2; to England, 223–24; knowledge and skill of, 263; in Philippines, 7; to Spain, 5. *See also specific allies*
Amerindian-European alliances: Christianity and, 29–31; failure of elements in, 31. *See also specific alliances*
Amerindian-European diplomacy, 23–27, 39
Amerindian military revolution, 55–56; firearms and, 56–61; fortification and, 62–65; political structures and, 67
Amerindian polities, 56; adaptations, 65–70; Amerindian military revolution and, 67; shift of power within, 66–67

Beilorussians, 110
Belbulatovich, Simeon (Khan), 130
Belgorod, 121
Bemoim, João, 168
Bengal arms race, 1760s, 93
Berbice, 10, 252–54, 264, 268, 269n4;
    Amerindian allies to, 252; authority in,
    251; Estates General, 272n46; internal
    conflict, 259; interpreters, 266–67; popu-
    lation, 253, 269n6; reinforcements for,
    256–57, 260–61; 1763, 250; trade posts,
    265. See also Society of Berbice
Berbice River: 1763, 250; sugar plantations
    on, 253
Berbice slave rebellion, 251–52, 254–63;
    Amerindian assistance in fight against,
    257–58, 266–67; Amerindian spies,
    258–59; Dutch losses as result of, 263;
    end of, 262; food and supply shortages,
    258–59; guns and, 268; internal battles,
    262; internal divisions over strategy
    within, 259; investigation and trials of,
    262–63; mutinied soldiers and, 259;
    organization within, 255; retreat, 261;
    support to fight against, 256–57, 260–61;
    suppression of, 260–63, 265–66
Bezopanost (security), 113–14
Bharatpur siege (1825), 83
Bilodeau, Christopher, 45n91
Blacksmith, 66, 76n65, 77n66
Blockade, 55
Blunderbuss, 96
Board of Trade, 236
Bogatyrs (knight-champions), 121, 123
Bogatyrskie zastavy (heroic frontier lines),
    121
Bomazeen (sachem), 35
Bombay. See Mumbai
Bosnia, 145, 155
Bosnians' rebellion, 155
Bow: arrow dodging and, 58; calculations
    of arrow, 57; efficacy of, 56–57; gun vs.,
    56–58, 78n80; kinetic energy expended
    by arrow, 73n31
Braddock, Edward, 60
Brant, Joseph, 58

Brazil, 10; African slave labor in, 197, 204,
    209; discovery of, 196; Dutch territory
    in, 1643, 192; European epidemics in,
    195–96; French-Portuguese rivalries
    in, 196–98; resources in, 196; Spanish-
    Portuguese Doublemonarchy and, 193.
    See also Portuguese colonists, in Brazil;
    West India Company; specific indigenous
    peoples
"Brazilians," 193–94; allies, WIC motive for
    recruiting, 201–2; autonomy granted to,
    209; auxiliaries and WIC expansion in
    South Atlantic, 1635-1642, 202–4; Dutch
    relations with, 198–99; recruited for
    labor service, 204; weaponry, 202. See
    also Tupi
Brazil sugar economy, 196, 205; African
    slave labor in, 197; "Brazilians" recruited
    for labor service in, 204; Dutch partici-
    pation in, 198
Breechloader revolution, 94
Brinjaras, 95
Brodniki (wanderers), 125
Broer family, 266–67, 274n69, 274n71
Burial mounds, 20
Burke, Edmund, 87
Burma, 94, 101
Burma War (1824-1826), 83
Buxar battle, 93–94, 100
Byzantium, 122

Cabo de São Roque, 197
Cabral, Pedro Álvares, 196
Cabral de Mello, Evaldo, 194
Caddo: French-, alliance, 28; Spanish
    colonists and, 28
Cadornega, António de Oliveira, 184,
    190n46
van Caerden, Paulus, 198
Calloway, Colin, 236
Callwell, C. E., 93
Calumet Ceremony, 21
Camarão, Filipe, 209, 211
Camel guns, 96
Canada, 225–26
"Canada Survey'd" (Vetch), 225

Enlightenment, 243
Enloe, Cynthia H., 16n27
Erickson, Edward, 145
Essequibo, 252, 259–60, 264–65, 268
Essequibo River, 257–58
Ethnic soldier, 10, 16n27, 268; Amerindians as, 263; Potiguares and, 194; Tarairius as, 215
Ethridge, Robbie, 69
Eurasia, 110, 130
Europe: absolutism in, 90; medieval, 169; weaponry development in, 169–70. *See also specific countries*
European bias, 90, 102
European domination, 84
European epidemics, 12, 208; in Brazil, 195–96
European military: gunpowder introduction into, 89; techniques, 68; in wilderness, 60
European military revolution, 12, 50–51, 57, 113
European military superiority, 81, 88, 167; Orientalism and trope of, 82–89; Parker, G., summary of, 90
European towns and colonies: Amerindian tribes and, 1650-1720, *18*; landownership patterns and, 68
Exchange, 20; commercial, 37; cultural, generated by conflict, 49; gift, 128; hostage, 120, 123, 128; of sacred goods, 22; technological, in India, 95
Exotic, 88–89

Fallen Timbers, 74n44
"Father" role, 25–26, 37, 42n43; violation of, 35
Fealty, 128
Felipe I (King), 183
Feudalism, 90
Fictive kinship, 21–22, 36, 40n5; real *vs.*, 27
Fiefs, 149. *See also Pomestie* land grants
Fifteenth Artillery Brigade, 140n111
Firearms, 51; Amerindian military revolution and, 56–61; appeal to indigenous peoples, 12; dependency on, 66; military

revolution and, 50; production in India, 91, 93–94; recruitment and, 50; supply, 33–35, 37; technology, 56–57. *See also specific types of firearms*
First Battle of Guararapes, 212
First Constitutional period, 144
Fitne, 156
Fixed prices, 36
Flankers, 63
Flintlocks, 51, 56–57
Forbes, John, 60
Fort Christanna, 68
Fortification: abandoned, 65; Amerindian military revolution and, 62–65; gunpowder and, 89; Iroquois, 63; in Steppe, 117
Fort Loudoun, 68
Fort Nassau, 253, 256
Fort Niagra, 67
Forts, 51, 61; adaptation of, 63–64; designs, 62–63; precontact, 63. *See also specific forts*
Fort Shantok, 75n53
Fort St. Andries, 255–58
Fort St. George, 92
Fort Toulouse, 68
Fort William, 91
Forty-third Highland Regiment deserters, 238–39
"Four Indian Kings," 226, 232
France, 11, 31; in Brazil, 196–98; Caddo alliance with, 28; in Canada, 225–26; English defeat of, 38; in India, 91–92; intermarriage with Amerindians, 27–28, 32; Iroquois-, alliance, 23, 25–26; in King Philip's War, 45n91; Portugal and, rivalries in Brazil, 196–98; prices for supplies, 35; Wabanakis and, 31–37; withdrawal of, 39. *See also* Amerindian-European alliances; Amerindian-European diplomacy; European military
Fraser, Simon, 240–41
Frederik, 266–67, 274n71
Fredriksburg plantation, 256–57
Free association, 15n16
Freebooters, 100
French and Indian War. *See* Seven Years' War

French dominion, 42n44
French military: King William's War
    strategy, 37; soldiers, 30
French Revolution, 86
Frontenac, 34–35
Fur trade, 25

Gallay, Alan, 78n80
Gangoe, 262, 272n53
Garcia II (King), 184–85
Gasco de Velasco, Luis, 7
"Gentry" militia, 117
Georgia, 224, 232; Common Council of,
    234; function and land laws of, 233; war
    with Spain, 236–37. See also Darien
German, 111; Baltic, 139n109
Gibbon, Edward, 84
Gift: exchange, 128; giving at Russian border,
    120, 123; redistribution of, 25, 67; refusal
    of, 24; to Tupi, 206–7; WIC and, 206
Given, Brian, 56–57, 65–66, 73n31, 78n78
Glorious Revolution, 34, 45n97
van Goch, Michiel, 213
Godparenthood, 29
Golitsyn, V. V., 118
Gommans, Jos, 95, 100
Gordon, Patrick, 118
de Gouveia Sottomaior, Francisco, 173–74,
    176
Gradeva, Rossitsa, 144, 153
Grand Alliance, 34
Grand Duchy of Moscow, 113
Great Northern War with Sweden (1700-
    1772), 117
Great Russian, 110–12
Great Swamp, 64
Greece, 141, 162n28; Christian paramilitary
    groups used by, 153; freedom fighters, 153
Greek Orthodox, 139n107; conversion,
    122–23, 138n86; Ottoman, 148
Green Corn Ceremony, 21
Grekov, Boris, 111, 123
Grenier, John, 223
Groups (moieties), 22
Gunpowder, 66, 77n69; dependence on, 61;
    European military introduction to, 89;

fortification and, 89; granular, 116; pre-,
    weapons, 96
"Gunpowder revolution," 116–18. See also
    European Military Revolution
Guns, 274n67; adoption of, 65; Akowaios
    and, 268; in Berbice slave rebellion, 268,
    274n67; bow vs., 56–58, 78n80; cutting
    off style and, 58; Narragansetts and, 69;
    open battle and, 59; wounds, 57. See also
    Firearms; specific types of guns
Gunsmiths, 66, 77n66, 93–94
Gypsies, 160n12
Gzak, 124

Habsburgs, 150; Ottoman contact with, 145
Haefeli, Evan, 29
Half-moon formation, 60, 74n44
Hancock's fort, 64–65
Hans, 24
Hari a Ngola, 186
Hayduts, 157
Headrick, Daniel, 94
Heigon, Mogg, 33
Hellie, Richard, 116–17
Highlanders. See Scottish Highlanders
"Highland problem," 234
Hill, John, 228, 230
Hostage exchange (amanat), 120, 123, 128
House of Commons, 240
Hundred Years' War, 169
Hunter, Robert, 227–29
Hunting, gun vs. bow for, 57
Hurons: Iroquois attack on, 53, 68; precon-
    tact forts, 63

Iberian powers, 193
Imbangala, 180–81, 183
Imperial conquest, 1–3, 9--13
Incas, conquest of, 14n8
India, 85–86; alliance politics in, 100;
    English economic factors of success
    in, 82; English forts in, 91–92; English
    immobility in, 94; European military
    superiority in, 81; firearms production in,
    91, 93–94; France vs. England in, 91–92;
    long-distance trade communities in, 95;

India (*continued*): ordnance factories in, 93; orientalist construction of, 88; polities of, 88; Portugal in, 81; Scott on, 86; in 1765, *80*; *silladar* practice, 99; south, 92; technological diffusion and exchange in, 95; technology impacts in, 91; warfare adaptation in, 82, 87–88, 97, 99. *See also* Colonial India; *specific places*

Indian allies, 91–92

Indian military, 86–87, 93–94; culture of, 97; distinctions, 101; history, 90–91; innovations in, 95; labor market, 98–102; organization and discipline, 85, 87, 96–97, 99; Orme on, 86–87, 97–98; sophistication of, 81

Indian rebellion (1857-1858), 94

Indigenous: defined, 9; forces utilized by Ottomans, 153–59; network exploitation, 8; Ottoman military and, 153–59; peoples and warfare in Ottoman Empire, 143; Steppe and, 111; technology, 97

Indigenous allies, 4, 167; recruiting, 9–10

Indios aldeados, 194, 197–98, 207; as loyal to Portuguese, 199–200; WIC and, 201

Indios mansos, 197

Industrial imperial power, 8

Inquisition in Mexico City (1663), 7

Intermarriage, 15n19, 32; alliance formation and, 27–29

Intermediaries, 6

Interpreters, 6; Berbice, 266–67; Potiguares as, 200; role of, 14n11

"Inverse racketeering," 162n28

Iroquois, 21, 23, 26; attack on Hurons, 53, 68; "council fire," 23–24; Delawares relationship with, 25; diplomatic prowess of, 47n122; in England, 226; firearm supply to, 34; fortifications, 63; French-, alliance, 23, 25–26; motive for attacks, 78n78; polities, 67; precontact forts, 63; raiding of Cherokees and Catawbas, 58–59; relations with colonists, 23; during Seven Years' War, 242; Toudaman killing of, 52; war party force on Squakheag, 59–60, 63–64; warriors *vs.* Scottish Highlander warriors, 241–42. *See also* Mohawks

Iroquois League, 22, 227. *See also specific groups*

Irregular units, 100

Islam: Christian conversion to, 153; education system, 147; modern terrorism of, 143

Islamic judge (*kadi*), 147

Islamic law, 147; on slaves, 151

Itamaracá, 201, 211

Ivan III (1462-1503), 113, 116–17; annexation of Novgorod, 1478, 119

Ivan IV "the Terrible" (1533-1584), 114, 116, 129; *oprichniki*, 133n23

Jacob, John, 89

Jacobite Rising (1715), 234, 236, 240–42

Jaenen, Cornelius J., 42n44

Jafar, Mir, 93

Jagas, 173, 189n16; invasion, 175–76

James I (King), 26

Jamestown colonists, 70n5

Janissaries, 149–54, 158

Japipe, 208

Jesuit priest, 30

Jew, 148. *See also* Ottoman non-Muslims

João I (King), 172–73

João IV (King), 204, 210, 214

Johnson, Richard, 221

Jones, David R., 3, 10, 12

Kabasa, 178, 181

Kadi. See Islamic judge

Kalka battle, 125–26

Kamen, Henry, 4, 8, 14n8

Kansanze, 176

Kanun. See Sultanic prerogative

Kars, Marjoleine, 3, 10

Kasanze war, 182

Kaye, J. W., 89

Kazakhstan, 128

Kazakh Steppe, 132n7

Kazan, 114

Keener, Craig, 63

Keep, John, 114–15, 128

Kennedy, Paul, 84

Kessell, John, 29

Khazars, 122

Khodarkovsky, Michael, 112, 119, 126
Kiev, 111, 126; *bogatyrs* of, 121; circuit wall, 121; techniques of steppe diplomacy, 121–22. *See also* Rus
Kilombo kia Kasenda, Njinga Ngola (King) (1575-1592), 176
Kiluanje, Ngola (ca. 1515-1556), 175
Kimbundu, 175
King Philip's War (1676-1678), 31; firearms and, 33; France in, 45n91; Narragansetts in, 64; refugees of, 32
King William's War, 32, 45n96; French military strategy in, 37; opening foray in, 33–34
Kinship, 21; Catholic networks of, 29; godparenthood and, 29; marriage and, 21; patrilineal system of, 26; ritual exchange and ritual, 22; roles and symbolic family structures, 25–26; trade and, 264. *See also* Fictive kinship
Kinship obligations, 21; failure to meet, 35, 37–38; reciprocal, 22, 24, 27–28
Kipchak, 114
Kipchak Steppe, 132n7
Kipling, Rudyard, 96
Kisama, 175–76
Kitombo, 186
Kliuchevsky, V. O., 110
Knaut, Andrew, 7
Kobiakovich, Danilo, 126
Kolff, Dirk, 98
Kombi battle (1647), 185
Konchak, 124, 126
Kongo, 175, 184, 185; Cão in, 172; civil war, 186; expansion, 173; failed invasion of, 183; mines of *nzimbu*, 174; politics, 177; Portugal battle against, 182, 185–86; style warfare, 171–72. *See also* Portugal-Kongo alliance; *specific places and rulers*
Kul, 149–50
Kunt, Metin, 145
Kurds, 145–46, 155, 160n12
Kwanza River, 177

Lachlan Mackintosh, Brigadier, 236–37
Landes, David, 84

Lawrence, Henry, 89
Leadership decapitation, 6
Lee, Wayne E., 2, 12
Lenman, Bruce, 91
Levend, 156–57
Life Guards Grenadier Regiment, 140n111
Lijnwaet, 206
Listrij, Johannes, 213
Lithuanian-Poles, 111–12, 116
Livingston, John, 225–32
Local, 9; cooperation and warfare, 1; ignorance, 6; mobility, 10
Long Island, 62
Lopes, Duarte, 173
Lorge, Peter, 96, 101–2
Loudon (Earl), 240
Louis XIV (King), 34
Lovat (Earl), 240
Lower Creeks, 232
Luanda, 174–76, 182–83; Dutch seizure and departure, 184–85; Mendes de Vasconcelos in, 181; WIC expedition to, 204, 206–8
Lukala River, 178–79

Mackay, Hugh, 234–35
Madockawando (sachem), 32, 35; negotiations with Andros, 45n97; peace treaty conditions set by, 33; Quebec travels, 34–35
Madras, 85
Magdalenenburg plantation, 254
Mahmud II (1808-1839), 145, 148
Maine, 31
Majeed, Javed, 86
Makdisi, Ussama, 161n13
Malcolm, John, 88
Malet, C. W., 100
Maliseets, 31
Malone, Patrick, 65–66
Mamelucos, 197
Mandell, Daniel R., 78n77
Maranhão Island, 203–4; rebels against WIC, 209; uprising in, 209; WIC conquest of, 203–4
Marathas, 85, 97

Marriage: dynastic, 124, 130; across kin
groups, 21; trade relations and, 264. *See
also* Intermarriage
Marryat (Captain), 94
Marshall, Peter, 91
Martial race, 16n27
Mason, John, 72n23
Mason, Peter, 231
Massachusetts Bay Colony, 51
Massasoit (sachem), 19, 25–26
Masters, Bruce, 161n13
Matamba, 185
Matchlock, 56, 70n5; muskets, 51
Maurits, Johan, 203, 207–8
Mayor, 7
Mbande a Ngola (King), 181–82
Mbundu, 175; innovation in, 178; style
warfare, 171–72
Mbwila, 185–86
McNeill, William H., 84, 110
Mehmed II, 148, 150
de Meijer, Joseph, 265–66
Mendes de Vasconcelos, Luis, 181–83
Merritt, Jane, 22
Meuwese, Mark, 3, 10
Mexico, 223; Spanish conquest of, 3–9
Miantonomi, 54
Middle Ages, 169
Middle East, 143, 146
"Middle Ground," 23, 41n25; Ottoman, 144
Mi'kmaq, 31, 68, 226, 230, 241; counter
attack threats from, 231–2322
Militarism *vs.* orientalism, 82, 88–89
Military: fiscalism, 101, 102; settlers, 121
Military revolution, 12, 49, 101, 109;
firearms and, 50; roots in eighteenth-
and nineteenth-century writings,
88–89; Russia's dual, 110–12, 115–19,
126; South Asia and, 89–98; start of,
169; theory, 83–84. *See also* Amerindian
military revolution; European military
revolution
Miliukov, Pavel, 116
Mill, James, 87–88
Millet, 148; population, 161n13
Millet, Pierre, 30

Milosevic, Slobodan, 143
Mineral wealth, 9
Missile weapons, 169–70
Mission Amerindians. See *Indios aldeados*
Mission villages. See *Aldeias*
Mississippian societies, warfare in, 53, 70n6
Mobility: local, 10; New World, 10–11;
operational, 65; steam-powered vessel,
94; in West Central Africa, 172
Mobilization, 13; of manpower, 89–90; of
resources, 84, 89–90. *See also* Social
mobilization
Modernity *vs.* tradition, 102
Mofussilite, 87–88
Mohawk fort: abandonment of, 231–32; in
Nova Scotia, 224–32
Mohawks, 22, 27; Jesuit priests in, clans, 30;
Livingston recruiting, 229; Nova Scotia
arrival, 230
Mohegans, 69; in Sachem's Field battle, 54
Mohr Mackintosh, John, 236–38
Moieties. See Groups
Moldavia, 155
Monghyr, 93–94
Mongol, 125–27, 139n106; Golden Horde,
111
Monhantic Fort excavations, 58, 66
Moradores. See Portuguese colonists, in
Brazil
de Morais, Manuel, 201, 206
de Morgues, Jacques Le Moyne, 53
Morrison, Kenneth, 45n91
Mortuary rituals, 20–21
Moscow: "colonialism," 112; "other's"
leadership within, 128; rivals, 114–15
Mose, 237, 239
Moxes (sachem), 35
Mpinda port, 175
Mpungo Ndongo, 186–87
Mstislav of Galich, 126
Mughal Empire, 96–97, 99
Mumbai (Bombay), 88
Munro, Thomas, 85, 94
Munza (Lord), 175
Murad IV, 155
Muscovite Great Russians, 111

Muscovite military: defense spending, 133n22; "new formation" units of, 118; reforms, 116; steppe and, 110; units, 129

Muscovy, 9–10; adaptations in, 12; diplomacy of, 12; expansion, uniqueness of, 111–12; expansionism *vs.* imperialism, 119–20; foreign and military policies in, 109–10; foreign wars, 129; "gunpowder revolution," 116–18; hostile neighbors of, 113–14; "imperialism" on steppe, 130; labor and, 2; as military national state, 115–16; "oriental natives," 128; polity as "garrison" or "service state," 116, 126, 129; provincial units, 116; state, 109; Steppe defense, 120–23; strategy, 114–15; techniques of steppe diplomacy, 121–22; technology transfers and imports into, 117, 135n42. *See also* Russia; Steppe

Musket, 51, 57, 95–96; shotgun-style loading of, 58

Musketball calculations, 57

Musketeers. *See* Streltsy

Muslim Caucasian, 139n107

Mysore, 99, 101

Narragansetts, 19, 27; advice to English, 53; guns and, 69; in King Philip's War, 64; language, 55, 60; in Sachem's Field battle, 54

Nation-building, 136n53

"Native Ground," 23

Naval power, 10, 89

N'dalatanda, 175

Ndjuka Maroons, 256

Ndongo, 168, 175, 185; alliance with Portugal, 175; defeat at, 181–82; defense of vulnerable areas, 178; elite, 180; politics, 177

Nelson, John, 35

Neoheroka, 64–65

Nevsky, Alexander, 113, 126

New Amsterdam, 253–54, 261

New England, 223, 226; burials, 53; recruitment practices developed in, 229

New France, 30

"New Inverness," 235

New Spain, 86

New World: gold and silver mines of, 8; mobility, 10–11; relations, 3; Spanish conquest of, 167

Nhandui, 201

Nicholas II, 131

Njinga Mbande (Queen), 182–84; army, 185; Portugal, Dutch and, war between, 184; treaty of 1657 and, 186

Njinga Mona, 183

Nkrumah, Kwame, 168

a Nkuwu, Nzinga (João), 172–73

Nogai, 114

Nomad: adaptations, 12; as *druzhinas*, 123; Muscovite-, relations, 109–31; Ottoman, 158; Pecheneg, 121–22, 124; of Pontic Steppe, 122; Rus relations with, 123–25

Norridgewock, 37

North America, 11; adaptation of forts in, 63–64; adaptation of warfare in, 15n19, 49; colonial powers in, 223; military tactics, 221; Scottish Highlander's dilemma in, 240–41; Southwest, 7. *See also* Amerindians; Dutch colonists, in North America; English colonists, in North America; *specific places*

North Yarmouth attacks, 34

Norton, John, 58

Nova Scotia, 227; financial accounts, 231; Mohawk fort in, 224–32; Scottish Highlanders arrival in, 239–40; 1713, 222

Novgorod, annexation of, 1478, 119

Nsanga, 171

Nzimbu, 174

Oborona (defense), 113–14

Oghuz, 146

Oglethorpe, James, 232, 235–37

"Older brothers," 22

Old World, 5

Olinda, 200

Oneidas, 22; Millet adopted by, 30

Onondagas, 22–24

Onontio, as "father," 25–26

Onúttug, 60

Open battle, 53–55; guns and, 59

Operational mobility, 65
Oprichniki (internal security force), 133n23
Oprichnina, 130
Organic colonialism, 119–21, 126
Oriental Herald, 83
Orientalism, 102; militarism and, relationship between, 82, 88–89; trope of European military superiority and, 82–89
Orinoco delta, 273n73
Orme, Robert, 86–87, 89; on Indian military, 86–87, 97–98
Osman, 146
Ottoman-Austrian border, 150
Ottoman Empire, 9, 10, 141, 142, 145; citizenship in, 144; "colonialism" and, 144; use of conquered peoples, 146; "ethnicity" and, 141; ethnographies of warfare, 1500-1800, 141–59; ethnohistorical identity, 148; identity, 146; use of indigenous forces, 153–59; internal threats, 158; labor and, 2; legal sources, 147; "Middle Ground," 144; millet system, 148; Muslim rivals, 155; nomad, 158; power extension into Balkans and Arab world, 145–53; Rumeli vs. Rum and, 145–46; settlement policies, 157; 1683-1800, 142; slavery and, 149–52; sources, 95; state policies, 160n12; subject categories, 160n12; warfare and indigenous people in, 143; warrior societies, 141. See also specific regions
Ottoman-Habsburg frontier, 150
Ottoman military, 150, 152; contractual military system, 159; derbend service, 154; "independent soldiery companies," 156–57; "indigenous" forces, 153–59; organization, 145–46; serhad kulu, 154; timariot system, 149
Ottoman Muslims, 146; ruling elite military class (askeri), 147
Ottoman non-Muslims, 146, 148–49; in Janissaries, 149–50; paramilitary groups, 153; tolerance of subject, 147–48
Ottoman-Serbian battle of Kosovo, 143

Pack train, 60, 74n44
Palestine, 143
Palisade wall, 53–54, 62, 65
Palmares, 205
Papunhank, 38–39
Paraíba, 197, 199–200
Paraupaba, Anthonio, 210, 212–14
Parker, A. W., 239
Parker, Geoffrey, 50, 55–56, 84, 90–91
Passamaquoddys, 31
Payment of tribute (dan or yasak), 120
Pazvantoğlu, Osman, 153
Peace chief, 66–67
Peace Indians, 8
Pecheneg nomads, 121–22, 124
Pedro II (King), 182–84
Peers, Douglas, M., 2, 12
Pemaquid treaty (July 21, 1693), 35–36
Penobscots, 31–34, 36
Pequot War (1637), 58
Pereiaslavl, 121
Pereira, Manuel Cerveira, 181
Pernambuco, 200; uprising in, 209
Persia, 96
Peru, 14n8; Spanish conquest of, 3–9
Peter I, 117, 130
Phase IV Operations, 8
Philip III (King) (1578-1621), 198
Philippines, 7
Pishchalniki (arquebusers), 116
Pizarro, Francisco, 4, 14n8
Plains Indians, 7
Plank, Geoffrey, 3, 10
Plassey battle (1757), 101
Plymouth-Wampanoag treaty, 26
Poland, 134n34, 135n42
Polovtsian attacks, 124–25
"Polyethnic" ruling class, 131
Pomestie land grants (fiefs), 117, 129–30
Pontiac's War, 75n50
Pontic Steppe, 112, 115, 118, 126, 130, 132n7, 139n106; nomads of, 122
Porter, Patrick, 82
Porto Calvo, capture of, 203
Port Royal, siege of, 226–28

Portugal, 11, 95, 174, 187, 198; adaptations, 12; Africa, arriving in, 172–87; allies, 183; Amerindian slave trade and, 196; Angola area controlled by, 168; Angola policies, 179; conquest of Angola, 168–88; European warfare and, 168–70; French-, rivalries in Brazil, 196–98; Imbangala alliance with, 180–81; "imperial" benefit, 187–88; in India, 81; Kitombo setback, 186; Kongo battle against, 182, 185–86; labor and, 2; Ndongo alliance with, 175; Njinga, Dutch and, war between, 184; slave trade and, 188, 226; treaty of 1657 and, 186; truce with Dutch Republic, 1640, 204, 208–9; WIC treaty of surrender to, 214. *See also* Spanish-Portuguese Doublemonarchy (1585-1640)

Portugal-Kongo alliance, 172–75, 187; struggle, 177

Portuguese colonists, in Brazil (*moradores*), 194; *Indios aldeados* as loyal to, 199–200; Potiguares, defeat of, 197; rebellion, 209–11; Tupi as auxiliaries for, 197; Tupi refuge from, 214

Portuguese colonization: efforts, 196–97; Tupi militarization during, 195–98

Portuguese military: art of war, 178–79; assets, 187; Kongo expansion and, 173; use of Kwanza River, 177; support to Bemoim, 168

Potiguares, 193–94, 213; allies, WIC motive for recruiting, 201–2; autonomy, 213–14; defense against Portuguese, 197; ethnic soldiering and, 194; interpreters and informants, 200; WIC alliance with, 199–201

Poty, Pieter, 210–12

Powhatans, 26, 53, 57

Precontact: Amerindian diplomacy in, 20–22; Amerindian warfare, 52–55; forts, 63

Prikaz (chancellory), 115

Protestant: Amerindian "praying towns," 31; Ottomans and, 148

Pudsey, Cuthbert, 202, 206

Pulsipher, Jenny Hale, 2, 11

Qasim, Mir, 93, 97, 99

Qazdağlis family, 152

Quadequina, 19

Quebec, 34–35

Queen Anne's War (1704), 31

Racism, 122–23

Raduschev, Evegenii, 153

Rafael, 186

Rajputs, 96

Ranger companies, 223–24; Algonquians serving in, 229

Reaya, 147, 148

Recife, 200, 212; WIC enemy in, 203

Reconquista, 6

Recruitment, 194; firearms and, 50; loyalty and, 100; New England developed, 229. *See also specific recruitments*

Regidores (magistrates), 209

Religious ceremonies, 21

"Requirement," 14n10

Restall, Matthew, 5–6

Rhode Island, 62

Richter, Daniel, 22, 25

Rifled guns, 74n38

Rio Grande do Norte, 197, 201, 208

Rituals, 20, 40n5; exchange, 22; mortuary, 20–21; warfare, 52–53

Road-width paths, 10

Roberts, Michael, 90

Rodrigues, Gonçalo, 173

Rohillas, 96

Roman models of discipline, 50

Romanov dynasty, 116–17

Roman roads, 10

Rumiantsev, P. A., 118

Rus, 110–11, 126; foundations of Muscovite Steppe defense and diplomacy, 120–23; hostility toward neighbors, 122–23; lands of, 112; nomads relations with, 123–25; Varangian, 121–22

Russia: alliance negotiations, 120; border agents, 120, 123; cannon and, 116; "colonialism" after 1480, 115; "colonization" of, 110–11; conceptions of defense, 112–14; diplomatic initiatives, 120;

Society of Berbice, 252–53; plantation slaves, 255, 263

Soldiering, 16n27

Song of Igor's Campaign, 124

South American. *See* Amerindians; Berbice; Brazil; *specific places and peoples*

South Asia, 95; European military superiority in, 81; historiography, 85–86; military revolution and, 89–98; "orientalizing," 12. *See also specific places*

Southeast Asia, 94

Soviet Union, 131

Spain, 198; Amerindian allies to, 5; contact, 15n16; Grand Alliance and, 34; imperial expansion model, 3–9; mineral wealth access, 9; New World conquest by, 167; in North American Southwest, 7; power, 4; supplies introduced by, 4; warfare adaptations, 7

Spanish colonists: Caddos and, 28; disease from, 4; indigenous relations with, 3; outside status of, 4–5

Spanish Florida, 233; war with Georgia, 236–37

Spanish-Portuguese Doublemonarchy (1585-1640), 193

Squakheag: fort, 63–64; Iroquois war party force on, 59–60, 63–64

St. Augustine, 68, 237

St. Castine (Baron), 32

St. Eustatius, 257–58

Stadial theory, 243

State: formation, 90, 109; war and, 90

State-based society, 9, 15n16

States General (Dutch), 183–84, 211–12, 214–15, 252, 261; Berbice and, 272n46

Steel: axes, 62; material advantages of, 5; swords, 4

Steele, Ian, 66

Steppe: bloody frontiers of, 114–15; caravan traffic, 122; changing cast of peoples, 111; Christianity in, 125; "colonialism," 112; defense, 120–23; defensive fortress and outpost lines in, 117; diplomatic systems, 12, 121–22, 125, 130; fortification in, 117; frontier zones and borderlands,

111; "governance" efforts, 111; Greek Orthodox conversion and, 122–23; horse archers, 10; imperialism before 1800, 119–20; "indigenous" inhabitants of, 111; khanates, 10; Muscovite and Kievan techniques of diplomacy, 121–22; Muscovite "imperialism" on, 130; Muscovite military and, 110; power politics, 127; regional political entities, 111; south-southeastern front, 110; trade, 121–22; vegetative bands, 131n3. *See also* Pontic Steppe; *specific regions*

Storm van 's Gravesande, Laurens, 259–60, 265–66, 268, 274n67

Strachey, William, 57

Strategic locations, 8–9

Streltsy (musketeers), 116

Subjection, Amerindian, 26–27, 39, 47n120

Sugar plantations, 253. *See also* Brazil sugar economy; *specific plantations*

Süleyman (Sultan) (1520-1566), 150

Sultan, Tipu, 92, 96–97, 99

Sultanic prerogative (*kanun*), 147

Sun Dance, 21

Suriname, 252, 269n4; help from, 256; mutiny of regiment, 268; rebel attack on, 254

Surprise attack, 53, 59; role of failed, 54

Suvorov, A. V., 118

Sviatopolk, 124

Sviatoslavich, Igor, 124

Sviatoslav the Great (ruled 957-972), 121

Svoboda, 124

Sweeney, Kevin, 29

Table of Ranks, 130

Tamara (Queen), 125

Tapuyas, 193–94; of Ceará uprising against WIC, 209; killing of, 213

Tarairius, 212; as ethnic soldiers, 215; to fight rebels, 210; WIC and, coalition between, 200–201

Tatar, 154; cavalry, 118; domination, rejection of, 119; Golden Horde, 112. *See also* Crimean Tatars

da Távora, Francisco, 186

Taxous (sachem), 36

Technology: as benchmark of progress, 102; differentials, 92; diffusion and exchange in India, 95; European, 12; firearms, 56–57; indigenous, 97; neutralized, 96; transfers and imports into Muscovy, 117, 135n42. *See also specific technology*

Tenochtitlan, 4, 5, 8

Territorial control, 9

Territory expansion *vs.* strategic locations, 8–9

Thanksgiving, 40n4

Thirty Years' War, 170

Thornton, John K., 3, 11, 14n7

Thrace, 146

Tilly, Charles, 90

Timar, 149

Timariots, 149, 152; to private regional armies, evolution of, 156; registers, 149

Timberlake, Henry, 75n47

Time of Troubles (1604-1613), 114, 116–17, 139n107

Tlaxcalans, 5

Todorov, Tzvetan, 15n14

Toledano, Ehud, 151–52

Tomochichi, 232–33

Tooanaway, 232

Torks, 124

Toudaman, 52

Trace italienne, 50, 61

Trade, 35–37, 265; alliance and, 24, 31; in Berbice, 265; in Brazil, 196–98; cost and supply of goods, 34–35; disappointments in, 31; Dutch and, 198, 264; fur, 25; Indian communities for long-distance, 95; interest in ordinary, 25; kinship and, 264; military assistance and, 31; steppe region, 121–22; WIC and, 265. *See also* Slave trade

Tradition *vs.* modernity, 102

Tribal society, 15n16

Tupi, 193–94, 212–13; abandonment of, 214–15; allies to fight rebels, 210; autonomy, 215; as auxiliaries for Portuguese, 197; in Ceará, 213–14; of Ceará uprising against WIC, 209; deteriorated state of, 211–12; ethnic soldiering and, 194; leaders, 207–8; militarization during Portuguese colonization, 195–98; military allies, 205–9; mortality rate due to disease, 195–96; at Palmares, 205; payment and gifts to, 206–7; population, 208; Portuguese-Dutch truce and, 208–9; refugee groups, 198; refuge from Portuguese, 214; resistance, 197–98; as separate from ethnic soldiers, 215; smallpox epidemic and, 208; traditional warfare, 194–95, 205; weapons, 195; WIC motive for recruiting, 201–2; WIC relations with, 208, 212–14; women, 206–7. *See also* "Brazilian"; Potiguares

Turks, 145; in Anatolia, early power base, 146

Turtle clan, 24

Tuscaroras, 22, 64–65

Ukraine, 110, 111

Uncas (sachem), 54

Uniform Recruit, 10, 16n27, 241

"Upside-down Capitalism," 25

Ural Mountains, 110, 135n46

uşaği, 152

Usner, Daniel H., Jr., 45n98

Van Hoogenheim, Simon Wolfert, 251, 254–56, 262, 266; correspondence with rebel leader, 256–59

Varangian (Norse), 111; decline, 137n71

Varangian Rus, 121–22

de Vargas, Diego, 29

Vasilii III (1502-1533), 116

Vassalage (*shert*), 120

Vaudreuil (governor), 37

Verónica I (Queen), 187

Vetch, Samuel, 225–32

Vidal de Negreiros, Andre, 210

Vidin, 144, 152–53

Vigilantie plantation, 256

Villebon, 36

Vladimir I (980-1015), 121; Greek Orthodox transition by, 122–23, 138n86

Voyvoda, 155